Take Care and Think Peace

Vietnam War Letters
between a Son and Mother, 1969–1970

Dail W. Mullins, Jr.,
and Virginia O'Donnell Mullins

Edited
by Ada Long

Copyright © 2019 Ada Long
All rights reserved.

For Christopher, Ashley, Cleo, and Fox Mullins

Acknowledgments

The primary consultant, collaborator, inspiration, and purpose for this project was Christopher Dail Mullins along with his wife, Ashley.

The project could not have happened without Jillian Woodruff, who initiated the recovery of the lost letters a few weeks before Dail Mullins's death and then, for the three days and nights following his death, started producing digital images of the letters so that they would never be lost again.

Subsequently, Beth Appleton and Dave Harbaugh, in a most loving gift to Dail, spent months digitizing the bulk of his letter collection, and they served as invaluable collaborators on the project. The letters they worked on included those to and from Dail's wife and friends, totalling 528 letters, more than twice the number of the roughly 200 to and from his mother.

Dail's brother, Denny Mullins, provided key information about their childhood and, especially, about their mother during long, fascinating conversations in St. Louis.

Betty Matejka, a "Savvy Secretary" in North Carolina, transcribed the digital images of the letters between Dail and his mother into Word documents, a process that took most of a year given the difficulties of reading their handwriting and the legibility issues in his mother's typed letters.

Jim and Tina Braziel provided valuable advice and proofreading along with their warm and unique encouragement.

Rachel Reinhart, Jeff Portnoy, and Linda Frost offered inspiration and friendship along the way.

Finally, this project could not have happened without the expertise, intelligence, patience, and friendship of Mitch Pruitt. Along with his ever-trusty sidekick Cliff Jefferson, Mitch runs Wake Up Graphics in Alabama, and both Dail and I worked with him on national honors journals for almost two decades. On this project, he deserves credit as a co-editor, not just working with Cliff on layout, typesetting, and graphics; not just paying attention to every minute detail; not just correcting all my errors; but deep-diving into the substance and spirit of the work with respect, inspiration, and love.

Foreword
Ada Long

The correspondence between Dail Mullins and his mother began on December 8, 1968, during his basic training at Fort Polk in Louisiana, and it ended with his first letter after returning from Vietnam, dated April 28, 1970. In the interim, they had exchanged over two hundred letters back and forth describing their daily lives. The correspondence reveals the intimacies and anxieties of a close family relationship during the most unpopular and senseless war in American history while providing windows into the realities of that war for a grunt in Vietnam and for a middle-class housewife back home in the United States. Each reality embraced distinctive fears, vulnerabilities, hopes, outrages, and agonies that consumed American culture during the Vietnam era. Displaying the importance and depth of close connections across a vast space during those years, the letters also reveal the barriers to understanding arising from such enormous disparities in daily experience, barriers that frustrated the families of American GIs and, far more acutely and permanently, the soldiers of a war they never wanted to fight.

The Vietnam era was transformative for individuals as well as American culture. The letters from Dail's mother reveal the racism and homophobia of Webster Groves, the suburban community outside St. Louis in which Dail grew up. His experiences in Vietnam belied all these stereotypes and prejudices, and his letters—usually with patience and tact—show him gradually trying to change his mother's perspectives while her letters show some earnest effort to see her world anew. Mother and son share a resistance to authority whether wielded by military officers, bureaucrats, or politicians, especially Nixon, and both enjoy a supportive circle of friends and supporters in their vastly different contexts, but with some stark contrasts: Dail's dependence on, loyalty to, and love of his "buddies" has a depth that accentuates the frequent quarrels and occasional pettiness among his mother and her friends. Many of these quarrels arise from the aggravation of Dail's parents with their friends' support for Nixon and the war, with their blind patriotism, and with the stereotypes and biases that Dail's mother is trying to leave behind.

BACKGROUND

The Son

Dail Weir Mullins, Jr., was born in the St. Louis Maternity Hospital on February 9, 1944. He attended Webster Groves High School in St. Louis along with his brother, Denny, and his sister, Linda. He then earned his BA from Rhodes

College, his MS from the University of Memphis, and his PhD in biochemistry from the University of Alabama at Birmingham. In 1967, he married his wife of sixteen years, Lucy Bartges Mullins, with whom in 1975 he had son Christopher, who became his lifelong pride and pal.

Meanwhile, in 1969 he reported for duty in Vietnam, assigned to Americal Division and stationed at LZ Baldy and later at LZ Hawk Hill when the U.S. started transferring bases to the ARVN. He was in an army division assigned to the marines, and he volunteered for demolitions for the extra pay. He was a mine sweeper as well as one of the men who went first into the Viet Cong tunnels while the rest of the unit kept a safe distance behind.

After his tour of duty, Dail became active in the anti-war movement, a cause to which he remained committed throughout his life. He wrote numerous newspaper articles, columns, and editorials as well as poetry, essays, and fiction. One of his short stories about Vietnam won first place in the Hackney Literary Awards of 1987.

Nevertheless, Dail spoke only on a couple of occasions about his personal experiences in Vietnam. As he says in one of his letters, he respected the men who never spoke of the war once they got home, and he had a hard time with what he called "professional veterans." He did give a talk in the early 2000s with one of his students, Eric Nguyen, not about the war but about the country of Vietnam, which he always described as beautiful beyond words.

In his life after the war, Dail became a biology instructor and bench scientist in biochemistry, with particular focus on Origin of Life science, at the University of Alabama at Birmingham. He published over thirty-five scientific papers between 1967 and 1984, when he became Associate Director of the UAB Honors Program, a university-wide, interdisciplinary curriculum and community serving a diverse range of students. He and Ada Long, the program's director, came together as colleagues and team teachers in the honors program and, starting in 1990, also as life partners. They carried their personal and professional partnership through and beyond their retirement to St. George Island in 2004, serving as founding co-editors of the two national honors journals and as co-organizers of the St. George Island Trash Patrol and yearly Franklin County Coastal Cleanup.

As part of the annual, semester-long teaching team in honors for twenty years, Dail lectured on scientific topics such as "The Fate of the Earth," "Dead Bees and Homosexual Flies," and "Human Rights and the Crunch to Come," earning the title "Dr. Doom." Colleagues compared him to Carl Sagan with a wickedly funny twist. As a teacher, Dail changed hundreds of lives, and this collage of his students' words about him after he died characterizes his legacy: "A legend is gone; the world is a darker place. . . . Dail Mullins, aka Dr. Doom, was irreverent, fun, open-minded, and blindingly intelligent. . . . Dail had a child-like curiosity paired with a fierce intellect. . . . He was hilarious, gentle but tough as old boots, loving, sharp as a tack, fun, intelligent, irreplaceable. . . . For all his Dr. Doom bluster, Dail Mullins was a sweet soul who liked to take care of others. He noticed the details not just of the universe, but of the individual. . . . He was a great guy who would make you have to think even if you didn't want to. . . . I am grateful for my time with him. My condolences to Ada Long and the universe. . . . I'll see you in the cosmos, dear teacher, dear friend."

He left an even more important legacy in his son, Christopher, and Chris's wife, Ashley, who had been one of Dail's students in the honors program. Chris and Ashley gave Dail the gift of a granddaughter, Cleo Grey Mullins, who was fourteen months old when Dail died suddenly, perhaps of a pulmonary embolism, on September 28, 2016. He never had the chance to meet his grandson, Fox Oliver Mullins, who was born on June 13, 2018.

Anyone who knew Dail knew that he was a devoted fan of the Allman Brothers, with whom he played a mean air guitar. These words of Duane Allman catch some of Dail's spirit: "I will take love wherever I find it and offer it to everyone who will take it . . . seek knowledge from those wiser . . . and teach those who are willing to learn from me."

The Mom

Virginia Lee O'Donnell Mullins ("Gin") was born at home in Chicago on June 18, 1917. Her delayed record of birth was not issued until August 29, 1977. As a girl, she was an amateur dance performer and, according to Dail, danced with the Chicago Ballet. She was also an accomplished swimmer who tried out for the Olympics. In the 1930s, her father, a federal mediator, moved to St. Louis, perhaps after the steel workers' strike and riots that resulted in the Memorial Day Massacre of 1937. In St. Louis, Gin attended Miss Hickey's secretarial school and became her father's secretary. Through mutual friends, the Hoffmeisters, Gin met her future husband, Dail Weir Mullins, Sr., who had started a dental practice in St. Louis in 1938. Because of her future mother-in-law's animosity, Gin and Dail,

Sr., eloped to Warrenton, Missouri; they kept their marriage a secret for at least a year after they got married on September 25, 1940.

Gin had four children: Dail, Jr., in 1944; Linda in 1947; Dennis in 1949; and Deborah in 1954. Born with Rh negative blood, Deborah died when only a week old. In 1953, the family moved to El Paso, Texas, and lived there until 1955 while Dail, Sr., was a major in the U.S. Army Medical Corps at Fort Bliss, after which they returned to Webster Groves, an inner suburb of St. Louis.

Gin died on August 20, 1987, at the age of 70, from metastasized lung cancer. Dail, Sr., died in 1990 of septicaemia, and Linda died of a heart attack in 2015. Dennis and his wife, Terri, and their two children and one grandchild live in an outer suburb of St. Louis.

Everyone who knew Gin remembers her as kind, warm, loving, and smart. Dennis remarked that, although she had no college education, she was the smartest of the Mullins bunch. Her grandson Christopher remembers her always in the kitchen, always greeting him with tender and loving hugs.

The Editor

Ada Long is Emerita Professor of English and Founding Director of the University Honors Program at the University of Alabama at Birmingham. She had the great fortune of working with Dail for thirty-three years and living with him for twenty-seven of those years. Together, they edited the two national journals of the National Collegiate Honors Council starting in 2000; she now edits them alone.

The Letters

Dail almost never spoke of his time in Vietnam and seemed to detach himself entirely from his war experiences, even to the point of losing all contact with his best friend there, whom he credited with his emotional and mental survival. One sign of the centrality of those experiences, though, was his near-obsession with the importance of his recorded history of those years in his correspondence with his mother. When he made out his will, the only request he specified was that the letters be preserved as his legacy to his son. At the same time, he revealed his ambivalence about what the letters commemorated in his relative indifference when the correspondence seemed to disappear for well over a year after he entrusted it to a typist who vanished along with all the letters. Only through the dogged determination of one of his former students—Jillian Woodruff—were the letters finally tracked down and later retrieved almost by accident in a chance encounter with the typist at a hardware store.

Two days after Dail died, Jillian came down to the island and spent three days working day and night digitizing the correspondence. Chris came from California soon after and oversaw the process (as a digital animator, his computer skills are exceptional and invaluable), and then two friends on the island—Beth Appleton and Dave Harbaugh—picked up where Jillian had left off, spending weeks digitalizing and labelling the rest of the letters. Ada photocopied and sent them to an excellent typist in North Carolina, Betty Matejka. The salvation of the letters was thus a truly cooperative project.

The letters to his mother are not the only ones Dail wrote from Vietnam, but they are the ones he most valued. He wrote more often to his wife, Lucy, and kept some of that correspondence as well, but it is not a complete set whereas his mother seems to have kept everything Dail sent from Vietnam. He also wrote to his mother that his correspondence with Lucy was a less revealing record of that era in either Vietnam or the U.S. as they were, above all, love letters.

All of Dail's letters to his mother were addressed to both his mother and father, and her letters were always signed "Mom and Dad." Apparently, his father did write to him a couple of times, but a reader does not get very far into the correspondence before realizing it was really taking placing between mother and son.

Many times, we wished that Dail were still here to answer questions about the letters and about his time in Vietnam. We expected that Dail would work on the letters himself as, starting at least in 1990, he often said he would do, but here again is a sign of his ambivalence. Nevertheless, we see this collection of letters as a tribute to him, a way of collectively honoring him and our love for him. We hope and believe he would be pleased.

A PRACTICAL GUIDE TO READING THE LETTERS

Determining an order for the letters was a significant challenge. Some of the letters were undated, and on some others the dates were clearly inaccurate. Guesswork, consideration of the context, and consultation of calendars from 1969 and 1970 went into assigning days and dates to several of the letters, and the dates thus assigned are indicated in brackets.

The biggest challenge was coming up with a way to order the correspondence. Putting all of Dail's letters in one section and his mother's in another would have been the easiest solution but would have erased the interconnection and flow of ideas. An initial hope was to print Dail's letters on the verso pages and his mother's on the recto, but their different lengths would have thrown off the balance between the two sets of letters. More importantly, the cross-references would have been lost given the problem of timing: mail collection and delivery in Vietnam was erratic at best so that letters from either Dail or his mother might take anywhere from three days to a month to reach their destination.

Christopher Mullins devised an ingenious way to resolve these problems: namely, to order the letters as Dail would have received and sent them. Readers need to imagine themselves as Dail; if he received two letters from his mother on

January 8, for instance, and responded to her on January 9, then the two letters from his mother precede his response. Ordering the correspondence in this way is a bit harder than it sounds, and no doubt mistakes have been made, but generally one can follow the flow from Dail's perspective and see the connections between the letters he received and the ones he wrote.

Another editorial issue was how to handle the grammatical and spelling errors in the correspondence as well as the typos in those of his mother's letters that were typed. All such errors have been preserved exactly as they appeared, with occasional clarifications indicated in brackets.

BASIC TRAINING: ONLY LETTERS FROM DAIL

Dail mentions three letters that his mother wrote prior to his deployment, but he didn't keep them. The two-way correspondence starts when Dail reaches Vietnam on May 17, 1969.

PVT. Dail. W.Mullins, Jr.
RA12927044
CoE, 1st BN, 1st BCT Bde
Fort Polk, LA. 71459

8 December, 1968

Dear Mom and Dad

I'm awfully sorry that I haven't written before now, but we've had about 0 free time—I called Lucy last night, but prior to that time I had only gotten one letter off to her. They keep us on to the move from 4:30 AM until about 7:30 PM—and since lights are out at 8:30 PM, I don't have much time for "fringe-benefits" like writing my wife and parents. We're supposed to take a shower and straighten up around our bunks before bed, too. And they have the gall to tell you that "the army likes you to write home."

I reported Wednesday as ordered, but by the time they had finished processing me in Memphis, the bus for FT. Polk had left, so I had to leave on the 5th—at 8:00 AM. I got to the base reception area at 9:00 that night—a lovely 13 hour trip. That same night I was blood typed, issued bedding and instructed how to make a bed before retiring. The next day we got haircuts and were issued duffel bags and uniforms. Friday we were photographed and fingerprinted, filled out more papers and had a few orientation lectures. Saturday was hot day and more orientation. Today, Sunday, we have off, so I'm skipping breakfast to write to you.

The place that I'm at now (The Reception Station) does not have adequate mailing facilities, so I can't receive my mail. Tuesday or Wednesday we're shipped out to basic either North Fort Polk or South Fort Polk, and I'll send my new address then.

We are going to receive a 14-day Christmas leave beginning on the 19th, so Lucy was happy about that. I doubt if we'll see each other for some time after that (approx. 4 months)—and preparing myself, psychologically, for that will probably be harder than basic.

We get $25 when we leave for basic and, supposedly, another $30 travel pay, but Lucy is wiring me $50 as soon as she gets my basic address. The army is supposed to guarantee every trainee a ride home, in one fashion or another, so I don't really know how I'll be going—I hope I make it before half my vacation is up. I'm not too worried about getting back on time, since if I can't get transportation in time, I'm supposed to turn myself into an MP, and they have to get you back.

I don't like the army, but I suspect that that's less the army's faults than it is my own thoughts about what I had to leave. Most of the fellas in this bunk are only high-school grads, if that, and I really think they don't know any better. It's harder on someone like me because I think too much—I guess. I just keep reminding myself of what you said—that when you're feeling low, just remember that it will all pass—fast, I hope.

Love,
Dail

Address will follow shortly—

PVT. Dail W. Mullins, Jr.
RA12927044
CoE, 1st BN, 1st BCT Bde
Fort Polk, LA. 71459
Platoon 2

13 December, 1968

Dear Mom and Dad,

I'm starting this letter now, but I don't know exactly when I'll mail it, so you best wait until after January 1st to send one back—I won't be here from Dec 19 until Jan. 4. My address at this hole is—

PVT. Dail W. Mullins, Jr.
RA12927044
CoE, 1st BN, 1st BCT Bde
Fort Polk, LA. 71459

I'm not real sure, yet, how I'll be getting home, but I'll make it somehow. We only got paid $25.00, so I may have to take a bus to Memphis, and then borrow the money from the Jackson's or Wintker to fly home on. I don't think there's anyone in our company who's as far away from home as I am.

We have shipped to basic, although real basic won't get down to the real nitty gritty until Mon.—then Wed. we leave.

I'm a little scared about what they seem to be pushing me into. As you know, I'm signed up for Infantry OCS—that's the main reason I came to Fort Polk—a big infantry training center. If they pay attention to my M.S., I should get AIT (Advanced Individual Training—comes after basic) at Fort Sam Houston in medical services. If not, and that's the rumor, I'll be here at Fort Polk for infantry AIT at a part of the base called Tigerland—that's the infantry's Viet Nam training ground. Then, after 8 wks. basic, 8 wks. AIT—its off to OCS for my commission. If I go to Viet Nam as a second looie (infantry) my life expectancy is about 2 weeks. Needless to say, I'll be dropping out of OCS voluntarily—course then they'll send me right to "Nam as a sp/5 infantryman—my last recourse will be either Peace talks coming through, cutting off my trigger finger or deserting to Sweden. You'd think with all their non-collegiate manpower around here, my damned master's degree would matter some.

I want you to do something for me if you will—send the name of the most dovish senator or representative from Mo. to Lucy's house so it will be waiting there for me—also his address.

Write me after New Year's here and at Lucy's after Dec 19. Also, I will call you Christmas eve or whenever necessary.

One more thing! If any emergency should arise which would require my presence, the fastest possible way to get me to St. Louis would be to notify the Red Cross in Webster Groves—they will contact the Red Cross here and this branch will speak to the commander about the situation.

The only good thing about this present situation is the fact that most of the guys in my barracks are college grads—

Love,
Dail

PRAY FOR PEACE
IN VIET NAM

13400 KINGSMILL RD.
MIDLOTHIAN, VA 23113

31 December 1968

Dear Mom and Dad,

Happy New Year! Hope you all had a pleasant Christmas and a nice New Year's Eve. I enjoyed my leave very much, even though it was somewhat clouded by the thought of having to go back to Fort Polk. It will be a long time before I get leave again, I'm afraid.

Thanks again for the check and presents—I'll probably use the money to get back to Louisiana.

Tonight Lucy and I and her folks are going down to Williamsburg for a New Year's Eve dinner—not exactly what you'd call a "swinging" New Year, but much better than being alone down at the post!

Sunday afternoon Lucy and I rode down to Williamsburg and visited with Currier. He has a nice apartment there with another Lieutenant, but he has to leave tonight for a 2 month course at Fort Benjamin Harrison in Indianapolis. He's due to return to Fort Eustis here in Va. afterwards, so he really doesn't know if he'll go to Viet Nam or not. Some army Captain who lives across the hall from him and is in intelligence said that there will be a major withdrawal of troops from V N within two months—course, that may be another rumor, but its the kind you want to believe.

Please thank Mrs. Seibert for the nice note and $5.00 that she sent—don't tell her I spent the money on such an unromantic thing as our ante inspection sticker, though.

Here's my address once again—don't forget to add the platoon #.

PVT. Dail W. Mullins, Jr.
RA12927044
CoE, 1st BN, 1st BCT Bde
PLT 2
Fort Polk, LA. 71459

Write as often as you can—the letters are awfully nice to get.
Well, you'll be hearing from me—take care.

Love,
Dail

PVT. Dail W. Mullins, Jr.
RA12927044
CoE, 1ST BN, 1ST BCT Bde, 2nd Platoon
Fort Polk, LA. 71459

6 January, 1969

Dear Mom and Dad,

Well, I made it back to Fort Polk on time. I flew to Atlanta, waited 2 hours for a flight to New Orleans, slept on the floor of a motel room that one of the guys in my barracks had checked into, and then rode from New Orleans to the fort on a bus.

We were issued field equipment (mess kit, helmet, tent, canteen, etc.) on Saturday afternoon and spent most of that day and part of Sunday squaring it away. Monday is when we get down to the real nitty-gritty of basic.

I am worried about Dad's back—maybe he should see a doctor, although I don't suppose that there is much he could do short of operating. Sometimes you can wear a brace, and I hear these help. Do take care of yourself though—I don't need that to worry about, too.

That old saying, ignorance is bliss, certainly displays its accuracy as far as the army is concerned. Undoubtedly, the happiest guys here are the ones who haven't even finished high school. In some ways I wish I were like them. Since I have the most education of anyone in the company, I guess that makes me the unhappiest—and sometimes I believe it.

By far, the hardest part of this whole deal is being away from Lucy, and you folks. In many respects, that Christmas leave was cruel—although I had a wonderful time. It's just that it was so short—at least it seemed that way—and made it so hard to come back. Also, I would liked to have spent some time with you and Dad.

If you get down this way, stop in—we are allowed to have visitors, although Sundays are really the only day that I can spend any time with visitors. In lieu of personal visits, however, your letters will be heartily received.

Take care of yourselves, please—say hello to Linda and Denny, and tell him he's a fool if he joins the Marines—

Love,
Dail

PVT. Dail W. Mullins, Jr.
RA12927044
CoE, 1ST BN, 1ST BCT Bde, 2nd Plt
Fort Polk, LA. 71459

Jan 16, 1969
Thursday night

Dear Mom and Dad,

I'm terribly sorry that I missed getting my letter off to you last weekend, but the circumstances, which you may or may not have heard about yet, prevented it.

Friday I reported for sick call, and when they found I had a temp of 101.4°, I was sent to the URI (upper respiratory infection) ward at the base hospital. There

I remained until the following Wednesday, fighting off a bad upper respiratory infection. At one time my temp reached 105°, and they had to cover me with ice to get it down. I was one lovely, miserable soldier that night—I even cried for Lucy. All is well now, though—I feel fine and I'm back at the company.

Got a letter from Denny tonight. It was awfully good of him to take the time to write. I was badly shaken to hear that Babbette had been killed—why didn't you tell me over Christmas instead of letting me find out down here? I can't believe I'll never see that little dog again—I'm very sorry for everyone—I know how much she meant to the family.

I did get a letter from Pete—thanks for giving him my address. He sounds like he's doing fine—that comment he made to you about wishing he'd signed for 3 years instead of the reserves—ask him if he'd like to trade places!

I was surprised to hear that Neil Tanner had been in the army, much less that he'd taken his basic down here at Fort "Puke". Is he in a reserve unit, or did he spend 2 years on active duty?

You remember that I had mentioned to you the possibility of dropping out of OCS and first going on an finishing as a non-com. Well, I still haven't decided, and I'd appreciate any comments that you might have. Here's the way the situation apparently stands. If I go to OCS, it will mean 10 months away from Lucy and 6 months of the worst (they call it the best) harassment that the army has to offer. The end result (unless I have a nervous breakdown) will be a second lieutenant's commission in the infantry, with only the slightest chance of a branch transfer to a more suitable area (medical services). All second lieutenants get a 4-6 month minimum stateside tour of duty prior to overseas assignment—if the Viet Nam War is on still, you can bet your booties that's where I'll go—as a combat officer.

On the other hand, if I choose not to go to OCS, I could take my chances on 2 years—most probably I'd go infantry (most 2 year enlistees do). An alternative would be to reup for a third year with the written promise of a school—I would choose med tech school and become a hospital assistant. I'd probably be in Viet Nam within 6 mos., but it would no doubt be a fairly safe job behind the lines. Well, that's it. Now like I told Lucy, I don't want you to decide for me, but I would appreciate your sending what thoughts you do have on the matter down as soon as you can. I'll be waiting.

Lucy's birthday is next Wed., the 29th of January. I'm going to call her this Sunday, but I won't be able to send her much more than a poem or something. I sure miss her and wish I could be with her now.

I understand Denny's dropping out of the fraternity to save money. Hard to believe, but wonderful news if true. I hope his sacrifice doesn't make him too miserable.

Here's hoping Bob and Linda are making it alright. I'll probably miss the wedding this summer, but my thoughts will be with them. I hope they'll be as happy as Lucy and I are, but I pray Bob is spared this hell!

I think of both of you quite a lot, and am looking forward to the time when Lucy and I can come stay with you all again. I think we have our best times there.

Love,
Dail

PVT. Dail W. Mullins, Jr.
RA12927044
CoE, 1ST BN, 1ST BCT Bde, 2nd Plt
Fort Polk, LA. 71459

Jan 26, 1969
Sunday Morning

Dear Mom and Dad,

I'm writing this letter mainly to clear up a misconception... more misinformation... that appeared in my last letter. Our drill sergeant, intelligent fool that he is, had told all 4 of us (OCS men) that we had received MOS' of 11B (that's infantry). You see, MOS' run like this (MOS, you will recall, stands for military occupational status): all MOS codes have 2 numbers and a letter. If the first number is a 1, the MOS is a combat arms. Thus, the 10 series MOS' (10A, 10B, 10C, etc.) represents artillery. The 11 series (11A, 11B, 11C, etc.) is infantry. 13 series is armor. Our MOS' are 12A—which is combat engineers. We will go to Fort Leonard Wood on February 23 for AIT in combat engineers. Actually, I'm somewhat relieved. This job can be dangerous, but certainly not to the extent that the infantry can be. So far, all I know this means is that if I do flunk or drop out of OCS I will be an engineer. What I'm curious to find out is whether this means we'll be going to combat engineers OCS instead of infantry down at Fort Benning. If so, I'd be delighted. For one, the job is safer as a 2nd Lt. Much safer. For another, the engineers OCS school is at Fort Belvoir, Va., and you know how much it would help to be closer to Lucy. Thirdly, I think I could get more interested in that field than I could as a ground-stomper. At any rate, I'll soon find out, since the other day I managed to wrangle into a conversation with our CO, 1st Lt. Jones, and he gave me permission to go down to building 314, which houses all the direct commission and OCS information. I have a lot of questions to ask and I'm hoping I can get some answered down there.

Fort Leonard Wood, although I've heard alot of bad stories about it, will nevertheless be a welcome change from Fort Puke. For one thing I won't have to look at these damn pine trees and swamps again, and for another, I'll be a little closer to something that I can feel associated with. I've heard that in AIT we get just about every weekend off, so since the Fort is only a 2 or 3 hour bus trip from St. Louis, I hope I can get home fairly often. Also I was thinking that it would do both Lucy and myself some good if she might fly down and spend a week with you all, and maybe I could catch her 2 weekends in a row. Would an arrangement like that be OK with you folks? I hope so.

Tomorrow we begin our 6th week of basic and it's a lulu. We have bivouac (camping out) Monday, Tuesday and Wednesday. We learn to live in the field and how to react to night attacks, gas attacks and the like. I just hope it doesn't rain too much and really make things fun and games.

Our company should have been given post privileges by now (i.e., allowed to go to movies and the PX on weekends and at night), but this upper respiratory infection epidemic has gone into a phase 2 quarantine status and keeps us more or less restricted to the company area. Every once in a while one of us manages to sneak off to the PX or phones at night, though, so life is bearable, I guess. But barely.

I don't know if I've mentioned the fact or not, but I have made pretty good friends with 2 of the OCS candidates in my barracks, Steve Loving and Bob Breugger. Both are unmarried, but we do have our educational and midwestern backgrounds in common. They're very nice guys, and I hope they can get to St. Louis one time with me so you could meet them. They'll both be at Leonard Wood with me; I hope in the same platoon.

Well, not much else to report. I'll write again next weekend and look for me after the 23rd of February. See you—

Love,
Dail

———————————

PVT. Dail W. Mullins, Jr.
RA12927044
CoE, 1st BN, 1st BCT Bde, 2nd Plt.
Fort Polk, LA. 71459

Jan 26, 1969
Sunday

Dear Mom and Dad,

Hi! How are you doing. We have Sundays pretty much free here (hard to believe), so I'm going to try and catch up on some letter writing. I just finished a marathon 6 page letter to Lucy, and I'd like to get one off to Denny.

I mentioned to Lucy that it bothered me that you hadn't told me about Babbette because I thought you were trying to hide all the families problems from me, thinking I had enough of my own. Well, you're right, but please don't keep all of them from me.

I got KP yesterday—its horrible, even though I didn't have to peel any of the proverbial potatoes—they have a machine for that now. The reason KP is so bad is because when you get it, you have to work from 4:00 AM until 8:00 that night.

Tomorrow we have hand grenade practice, Wednesday we crawl under the line machine gun fire and Friday we get to see what a tear gas attack is like. Last week we had bayonet practice and quick kill. Quick kill is where we walk through woods and a mock Vietnamese village with a BB gun and shoot pop-up targets. You learn to engage a target without aiming the rifle—just pointing it.

You really ought to see the bayonet practice—every time you make a thrust with the thing you have to yell KILL! And there are some other delightful conversations that we go through with the instructor: for example:

INSTR: What is the spirit of the bayonet?
US: To Kill!
INSTR: What are the 2 types of bayonet fighters?
US: The quick and the dead. We're the quick.

All the college guys in our platoon refuse to yell all this crap—I'll be damned if I'll let them turn me into an animal.

Still haven't made any decisions, and would appreciate any thoughts you may have on the matter as I said before. I waver between OCS and a nice quiet med tech school.

I really got homesick for Webster the other day—I got to thinking about what good times Lucy and I had when we stayed there, and hope it won't be too long before we do so again.

Denny said that Bob and Linda had come home last weekend, but that Bob had gotten the flu, so they had to stay over some. I hope he's feeling better, and that they got back alright.

Well, we have to go eat breakfast soon. Please keep me posted on what's going on—I know what with trying to write to everyone that its hard to find the time and the words, but the letters really are appreciated. Take care and will see you.

Love,
Dail

PVT. Dail W. Mullins, Jr.
RA12927044
CoE, 1ST BN, 1ST BCT Bde, 2nd Plt.
Fort Polk, LA. 71459

Friday night
Jan 31, 1969

Dear Mom and Dad,

How are you all doing? I want to thank you, first, for the nice long typed letter I got the other day (your's and Lucy's letters are about the only intelligently written pieces of literature I get to read down here), and second, for the nice box of magazines. At first I thought they were going to take them away from me, since basic trainees (quote) "aren't supposed to have any time to read magazines" (unquote), but they finally consented and I stuffed them all in the bottom of my wall locker. I don't know when I'll get a chance to read all of them, but maybe between myself and some of the other fellas in the barracks, we can put them to some use on Sundays.

I did find out that we can receive food through the mail, except that we have to share it with the rest of the fellas in the barracks after we get our fill. Thus, if you want to send some cookies down, go ahead. There are 45 men in the 2nd platoon + 1 drill sergeant.

I found out today that the 4 OCS candidates in 2nd platoon, Mark Buls, Bob Breugger, Steve Loving and myself, are all scheduled to go to Fort Leonard Wood for AIT (advanced individual training) in infantry right after basic. It isn't what I wanted, of course, but at least I won't be taking AIT down here at North Fort Polk (little Viet Nam)—instead it will be little Korea. That doesn't mean, by the way, that I won't go to Viet Nam. What it does mean, however, is that as of right now, my MOS (Military Occupational Status) is ground-stomper (infantryman), and that I will go to infantry OCS with little chance of a branch transfer into another area. They sure do make good use of their educational power, don't they! So, if I choose not to go to OCS, I'd definitely have to re-up for another year, to get my MOS changed. Well, at least I won't be too far from St. Louis, and if I can squeeze a 3-day pass out of AIT, maybe Lucy could meet me there for awhile. Would that be alright?

Another fine example of the Army way. There's a guy in our barracks named Danny Yeager, who was drafted out of theoretical chemistry graduate school at Cal Tech. What are they going to make him—why an MP, of course! I don't know where Neil Tanner got his info about the army doing their best to give men jobs along with their training and education, but it sure doesn't seem to work that way. Yeager says he's going to desert to the first Swedish embassy he can find on his next leave! Sounds like Cal Tech talking there.

I want to apologize for not writing more, but what little time I do have to get a letter off during the week I try and use to get one to Lucy. I'm sure you understand. I do try and get off one each weekend to you, though.

I remember one time you asked me what all those letters and numbers on my address meant. I'll try and explain. RA12927044 is my serial number. The RA stands for Regular Army and appears before the serial number of anyone who enlists in the service. This is opposed to the letters US, NE and ER, which appear before the serial numbers of draftees, national guard and reservists, respectively. CoE stands for Company E, or, as the army calls it, ECHO COMPANY. 1st BN stands for the first battalion, and 1st BCT Bde stands for the first basic combat training brigade. In the army then, CoE, 1st BN, 1st BCT Bde is translated as ECHO-1-1.

Don't let anybody back there get you upset by stories about Fort Polk. The place is a hole, there's no doubt about it, but that's mainly due to the fact that all the buildings were built before WWII and remain largely unchanged since then. As for snakes, there are plenty of them—water moccasins, rattlers, coral snakes and copperheads. The only thing is, they're all hibernating now, and will be until I get out of here. The weather is the worst thing. It rains alot, getting everything wet and muddy, and you don't know how to dress, since its bitter cold in the morning and then hot by noon. If the weather and snakes were all there was giving me a hard time, however, life would almost be pleasant down here! There are the drill sergeants, though. SOB's.

I don't know whether I told you or not, but I am following up, or trying to follow up, on the suggestion by a 1st lieutenant at battalion headquarters that I try for a direct commission in the chemical corps. I've written to this guy, but as of yet I haven't heard anything—a few more days and I think I'll try and call him.

Well, not much else to report, I'm doing as well as can be expected under the circumstances, I guess, huffing and puffing trying to keep up with these 17 and 18-year olds.

Keep me posted and write as often as you can. Will do same—

Love,
Dail

P.S. Managed to get a letter back to Denny . . . also got a rather interesting letter from Bobby Paschen, I guess much on the same order as the one Linda got. The envelope he used was big and off-white colored, and was sealed with sealing wax! I thought when I first saw it that the army was transferring me to Williamsburg!

PVT. Dail W. Mullins, Jr.
RA12927044
CoE, 1ST BN, 1ST BCT Bde, 2nd Plt.
Fort Polk, LA. 71459

Feb 8, 1969
Saturday night

Dear Mom and Dad,

Hope my weekend letter finds you all well and as happy as possible. I enjoyed talking with you, Mom, even though I had to call collect. I'm always hesitant about calling long distance on a pay phone, as I am never sure if I'll have enough change, when I'm through talking.

Let's see, I told you about having to drop the medical services corps as one of my OCS choices and pick up transportation instead, and I think I mentioned that I had at long last obtained the forms necessary for application for a direct commission. Like Dad, I'm not very hopeful of the outcome of such proceedings, but I certainly can't lose anything by trying. I think I did neglect to mention one other "angle" that I'm working on. Mom, do you recall my mentioning on the phone the boy in our platoon, Danny Yeager, who had threatened to go to Sweden if he had gotten an infantry MOS? Well, this guy was drafted out of graduate school at Cal Tech, and before he left one of his professors gave him a list of addresses to write to after he got in the army in his search for a scientific job. One of these was a Major Coblentz, c/o the Army's Natick Laboratories in Natick, Mass. Well, I obtained the address myself and wrote to Major Coblentz. About 3 days ago I got a rather encouraging reply to the effect that the Natick Labs did indeed employ persons with my background and qualifications for work on CBR weapons system and other biologically related areas, such as food microbiology, etc. They sent me an application form and encouraged me to apply as soon as possible. As you can see, most of tomorrow will be spent filling out all of these forms I have. That's why I decided to stay up tonight and get some letters written. Saturday night is one night when you don't have to worry too much about getting as much sleep as possible, since Sundays are usually pretty slow. We get up at 6:00, eat at 7:00 and then head out to "church"—actually we go to the service club across the street from the chapel and listen to music, have coffee and doughnuts, watch TV, read, write and just generally do everything that we don't get to do during the week. In short, we relax for 2 or 3 hours.

Well, Monday we start our 7th and, training-wise, last week of basic. The 8th week is spent in review of all the crap we've learned in preparation for our practical and written exams. We graduate from basic on the 21st of February. That'll be one diploma you'll never see on my wall.

All of us that got preliminary MOS' of combat engineers at Leonard Wood are keeping our fingers crossed that, come graduation day, our final orders will be the same. It's either that or Tigerland—and you know what I think of that. I never was overly crazy about Tigers.

At most military posts, basic trainees in their 6th week, as we are, get post privileges, and are allowed to go to the PX at night and to a movie or something on Saturday night. Not Fort Polk. This spinal meningitis phase II thing has kept our extracurricular activities out to a minimum. Tonight, however, we were allowed to go to the PX for an hour—boy did everybody go wild. I bet our company alone drank 10 gallons of Budweiser and sneaked back 500 lbs. of candy bars to the barracks. I had one beer and managed to get back with about a dozen candy bars. That, plus your cake (which was very good), plus the two boxes of cookies that Lucy sent me—I'm in good shape, food wise. I am going to sneak down to that PX tomorrow with Steve Loving and have another beer on my birthday come hell or high water.

Really, there's not much else to tell you. Basic training is moving along fairly fast for something I don't particularly like, and it won't be too much longer before we're through. Like I've heard so many doctors say about med school. "Its something I'm glad I went through, but I wouldn't care to do it again." I have a feeling I'm going to feel much the same way about the whole army when its all in the past.

I haven't heard any more from Linda or Denny—trust they're doing alright. Tell Denny to write some more if he gets the chance—I enjoy reading his mail.

Well, adieu and farewell. At least for now. Providing I will be at Leonard Wood for 8 weeks after basic, keep the icebox stocked with beer, the bed warm and the TV in good repair, because PVT MULLINS, RA12927044, will be dropping in. I hope. Write soon and I'll get to you next weekend—

Love,
Dail

PVT. Dail W. Mullins, Jr.
RA12927044
C-3-1, 2nd Platoon
Fort Leonard Wood, MO, 65473

Feb 11, 1969
Tuesday night

Dear Mom and Dad,

    First off, I want to thank you both for making last weekend possible. All the little "extras" you supplied—the fire, the champagne and the supper—really went toward making it one of the most enjoyable weekends I've ever had. The time went so fast, though, and Lucy was pretty upset when time finally did run out and I had to leave before taking her to the airport. We had both counted on being together for that "one last hour", but when I saw what time it was, I knew there was no chance of making it back here by 8:00 if we went out to the airport first. I hope she got away OK—I was a little worried about her having to drive all the way from D.C. to Richmond—she was pretty tired after such a hectic 2 days. I wanted to call her last night or tonight, but I've had too much to do around here, and haven't been able to get away.

    Monday, the 17th, our company is being inspected by the Inspector General's office of the Pentagon—they do that to all military units every few years. Needless to say, we're going to be busy getting things ready. If the sergeant thinks most everything is in pretty good shape, we'll get passes this weekend—I don't know, though, what time I'll get in if we do, so if you have plans, go right ahead—I have a house key. If I come, there's a chance that Steve Loving might be along too, but he's a short, quiet fellow, and no trouble. All we want to do is relax, watch some TV and maybe drink a few beers. I want to finish up on these direct commission forms and also begin writing to some schools—including Alabama—about getting accepted for the fall semester of '70. That way I can get out of this fool organization 3 months early.

    I know you both are anxious about my having dropped OCS, wondering if it was the best thing to do under the circumstances: Well, only time will tell on that account, but I do know that that discharge late next year means more to me than eating in an officer's club for a year. If I do have to go to Viet Nam, I'm sure there will be many times that I'll wish I was back at OCS in the states; nevertheless, other married men have made it, and besides, I'd rather go as a private in the Corps of Engineers than as an Infantry lieutenant. My going overseas for a year, whether to 'Nam, Korea or Germany, will be awfully hard on both Lucy and myself, but I think we have the stuff to make it. I have to believe that, or I'd desert.

Well, hope I can get in this weekend. Getting out of this hole really helps my morale alot.

Love,
Dail

PVT. Dail W. Mullins, Jr.
RA12927044
C-3-1, 2nd Plt.
Fort Leonard Wood, MO. 65473

March 2, 1969
Sunday night

Dear Mom and Dad,

Thanks for the weekend—again! I think you know how much I enjoy coming home for those few hours!

Had an uneventful trip down—not a bit of trouble, although it rained quite hard nearly all of the way down. I parked the car in a fenced, guarded lot for $1.50 per week. I locked it up, so it should be safe.

One of the little things that drives you crazy in the Army—when I got back to the barracks I hauled out my radio to listen to music while I packed up for bivouac—I put the dial on 1150 and lo and behold, guess what station I picked up—WRVA, Richmond, Va. I about went out of my mind!

I looked up Dr. Fattig's address in my book—it's

Dr. W. D. Fattig
713 Comer Dr.
Birmingham, Ala. 35216

When you send his note, you might first mention at the bottom that I apologize for not writing him myself, but that I just don't have too much time right now—tell him I'll try and write during any leave I might get after AIT.

I probably won't have too much free time in the field, so if you don't hear from me again, don't worry, and I'll look forward to seeing everyone next weekend.

Love,
Dail

P.S. Lucy said on the phone that she had to buy her ticket for St. Louis Thursday. I hope she can use this ticket anytime, since if anything came up that forced us to postpone our visit for a weekend, I'd hate to have her waste the money—though, perhaps—they'd buy the ticket back. The reason I bring this up—we won't get back to the company area, as I said, until Friday afternoon. Thus, I won't know until then if I have CQ this weekend. I don't expect it, since I had it Wednesday, but I've learned to expect anything in the Army. If, by some chance, I do get it, I'll try and call Lucy—I'll have to call Lucy—Friday night. If I can't get her, I'll call you and you'll have to call her. OK, As I said, I shouldn't get it, so here's hoping I'll see you all again next weekend.

PVT. Dail W. Mullins, Jr.
RA12927044
C-3-1, 2nd Platoon
Fort Leonard Wood, MO. 65473

Tuesday night
April 1, 1969

Dear Mom and Dad—and the rest of the family,

Well, its time to thank you again for your weekend hospitality. Lucy and I had a wonderful time. She feels bad about not helping you more when she's there, but you know how precious those few hours are to us. I was relieved to hear that she had gotten home OK—though when I called I wasn't really worried, since I figured you would have gotten in touch with me by then if anything had been amiss.

I called you—or Denny, as it turned out—from Rolla. I was a little depressed at the time, and wanted someone to talk to. We got up Monday morning at 7:30, ate breakfast, had a police call (15 minutes) and, after getting paid, got out on pass the rest of the day! All I could think about was that, had I not come back, I could have had all that extra time with Lucy—what they would have done to me for coming in Monday night instead of Sunday, I don't know, but it may have been worth it. Steve Loving and I found the post too depressing that day (everything was closed), so we caught the bus to Rolla with the intent of seeing a movie. All the theaters were closed, however, so we ended up just walking around downtown Rolla (which takes about 15 minutes) and looking in the various stores. Whoopie!

We are scheduled to make up the training we missed on Monday this Saturday. Thus, we'll be out in the field on Saturday until around 4:00 or 5:00. Whether or not they'll let us off on pass after that, I don't know. If they do, I'll probably catch the evening bus to St. Louis and bring Denny's radio then. If they don't, well, I'll just have to skip this Easter with you. I'll bring the radio the next chance after that, though, and maybe you can send it down to Denny through the mail. If we do get off on pass, would it be alright if Steve Loving came again? I know you'd be crowded, but he lost his pass last weekend, and if we get off at 4:00 or 5:00, that's a little late to be leaving for Iowa—and it sure means a lot to us to get off this damn post for those few hours. About all I can say is don't look for us, but we may be in.

Well, that's about it. Oh, I wanted to tell you something funny. There's this kid in 1st platoon named Cooklin who apparently thought he was getting an extra bad deal, so he wrote President Nixon, of all people, and complained of being mistreated. Well, believe it or not, Friday afternoon the White House called our orderly room to check up on it. I think Sergeant Hess was speechless for the first time in his life! I thought that was hilarious.

Love,
Dail

D. W. Mullins, Jr.
13400 Kingsmill Rd.
Midlothian, Va. 23113

Thursday
May 1, 1969

Dear Mom and Dad,

If I seemed to be in an awfully big hurry the other day at the airport, its only because I hate "goodbyes" so much. Even now, I am dreading the tears on the day I leave here.

I'm having a wonderful time, but the days are sure slipping by fast. Tomorrow we leave for a week at the beach—we finagled (?) a free cabin in S. Carolina, a few miles south of Myrtyl Beach. Lucy and I are both looking forward to it, even though we know that the 13th is fastly approaching. Oh, well—that first means next May 13 is coming too—I guess.

About all we've really done so far is to go shopping—Lucy's bought more clothes in the past week than she has since we got married! Today (Lucy had to go to work) I went down to Fort Eustis to see Frank Currier. He got me an appointment with a lawyer in the AG building, and I got my will and a power of attorney made out. Lucy and I both have to go back tomorrow so I can get her military dependents ID. I found out, by the way, that the GI bill has gone up, so that, after I get out, I'll get almost $225/month to go to school on!

Well, not much else to say—first wanted you to know that I arrived safely—it was really a beautiful flight over the mountains. I leave Richmond on United Airlines, May 12 at 4:00, and I arrive in San Francisco at 8:30—4 hours—that's fantastic, isn't it!

I'll drop you a postcard from the beach. Stay in touch.

Love,
Dail

PFC Dail W. Mullins, Jr.
RA12927044
Personal Mail Section
APO, SF. 96381

May 12, 1969

Dear Mom and Dad,

While Lucy and I were down at Myrtyl Beach, we chanced to stop in at a small antique shop which specialized in the buying and selling of books—so many different types you wouldn't believe! I couldn't resist, of course, and bought two—one Agatha Christie collection of short stories and a large, hard-cover book entitled "The World's Greatest Letters". The latter is a fascinating anthology of letters written by various and sundry famous and infamous people. Well, after reading these, I have resolved to try and compose somewhat more interesting letters than in the past—after all—someday I may be famous (or infamous?), and I'll want to afford any anthologist a wealth of material from which to choose.

At the moment I am 35,000' in the air, somewhere over Ohio or Indiana; heading toward San Francisco. It's 6:30 PM in St. Louis, but my watch says 3:30, since I set it for Pacific Daylight time when we left Dulles Airport about 1 1/2 hours ago. We're due to land in Frisco at 8:30, so I should get my first glimpse of a Pacific sunset.

I could have arranged to stop-over in St. Louis enroute, I suppose, but I'm awfully tired of saying goodbye to everyone—frankly, together with the prospect of spending a year in that hell-hole, Vietnam, saying goodbye so many times has just become too emotionally exhausting. While it is fine that you and Lucy can accompany such partings with the customary, and, somewhat strangely, comforting, tears, our society, unfortunately, forbids crying on the part of men. Consequently, the emotion of having to say goodbye must necessarily remain locked within us—and it makes you weary. I hope you understand. As I explained to Lucy, I'd just as soon get on with it and get this over with. The sooner I leave, the sooner I'll be back—that's why I hope they don't keep us in Oakland too long.

I am enclosing a copy of the will that I had drawn up at Fort Eustis, solely because I had named you as my alternate executor. I hope you are not offended at having been "cut-out" of my will, but upon checking my "estate" out, I discovered that there just wasn't enough to go around! Perhaps in time. . . . .

About that hand gun, again. Don't go and buy one yet, please. Let me find out what my units policies are toward that sort of thing, first, and if I think I'd feel better having one around, I'll, of course, let you know. But I would hate to get fined or court-martialed for breaking any rules.

Later on this evening we're to see a movie in flight—"Backtrack", a western based on the TV "Virginian" series. At least it will help the time pass.

I'll get a hotel room in San Francisco tonight and maybe see a movie if there's one close by. Tomorrow, then, I'll take a bus over to Oakland and report in for the start of my "great adventure".

So, until I have more to tell you, take care, don't worry about me (HAH! Lucy said) and write when you can.

Thinking about you both,

Love,
Dail

PFC Dail W. Mullins, Jr.
RA12927044
Personal Mail Section
APO, SF 96381

14 May, 1969

Dear Mom and Dad,

I guess it doesn't take much common sense to realize that most of what I had to say on the phone this afternoon could very well have been taken care of by letter—in fact, I am enclosing the fact sheet from which I got all the information so you can put it on that catch-all bulletin board in the kitchen. The main reason I called, of course, was just to have someone to talk to. I've always told you that I thought the worst part of any assignment was the first few weeks—the breaking in part, so to speak. Even though its the same old Army, the faces are always different, as are the places—and being "alone" (which we all really are, no matter how many other fellas are in the same boat), especially having to face a year in a combat zone, almost forces one to seek out a familiar voice, even if that voice is 1500 miles away, I realize that kind of loneliness can get expensive though, so if I do call from 'Nam sometime this year, I'll foot the bill—I understand that a 10 minute conversation to the East Coast is about $24, which means it would be a little less to St. Louis.

I was just talking to a nice young fella from Chicago who's mother just died—he was in Vietnam when it happened and got a 30-day emergency leave, but, of course, has to return now. He said the only thing wrong with coming home like that is that you have to go through all the depression of returning a second time. I feel awfully sorry for the poor guy—he's in the infantry, which didn't seem to bother him too much—he's mainly worried about his Dad, who's an aging diabetic. I swear, you'd think the Army would have some compassion on fellas like that. Anyway, the fella said that he was in Vietnam almost a whole month before he got any mind at all—that just added to my depression. I hope I get those letters you and Lucy have sent and will be sending before then! Oh, well, if I don't I don't, that's all. If your puzzled by the fact that my letters may not be making any appropriate references to yours, you'll realize that I probably haven't gotten any yet—but keep them "cards and letters comin' in"—I'll get them eventually. I've decided that a soldier's need for mail is a product of both his contentment at learning that everything at home is proceeding normally and a desire for these people at home to know that he's alright too, and needs to be remembered now and then.

I listened to Nixon's speech tonight—it was alright except that tomorrow Hanoi will call it a capitalist trick, so I doubt if very much will be accomplished. Well, the chance of maybe coming home sooner is something to dream about anyway.

Well, when I told you I thought we'd be leaving tomorrow (May 15) I wasn't wrong. We leave on a United Airlines chartered flight from Travis Air Force base tomorrow at 3:00 PM. We'll either fly to Honolulu and then Japan before Vietnam or to Anchorage, Alaska, Japan and then 'Nam. We're scheduled to land at Bien Hoa and then travel 7 miles by bus to Long Binh for our inprocessing and such. That information was provided in case your following my movement on a map. I believe I'll stay in Long Binh for approximately 2 weeks for climate training (the heat, you know—135°!) and more orientation on the strong and varied behavior of Charlie Cong.

Well, my next letter should be from that Southeast Asian Vacation Paradise, South Vietnam, and marked "FREE" where a stamp should be. I think that's awfully considerate of Uncle Sam, don't you? The scarcity of post offices in the jungle being what it is, and all.

I shouldn't be so bitter, I guess—that doesn't make it any easier. Some confirmed anti-war pacifists who've been to Vietnam have told me that, while you're there, the only way you can stand it, psychologically, is to convince yourself that you really are doing a just and noble job for the "greatest country on earth" and that the United States is doing the right thing there. Perhaps it will come to that, since I can see the difficulties in trying to do as tough a job as this one and hating every minute of it. Nixon was right tonight, I think, when he said that the American soldier has never had to fight such a thankless war. Even when you consider the fact that most of these young fellas are here only because of the consequences they must face if they refuse, their courage and fortitude is striking. Then again, it may just be natural self-preservation.

Well, so long dear Parents—I am off on my greatest adventure to date (and hopefully my last, if they're all as "great" as this one!)

Remember to keep me in mind, but don't worry excessively (I know it doesn't do any good to say don't worry at all). I may be a representative of my country in a foreign land and all that jazz, but first of all I'm going to look out for the big I. I doubt if the National honor will be too much affronted if it were to know that I'm fused with the dirt at the bottom of my foxhole—too bad if it is! I'll be thinking about all of you constantly—and please take care of yourselves too. I'll write soon.

Love,
Dail

THE VIETNAM CORRESPONDENCE

17 May, 1969

Dear Mom and Dad,

    Arrived safely at Bien Hoa, Vietnam around 1:30 AM, Saigon time. When we arrived at the replacement center here, was told that I'd be joining the 39th Combat Engineer Battalion. I haven't been shipped out yet, though, so I don't have my complete new address. Will send it as soon as possible. Meanwhile, send all mail to the address I gave you, as it will be forwarded to me. This place is hot as blazes (90° at 8:30 AM) and smells somewhat. Please take care and you'll be hearing from me. Please write!

Love,
Dail

PFC Dail W. Mullins, Jr. RA12927044
CoA, 26th Engr. BN.
APO SF 96374

May 19, 20—I don't know

Dear Folks,
    You'll probably have to excuse the appearance of this letter, since I usually have to carry the thing around in my pocket for a day or two before I get a chance to finish. With temperatures into the 100°'s and a standing humidity of about 93%, things, especially paper and people, get pretty crumbly.
    After arriving at Bien Hoa airport, as I had mentioned in my postcard, we were sent to the large replacement company at Long Binh, which is about 22 miles NE of Saigon, to await further orders. Mine said I had been assigned to the 39th Engineers Battalion, combat. I didn't know, nor could anyone tell me, where this unit was located—a guy that worked in the post office at Long Binh said that the APO number was up north, in the Americal Division. Sure enough, the next day my name was called out for the group going to Chu Lai (pronounced chew lie), which is in the I corps area, about 50 miles south of Danang. The Americal Division, which is composed of 3 light infantry brigades and several artillery bases, is based at Chu Lai. All but a few of the fellas travelling in my group to Chu Lai had orders assigned to the adjutant general's office, headquarters—this means that their final assignments were to be made by the people up at Americal Division headquarters. The sergeant who talked to us when we first arrived said that all of our orders might be changed, and that some guys with non-infantry MOS' might be put in the infantry, since the Americal Division had been hit so hard lately. Other guys I've talked to say that they are sticking pretty much with the MOS', though. I sure hope so—I'd hate to be part of an infantry unit alone, much less one that had been getting hit hard lately! I did find a guy from the 39th En. Bn., and it is here at Chu Lai, so I hope my orders will hold. This guy said that the two most common things they did were minesweeping and bridge building. This guy also said that he had had malaria and had also been shot twice—he may have been telling a story, though.
    Last night was Ho Chi Minh's birthday, and they told us to expect either a rocket and mortar attack or a ground assault sometime during the night. This made me somewhat nervous, as we have, as yet, not been issued our weapons. Well, about 3:30 AM, the sirens started—everybody jumped out of their beds, ran out of the barracks and into the bunkers—I sat there cringing for the first rocket to hit. The bunkers afford good protection unless there's a direct hit—then you can hang it up. Well, after about 5 minutes of no mortars or rockets, we realized

that it must be a ground assault. Earlier in the day some guy said the 3 divisions of NVA troops had been spotted in the mountains in front of us. Off in the distance we could hear small arms fire and mortars going off, and after about 1/2 hour, we got an all clear. Thank goodness they didn't break through—what could you do with no weapon? I was planning on running down to the beach and hiding in the water should they have gotten in.

Well, I just wanted you to know that I was still kicking. Of course you both and Lucy are on my mind constantly—it is terribly lonely and frightening here with no mail from home. Oh, about the mail. I should get my orders today or tomorrow, with my address on them. I'll send it to you, and you can begin writing. I'll still be in this replacement company for about another 5-days, however, for a week of RVN training when I get to my unit, I hope there'll be some mail waiting. I'll wait to get that address before I send this off.

Later in the day

Well, they changed my orders some, but at least I got another engineer unit. Please write at the following address so there'll be a letter awaiting my arrival.

PFC Dail W. Mullins, Jr. RA12927044
CoA, 26th Engineer BN.
APO SF 96374

Please don't forget about me—it's awfully lonely and scary over here, and when I start out into the bush and mountains around here, it's probably going to get more so. I'll be as careful and alert as I can and don't you folks worry too much.

Love,
Dail

PFC Dail W. Mullins, Jr. RA12927044
CoA, 26th Engr. BN.
APO SF 96374

May 23, 1969

Dear Mom and Dad,

I guess you're both pretty anxious and worried about me, not having heard in a few days—this training and the heat really takes it out of you by the end of the day, though, so that I have trouble keeping my eyes open to even write a letter to Lucy. Now, however, before our night class on flares, I shall try and at least start a letter to you. I may have to finish it tomorrow, though.

As I indicated, we're still here at the Chu Lai replacement center taking a cram-course in subjects valuable to the combat soldier over here in the sun-and-fun capital of the world. Last night our group had to pull perimeter guard in a few of the bunkers down by the beach—Chu Lai's eastern perimeter boundry. All this necessitated was sitting in a bunker with umpteen rounds of ammo and a flak jacket, watching to see that no VC tried to swim across the Chu Lai bay of the S. China Sea with snorkels and penetrate our defense. Fortunately, they didn't try. I think if I had seen one Cong I'd have thrown 12 hand grenades and fired 200 rounds at him. Pulling perimeter guard is one thing I will definitely be doing at the LZ where I'll be stationed, so I'd better get used to it.

Today we took a convoy out to LZ (landing zone) Bayonette, one of the many smaller sub-bases which surround Chu Lai, for one final training period with some of the weapons most commonly in use over here.

I understand that we'll be shipping out to our units on Sunday or Monday, so I have just a few more days to go without mail. It's a horrible feeling not to know what's going on back home with your loved ones, but hopefully there'll be some mail waiting. I found out that Company A of the 26th engineer battalion is stationed at an LZ just outside of Duc Pho, Vietnam, about 20 miles South of Chu Lai. My address, of course, will remain the same.

Later that night

Well, I found out this evening that we won't be shipping until next Wednesday—not Sunday after all. I'm of two minds about it, but not really. On the one hand is relatively safe here—on the other hand, I receive no mail whatsoever, and that makes it awfully hard.

Well, about all I can say is, write, so those wonderful letters will be there when I arrive, and keep wishing me the best—I know you will, and I shall stay alert. I miss you all terribly much and am already longing for the day when I can return home to you all.

Your loving son,
Dail

———————

PFC Dail W. Mullins, Jr.
RA12927044
488-48-0511
CoA, 26th Engr., BN.
APO, SF, 96256

27 May 1969

My dear Parents,

    Well, tomorrow is the big day (Wednesday here, Tuesday where you are)—I ship to my new unit. I got quite a jolt yesterday when I heard on the Radio that 10 engineers had been killed in an ambush while on a minesweeping operation 16 miles south of Duc Pho. Duc Pho, as you know, is where I'm headed. Whether or not these 10 boys were from company A of the 26th engineers, I don't know, but I have a sneaking suspicion they were. It seems that every engineer to come into the replacement center here is going to the same unit I am. I hope that doesn't mean they need alot of replacements because they're all getting killed—that's a jolly thought.

    I was on bunker guard last night, again, down on the beach. About midnight a red flare went up from down the beach about 1/2 a mile. We had been told that a red flare meant enemy penetration, so I immediately grabbed my rifle and waited, not really knowing what to expect. Well, I heard about 6 shots in the distance, then saw a white flare (for illumination), and then about 2 minutes later, a green flare, which supposedly means all clear. I waited awhile longer, shaking in my boots, but all was quiet. Other than that, the night was fairly uneventful.

    I volunteered for barracks orderly today. That's when you stay in the barracks all day to clean up some and then guard the other peoples gear so that no one comes in and steals it. It's a little lonely here all alone, but it gives me a chance to write and do a little thinking. You think about so many things over here, and can really get yourself in a turmoil. If you start to worry about yourself too much, you begin to feel guilty about not thinking of your loved ones, who are worrying too, at home. And, if you start thinking about them too hard, you go nuts. I miss everyone so much already I can hardly stand it—how I'm going to make it a whole year over here I don't know. I try and act brave like all these young kids over here, but the facade breaks down when I'm alone. I am frightened—frightened to death, but what can you do except go on, hoping that that bullet, or rocket or mortar doesn't have your name on it. War is so stupid! Why must man fight his brother?

    I've noticed, like you said I probably would, that most of these guys over here have pretty bad backgrounds—broken homes, divorces, etc.—and I wonder if that doesn't have something to do with bravery? Is the reason I'm such a coward when it comes to something like this because I have so much to live for? A wonderful wife, wonderful parents and a fairly bright future. All of these things seem so very, very far away. But, I know you're all pulling for me, and perhaps that is what will keep me going. I hope and pray it is.

I'm sorry for the depressing letter.

Love,
Dail

PFC Dail W. Mullins, Jr. RA12927044
CoA, 26th ENGR. BN.
APO SF, 96256

29 May 1969

Dear Parents

Well, George Norris (the other guy going to A company) and I have left the Replacement Center at Chu Lai for our units. Right now we're at the 26th engineer's battalion headquarters here at Chu Lai, waiting for a chopper to take us to Company A. When I got here I found out that Company A isn't at Duc Pho at all, but, rather, is further up north, toward Da Nang. We'll be located at a place called LZ Baldy. Also, I was talking to another guy here who's been up at LZ Baldy awhile, and he says the APO number is 96256, not 96374, like I've been using. Well, my orders say 96374, and the postal clerk says its 96374, so I don't know what's coming off now. No matter what the APO number is, any letters you've sent will reach me sooner or later, but a wrong APO can hold up the mail for several weeks—So, when I get up there I'll get the right address and send it to you right away. I was so hoping there would be some mail waiting, but if that number really is wrong, I guess I'll have to wait some more. Oh, folks, its so lonely and frightening over here.

Talking to these guys from LZ Baldy around here, the engineers up there are currently carrying out mine sweeps, building bunkers and culverts under roads and blacktopping a road—plus dodging bullets. Apparently there are alot of VC up there. I'm sure not looking forward to getting shot at—in fact, I'm rather scared to death. But, I guess if other guys can make it, I can too. Please don't forget about me, Mom and Dad, and keep writing.

Love,
Dail

P.S:—Start sending the mail to

PFC Dail W. Mullins, Jr. RA12927044
CoA, 26TH ENGINEER BATTALION
APO SF 96256

↑

Note the new APO #

As I said, any mail you sent will get to me sooner or later (knowing the Army, later), but this new address should get it to me fast.

PFC Dail W. Mullins, Jr.
RA12927044
488-48-0511
CoA, 26th ENGR. BN.
APO SF, 96256

30 May 1969

My dear Parents,
   Please excuse my rather short, impersonal Memo that I sent yesterday, but I was rather pressed for time.
   Both George Norris and I were put into 2nd platoon, but when we got here, they were all out at LZ Ross, just finishing up their turn out there. They're due back today at noon, and one of the other platoons will go up there. Second platoon will probably mine-sweep this end of the road and begin pulling maintenance on some of their equipment. We have an IG inspection coming up, and the stuff has to be in pretty good shape.
   As I told Lucy in a letter, it's no fun not having any mail coming in, believe me. I sent you my final, correct address, so when you start using that, we should be able to establish fairly regular contact. Even then, though, I understand it takes my letters approximately 7–8 days to reach you, and if it takes that long coming back, messages will be, what, about 2 weeks to have an answer. The letters you sent to the old APO numbers will eventually get here, but until they do, I'll just have to hope and pray everything comes out alright—that you folks and Lucy are all OK.
   I've been trying to figure out how dangerous it's going to be around here. Actual mine sweeping isn't too bad, since just walking over an anti-truck mine

doesn't supply enough weight to detonate it—it takes something like a truck. After the sweep, however, and before a convoy proceeds along the road, someone (an engineer) has to drive the pressure test truck along it. This is a 10-ton monster you drive backwards by sitting on the hood—if a mine blows the truck, you then have a good chance of being blown off. I'll never volunteer to drive the thing, but, of course, if I'm ordered to do so, I'll have to.

Whenever we go out on a sweep we have an infantry unit along as security—there's always the danger, of course, of an ambush or sniper fire. All the engineers have M-16 rifles with 7 magazines, 18 rounds each, for self-protection.

The engineers also have part of the perimeter to defend here at LZ Baldy. Usually there are 3 men to a bunker, unless there's an alert, then the number will rise. Bunker guard isn't bad unless there is a ground assault or a ZAPPER SQUAD of VC tries to sneak in—then it can get pretty hot.

I guess you were right about religion coming to a person in time of stress, because I'm starting to do some serious thinking and praying. Last night I lay in bed and asked God to take care of all of you and to see me through this, my time of greatest need. All of the other fellows around here seem fairly happy and carefree—perhaps I will to, in time. Most have the attitude that if its their time to go, they'll go, and there's nothing going to stop it.

This idea has always been foreign to me, but if that's the only way to remain sane over here, I guess I'll just have to adopt it too. I'm really not so afraid of dying as I am afraid of knowing what it would do to Lucy and you all. If anything does happen to me, Mom and Dad, I want you both to promise that you'll take care of her for me—I love her so much, and want her always to be as happy as possible.

Well, enough of that morbid talk. I am going to make it, I've got to—as I said before, I have too much to live for.

I miss you all, and hope I soon get some mail from you folks and Lucy. Keep writing, something's got to get here soon. Don't forget to use that new APO number and my social security number on the address.

Love,
Dail

PFC Dail W. Mullins, Jr.
RA12927044
488-48-0511
CoA, 26th ENGR. BN.
APO SF, 96256

2 June 1969

Dear Mom and Dad,

Please excuse the dirty paper, but I have perimeter guard tonight and I didn't get a chance to take a shower this evening. Needless to say, your hands get rather dirty over here.

Yesterday I went on my first mine sweep! Surprisingly enough, I rather enjoyed it—I guess that's because we didn't really run into any trouble. My platoon, 2nd, swept 1/2 of the dirt road between here, LZ Baldy, and LZ Ross, while 1st platoon, which is now stationed out at Ross, swept their half. The entire road is 12 miles long, so by the time we walked out 1/2-way and then back, we had a good 12-mile hump. I was pooped when we got back, and was rather glad we didn't have to sweep again today.

I enjoyed the sweep also because it gave me my first real contact with the rural folk of Vietnam. My heart really went out to these brave and battered little people, and for the first time I actually felt that my presence over here might be doing someone some good, if not myself, Lucy and you folks. After seeing these small, grass-hut villages along the road, with one-room, dirt-floor shacks housing five or six children, a papa-san and a mama-san, a couple of chickens and two water buffalo, you really have trouble understanding how Vietnam could be one of the wealthiest countries in SE Asia. Wealth is a relative thing, though, and I guess to the average American it implies two cars instead of 3 bowls of rice a day.

As soon as you walk out the main gate at LZ Baldy and start out on your sweep, you're surrounded by a bevy of 12, 13 and 14-year old girls carrying cans of cold soda and beer in a cardboard box mounted on the rear of a bicycle. Each GI is expected to "choose" a girl at this point. She then peddles along side you or behind you for the entire sweep, ready and willing to sell you a can of Coke or Budweiser for 50¢ whenever your water runs out (in about 1/2 hour in this heat). After walking 3 miles in 105° heat, you don't mind paying that price for a cold soda or beer, believe me! Besides, there's nothing else to spend this damn money on over here.

I mentioned that you "choose" a soda girl to follow you—and choose you do. Because you'd better not buy anything from one of the other girls or you get a good old fashioned Vietnamese cursing-out—and it sounds all that much worse when you can't understand what they're saying. If, on the other hand, you play by the rules, and buy 4 or 5 Cokes along the way, you become number 1 G.I.—and that is a real honor. By being a number 1 G.I, you are automatically subject to receiving various small gifts from these girls. The one I picked was an 11-year old doll named Lân—she was cute except for rather badly tobacco stained teeth. Oh, yes—the children start smoking over here at about age 5! Regular tobacco and not.

Lân, I believe, is the Vietnamese equivalent of Linda—at any rate, she seemed delighted when I told her my sister's name was Linda. She was fascinated by Lucy's pictures and thought my "wife boocoo (very) pretty". Apparently I made the grade of number 1 G.I., because she gave me a small comb for my "messy hair" and a little round, yellow mirror. I really felt sorry for the poor little thing—I guess she's seen more death and suffering in her short 11 years than most people see in a lifetime—and her eyes showed it. I'm looking forward to seeing her again on Wednesday when we make another sweep—these girls do add a few smiles to a tiring and dangerous job.

We found one mine Sunday—a 500 lb block of TNT with the words TO KILL AMERICANS AND ARVNS scratched on it. It shocks you back into the reality of what you're doing to see one of those lying in the road.

Well, folks—guess I'll close—it's getting too dark to see now and we're not allowed any prolonged lighting on the bunker line because it affords too easy a target. No letters have arrived yet, but I keep hoping they'll come in soon. Take good care of yourselves, please—I do worry about everyone as I know you do about me. I'm alright so far, though.

Love,
Dail

PFC Dail W. Mullins, Jr.
RA12927044
488-48-0511
CoA, 26th ENGR. BN.
APO SF, 96256

6 June 1969

Dear Mom and Dad,

Well, we just got back from another long sweep, and I've got a little time before I have to go on bunker guard, so I thought I'd at least begin a letter to you.

George Norris, a guy from my AIT Company who came to LZ Baldy with me, has been getting all kinds of mail, but, so far, I haven't gotten a one. I realize that, since it takes about a week for mail to get from here to you, you probably have only had my new address for a day or so as I write this now. Nevertheless, I do wish some of the letters you've written to the other addresses I've had would get here. I'm worried enough as it is about you all and Lucy, much less not having heard in almost a month. Perhaps they'll be coming in soon. I sure hope so. If I don't hear in a couple of weeks, I'm going to try and call on the MARS telephone line to make sure you're all OK and that you do have my address.

On the way home from the sweep today we stopped in a small village (about 50 huts) to eat lunch. It was pitiful the way all the people, young and old alike, flock around you begging for some of your C-rations to eat. I give away all I can, but I refuse to throw it at them like some of the fellows do. If you don't hand a can of crackers or a piece of chocolate to someone personally, they first fight over it like animals. I think that's terrible.

We found two mines today and blew them both up in place—one of them left a hole in the ground 10' deep and 10' wide. Can you imagine what that would do to a truck filled with AMMO or jet fuel?!

The lieutenant in charge of our platoon put me in charge of one of our platoon's two chain saws—Wow! I'm the only one who is allowed to operate it, and I also have to take care of it if something goes wrong. I understand we're going out to the field soon and spend a week building a suspension bridge across some river near LZ Ross. It shouldn't be too bad if the VC leave us alone.

Well, so far I'm OK. It's hot, dirty and lonely over here, but all the other fellows over here are in the same boat, so I guess I'll make it. I just hope everybody back home is taking care of themselves—please do, so I don't have to worry so much.

I'll write again as soon as I can.

Love, Dail

[Unclear when Dail got this letter or the next two]
Sunday [in Dail's handwriting: Probably May 11, 1969]

My dear Dail,

Perhaps this letter will be winging its way west the same day you are, I hope. Figure it will be a lonely few days until you get over the strangeness so hope this letter is waiting for you. Denny had said he'd try and have a letter waiting for you too.

When you called I had just been lying down getting a little shut-eye. We had been invited to the Hester's last nite for dinner and about five o'clock she called and said they hadn't had any electricity since 11 o'clock that morning and as she cooks by electric, she was having trouble. She had all the food prepared but couldn't cook it, so I told her to bring it over and we'd have dinner here. They didn't leave until two and these late hours just don't agree with your father and I.

Had the Skillings and their son Van and his wife and children over for cocktails Thursday nite. This is the son who lives in California, with good reason. Anyway they had just gotten back from eight weeks in Europe, England, Ireland, Spain—you name it and they had been there. Her parents both died within weeks of each other last year and they decided to use the money she inherited and see something before they were both too old to enjoy it. They evidently had the time of their lives and it really made me think when they mentioned how safe it was over there. At nite when Van and his wife would linger over their coffee the two children, who are 12 and 8, would often take a several block walk by themselves in whatever city they happened to be. If they did that in any large city in America, they would be either mugged, robbed, stabbed or killed. And here we are 6000 miles away trying to convince the rest of the world what they are missing by not living as we do. What a joke!

Thought you would be interested in the enclosed article which appeared in the Post Dispatch Friday evening. As I mentioned, I was talking to Bill Colbert's father Saturday and it's funny how compatible two people, who ordinarily would have nothing to say to each other, can be when they have sons in the Army. He was mentioning Bill's complete distaste for Seargeants. He especially hated one he had at Fort Leonard Wood whom he said spent the entire eight weeks telling them one filthy story after another or telling them how brave he had been in Viet Naam. Guess they are a breed.

Have a new suggested name for the puppy. Liberace, because she's the peeanist. We have got to have a name for her soon or she is never going to answer to anything.

Dad heard a joke he said I should pass on to you. Do you know how to tell the difference between girl chromosomes and boy chromosomes? You pull down their genes. Funny!

I thought the enclosed pictures on "Silly Saguaros" was clever. Often wished I had the imagination and mentality to see things in perspective like this.

Wanted your father to take your grandmother to dinner today with Basil. But I'll never be able to figure this family out. He is going to take her fishing Wednesday and says that will be in lieu of a mother's day present. Which it probably will be, altho they will probably both come home upset with each other. He's just going to take her to one of those stocked lake places, where you have a little chance of catching anything. We took a drive the other nite to check on some and he'll probably go to one that is out 66 near the Meramec. They both like to fish but after your father is with her more than two hours things begin to happen. I plan to make myself scarce when he gets home.

Well you be sure and keep in touch as often as you can and you'll hear from me if the mail service is any good at all. Please let us know if there is anything you want or need and we'll try and get it.

We'll be thinking of you often and all our love,
Mom & Dad

[undated; May 14 or thereabouts, 1969]

My dear Dail,
 Hope I didn't get you too down with the tears the day you called, but as you say, women have this advantage. It's funny, but after I talked to you I thought of all the times in my life when I said never again would anything ever make me cry—that I had no tears left. What a joke?
 I had thought at first that I would make a determined effort to make all my letters to you light and gay and frothy. And then on a second consideration it dawned on me that then is when you would think something is going on and she is not letting me know. In other words, it would be very abnormal for me not to gripe; so you'll be getting my typical letters. For some reason I always used you for a battering ram in getting things off my chest, simply because you are the only one in this family I was ever able to talk to. This is one reason I will miss you so.
 Tried to get Aunt Dotty on Mother's Day but never could get through. Talked to Mr. and Mrs. Paschen tho and they are leaving for Louisville on the 26th of May in order to see Wendy graduate from high school.. They were upset in that young Bob had passed his physical and I guess it is a matter of time with him. Kurt Eisleben was at Fort Leonard Wood when you were, except he was going through basic. All the men from his class went to Fort Sill, except Kurt and a few others. Kurt, having majored in business administration happened to fill a needed vacancy on the post so he is still at Fort Leonard Wood doing administrative work. He'll probably luck out.
 Thank you so much for my Mother's Day card and as you say, this is one I'll remember. I got my usual original missile from Denny and a poet laureate he ain't. He had drawn a picture of a flower on the first page and inside was the following verse—

> If I had a choice of all the mothers;
> And if I could, Id' have my druthers (don't get this)
> You're the one who's tops with me;
> It's your day, relax, and have some tea.

From the youngest.

Doesn't that grab you! He's another Rod MkKuen.

Speaking of mothers, your grandmother was her usual cheerful, beautiful, wonderful self. I had told your dad that he and Basil should take her to dinner, but he was going to take her fishing today in lieu of this. He did send her a card and some flowers and then around 7 O'clock Sunday nite he took a ride over there. He was home again by 7:45 and said that no one was home and he assumed that she was at Basils. Monday all hell broke lose. She evidently called him at his office and claimed she was home all day alone and that he didn't come over and it went on and on. I really think she pretends she is not home so she can carry on like this. The sad thing is it really gets to your father and between his office, his help and his mother, along with you being on his mind—he's pretty down.

Speaking of the books you had acquired and particularly the one relating to letters. If there is any possibility of your keeping a diary I think it would be well worth your while. You do have the ability to convey thoughts on paper and who knows what could be done with one boy's (man's) personal record of Viet Naam. I'm quite serious. I just finished reading two books which impressed me. Perhaps not so much for any deep hidden meanings they conveyed but possibly because for the moment they penetrated a mood or perhaps a time of my life. One was Sloan Wilson's "A Sense of Values", which is about a modern suburban middle age marriage—and rather bitter. The other is a rather new publication entitled "Mr. Bridge" by Evan S. Connell, Jr. This last book has been reviewed as taking the place of Sinclair Lewis "Babbitt" as the typical American husband, father, and businessman. In other words he is the archetypal White, Anglo-Saxon, Protestant, middle-class, right-thinking pillar of society. It's written in almost grade school sentence structure and the entire book is short paragraphs which you at first think are trite, but they take a second scanning. For instance one section entitled Love—

"Often he thought: My life did not begin until I knew her.

She would like to hear this, he was sure, but he did not know how to tell her. in the extremity of passion he cried cut in a frantic voice: "I love you!" yet even these words were unsatisfactory. He wished for something else to say. He needed to let her know how deeply be felt her presence while they were lying together during the night, as well as each morning when they awoke and in the evening when he came home. However, he could think of nothing appropriate.

So the years passed, they had three children and accustomed themselves a life together, and eventually Mr. Bridge decided that his wife should expect nothing more of him. After all, he was an attorney rather than a poet; he could never pretend to be what he was not."

His contacts with his three children are in the same vein. I keep thinking of your father and his standard remark "nobody understands me." By golly, you be sure Lucy understands you.

As I mentioned we met Mr. Lake and his "new" wife; only believe me she isn't so new. She looks like she has been around a long time (meow, meow). Really, Jane looks like Raquel Welch compared to her—guess she either has personality or money.

Does this sound like one of my usual letters—I hope. The weather has been so rainy and dark haven't been able to take any pictures but I promise some soon. Take care, God speed, and we all miss you like the very devil.

With much love,
Mom & Dad

Sunday, May 18 [1969]

Our dear Dail,

Were your ears ringing last nite, or were you too busy avoiding shells? I've been promising Joan Seibert for years that I would have them over for Tacos. She has been so great for me this past week that I fixed a Mexican dinner for them last nite with Tacos, guacomole salad, chili con queso, the works and they seemed to enjoy it as much as you always did. When Charlie left he said it was the best meal he had in years. All during the dinner we talked about you and how much you would have enjoyed it. Soon this will be and hold on to that thought with all your might.

This morning for some vague reason I decided to go back to our old church. You know Mr. Murphy resigned about three months ago and they have had two young men taking over the pulpit on alternate Sundays. One is the student minister at Washington University and the other is a presbyterian who teaches theology at St. Louis University and who is currently under fire by the new Cardinal Carberry who has decided they have too many Protestants influencing the new young priests. Any way, I was so glad because it was so what I needed. His sermon was on Optimism and the old testament text from Psalms 121.

Your father has gotten a large map of Viet Naam which he is charting, but it is almost more than I can bear. I'm sure you know that the day after we received your last letter stating your destination—the next night the paper announced the hell that was breaking loose at Long Binh, Bioh Hoa. Neither of us slept a wink all night. As you have said—we women can release our emotions through our tears and for some reason it helps momentarily. But your Dad can do nothing but walk the house, rush to hear the news every hour and talk to everyone who comes in his office who have had sons or relatives in Viet Naam. He can't talk about it to me and as usual his manner in trying to express his feelings is to hand me a $100 and tell me to go buy something for myself. It breaks my heart.

By the way, you'll notice that on the back of this envelope I have started numbering my letters. Mailed one a week age Sunday, last Wednesday, and this is No. 3. That way if the mail gets held up and is delivered in bunches you can put them in sequence. Also, before I forget I am going to send you Dad's credit card from the phone company and if you get a chance use it to call Lucy and then she can write us. Now this doesn't mean every week. May be once every two months.

Dad wants me to head down to Aunt Dotty for a day before I go on down to Athens, if I pick up the children. But Uncle Bob's parents are going down there the 26th for Wendy's graduation so I think I'll just wait. We'd probably be such dampers on every one that I'd rather postpone it untile we can console each other in private. Altho at this point I don't know what to do about going down to get Dennis and Linda. Linda called the other day and said Bob wanted or was willing to drive them home. Now this is quite a bit out of his way and with the way Linda treated him I wouldn't blame his parents if they became quite upset about his driving her home.

Joan and Charlie were talking last nite about a recent (Mike) experience he had. He was alone in his patrol car and had picked up three negro suspects whom he put in the back of his car. As he started to take them to the station another car with two young fellows in it tried to squeese him to the side of the street. He out-maneauvered them and pulled his gun as he went over to interrogate them. As he reached into their car they rolled up their window on his arm and dragged him about 50 yards. He managed to pull loose finally with his arm lacerated and wired for help. They managed to capture the two fellows in the car and Mike said it's hard not to take a poke at fellows like this. Then two nights later he captured two hopped up parole violators in some woman's basement. As Joan said, he was a lot safer over in Viet Naam guarding his officers' clubs. Of course, he was lucky. Tom Lake was telling us that he thinks young Russell is on Hill 129, which doesn't sound good.

Right now I don't know if I went you to tell us what you are doing or where, but this again is not facing facts and we are all going to have to live with a lot the next year, so tell us all you can. You just keep watching out for No. 1 and we will all keep praying and thinking of you constantly.

I'll probably keep enclosing little clippings from the newspaper even tho, if I were where you are, I would be inclined, to be a little bitter in that life was going on back in the states with births, weddings and deaths. But maybe when you are far away your perspective changes about things like this.

Again please let us know if there is anything you can have that you would want us to send you. What about paper back books. I was going to take a trip up to the Webster Red Cross and ask them what their experience has been regarding what boys in Viet Naam need. I thought while I was there I would also inquire if they could use me one day a week doing something. I feel so damn useless. I've been knocking myself out working in the yard, waxing the cars, cleaning the house but all I keep saying is "what for".

God willing this thing will be over soon.

With all our love and thoughts,
Mom & Dad

Wednesday May 21 69

My dear "GI Joe",
Frankly I'd rather be addressing you as just plain John Doe and I'm sure you feel the same.

You'll never know how glad we were to get your post cards. I've been a nervous wereck about the plane ride and I don't know how I'm going to tolerate this year ahead of you. We received the card from Honolula, Wake Island (lovely spot), and the one you sent from Viet Naam. Too Bad you couldn't have landed in Wake when Nixon and old Thieu were there; you might have given them a neutral opinion about this stupid mess.

I've been watching the Apollo shot and I don't know whether you are kept abreast of these events, but everything has been going almost too perfect. How man can accomplish feats of this magnitude and can't learn to live with one another.

Took the puppy out to the Veterinarian today for her rabies shots and to have her ears cleaned and her toenails clipped. I spend more time on that stupid dog. Anyway I was asking Dr. Murphy about Tommy Rowe that worked for hime during the summer. I just wondered if he had gone on with veterinary training. He said = "Hell no, he's got some job in an office down town doing clerical work and drives a Cadillac." This dog is going to be worse than Babette ever was. She is absolutely nuts; and you should see her show off when we have company.

Do you remember a girl named Susan Heinrichs. She is a very attractive tall, thin blonde. I met her mother through Eloixe Skilling. She belongs to the Presbyterian church and twice when Eloise has invited me to lunch she has had Mrs. Heinrichs along. I believe this Sue used to date Harold Zeabold. Anyway about two years ago she had a few very short black out spells. The doctor they were going to thought it was all emotional and shrugged it off. The other day she had a sever spell while driving her car and managed to pull off to the side of the road. The police took her to County Hospital and her mother asked Dr. Skilling if he would have a look at her. After a series of tests they discovered the youngster has a brain tumour and they are operateing Friday morning. To add to the sadness, her father died about two months ago. I guess if we look hard enough we'll always find someone with problems.

Went shopping today and I met little Gail Goetz, who graduated with Linda. She is married and evidently her husband was tabbed the same time you were. He is in Georgia at OCs and as she says, hates every minute of it, but he is just playing for time, hoping it will be over by the time he has finished.

Well your father just walked in after his fishing trip with your grandmother. Evidently it wasn't too bad except we had quite a storm blow up here today and on the way home some physicisan skidded into the back of your father's car. No car damage was done but your grandmother complained about her neck. The doctor thought she should be watched and should be with someone so now Dad has this to worry about.

As you know, we are supposed to leave Saturday morning for Tan-Tar-A and I am not looking forward to it at all. I'm resenting anyone daring to have any fun while you and Lucy are so miserable. Anyway my next letter to you will be from Tan-Tar-A.

Linda called last Thursday to tell me she was going to Florida with Bob and Lenny. She isn't supposed to be unavailable while she is Sweetheart of Denny's fraternity so no one was going to know where she was (isn't that stupid). Anyway I sort of "blew my stack" and said that with you headed for Viet Naam I couldn't care less about her plans and that she had better give some thoughts to things besides her pleasure. Of course I regretted this as soon as I had said it. She said "Mother, there isn't a morning when I wake up that my first thought is Dail and I have had a long talk with thier minister down there and he is mentioning you in his prayer service every Sunday". She said I'm not going to tell Dail because I know how he feels about things like this, but I just know everything is going to work out alright and he and Lucy are going to be together soon. So then I feel like a heel.

The Reinhards were here for dinner Sunday and she asked for your address. So you might be hearing from them. She said she was going to send you something and write. I really hope you start getting some of this mail. I'd rather you would get two or three letters a week than a dozen in one bunch.

Well you know we are thinking of you every minute of every day and will be anxiously waiting to hear from you.

With all the love there is.
Mom & Dad

Friday, May 23 69

My dear Son,
    We are always so relieved when we hear from you and then when we read what you are going through and where you are I think sometimes I'd just as soon not know where you are.
    It makes it a little confusing wondering whether you will get this letter first or if the mail piled up at San Francisco will meet you first. But after I received your letter today I had made up my mind I'd get a letter off if I did nothing else.
    As you may remember, we are to leave tomorrow for Tan-Tar-A and I had planned to take some pictures and write my next letter to you from there. I'll do this anyway but I did want something to reach you. Still don't know if I am to drive to Athens to bring Denny and Linda home. I wrote Bob a long letter trying to tell him how we felt about Linda and about him. I'd much rather stay out of the whole affair but he wanted me to write to hime. He has said he would bring the children home, but I have told him if it would anyway cause trouble at home I would rather he didn't. They are to call me tonite.
    Perhaps you will be interested in Bob Kaspareks latest state of affairs. In order to fullfill all the requirements of this Fullbright he should stay over there until July 7. The Webster Draft board started getting a little testy and wanted him home for his physical. He cabled and asked if he could get his physical over there. They said yes and so he had a Swedish physician examine him and of course the form was filled out in this language. No one at the draft board could read it so they have asked hime to have it translated into either German or English. His idea is that all this fooling around will take him until July 7. Watch this wheeler and dealer get some soft berth or be rejected.
    In my last letter I mentioned Susan Heinrichs going in for this brain tumour operation. I talked to Dr. Skilling today, as they were leaving for Florida, and he tells me the prognosis for her is very bad. The tumour is in such an inaccessible place that they are quite afraid she might not make it throught the operation. She is such a pretty girl.
    Had bridge club Wednesday nite and Winnie Bill was talling me that Wayne was home for his last leave before he heads over to Viet Naam. I'd give anything for her faith.
    Are you able to see or hear any of the news going on over the world. I was thinking of the Astronauts. Of course, I have the raido and television on all day

listening for any news I can hear. This latest Apollo shot has been quite exciting. I was watching on television when they ran into a little trouble as they neared the moon. It was quite a shock to hear one of them yell over the air "Son-of a Bitch" what the hell is happening. This is when they failed to flip some switch and went into their wild gyration. This is probably the coolest group ever to be in this program. You know one of the guys is called Charlie Brown and the space capsule has been named Snoopy. The other day when I was watching their showing shots of the earth and moon and the inside of the capsule, they said they were going to have their music hour. And out of this capsule comes a recording of Frank Sinatra singing "Fly Me to the MOOn". Boy, thats being cool.

Received a letter from Denny and that school they are going to is having its problems. They have three of the top men resign. If things don't straighten out I'm afraid we are going to have to look into a new school as we can't afford to spend this kind of money for a school that might lose its accreditation. Denny is showing a lot of maturity in staying in the middle of the road down there in this issue between school and student.

Well the Vermillions are coming over for bridge tonite so I'd better get on the stick.

Does all this chatter seem trite to you while you are running from town to town, trying to avoid being hit by shell fire. I just don't know what kind of letters you'd like to have. The world does go on in its usual gay fashion and I know this must be compeltetely maddening to you. It would be to me. Just don't forget there isn't a minute of the day that you arent't in our thoughts and I've got my fingers crossed, my knees, and my ankles while I pray constantly.

You are missed more than you will ever know and we are all with you every minute. I do hope you get your mail soon and please let us know if there is anything we can send you.

With all the love in the world—
Mom & Dad

What a typist

———————————

PFC Dail W. Mullins, Jr.
RA12927044
488-48-0511
CoA, 26th ENGR. BN.
APO SF, 96256

7 June 1969

My dear Parents, Linda, Denny and houseguests,
    Well, today I hit the jackpot. I got 3 letters from Lucy, 1 from Lena and 3 from you all. I got 1 from Lucy and 1 from you (Dad) yesterday, dated June 1, and the ones I got today were all dated the end of May. Even though they're out of sequence, I can't tell you what a relief it was to hear from everyone.
    Thanks so much for the picture—anymore you send will be most welcome. I trust that by now everyone is aware of the fact that I am not at Duc Pho, but rather North of Chu Lai, at LZ Baldy, near Da Nang. We have our own APO number here at Baldy, 96256, and when you start sending the mail to that APO number, I should get letters in 5 to 6 days. I assume my mail takes approximately the same length of time to reach you.
    It sounds like you both had a wonderful time at Tan-Tara, even though, as you said, such seems unreal to me now. Everyone over here refers to the United States as "the world"—and, believe me, it is true. When someone asks you, "Where are you from in the world?" you know right away what they mean. Places like Tan-Tara, St. Louis, Richmond, all seem so very, very far away. I don't think it would be half as bad if we were fighting this war in Mississippi or Canada—the distance that separates us from our families and loved ones is enough, in itself, to depress you, even in this, the jet age.
    I appreciate the invitation to call you and Lucy on the phone. There is a MARS station here at Baldy, and I will call someday. I'm tempted to now, but I best wait awhile—otherwise I'm lible (sp.?) to get in the habit of making too many. I think the rate to the east coast is about $8.00 for 3 minutes. I'll have to call collect—that's the only way we're allowed to use MARS.
    I'm enclosing a few choice cartoons from Cavalier Magazine and the Army Times—I particularly like the one which shows the GI in "Nam planning to attend college when he gets out of the Army. I like the one from the Army Times by Oliphant—you, of course, have heard of Hamburger Hill?
    I didn't know that David Emerson was stationed near Da Nang. Please tell the Emerson's to mention in their next letter to him that I'm with the 26th engineers at LZ Baldy—he'll know where that is; perhaps he could make a run down to see me.

During the day I always think of a 1001 things to write about, but when the time comes to put them down in print I lose my memory.

We went on another long sweep the day before yesterday. I think I enjoy those sweeps more than anything, because we get to get out and see the people and talk with them. We found two mines along the road and blew them both in place with dynamite. They made two rather large holes in the ground.

They issued us all brand new M-16's when we got to the company area, so I doubt that I'll need a pistol. Moreover, I might get in trouble carrying an unauthorized weapon around here. Let's hold off on it until I become a little more accustomed to the rules and regulations around here.

About your letters not containing any interesting information—believe me, folks, all I want to do is be able to hear that everything is going on about the same as usual back home. Let me supply the adventurous stories this year. I'd probably just worry if I knew that anything out of the ordinary were occurring back in "the world".

About all I can say to those people who ask you if you aren't proud that I'm over here in this hellhole is to tell them to kiss my a__! Why don't all these patriotic hawks say goodbye to their families and join the party so us less patriotic doves can go home! How many of those people who have stars and stripes in their eyes would like sleeping in rat and mosquito infested hooches, wake up to the sound of rockets and mortars coming in at 3:00 AM and sit on a dark bunker line scanning the black horizon for a sign of Charley crawling up on you through barbed wire with a satchel charge of high explosives ready to throw at you. Glamorous, huh! Thanks, but I much prefer Lucy and my work to this crap. If I make it back to the world I can't wait for the first person to ask me if I'm not proud of myself. I may value what I learn about oriental culture and the people of Vietnam for the rest of my life, but as far as my own country is concerned, this experience will only further disillusion me as to the great and wonderful America—for the people, by the people and of the people—BALONEY. Sweden may not be heaven on earth, but my children will never serve in the Army of the United States, I guarantee you!

I'm sorry I spouted off like that, but when you live right next door to the MEDIVAC hospital here at Baldy and see about 15 choppers land everyday with young kids who have been killed or wounded up in the mountains—well, it's a lot different than sitting in front of Huntley-Brinkley with a martini.

I'm afraid my mood has deteriorated to the ridiculous, so I'd better sign off. I really do appreciate the letters from home, folks—please, please keep writing—Anything! I miss all of you terribly much.

Love, Dail

P.S.—Try and keep Lucy cheered up as much as you can—you might send her these cartoons if you write to her.

———————————

Monday June 2, 1969

Our dear Son,
    Well today we received the letter you had written on May28 with another move and this time I can't even find the damn place on the map. And I am sick that you haven't received any of the letters we have been writing you. Is there anyone I can write to that will do any good. I'm just beside myself with frustration. Your father wrote to you Sunday and he is feeling the strain too. He very seriously asked me Sunday whether I thought there would be a possibility of his replacing you in Viet Naam (in the Dental Corp, of course.) I said knowing the Army they would probably make him a cook. I mean it, if there was any chance that they would replace you with his efforst, he would be packed tomorrow.
    Our hearts are very heavy and God how we have prayed, thought and cried. And then we keep asking the eternal Why! Why!. Of course, I've asked myself this many many times in my life and all things do pass. Know that we are going through everything you are and that you are not alone.
    Well the final troop came in this evening. Bob and Linda got in around 7 PM with an aquarium of turtles and a large glassy tank with two gerbels. Of course, the dog can't understand all this commotion but does she love it. In the two days Denny has been with here she is completely impossible and now I have Denny to contend with. Bob was informed about his mothers call as she had asked me to have him contact her the minute he arrived. He is evidently trying to definitely break the strings and he told them if there was any discussions he was going to move out and get his own apartment. He is very emphatically trying to get across to them that he is going to live his own life the way he wants it and he doesn't want them to think he is ungrateful for what they have giveen him but he must break the ties. Well, we'll see.
    Dad wants Linda to start working with him right away and this is going to be an interesting summer. He is at his all day and night seminar at the moment so he hasn't seen the kids yet. Linda has an idea he was going to have her at the desk and Christine in the room with him working on patients, but it is going to be the other way around. I'm sure you can hear her response to this. EEEK, I hate looking at tonsils and teeth and I can't stand all that blood. I know one thing, I'm going to make myself scarce when they come home at night until they both cool down.
    Denny is to see the man he worked for last summer on Wednesday and he is fervently hoping he will be able to use him. Summer jobs are again extremely

scarce and I sure hope he gets something. For the money and also for the keeping busy.

Talked to Jane Lake today and she said she hadn't heard from Russell for so long and then finally go a letter stating that his group was going to Okinaw to clean up their tanks and then to the Phillipins for some specialized training and then back to Viet Naam. I asked her how long he had been over there and she said it would be a year in September, and I thought it just isn't possible he has been over there that long—and in the next moment I thought how irrational as it seems you have been there forever. David Emerson is on his way to Australia for his R and R, for two weeks. I didn't know this was a spot you could pick.

Dr. Sprengnether was here Sunday with his dog. You know he has this little poodle that he takes to his office every day and it travels with him wherever he goes. It's funny to see a grwon man walking around with this little dog.

Want to take some pictures of the kids in the next day or two and send to you.

Well we wait so anxiously for your letters and Dad calls every day to see if I heard from you and then when they come I cry and walk around talking to myself and swearing at the whole world.

Went over to South Webster Pres. church Sunday and I do like this new young minister they have subbing. They sure ought to try and get him permanently. I talked to him after the service and he was telling me that his younger brother is in Viet Naam right now. This fellows name is Muffey.

Be good, be alert, and you take care of yourself and we love you much and miss you much much and think of you much much much.

With all the love in the world,
Mom & Dad

June 7, 1969

Dear, dear Dail,

We have been receiving your mail in around five days. The last letter which we received Thursday, was dated May 30. We haven't received any letters since this date and of course we worry, but it is still better than Jane Lake's problem. She doesn't hear from Russell for several weeks and then she again goes up to the Red Cross and they put their wheels in motion and she is informed that he is alright.

Now! We are all going to have to settle down. This morning your father came down for breakfast and he hadn't closed his eyes all night. He'd been fighting the Viet Naam war every step of the way with you. I have the release of tears, which helps; but he can do nothing but bleed inside. We were out for dinner with the

Seiberts last nite and he and Charlie got into a violent discussion of American Policies and old "tricky-dicky" Nixon, and it is foolish because it just tears you apart inside and you can do absolutely nothing. You wonder how anyone can assassinate people when you read about the Kennedys and Martin Luther King, but I believe if your father were to meet Nixon he would find it hard to restrain himself from beating him.

YOU must stop worrying about us, Lucy or anything but yourself. You know that if Lucy needs anything we will be right there. We have informed her of this and we never go anywhere that we don't let her know exactly where we are at all times. She is as much loved as any of you children and we consider her in all ways our own daughter and she also has two very devoted and loving parents who are watching over her. Then too, you can have the peace of mind about her conduct while you are away, knowing that she will be true and waiting—which is a lot more than a great many fellows over there have. As you say, a great many of the dare-devil boys feel they have nothing to lose, as they left nothing of value behind. By the same token, these same fellows have nothing to come home to, which, By God, you do. So just keep remembering that, don't worry about us, and keep your wits on our No. 1. Man. As far as I'm concerned you are the only person in Viet Naam and if they dare let anything happen to you they are really going to heave a wild cat on their hands and I mean this with all my heart. You'll see my name in print.

When you talk about doing a lot of thinking about God and the whole scheme of things, I can't help but think back to all of us around our kitchen table. When we have youth and no serious problems we can feel we will handle things by ourselves. But unfortunately maturity brings many situations and tragedies which we must have something besides ourselves to call upon. Believe me, your father and I know. He was talking the other nite about the first time it was hinted he had something wrong with his lungs, which was about age 21. And then before then, at about 17, he went through this mental turmoil, brought about by religious fanatacism.

As he says, he has spent his whole life "running scared", expecting death at any time and he is still kicking at 57. His whole point was that how much more enjoyment he could have had out of his life and how much more of himself he could have given to you children if he hadn't constantly been worrying about himself. The old truism is pretty right—"There are not atheists in fox holes." You call on God anytime you can and you gripe to us all you want, but just don't worry about anything but your own skin.

Thursday night about 11 PM the phone rang and it was a long distance call from Birmingham, Alabama and Dr. Fattig was on the phone wanting to know about you and if I had your adress yet as he wanted to write you. We had such a nice talk and he was telling me his feelings were very akin to yours when he was in Korea and he said he thinks back now to the letters he sent his mother. Anyway he will tell you and he wants me to let you know that some good things are happening down there and he thinks some good plans are in store for you. I have been checking on the Genetic Building here, but they seem to have run into a serious financial snag and you can't, at this time, get any information as to when they think the whole set up will be in operation. Anyway, just know that a lot of people are pulling for you and thinking of you.

Bob is still here and things are a little confusing with trunks being delivered, dirty clothes and the usual mess. I've been washing and ironing for two days straight but I'm so glad to be busy as it keeps me from thinking. We tried to have a serious talk with Bob and Linda the other night but as usual, Linda had to leave at the critical point to go to a showere for Ann Sloss, who is getting married next Saturday. Bob said this was typical, whenever they get to the crux of a problem she walks away. We tried as much as we could to make him understand that, as of now, we are not receptive to any marital plans as I still feel she is not ready. Linda still wants "fun and games". Perhaps that is all she will ever want. Bob tried to explain to us why Linda feels about his parents. He said she keeps comparing them to your father and I and he says they are different. Evidently no outward signs of affection is ever shown by his parents toward one another, or really to the children. Evidently the only way his Dad can show how much he loves his children is with his money and Linda just doesn't get this coldness. Well we gave them our thoughts and if they go their own way, then it is their baby. He had better have a definite plan for supporting Linda as I don't think he'll be able to count on her ability to get a good job.

Think I told you that Linda is going to work for your Dad this summer and this is going to be great. As I told Lucy, I'm going to make myself very scarce for about an hour every day after they get home. Poor Denny is quiite down in the dumps as all his jobs are not panning out. He is going up to Walter Weir later on today and see if Tommy Weir will take him on in Mike Sherman's place. I really hope he gets something as it is miserable at his age to have nothing to keep you busy. I even thought of letting him paint the house but I can't afford it.

Dad is leaving for Canada this coming Tuesday and is so hating even the thought of it. It is really too late to back out and now I wish I hadn't encouraged him. I do feel he needs the rest and relaxation, but I don't think he is going to get it. Mainly he likes to be around to see if we hear from you. He calls every day from the office with "did we get a letter from Dail". I do have the number where he can be reached up there and I'll just call him whenever I get a letter from you.

Went to a luncheon last Thursday at Jean Brown's and Ruth DuBous was there. Terry is leaving for Houston, Texas in the Air Force on June 16. When he enlisted the seargeant asked him if he wasn't General Du Bois' son and if he didn't want his father to swear him in. Terry said he didn't want it made known on any of his records that his father was in any way connected with the Air Force as he knew what the seargeants would do to him.

It's been very hot here, usual St. Louis summer weather, and of course our big air conditioner in the living room konked out and because it is 10 years old they don't know if they can repair it. Everytime someone gripes about how hot it is, your Dad reminds them of the heat and horror you are putting up with and it shuts them up in a hurry.

Thought you might like the enclosed picture of Margaret Mudd and also the candid shots. The picture of Dad and myself was taken by Dr. Sprengnether, who was in town last week end.

You know all the rules and regulations I laid down about the puppy? Well they have been blown to the wind. She is worse than Babette ever was and of course sleeps in Linda's bed every night. When she isn't loose with Linda, Denny has her in his room. By the way, her name is Chanel—take it for what it is.

God be with you and again you worry about nothing but yourself.

With all the love in the world,
Mom & Dad

Memorial Day May 30, 1969

Our dear son,

What a day to be writing a letter to Viet Naam. Wanted To write you yesterday but things started breaking loose around here with the beginning of the trek home from school. We got back from Tan Tar A late Wednesday and then Thursday Denny drove in with a boy that lives in Glendale. Linda and Bob are driving in Saturday or Sunday.

That was another reason I didn't want to write you yesterday as I needed to cool down after a telephone call from Bob's family. Evidently Bob and Linda have another understanding and are trying to work things out. Granted they have a legitimate complaint about some of Linda's behavior, but I'm afraid I'm beginning to think Linda had some very concrete reasons for getting in the mental turmoil she was in, and right now I feel she'd better stay out of that situation. The sister called and started in immediately on an aggressive tone, telling me that Mother (DeCurtis) was too upset to talk and had been crying and actually been made ill by reports coming from Athens College via "little snip" Suzie DeCurtis who had barged in for a week end. Evidently Bob finally told Suzie off in no uncertain terms that she should mind her own business and this lit the fuse. The first sentence from big sister Beverly lit the fuse with me too. I said she had better have her mother save her tears for Bob's possible tour of Viet Naam; that she might need them then more than now. I said I had just too many important things to worry about right now other than the "big shot" DeCurtis'. I'm sure Bob and Linda are going to want to discuss a lot of things when they come home and Dad has warned me to stay out of it. He is going to insist on her finishing school and that we are not going to be involved in any rush marriage plans. If they don't accept this then they will have to be on their own. As you can see, things are proceeding normally on the home front.

Ironically, right after that called, I recieved a letter from Lucy's mother and the complete difference in their thinking is such a contrast. I had written her thanking them for opening their home to you and Lucy for your last leave and I said I knew it must be hard, knowing that this is not the type life they had planned for Lucy. She couldn't have been nicer and said they never felt a life of complete pleasure was the best thing for young people. Her point was that we must take the bitter with the sweet and the dissappointments with the pleasures, in order to fully understand how to appreciate the good things that come along. She said Lucy is doing fine, very busy at her work and she and Clyde try and make her week ends as pleasant as possible. She said Lucy just goes around daily planning and saying constantly—"when Dail comes home." Both she and Clyde thought you looked so good and they were very proud of your attitude. I truly do wish Linda could have at least a semblance of this type relationship; of course Linda is not Lucy and Bob is not you—which is one of the problems. Bob is still finding it very difficult to cross his father and stand up on his own two feet.

Afraid that was our last trip with the Meachams where we split the bill down the middle. You know how shintzy he has always been; for instance when he and your Dad have lunch together on Wednesday, if your father orders something that costs a dime more, by golly he lets him know. Well down at Tan Tar A, they invited a couple who have a summer home down there to come over and go to the champagne breakfast with us. Then Sunday Patty Meacham and her husband come down to spend the night and we all go out to an expensive dinner. The next night we go to a little night club on the grounds for dinner and the bar bill alone was $28, of which your Dadand my share amounted to $4. Then Rosemary is constantly asking all the "party boys and girls" to come over to our place for drinks—some of this at 1o o'clock in the morning. Of course, when it came down to paying the bill it was divided right down the middle. Those few days cost us at least $60 for people and drinks we had nothing to do with. So I think your father finally has had his eyes openede regarding "old tight Meacham". He still feels closer to hime than anyone else, but I think he's been taken for the last time.

See what I meant when I said I couldn't write a letter to you constantly without griping. And I'm sure it all sounds so petty under your circumstances—but life is normal back here; which is the biggest fallacy—it is too damn normal and I for one am letting everyone within ear shot know this. Dad said no one is going to have anything to do with me if I Keep up on this theme, and I hope this happens. When I'm around people now I look at all of them and I think—"not one of you is worth for one minute that boy sitting in some bunker God knows where."

We are so relieved when we get your letters; not at what you are doing—but just hearing from you. You won't believe this but there are still many people here who are thinking of you constantly. One is Joan Seibert. She invited us over today for swimming and a barbecue and when asking me—she said—"God how I wish young Dail could be included in this invitation." Of course, this is how the people are who have sweated a boy over there for a year.

Our thoughts and prayers are with you every minute. Dad said to tell you if you get a package some day don't be surprised if when you open it our new puppy jumps out. She is really the wildest, pestiest, irrascible dog I have ever seen. You should see her with Denny. She won't leave him alone and she keeps biting and pulling the hair on his legs. The other day he was trying to watch television and she wouldn't leave him alone so he put her in that closet in the family room. He said to tell you hello and that he would write you this week. I do hope you have gotten some of the mail we have been sending you.

Take care and all our love always,
Mom & Dad

PFC Dail W. Mullins, Jr.
RA12927044
488-48-0511
CoA, 26th ENGR. BN.
APO SF, 96256

10–11 June 1969

Dear Mom, Dad and kids,
    If I remember right, Dad has left for Canada as I write this letter. I sure hope he has a good time and catches a lot of fish—I'm sure the trip will do him good, if for no other reason than it will get him out of that office.
    I must apologize for not having written to you all more often, but my free time is somewhat limited, at least to the extent that if I don't get a decent night's

sleep once in a while, I have trouble putting in a full work day in this damnable heat. I do try and write Lucy at least once a day, but I know you folks worry just as much as she does when my letters slack off.

Apparently there's no need to worry anymore about my not getting any mail. Today I got two letters from Lucy and one each from you, Denny and Linda. Thanks, everyone, for writing—I can't tell you how much I appreciate the news from "the world". I notice from the address you used that you finally have my correct APO number—by using it you cut off an extra day, so that letters get here in 4–5 days.

I was glad to hear that the kids made it home from school safely—I hope that their grades come out OK and that they both have nice summers.

I'm sitting here with your letters in front of me, hoping that I can answer some of your questions and comment on some of your observations and statements. Perhaps my letters will be somewhat more interesting that way.

No, I don't think the Army would allow Dad to take my place over here (get serious), and even if they would, what on earth would that solve. What difference does it make which member of our family is over here—we'd all still worry just the same, whether it be me, Dad, Denny, Linda, Lucy or Channel. Channel! That's the craziest name I've ever heard. If she has puppies someday, you could call them My Sin and Arpegé!

You seemed surprised to learn that Australia was an R&R center from Vietnam. Yes, and quite a popular one—probably because it resembles the world more than Hong Kong, Taiwan or Kuala Lumpur. Most of the married fellows, of course, go to Hawaii and meet their wives—which is what Lucy and I would like to do. David Emerson is on his second R&R—you get another one if you extend over here for 6 months or more. There is no way in hell I'll ever get 2 R&R's.

I can't recall whether or not I told you folks about my money problems over here, but I finally got them straightened out today. You see, when I went through in-processing down at Chu Lai, they told us that it would be wise to open up a combination savings and checking account with American Express—5% interest on all savings. Instead of getting paid in cash each month, the government would simply deposit my pay in my account. The only problem with this deal was that there is no place on LZ Baldy to cash a check. So, up until today, I was broke. It does no good to write home for money, since we're not allowed to have any American money—only military currency. Well, to make a long story short, the lieutenant let me catch a chopper down to Chu Lai, where I dropped the account and arranged to get paid in cash up here. I didn't really close the account completely, so that any money I want to save I can just send to the bank as a money order.

The helicopter ride down to Chu Lai was something else. The choppers over here don't have any doors or seat belts, but you remain seated rather steadily because of gravity and centrifugal force when these birds make a sharp turn—and believe me, they do.

Vietnam from the air, as I told Lucy in a letter, is a study in stark contrasts. At times it looks almost like an oriental fantasyland, what with the hunched figures under those famous straw hats digging in the rice paddies, small children running into the pagoda-like schools for their classes and the women, walking along the dusty roads in their colorful, silk dresses and parasols. But you don't have to look too hard to see the effects of the war. If you look closely at the pagodas you see that they are all riddled with bullet holes; over there under that coconut tree is a rusted and gutted tank, left over from a previous battle; and here, in the middle of a rice paddy, lies the charred skeleton of a downed helicopter. It's really amazing how the land can look so peaceful and sinister looking at the same time.

Vietnam during the day and Vietnam at night are also two different places. During the day you can travel by truck from Chu Lai to Baldy, about 50 miles, in relative safety—I did today on my way back from the bank. There's one large village on the way, Tam Ky, and it is fascinating to drive through. I don't know how to describe it, really, except to say that it's much like Juarez, the only differences being that the people are all oriental, the kids all naked and the streets and buildings dirtier.

Vietnam at night, however, is a place of terror outside the security of the barbed wire—and sometimes within, when the rockets and mortars come in. You have to get used to sleeping with flares lighting up the room and artillery shells whistling overhead. The VC and NVA do their thing at night, so that's when our security is the tightest.

I meant to finish this up tonight, but its late, and I need to get some rest, so, excuse it being an extra day late and I'll add a little tomorrow.

11 June 1969

I hope to have a camera soon, so that I'll be able to supplement my letters with some film. It's too much trouble to get the film developed over here, so I'll probably just send undeveloped roles home and let you folks get that done.

I thought I'd try and give you a brief itinerary of what the 26th engineers will be doing for the next few months, at least as far as we've been informed.

Until around the end of this month will be here at Baldy, repairing bunkers, laying barbed wire and mine sweeping. At the end of June we're supposed to go out in the field for a week and build a suspension bridge across some river near LZ Siberia—don't ask me where LZ Siberia is, because I don't know yet. Then, later on this summer I understand we're supposed to go into the A Shau Valley to build a series of fire support bases for the artillery and infantry. Hamburger Hill is over there, and I'm glad they've already taken that thing.

If you're confused as to my exact location at the moment, perhaps the enclosed map will help some—its on the next page.

I just now got another letter from you all, dated May 30—I have gotten some dated later already, so you can see they haven't been received in order. Now that you have my correct address, though, I'll be getting them quite regularly.

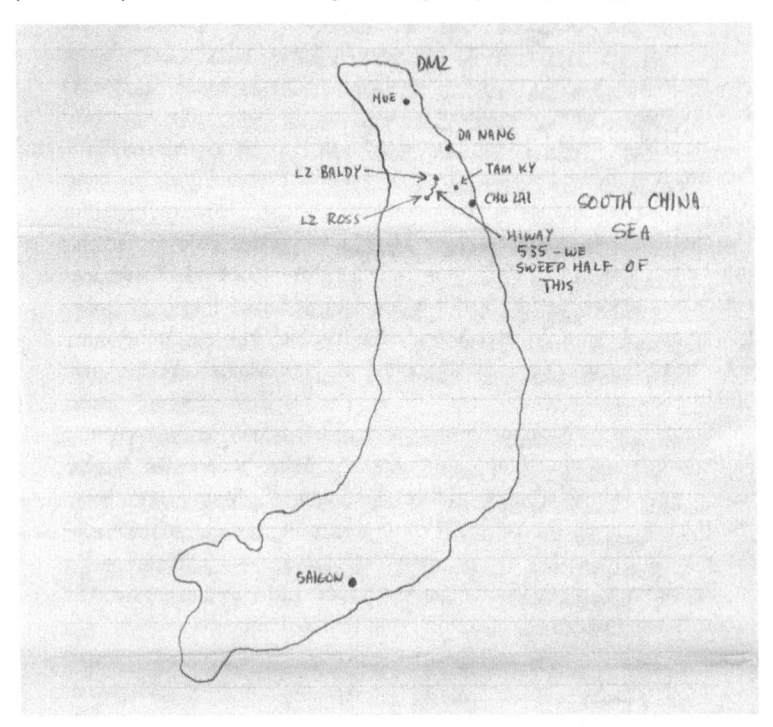

[Hand-drawn map of Vietnam with the following labels: DMZ, HUE, DA NANG, LZ BALDY, TAM KY, CHU LAI, LZ ROSS, SOOTH CHINA SEA, HIWAY 535 - WE SWEEP HALF OF THIS, SAIGON]

Well, not much else to tell. We haven't had a mortar attack in 3 days, so right now, things are pretty quiet. Our chaplin here at Baldy was killed 2 days ago when his jeep ran over a mine—its a shame so many good men have to die for this damnable war. I'll write again soon, and you do the same—your letters are Godsends.

Love,
Dail

June 11 69

To our dear "Number One GI",
We read your letters with utter fascination, enjoyment and fright—all mixed. You just be very careful that these little "coat-tail hanger ons" aren't booby traps. Keep your wits about you at all times.

If you still aren't getting your mail I've got to do something desperate. I talked to our mailman and he just doesn't understand this. He says the way they have all this army mail coded and the number of ships and planes doing nothing but carrying soldiers mail, there is no excuse for boys not receiveing their mail. Little Gay Reinhardt called me last night and she has even written you a letter. When you do get it they are going to have one sackful for Pfc Mullins.

Well your father finally got off, reluctantly—very reluctantly. Never have I seen him so adverse to going fishing. He had office hours Tuesday morning and then was going to come home and start out and try and get to Keokuk, Iowa that evening. Well he sat on the edge of the bed wondering what to take and the best way to go. This wore him out so much that he decided to take a nap, which lasted four hours. I get so irritated at people that will not make decisions that I went out and started digging in my yard. This is my way of getting rid of all my pent up emotions lately and by the time you get home the yard will be filled with holes. Anyway, he then decided he'd get up at four AM and start off. He got away by six and I hope the trip wasn't too tiring and that he has fun. He will be up their over Father's Day so I sent him a very nice little book about Fathers from you, Linda, and Denny. One article in their I thought so appropriate and provoking and I think you'd get the message.

"What is a Father?

A father is someone who is forced to endure childbirth without anesthetics. Fathers usually growl when they feel good and laugh very loud when they're scared half to death. A father never feels entirely worthy of the worship in his children. But he keeps trying to be the hero his daughter thinks he is—the man his son believes him to be.

Sometimes fathers go to war. They don't want to. But as always, they know that war is a part of their most important job in life . . . which is to make the world a better place for their children than it has been for them. (you can forget this)

Fathers grow old faster than other people. Because they, in other wars, have to stand at the train or airport and wave goodbye to a son in uniform. And while mothers cry where it shows, fathers have to stand and beam outside—and die inside. (how true)

"Fathers are men who give daugthters away to other men who aren't nearly good enough . . so they can have children who are smarter than anybody's.

Fathers fight dragons almost daily. They hurry from the breakfast table . . off to the Arena which is sometimes called an Office or workshop. There they tackle the obstacles that stand in their way, schedules, hard work, and occasionally, the boss. They never quite win the fight but they never give up.

I don't know where father's go after life, but I've an idea that a father doesn't just sit on a cloud waiting for the girl he's loved and the children she bore. He'll be busy there too . . . repairing the stairs, oiling the gates, improving the streets, smoothing the way."
Unknown.

Denny is getting so discouraged about the job situation and the thing that bothers me is he talks about "he might as well join join the Army." Pete Merril gave him the name of a man who owns a towing service on the river and he is to see him today. The trouble is that most of these jobs are on a permanent basis and they just don't want summer help. He says he could get better jobs when he was in hight school and that the more education he has the less he is able to find.

Linda of course is with Dad and she is already trying to tell him where he runs his office wrong. She thinks Christine works so hard and that your father is just too unkind and rough on her. I'm sure you know how this goes over with your father. He said—"two days and she thinks she knows more about dentistry than I do, after 35 years." It's going to be interesting. He doesn't realize that someone who stands on the outside can sometimes come up with some valuable ideas.

Pete in talking to Denny, of course, made a luncheon date with Linda. I just cannot figure her out and I've reached the point where I can't even try any more.

Now you take care of yourself and pray and know that we are missing you every minute and I'm marking the days, but they go so slow. It's better if I skip a week and then mark several at a time.

With all our loeve and our prayers—
Mom & Dad

PFC Dail W. Mullins, Jr.
RA12927044
488-48-0511
CoA, 26th ENGR. BN.
APO SF 96256

15 June 1969

Dear Mom, Dad and Kids,
I hope this letter finds you all well and happy. I received two letters today, one from Dad and one from Mom (letter #11), and from the sounds of things, everything is proceeding as usual. I've no doubts, Mom, that you've started sitting

up nights, now that Linda and Denny are home for the summer and "running free" again.

I suppose that when this letter reaches you all, Dad will have returned from his fishing trip—I do hope he caught some fish and was able to relax some. As I told Lucy not too long ago, one of the things I hate about being over here is knowing how much I have upset a lot of people back home. But, first as I'm going to have to get used to Vietnam, I guess you're going to have to get accustomed to my being over here.

I'm really at a loss of what to write about, folks. In your next letter, if there's anything you want to know or are curious about, please ask away. I'm hoping that Lucy will get my camera over here soon (I've asked her to send it), and when it arrives, I'll be able to liven up my letters with a few pictures—much as you've done. By the way, those letters and pictures are wonderful—keep them coming.

I must apologize for not having written for some time. The work is pretty hard around here, though, and after walking on a 10 mile mine sweep followed by bunker guard that night, you're pretty pooped. Today is Sunday, however, and the CO gave us the whole afternoon off, so I finally have time to get off a few letters. The mess hall found itself with a few extra steaks and chickens today, so the company is going to have a barbeque with free beer tonight! It's a little touch of home, except that we start our fires with JP4, jet helicopter fuel!

Intelligence reports had it that Baldy was supposed to be hit sometime between the 10th and 14th, but nothing happened. Actually it's been fairly quiet around here, although a couple of trucks have been blown up by mines (we don't find them all) and will stay on a yellow alert for a few more days. I imagine the VC will be starting one of their summer offensives before too long, but I hope not. I only wish all those idiots in Paris, Washington and Hanoi would get on the stick.

Yesterday, as I mentioned above, we went on a long sweep. The temperature was 102°, but there was a fairly nice breeze blowing, so I didn't mind it too much. On the way back to Baldy we stopped in a small village to eat (C-rations), as usual, but this time one of the local mama-sans invited me and two other guys into her hut to get out of the sun. After lunch I couldn't decide whether eating in the shade was worth sitting in that fly-infested straw hut with 1600 naked kids, 5 chickens, a cow and a toothless old lady staring at you. One little girl (she couldn't have been more than 3) had the most horribly infected ears I've ever seen. They were 3 times normal size and just dripping with pus and covered with flies. One of the fellas with me said all the girls have their ears pierced when they're that age—usually with a nail! I sure am seeing some sights over here.

Well, I guess I'll close. Please try not to worry about me too much—I'm doing my crummy job as best I can over here without taking on unnecessary risks, and I have faith that, somehow, I'll pull through it all. A lot of other guys have, and there's no reason why I shouldn't be able to keep pulling for me, and I'll take care of myself.

Love,
Dail

P.S.—If you'd like to send a package of any type, you are welcome to. Most of the fellas' parents send canned and boxed food (soup, cookies, peanuts, etc.), books and magazines and anything else they feel might help pass the time. Be sure and keep any package under 5 lbs., or it won't come by air.

PFC Dail W. Mullins, Jr.
RA12927044
488-48-0511
CoA, 26th ENGR. BN.
APO SF 96256

15 June 1969

My dear Parents,

Well, I got another letter from you today—seems I get one almost every day. Lucy's don't come in near that often, and I don't know whether it's because she doesn't write as much or whether it's the mail system. Any day now I expect a dozen back letters to pour in. Anyway, keep witing and I'll do the same—I really appreciate the letters, and am looking forward to hearing from Dr. Fattig and Gay Reinhardt, and only hope I can find the time to answer them all. I must, above all, keep you all and Lucy informed as to what's going on.

My DEROS date (the day I leave Vietnam) is May 14, so yesterday was the end of my first month over here—only 11 more to go! That first month did go by pretty fast, I'll have to admit, but the rest of the time still seems like it will last forever. I'll just have to keep plugging away, I guess, and hope for the best.

We had a short sweep this morning—no excitement, no mines, as is usual with a short sweep. We usually work when we get back until 11:30, break for lunch until 1:00, and then go back to work until 4:30. At night they usually try and have a movie for us (sometimes they're good, sometimes not) and, of course, the "club" is open, selling cold soda and beer for 15¢ each. Seems whenever they have a good movie, though, I'm pulling bunker guard. I did get to see "For the Love of Ivy" the other day, so I can't complain.

LZ East, which is several miles up into the mountains, got hit pretty hard about a week ago, so they sent the second squad of the second platoon (I'm in third squad) up there to repair the damage to the bunker line and the headquarters. That left only third and first squads here at Baldy, and we've had to work pretty hard. Today and tomorrow we'll be building two hollow-wall bunkers on the bunker line over near where the infantry stays, and, believe me, that's hard work in this heat (110°)—each bunker is about the size of a two car garage with 3 foot thick hollow walls filled with dirt.

I thought you might find it interesting if I described Baldy for you—I'm sure you probably have no idea what an LZ is. LZ, which stands for Landing Zone, is just that—a place where helicopters can land enroute from a large base, like Da Nang or Chu Lai, to the infantry, artillery or engineer units out in the field. LZ Baldy is a fairly typical LZ, although it may be somewhat larger than most. It is roughly 8-shaped; that is, the barbed wire perimeter defines the figure 8. Baldy is about 1 1/2 long and maybe 3/4 of a mile wide across the two loops of the 8. The upper loop of Baldy is manned by 2 battalions of the 196th light infantry brigade. At the very center of the LZ there is a large hill, the left side of which houses an artillery unit, while F Troop, an independent infantry unit, lives on the right side. The lower loop of the figure 8 is manned by 1 battalion of the 196th, the 9th marine engineers, the 26th engineers (us) and an airfield with a weather control station. Thus,

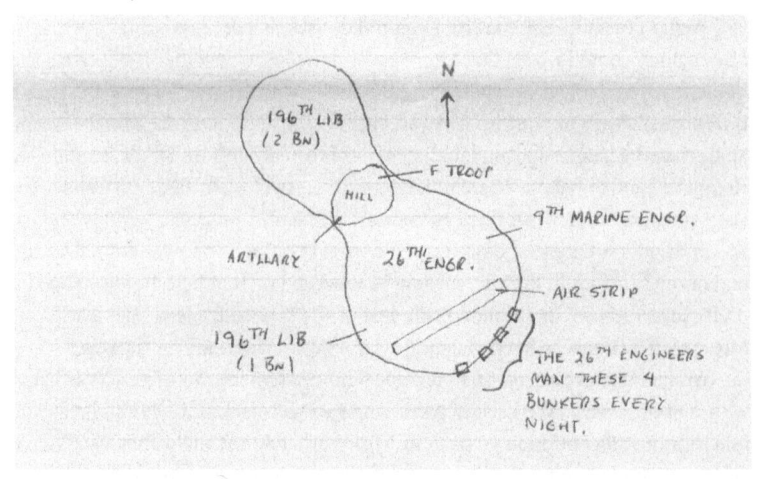

To the north, east and south, it is fairly flat and sandy (the South China Sea, of course, is only about 10 miles to the east), with numerous small oasis-like clumps of thick vegetation, rice paddies and villages. At night, if it's clear, you can just make out the lights of Da Nang way to the northeast. To the west, the coastal plains gradually give way to the infamous central highlands with their jungle-covered mountains. We haven't been over there yet, but I have no doubts that I'll make it.

I think alot of people back in the world get the idea from watching TV news reports that Nam is one big battle which never lets up. Actually that's not true. By far, the majority of days are relatively peaceful, at least by Vietnam standards. There are some clerks and cooks over here that never have a round fired at them or hear a mortar go off—that, of course, is rare, but it happens. I'm considered a front line troop, so, no doubt, I will undergo these experiences—nevertheless, its not like it was a daily occurrence. The only time you ever see any of the enemy, in fact, is when they're charging your bunkers or when they're already dead. Usually, they make their presence felt only through rockets and mortars—not that these can't be dangerous, mind you.

Most of the troops over here are too preoccupied with the day to day business of staying alert to their surroundings to be overly concerned about why they're here in the first place—philosophical discussions of this type just don't come up that often. When they do, however, it is the rare soldier who really understands what he's doing over here. I don't know anyone who wouldn't like to get the hell out of here and go home—but most fellas are fairly well resigned to the fact that they're here and that they might as well make the best of it. Well, enough of my rambling. Just trying to make my letters more interesting.

Keep writing, folks—I really appreciate your letters.

Love,
Dail

P.S. Would it be too much trouble to send me one of those Polaroid cameras you have laying around the house? I'd appreciate it, and could get pictures right back to you and Lucy—I'm sure you'd appreciate some pictures of my surroundings. I won't keep the camera for a year—just a few months. If you do send it, remember to keep it under 5 lbs (or I won't get it for several months) and, also, to enclose some film—film is awfully hard to get over here. Thanks a lot.

PFC Dail W. Mullins, Jr.
RA12927044
488-48-0511
CoA, 26th ENGR. BN.
APO SF, 96256

17 June, 1969

My dear Parents,

I thought I might have bunker guard tonight, but since our platoon has a long sweep tomorrow, they gave us a free night tonight—I'll catch it tomorrow for sure. Right now its raining cats and dogs, which ought to make it especially pleasant on the road—the mud gets knee deep, I understand.

The past twenty-four hours have been rather exciting around here—maybe a little too exciting. Last night I had interior guard—this is where two men walk around the company area for 2 1/2 hours. There are three shifts—10:30 to 1:00, 1:00 to 3:30 and 3:30 to 6:00. A guy from Illinois, Reiteman, and I had the middle shift, 1:00 to 3:30. Well, we were both tired and it was kind of dull, so we decided to sit down for awhile and just shoot the bull. We sat down against the wall of an old sandbag bunker, no longer in use except as a position for secondary defense. Well, about 2:15 I heard this WOOSH! KA-BOOM! I didn't know what it was at first—there are all kinds of weird noises around Baldy at night—flares, artillery firing, the bunker line firing, etc. Well, when I heard the second WOOSH!—KA-BOOM! I knew we were getting mortared. Reiteman and I both jumped over the bunker wall and hit the dirt just as a third one came in—really close! It blew dust and rocks all over us—boy, I was really scared. I knew the next one was coming in right on us! Luckily, however, they stopped. Taking advantage of the sudden break in the action, Reiteman and I decided to make a break for our platoon's regular bunker, located next to our hooch. When we got there, at a dead run, incidentally, the rest of the guys were all out of bed and in the bunker. Just as we crawled in, some more rounds started coming in, only further away, over near the Marines. One mortar hit a gasoline storage tank over there and started a big fire, but it died down fairly quickly. Altogether the VC hit us with 18 mortar rounds, causing 28 casualties—nobody killed. The attack was over by 3:00, and everything remained quiet the rest of the night. Yes, I'm OK.

Tonight we had a little more thrills. This afternoon they installed some CS gas bombs on our bunker line for defensive purposes. CS is much like tear gas, only much more powerful. These bombs can be detonated from inside the bunkers out there by electrical means. When they go off they shoot CS gas out towards the enemy for a distance of about 200 feet. Well, we had an electrical storm tonight, and as luck would have it, one of the things was set off by a lightning bolt. Of course, all the gas drifted back toward Baldy, so we ran around here with our gas masks on for about 1/2 an hour until it dissipated. Never a dull moment—unfortunately!

I didn't get any letters today, but neither did anyone else, so I guess the mail got messed up. You know, for awhile I was getting letters from 3 to 4 days after they were postmarked, but lately they've been coming in about a week or 10 days after mailing. At least I'm getting letters. Keep writing folks, I love to hear from you. Find out if Lucy is writing or whether the mail is messed up—I haven't heard from her in about a week, and you know how I worry when I'm not in touch. Take care, please, and I'll let you hear from me again soon.

Love,
Dail

Tuesday—6/15/69

Dear Dail,

Well, it's rather quiet here tonite—which is probably more than you can say. I actually flinch reading your letters. It's going to be a long year.

Linda is next door baby sitting for Larry and Judy. She was out Friday nite, Saturday nite and Sunday nite with Pete Merrill and I finally put my foot down. When here Dad comes back he is going to have a fit if she is running around every night and gripes about getting up at 6;30.

Denny is working. He got that job at the service station on Lindbergh Blvd and I wish you could see him when he comes home. I look at him and wonder if any grease, pil or gas got into the cars—it all looks like it landed on him. He really seems to like it and believe it or not, is doing a lot of repair work. This bothers me as I didn't think he knew what a motor looked like, but he puts in brakes, mufflers, lubricates—the works. One thing I don't like: the owner showed Dennis where he hides his gun but he told him to use it only in self defense and to just turn over the cash when they are held up. So now I've got that to think about. Isn't this whole world a mess.

Just finished a long letter to Lucy. She sent the nicest Father's day card to Dad and I know he will be so pleased. Also received yours for him to enjoy. We called him long distance Father's day and he said the fishing hadn't been too good. Of course, the first thing he asked us was—have you heard from Dail.

You know I've been going back to our old church and I really enjoy it. I hope they never get a regular minister as, to me, it's very stimulating having the different views each Sunday. Last Sunday we had a Lutheran minister who has what they call an "inner-city" church. He really made a lot of people think, myself included, when he said we must get involved with the cities or they will bury us. Afterwards I talked to him and told him how he had made me squirm and how I kept constantly trying to figure out wht I didn't get involved and it got down to nothing more than I was very much afraid. His response was that "if you have faith, you are never afraid." This bothers me and I know I talked to your dad about it and he thinks this is ridiculous because you also have a brain and intelligence which tells you it is foolhardy and dangerous to go down into these neighborhoods, where they really don't want "the white good works!".

St. Louis is really having quite a problem on Sundays. The Black Panther organization has been walking in on different church services. They seem to be concentrating on the large wealthy Presbyterian churches and the Catholic churches. They want all ghetto businesses owned by the churches turned over to them and they want a complete financial resume of every church and 3/4 of all holdings given to them—plus 3/4 of everything collected each week in the individual churches. Our new Cardinal Carberry, who is more extreme than the Pope himself, is really up in arms about this, especially since they said they were going to spit in the Eucharist. Sunday all the black people who interrupted a service in a catholic church, were arrested. A group visited and Episcopal church in Ladue and were invited to take over the pulpit and wound up staying for the coffee hour. I don't feel they will try and interrupt South Webster's services as it is well known the financial difficulties they are in, but I am looking for them to interrupt the big Pres. church and can't you just hear old Eloise Skilling?

Well did you hear from Dr. Fattig and what did he have to say? I hope some of his information gives you something to look forward to.

The enclosed picture is one that Linda took up at Stix Westroads, and if you don't recognize it—it is Tiny Tim. She had Pete drive her up there Friday at noon and believe it or not, while the world is burning the stupid females are still screaming and fainting over "queers" like this. I just don't get it. I never did and I do less now.

Thought you might enjoy the enclosed which is from the last issue of Life magazine. Frankly it's just another thing that makes me sick to my stomach. I'm really glad I won't have to participate in such goings on.

Well, my dear, we live through and share every ordeal you are going through and I'll be so glad when you are back home. God speed and our love and prayers. Your Dad should be home this Thursday or Friday and I'll be so glad to see him. I've been alone a lot the last few days and I'm beginning to understand your grandmother a little but I guess it's too late—

With much much love
and please let us know if there is anything you need,
Mom & Dad

PFC Dail W. Mullins, Jr.
RA12927044
488-48-0511
CoA, 26th ENGR. BN.
APO SF, 96256

19 June, 1969

My dear Parents,

 I got your letter dated June 15 today, and it was such a relief to hear from someone. I haven't heard from Lucy in about a week and a half, and I'm sick with worry—I'm sure she's writing, and I can't imagine why her letters haven't been coming in. This stupid mail system is something I just can't get used to. I get some letters in 4 days, others in 10—and I still never got the first 5 you sent!

 I'm rather tired this morning, folks. Intelligence reports indicated that Baldy was supposed to be hit with a ground attack on either the 18th or 19th, so, of course, the entire LZ goes on a red alert at 1:00 AM each night. I had bunker guard last night—red alert means all 4 men in each bunker must be awake during the hours of the alert. They also brought out APC's (armored personnel carriers) and parked them between each of the bunkers. Each APC carries 6 men with personal weapons, 2 M60 machine guns and 1 50 cal. machine gun. Nice to have around when things get tight. What the enemy usually does when they attack, I understand, is to either mortar the whole LZ from in front of the engineer bunkers and, while this is going on, to try and get through the wire on the opposite side of Baldy, OR, to mortar the engineer's bunker line itself and, while all the guards are hugging the floor of the bunker, to sneak through our wire. The VC use what are called Sapper squads—a group of 5 to 10 men, stripped down to their shorts and carrying canvas bags filled with explosives, who crawl under, through and over the wire—a suicide mission, really, and most of the Sappers are high on pot. Nothing happened last night—in fact, it was relatively quiet—but, of course, we'll be on alert again tonight. However, I won't have bunker guard tonight, so that's something. It will be somebody else's turn to sit out there and stare into its flare-lit night.

 You know, it's funny. Last night, while I was sitting out there in that bunker, I wasn't nearly as nervous or depressed about my present predicament as I am this morning. Adrenalin, I guess. Of course, that's not to say that I'm not scared when those mortars start popping in. What is so damn horrible about mortars is their sheer impersonality—they fall where they please and you better not be there. I don't think I'll ever forget the sound they make.

Every morning when we get up, I ask myself—what are we doing here? I hope I can get used to this life soon.

I don't know what gave you all the idea that mail from home upsets me more—true, it sometimes is hard to believe that everything is quite the same back in the world, but at the same time, it is encouraging.

It's awfully nice to know that there are alot of people back home pulling for me—tell them all thank you for their prayers and thoughts—I really appreciate it. You didn't mention anything about Carol Kreyling Knight's husband—how are they getting along? Wasn't her husband in the Army?

I thought it was funny when you mentioned that the Kenny's were afraid their son-in-law was going to be sent to Vietnam after taking a course in Vietnamese—where did they think he'd be sent, Germany!

I really don't mean to break your heart with my letters, Mom—but sometimes it helps to just spout off to someone about all the injustice and cruelty you see over here. I'm not completely disgusted with my country—really, I'm not—who can ignore what living when and where I have has enabled me to achieve with respect to my work and marriage. But nothing—absolutely nothing—can change my opinion of what this war is doing to America. It's tearing its soul in two pieces, and its men in more pieces than that. I don't have time right now, but in my next letter I want to tell you about the American-Vietnamese personal relationship at the enlisted man's level. It's something that is so horrible and disgusting—and just as frightening to me as getting killed over here.

Well, I guess I'll close. I want to try and at least start a letter to Lucy tonight. I sure hope I hear from her soon—I worry so, even though I know you all tell me not to. Be good, keep writing and praying for me—I'm sure it will help—I really am.

Love,
Dail

PFC Dail W. Mullins, Jr.
RA12927044
488-48-0511
CoA, 26th ENGR. BN.
APO SF, 96256

22 June 1969

My dear Parents,

It seems awfully long since I last wrote—time does, amazingly enough, go rather fast over here, and I suppose that's because we keep pretty busy. Come July 13, I will have been here 2 whole months—1/6 of my time!

If I remember right, in my last letter I was complaining because I hadn't gotten any letters from Lucy in some while. Well, as I knew would happen, I got two from her shortly after that—apparently I'm just going to have to get used to erratic mail—along with soggy toilet paper, flies, heat and diarrhea.

Not much has really happened since I wrote you last. Yesterday we were supposed to have had a long sweep, but since the VC had blown up a bridge between here and LZ Ross, the convoy couldn't have made it anyway—the sweep was cancelled. Third platoon swept today, and lost two pressure test trucks to mines. Have I mentioned pressure test trucks? It's a 5-ton cargo truck which is heavily sandbagged around the driver—the bed of the truck is filled with wet dirt to make it heavier, and also to absorb some of the shock when the truck does hit a mine. The driver sits on the rear edge of the hood of the truck, facing to the rear of the truck, and drives backwards behind the sweep team. Hopefully, if the truck does hit a mine, it will be the rear wheels (those farthest from the driver) that find it. Usually the driver is unhurt, although most suffer broken eardrums. It is, I understand, a voluntary job—if so, I hope they don't run out of volunteers before I leave.

Since I don't have a camera yet, some of the fellows agreed to give me a few of their extra pictures to send home until I could begin taking my own. I'm not in any of these, and, in fact, except for the one showing the air strike, all of them were taken before I arrived here. Unless there's some reason why you'd like to keep them, could you send them on to Lucy for her to see. I'll explain each one so you and she will understand them. I numbered each one on the back to accompany the explanation.

(1) This is an air strike by a couple of Phantom jets that we watched while out on a sweep. One of the jets has just dropped a couple of napalm bombs on a target and is pulling up into the sky again. I don't know what they were bombing, and I wasn't about to walk over that little hill to find out.

(2) and (3) are just pictures of the Vietnamese countryside around LZ Baldy, taken from a helicopter. You can see the beginnings of the Central Highlands off in the distance, and below, the blue and green colored, rectangular rice paddies.

(4) is a U.S. Army forward observation plane. This thing flies around looking for large concentrations of enemy troops; when it spots them, it starts circling over head and directs artillery fire onto them. This, by the way, is the type of plane they were training Bill Colbert to fly around in. Can you see the ace of spades marking on the tail of the plane? The VC and NVA are very superstitions of this symbol, and whenever this unit kills an enemy soldier, they leave an ace of spades playing card in his mouth—this really scares the other enemy soldiers. This plane, by the way, is sitting on the runway at LZ Baldy. That large hill in the center of Baldy is behind the plane. Our company area is almost directly behind the cockpit of the plane.

(5) is a pressure test truck (the kind I described above) just after it has hit a mine. Notice the sandbags and the dirt on the back of the truck. You can get a pretty good idea, I think, of the size holes these mines make from this picture.

(6) This is a picture of one of the villages along the road that we sweep. The guy that took this picture said that their pressure test truck had hit a mine just outside of the village. The engineers and their infantry security rounded up some of the people to ask them who planted the mine. All of a sudden no one in the whole village spoke any English. The result: they burned down the village. I can't see where this wins any friends, but it is done all the time.

Well, that's about it. Be advised, as they say in the Army, that I am fine and miss everyone very much. Give my love to anyone who asks about me—keep writing and I'll do the same.

All my love,
Dail

PFC Dail W. Mullins, Jr.
RA12927044
488-48-0511
CoA, 26th ENGR. BN.
APO SF, 96256

25 June 1969

My Dear Parents et al,
    Again I must apologize for not having written for several days—I know everyone of you becomes as anxious as I do when the letters don't come in for awhile. You'll also have to excuse this horrible paper—it was all I could dig up at the moment.
    For the past several days my squad has been constructing two permanent fighting bunkers on the Northeastern perimeter of Baldy. These are heavy, wooden jobs, designed to replace the old sandbag bunkers that were out there before. As I told you before, these are about the size of a two car garage, and believe me, you work hard in this heat putting one of them up. Anyway, our platoon had a long sweep today, but the Lieutenant asked me and another guy in my squad, Mike Taylor, to stay behind and put the finishing touches on these bunkers. So, since both the Lieutenant and our platoon sergeant went on the sweep, Taylor and I had the day pretty much to ourselves—of course, we did have to work on the bunkers some.
    At 11:30 we came back to the company area for lunch, and were just getting ready to go back out, when word came in over the radio that the pressure test truck had hit a mine. When this happens, the motor pool here at the company area has to send a wrecker (tow truck) out to pick it up. This wrecker, of course, needs a jeep escort (the jeep has an M-60 machine gun mounted on it). Well, Taylor volunteered for jeep driver and I volunteered to be gunner. However, one of the Lieutenants back here said he wanted to be the machine gunner, so I didn't argue. Now, I'm practically alone back here, so I thought it would be a good time to get a letter out.
    I'm enclosing a Chieu Hoi (pronounced chew hoy) pass for you to see. Chieu Hoi is Vietnamese for "open arms", and these papers, which are dropped by the millions all over 'Nam, are safe-conduct passes for both VC and NVA soldiers who want to surrender. The Chieu Hoi program, operated by the psychological warfare operation's branch over here, is fairly successful, except that after a firefight, especially one in which some Americans have been killed, most GI's aren't in the "taking prisoners" mood—so when a VC pops up out of the bushes and starts yelling "Chieu Hoi, Chieu Hoi!", he very possibly may wish he hadn't. At any rate, I thought you might like to see a Chieu Hoi pass.

Thanks for sending the pictures of Tiny Tim (hmmm!) and the article from Life Magazine. I really enjoyed reading the latter, as did Hugh, another college man in my squad. Hugh has a master's degree in English and was teaching at Murray State in Kentucky when Uncle Sam grabbed him. At least there's someone to talk to once in awhile. He's also married.

Lucy sent me a nice letter and 3 more pictures from our trip to Myrtyl Beach—one of her in her new bikini! Wow!

So Denny's working in a filling station, huh! I can just see the fits your having when he gets home at night—but you ought to see me after 2 hours of work. During the summer months it doesn't rain very much at all here in Vietnam, and these military installations around here become virtual dustbowls, what with all the trucks and tanks churning up the earth. And what's really bad is when a big Chinook helicopter lands 50 feet away on a dusty chopper pad. Out on the bunker line we've actually had to put our gas masks on the dust has gotten so bad.

You asked me one time whether I was able to get any of the news of the world here. Yes, I am. There are two "stateside-type" rock and roll radio stations here, one in Saigon and one in Danang. The Danang station, AFVN, comes in real clear on my radio, and they have hourly news reports, just like KXOK. We even get the "Adventures of Chicken Man". Also, we get a newspaper every day, the "Stars and Stripes", although it is about a day old when it arrives at Baldy. Time and Newsweek aren't any fun to read because they're at least 2 weeks old. War is hell, I guess.

Well, keep me informed with all the news from home—I love to hear from everyone. I'll keep writing as often as I can. Take care all—I miss you.

Love,
Dail

Saturday June 21, 1969

My dear Son,

Just came in from mowing the yard. Whenever I mention cutting the grass or working out in the yard you will know that I am working off all my troubles, tensions, and frustrations. Received your letter this morning in which you mentioned your bombardment attack and of course, I cried and then I became so g-d mad that I must do something extremely physical or I'd burst. I know the other nite when listening to the news they recounted the same attack you mentioned. When your father got home from Canada I told him I was afraid you had been having it over there and of course he always tells me—"every raid they have you just know it is where Dail is." But this nite they showed a map and I had just received your letter on which you had drawn your location and it was the same. You can't know how all this affects us but we must know and please keep giving us the details.

Denny is still working at the filling station and seems to like it very much. In fact, he got an answer from a camp consouelling job he had applied for and he decided to keep the one he had because he thinks he can work for this fellow when he comes home on holidays. I'll say one thing for it, it's dirty. It's rather funny in a way; as he now informs us all about how we should take care of the cars and he's always pouring cans of STP in the oil and other various gimmicks. You know what your father thinks of all this.

Linda! Now there is something else again. Since she has been home Pete has been taking up every spare minute of her time; which I guess is alright except she had told Bob not to date and she wouldn't, even tho they are notengaged. Again—she wants her cake and eat it too. The other day Pete took her to lunch and she was about ten minutes late in getting back to the office and your dad really was furious. Here Christine and the hygenist, Beverly, don't dare be a minute late and she breezes in ten minutes late. Of course, that night at the dinner table she hopped on him for embarrassing him and he blew his top. He also said that Pete was as far as he would go because he conducted a business at his pleasure and of course, your father is right. Many times he would love not to go in to the office but he knows you cannot do this and you have to discipline yourself at all times. Then I got in the act and of course Linda is not speaking to any one. She mentioned her depressions start when she is around me and this is probably true. So I suggested she try getting a job which would pay her enough to go out and live somewhere by herself. I am at my wit's end as to how to handle her. The thing is she has so many endearing qualities. Wednesday was my birthday—yes, I'm 52 and I couldn't be prouder as I thought I'd never make it—and she got up at 6 o'clock and fixed my breakfast and brought it up to me and cleaned the house and fixed my hair and then wanted to take me to see "Goodbye, Columbus", which I wouldn't do. I had heard it was just another deal of hopping in and out of bed and they are not going to get my money to see this stuff. This, of course, hurt her— even tho she has seen the movie twice and says it is terrrific. I was glad when my birthday was over.

Hers is tommorrow and I wanted to have some of her friends over but she is not speaking to me so I don't know what to do. If you only knew how relieved I would be if she could find the right "older" man for her and settle down so I could quit worrying about her.

I can't understand why you are not receiving Lucy's letters as her mother wrote and told me she is writing you almost every nite. So I thought tommorrow

I would give her a phone call and then I will write you as you seem to be getting our letters.

Haven't said anything about your fathers's trip as he is going to write you tomorrow and tell you all about it. He did seem to have such a good time and I'm so glad. Ashton Wick and he have always had such fun together and I know he drove from Fort Francis to Duluth with Ashton. One of the other men told your father to drive with Dr. Wick and he would drive your father's car and they would all meet in Duluth. He said you really haven't had a chance to talk to Ashton so go ahead. Ashton was so grateful as he told your father that he and I were the only ones he could still tell how he misses Dorothy. He doesn't seem too happy in his second marriage—now he doesn't say anything against Helen, but he did say he constantly wonders if there wasn't something, he should have noticed about Dorothy that could have prevented all this. I've told him this is foolish, because she really had more love and attention than most women receive in 70 years. Your father does like him so much and I wish he were closer.

Ran into Susan Pratt today and she was telling me that it is just a matter of time with her mother Dee Dee. She is really so young and she was so alive and it seems like such a shame. So we are in the midst of death here too.

I am sending you two packages. Look for them. I'll probably mail them Monday. One will have the Poloraid Camera and film and I hope you know how to load it. The other will have a few snacks. Won't be much as five pounds comes around quite soon.

Again all our thoughts prayers and love go with you always and don't worry about a thing but yourself and I'll let you know what Lucy has to say.

Love,
Mom & Dad

[No Envelope]

27 June 1969

My dear Parents,

I hit the jackpot on mail yesterday, folks—a letter and some more pictures from Lucy, and a letter from each of you. I can't understand why Dad has never written before—his letters are really interesting and fun to read.

Some bug has been going around A Company for several days, and yesterday I got it. I went to the medics yesterday, along with several other guys from my squad, and after giving us a blood test and taking a stool sample, they gave us bed rest for 24 hours. It was nice just to lie around for a change, although I didn't feel up to doing much of anything—either reading or writing. I still don't feel real well today, so I guess I'll go on sick call one more day to see if I can't get rid of this. I think what we've got has been diagnosed as amoebic dysentery, and I understand that nearly all men in Vietnam come down with something like this sooner or later. I'm taking some small white pills and Kaopectate, so, hopefully, I can lick this today. Don't worry, though, I'm not really that sick. I think the worst part of it is the depression that can set in when all you have to do is lie in bed and feel sorry for yourself.

All the guys in my squad who aren't sick took a chopper to LZ Center this morning. They'll be out there for a day or two, building a bunker to store ammunition in.

We're supposed to go to the field sometime after July 4 to build that bridge I was telling you about. It will be a suspension-type bridge for pedestrians across some river that flows through a narrow valley between two LZs near hear, LZ Siberia and LZ Karen.

I just now got back from the medics again, and the doctor gave me some more pills. He told me he thinks I have a mild case of gastroenteritis (?).

Last night my assistant squad leader came in and asked me if I would like to be put in for demolitions expert—actually he didn't ask me, he said he was putting me in for it, since the lieutenant and the platoon sergeant thought I had enough intelligence to work with explosives. You see, each engineer platoon has 3 demo men, one from each squad. Being a demo man has its good and bad points, and, consequently, I'm of two minds about it. The good point is—I'll be making an extra $55/month hazardous duty pay. Don't let that hazardous duty thing scare you, now. While all explosives can be dangerous and have to be treated with respect, all of the Army's explosives are very resistant to shock, etc., and can only be set off by a blasting cap. There is one type of explosive we use quite frequently, called C4, which can actually be burned like canned heat to warm C-rations. However, when you use a blasting cap on it, look out. The bad point about being a demo man is that you sometimes have to go out with the infantry for a week or so at a time, blowing up enemy bunkers and tunnels. This I won't be looking forward to, but I guess I can do it. Of course, I'm not a demo man yet, and the orders will probably take awhile to go through.

Well, folks, guess I'll close. Thanks so much for sending the polaroid and film—when it arrives I'll take some pictures of the area around here and get them off. If you need the camera back soon, let me know and I'll mail it back to you. Also, thanks for keeping the letters to me rolling in—they really help ease my mind about everything back home and do make it seem like I'm not so very far away. I'll keep you posted on everything that goes on, although sometimes I feel like maybe I shouldn't worry you all so much with my letters. You'll hear from me soon.

Love,
Dail

P.S. I'm awfully sorry I missed your birthdays for the 25th straight year—it's hard to buy cards and gifts around here though, so I'll just wish you all a big HAPPY BIRTHDAY and to say that I will be there for your next one.

Tuesday June 24, 1969

My dear Dail,

    FIRST—I called Lucy Sunday evening and she is fine and everything is alright but now she is upset because she doesn't understand why you are not getting her mail. She is writing almost every day and once in a while twice a day and she thought you were getting all her letters now and she wants you to tell her if you don't. She and I are planning a two women march on Washington and don't think we won't do it. Enjoyed talking to her and we spent the entire time talking about the stupid administration, the stupid military, stupid friends, stupid members of her father's congregation—who irk Lucy when they make the comment—"how well you are taking all of this." She said her job is keeping her very busy and very frustrated but for this she is glad. She said she is beginning to understand my philosophy of "hard work taking care of a lot of problems". Wish I could make Linda understand this. Anyway, everything is fine in Richmond and it is just the g.d. mail system, which like everything else, needs overhauling.

    The polaroid camera and some film is on its way. My other package with a little food and reading material won't get off until today and all because it was 1/2 pound overweight. How ridiculous! You really can't get enough food in one box to weight less than 5 lbs, to make one good midnite snack and then they charge you $1.50 to mail it. Really I'm mad all the time and Dad keeps telling me if I don't simmer down I'm not going to last until you get home.

    Pete was here Sunday evening for Linda's birthday dinner and I wish you could see him. He must weigh 230 lbs and he better not dare make fun of your bald spot. I told him his forhead is just about meeting the back of his neck. Linda gets very perturbed with me about my comments to some of the "hot shot" Websterites. I know I asked Steve Parsons why he wasn't in the army. Of course, this is my standard question to any one I meet now. It really seems like every time I turn around I stumble over Pete. I'm still trying to find out what happened to the nun.

He's still going to everyone's wedding and I think then he spends the rest of the evening at the food table. He's really something. Last week he had to make a flight to Topeka, Kansas on some barge business (I'm still also trying to figure out what he does for a living) and the last nite there he evidently went out on the town (in Topeka?) and when he got on the plane the next morning he must have been just a little hung-over. Instead of getting off in St. Louis, he slept through this landing and wound up in Baltimore Maryland. He said luckily it was a TWA flight and he convinced them that it was the fault of the Stewardess so they flew him back to St. Louis. I really never know when to believe him or not.

Really, I don't know how much longer I can tolerate this puppy. Still can't get used to calling her Chanel. She is without a doubt, the most spoiled impossible animal we have ever had in this domicile. Saturday nite we went out with the Seiberts to celebrate their anniversary. When Joan called me to ask if we would go over to Stockyard Inn, she said she didn't know if Charlie knew it was their anniversary or not as he hadn't said anything, but she said "what difference does it make—we might as well start out our thirtieth year the same way we've started the last 29." Anyway, before we left I had a little time so I took my last letter down to the mail box at the corner and thought I'd take the puppy with me, on a leash. Well on the way she spotted that dog of the Wellingtons and she pulled loose from me and I guess for anyone watching, it was quite hilarious. I was screaming for your father and anyone withing earshot. We chased her through back yards, over fences, under cars. It was really horrible. When we finally caught her I would gladly have choked her—especially as I was all dressed up for an evening out on the town. You don't dare put her down in the yard without tying her to a strong chain. And she eats everything and anything—from charcoal to grass to bushes to shoes to stockings to furniture, and once in a while—dog food.

You know after Saturday and Sunday nite I'm beginning to understand perhaps a little of the fright you are going through. First of all, as far as I'm concerned—The Stockyard Inn is off my list. Dad drove over there and after you leave the freeway to East St. Louis you have a short section of the Black aread to drive through before you come to the restaurant. Going over was alright, but coming home we arrive at this section, and there is a 4 way stop about two blocks before you get onto the highway that takes you in to St. Louis. As we came to this stop, as car pulled up on the cross street and there must have been about 8 "zulu" type characters in it with the afro haircuts and each with their bottle. On the opposite corner was another group of the same standing cat-calling. Your father at this moment said—"I sure don't like the looks of this and if I pull in front of them they will think I'm antagonizing them and if I wait they might get out." With this, Joan and I are both laying down on the floor of the back seat. Your dad takes off and then says—"yep they are going to follow us." Charlie, of course, is just saying "if they take after us plow into the s-o-b's." But we made it to the highway. Then Sunday we had Tornado alerts the live long day. And the new siren system is a prolonged eerie whine that just goes on and on. It seems a little foolish as you get so tired of hearing it after awhile you just ignore it.

With these church confrontations and some of the other things taking place I'm a little afraid St. Louis might have some trouble this summer. Your father has a patient who has a special interview type radio program. She herself is a singer and she and an announcer and another fellow who sings, go to different night spots and interview guests. I know the night Bob DeCurtis was here we took him to the 230 Club in Clayton and she was there and wanted to interview your Dad. Anyway, they were at the Stadium Club the other nite and when she is working, rather than have her husband come and get her at 1 in the morning, she has an arrangement with the Yellow Cab company to pick her up. This night instead of waiting for the driver to come up to the Stadium Club, she walked down to the foyer of the club. She went out the front door to see where the cab was and these three colored fellows grabbed her and pulled her into a car and your father said you have never seen anyone beaten the way she was. They broke her nose, knocked out several of her teeth, broke her finger getting a cheap piece of jewelry, took her purse and threw her out, unconscious, in front of a church downtown. She doesn't remember too much of the ride as she passed out when they broke her nose, but she said the hospital said she hadn't been raped. And this is not a young girl. She is around 45 years old. Pete has been taking Linda to a lot of the nite spots down in that area—The Levee, The Garage, The Brathaus and several others. They are quite the night spots in town right now, but I just can't help worry every time she is out—and you know how Pete can get if anyone says one word to him. I sure wish she would settle down and marry some nice quiet older man.

Denny is still working hard. Sunday he opened the station at 8 A.M. and worked until 10:30 that night. He was so tired when he came home. He said he changed 20 tires that day, along with all the rest of it. You know he is still carrying a torch for that darm Lambert girl. He doesn't say much and sometimes I think it would be better if he would talk about it, but he has pictures of her in his wallet and in his room and poetry he has written to her. He won't even give himself a chance to get over her.

Well tomorrow is your father's 57th birthday and I really think it bothers him. Lately, for some reason, he has been ruining every tie he wears, with food. The other nite he wore a brand new sport jacket for the first time, and got something all over the sleeve. When I showed it to hime he looked at me so dejectedly and said—"you know it makes me sick to think I'm turning into one of those typical "dirty old men", with gravy and slop all over their ties and clothes." Then he gets mad when I laugh.

Well, my dear, I just don't know how to comment on your letters—just believe me when we both say we are actually sharing all this pain and horror—spiritually, and we'd give our souls for just some way to alleviate it. Keep griping and writing and get it out of your system. Man's inhumanity to man has allways been something beyond comprehension.

Sunday at church we again had this young fellow who teaches theology at St. Louis University. As he stands at the lectern just before he starts his sermon he always raises his hands upraised and says "let us unite in prayer before we hear Christs teachings", and then he prayed for the sick and the poor and those in mental turmoil and for those away from home and for the brotherhood of man all over the world. As he said "Amen", there was the loudest clap of thunder and lightening you have ever heard. He just looked out at all of us and said—"A Warning?" I really like this guy.

Keep alert, keep hoping, keep loving, keep praying and we'll be right with you.

All our love,
Mom & Dad

PFC Dail W. Mullins, Jr.
488-48-0511
CoA, 26th ENGR. BN.
APO SF, 96256

29 June 1969

My dear Parents and Kids,

Well, how is everyone doing? I trust that Denny is up to his ears in grease and oil at the end of each day, and that Dad and Linda are having words on occasion. Actually, I hope your problems are no more serious than those and that you're all doing fine.

I'm feeling fine now—the pills that the Doctor gave me apparently did the trick. I certainly wasn't the first to come down with this bug, nor the last. It seems that every day two or three more guys from our company are over at the medics.

We only worked half a day today, Sunday, and its a good thing. The heat has been terrific lately—upwards of 115°. I find that you have to work in spurts when its that hot—you'd collapse if you kept any kind of hard labor up in this sun for more than 15 or 20 minutes. Also, I wish someone would invent a canteen which would keep water at a temperature slightly below the boiling point. Have you tried hot water lately? It's just wonderful. I swear to God, how anyone with an ounce of gray matter could make this miserable life a career!

I'm sure you are familiar with those U.S. Army Reenlistment Posters which show a Rock Hudson type G.I. in brand new dress greens standing in front of Old Glory and the words: Your Flag, Your Future—Stay Army emblazoned across his chest. Well, we have a satirical poster based on this thing in our hooch. It says, Your Flag, Your Future, Your Life! Stay Civilian. Pretty good, huh!?

I got 4 letters from Lucy yesterday—3 of them were postmarked back near the beginning of the month, so I guess that explains why I didn't get any letters from her for awhile. It was wierd to read on one day about what a wonderful time she had visiting her relatives in Philadelphia, and then hear in a letter one week later that she's planning to go to Philadelphia to see her relatives. I'm still anxiously awaiting the arrival of packages from both you and Lucy, and I hope the Army doesn't manage to get those lost.

The day before yesterday I received a nice letter from Wintker. He's living in Nashville now, in his own apartment, and working on his master's at Vanderbilt. He seems to be doing OK, except he said the girl he had been dating up and married someone else! At least that's one problem—thank the good Lord—I don't have to worry about.

Well, we'll be going out to the field to build that stupid bridge the first of next month (I think I may have already told you that). The Lieutenant wants to put it off until after the 4th, as that's a holiday. HAH! Do you know what they did on Christmas Day here last year—went on a long sweep. Yeah, I know, war is hell! He also wants to try and have us back here at Baldy before the middle of the month, as that's when the moon is new. You don't want to be camped out in the field with no moon any longer than is possible. I would hope, at any rate, that we could get that bridge up in less than 15 days. What I'm getting at, anyway, is that I don't want you to worry if my mail seems to slow down more than it already has if that's possible to you. I will take my writing equipment out there, of course, and will get off just as many letters as I can, but they may not come as often. They'll still bring my mail out to me, though. I hope all these packages arrive before we leave.

I have that stupid bunker guard again tonight—I also had it last night (this happens occasionally, since they keep a separate roster for Saturday nights). They try and make sure you only have Saturday night guard once a month. I have to leave now for the bunker line, so I'd better close. I'll add some more tomorrow and get it off then.

30 June 1969

An uneventful night on the bunker line—some idiots are disappointed by that; I'm always rather ecstatic.

Oh, before I forget. The army is dropping all US and RA service numbers from their records—why, I don't know, but they are. They're switching over to social security numbers as a means of numbering their expendable masses. So, you won't have to put RA12927044 on my letters anymore—just 488-48-0511.

Lucy mentioned in one of her letters that she and her folks enjoyed my descriptions—perhaps that's what you'd like to hear too. I really don't know what else to write about except my personal opinion of this war—and you already know that. No doubt this year would be much easier on me and everyone concerned if we all felt that I was helping to fight for a worthwhile cause (indeed, if such a thing exists), but right now that's impossible. Maybe after I see a couple of my friends over here killed I'll learn to hate those dirty communist gooks as much as everybody else and really feel like getting in and knocking heads off.

Well, let me talk about the people over here—the Vietnamese. Like people everywhere, the Vietnamese come in all shapes and sizes (though, it's true, I've never seen one whom I'd call tall). Some are very good looking and some are extremely ugly. Those that live in the larger cities and villages appear to me to be cleaner, healthier and somewhat more sophisticated than their rural counterparts. This is due, undoubtedly, to the fact that the urban (I use the term loosely) dwellers are exposed to American culture and medical facilities. The men in these large population centers all own expensive Honda motorcycles and dress in American-style clothes (tapered pants, ivy-league shirts and Italian-style loafers), while the women wear the more elegant types of Vietnamese dresses—the brightly colored slacks worn underneath the skirts that are slit up the side all the way to the waist. I've noticed too, just as a matter of course, that all of the city-dwellers, at least the younger ones, have beautiful teeth.

All of these things I've told you about the urban people are in striking contrast to the inhabitants of the rice paddy villages. These poor creatures live under such miserable conditions that I am often amazed to find that there are actually elderly villagers—how they manage to live so long in the midst of all that filth and poverty I'll never know.

Because of the war, of course, these small villages have a preponderance of females and small children—all of the military age males are either fighting for the National Government or the VC. Quite often, however, these villages will be guarded by ARVN or PF (popular forces—like our militia) troops who live there—so I can't actually say that there are no young males at all in the farming communities.

As I said, the people exist in filth. Most of the women have but one dress—usually a cotton pullover type affair—which they wear for weeks at a time. The women (except some of the younger girls) don't wear bras as we know them, but rather, wrap a piece of white cloth around their breasts, more to bind than support. The children are all dressed alike—no shoes, no pants at all, a colored T-shirt and a hat. All Vietnamese children have to have a hat! Usually it's a G.I. discarded baseball cap or jungle hat, but many wear those African pith helmets. One thing you do not do in Vietnam is pat a small child on the head, especially in front of his mother. The head is considered by these people to be the most sacred part of the body, and is strictly hands off! The Vietnamese are extremely shy about sexual matters, which is surprising, considering the fact that all the children run around with no pants on up until the age of 10 or 12. The worst thing about the children not wearing trousers or dresses is the fact that their genital regions are nearly always covered with flies (I don't mean to be crude—I'm just telling you like it is). The females, too, are often badly infected in that region. Apparently the children are rather badly subject to dermatological infections on their scalps, too, because by the age of two, every child has his head shaved, except for one patch of hair up front.

I believe I've mentioned in past letters the early age at which children smoke over here. Every child three years old carries his own pack of cigarettes. It's really strange to see two 4-year olds standing on the side of the road, stark naked and with their bellies sticking out, puffing on a couple of Marlboros!

Well, I've taken up enough of your time. I'll try and relate more of what I see over here in each of my letters, in the hopes that they'll be more readable. You do the same, hear, so I don't forget about "the world". I've stopped counting days—it only depresses me.

Take care, please, and try not to worry too much. You'll hear from me again soon.

Love,
Dail

Sunday, June 29, 69

Dear Son,
    Whenever 3 or 4 days pass and I haven't written you, I feel so negligent as I know what letters must mean to you, but at times I find it so hard to think of any news.
    Just got back from church and I certainly do enjoy hearing these two young fellows they have conducting the services, which I know I've mentioned before. This morning we had the young chaplain from Washington University and he based his sermon on the parable of the "Prodigal Son". He brought out all the "hippies" and "Wierdos" that Christ had following him in his days upon earth and how the then Establishment hated this group—the Establishment being the men of the temple, the scholars, judges and men of dignity and means. He said it was so in keeping with the student world of today and the bankers and lawyers and the pompous Wasps. It always strikes me with more impact when just last nite we had heated discussions with Joan and Charlie Seibert about this very thing. I know Charlie is very sincere in his belief of heritage, patriotism and the whole bit. He again is one who firmly believes we have a communist in every corner and how can you convince someone like this?
    What makes this so ironical is Joan's involvement in the sordidness of the slums and ghettos, and what for! She is now taking a five week course under Webster College, sponsored by the Head Start Program, which is giving her five hours of credit. Three days a week she drives down to Flat River, Missouri with three carloads of "students" and a Dr. Pitts. They are working with a group of children from below poverty conditions. Most of the children have serious speech difficulties, even tho eight and ten years of age, and some have never spoken at all. Each one of the group have two children they are responsible for and work with constantly the six hours they are with them. Then they meet at nite with Dr. Pitts to evaluate. Joan is her typical self in her remarks about her charges. She has one little boy of eight who, to date, has uttered just a few words. Dr. Pitts asked her the other nite if she had noticed any progress with the child and her answer to him was—"if you could ever get that child to stop masturbating he might have time to talk—either that or his underwear is too tight". I just wonder why she goes to all this time and effort when basically she feels very much the way Charlie does

about the colored and the poor—that it is just because they are to damn lazy to earn a living. Of course, these are all white people she is dealing with in Flat River.

Wednesday was dad's birthday and he received the cutest card from Lucy. That evening Pete Merrill came by and we went out with him and Linda to play miniature golf and to also hit some golf balls. He left Thursday for his two week summer camp training up in Ripley, Minnesota. Isn't that tough.

Denny is still plugging away at his gas station job and I'll say one thing for him—he has fortitude. The sad thing is that everything he has made so far has gone to pay bills he obligated for. $50 for a stereo tape, $50 to his fraternity for a cabin they are buying in Athens, and then his monthly dues. He really hasn't cleared a penny yet and he works so hard for that money. In fact the owner of the station had a difficult time getting anyone to work for $1.50 until Denny came along. He tried to hire some of the colored boys as his station is near Meacham Park but none of them want to work that hard for that money. He comes home just exhausted, especially when he works the 8:30 AM shift until 10:30 at night.

Believe it or not, Linda is enjoying her working at dad's office very much, altho she thinks most of his patients are nuts and as she tells him—"why do you put up with people like this"; not realizing that his taking this stuff all day long is what has kept her a lady of leisure on various campuses. He gets a little irked at her once in a while, and then she stomps off for awhile. The other day she mentioned that Christine and Beverly were so floored when she told them Dad was going to be 57 as they thought he was much younger. He was just furious because she had told them how old he was—which is really silly. He's like his mother about his age, altho he doesn't mind telling everyone how old I am. He and Basil are taking your grandmother to dinner today to celebrate her birthday, and only God knows how old she is.

We enjoyed your pictures so much, but it does also make us sad when you look at an area so many thousands of miles away and you wonder what it is all about. I'm almost afraid to ask, but how far are you from Ben Het and Dak To. The news about these two places just makes my hair stand on end, and it sure looks close to your area I have mapped out. I'll send the pictures on to Lucy. By the way, after I sent the camera your Dad happened to mention the possibility that the batteries might be old. Let me know if you need replacements. Think after this I'll send your packages via PAL. They will take things over 5 lbs and delivery is flown all the way and reaches you in 5 to 7 days—supposedly, for $100 extra.

Do you remember Jon Custer that Linda dated for awhile. He dropped in the other day. He has been back for several months after a year in Viet Naam and spent a lot of time in the general area you are in. He was saying after a time you sort of become impervious to the mortar attacks. He also had mentioned this black Ace of spades symbol which was shown on the plane. He said you soon learn to carry this marking with you to get rid of the beggars whom he said beseech you constantly.

The weather here has been 95 to 100 with typical St. Louis humidity and we have had Tornado warnings almost every day for a week. We have all gotten to ignore them except Linda, and she still goes into a tizzy every time the sirens blow. The other nite she and Denny and I were up at Velvet Freeze to get some ice cream and I was out in the car while they went in to get the cones. They had been in the store just a few minutes when the Tornado sirens started blasting. One must be on top of the fire station across from Velvet Freeze as the sound was ear shattering. I looked up and Linda was catapulting out of that shop as tho she had been attached to a lighted fuse. It was so funny.

The enclosed pictures were taken today out in the back yard after Linda had given the puppy a bath. I really shouldn't send the one of me. Your father said he could count five rolls of fat very visible. It is really just that the dress is tight.

We are supposed to go down to the Lake of the Ozarks over the 4th and sleep on Reinhardts boat—but I am really going to try and beg off that trip. That place is completely inundated with hordes of people and sleeping on that hot boat with the Reinhardts is not my cup of tea. Then too, I hate to be away Denny's birthday. Thank heavens, that will be the last one for awhile.

The Paschens called me the other day. They had just returned home from Aunt Dots. They said they had such a good time, altho it was rather difficult keeping their mouths shut regarding Wendy. I know what they mean, as she is really unbearable after you are with her for awhile. They were a little upset as young Bob is planning to enlist as he is getting tired of the Army bit hanging over his head. This would be a 4 year hitch. I'm hoping some week end I can drive down to see Aunt Dot. I'm going to have to learn to do some highway driving sooner or later—by myself. Linda wants to go with me but I'm afraid your father will not let her off as she is to set an example for the other help. Lucy asked me to take a trip down to Virginia and this too I'd love to do, if it just wasn't so expensive. We've got the kid's down payment on their tuition next month and then the full tuition by September so air traveling is pretty much out of the question.

Well God bless you and keep you and several times a day I just stand and send my pleas heavenward. We miss you and weep for you and mark off the days.

With all our love,
Mom & Dad

Lucy said you want cigarettes? Is this right. Let me know anything else you would like to have. I'll try and get another package off to you later this week.

_____

PFC Dail W. Mullins, Jr.
488-48-0511
CoA, 26th ENGR. BN.
APO SF, 96256

5 July 1969

My dear Parents and Kids,

Well, I made it back from my first trip into the field relatively unscathed save for some sore muscles and a rather badly sunburned hand. The work was awfully hard, and we had to contend with afternoon temperatures of 130°, but we got the job done in something less than 4 days without incident or injury. As I had suspected, I wasn't able to get any letters off from out there—even if I had had the time to write, I couldn't have sent them out anyway, since the choppers don't pick up outgoing mail if you're to be in the field for any less than 5 days.

In case you're still following my travels on that map you've mentioned, I'll try and pinpoint where we were, although you're map may not be very detailed. Look about 25 miles West-South-West of where you think Baldy is, and you should see the Song Tran River. Somewhere along the eastern bank of this river is the province capital of Hiêp Duc—we put the LTR ferry in at this point.

Actually the place was quite beautiful, if you could divorce the view from the activity. The Song Trau is a tortuous, twisting river that runs down from the higher mountains toward the Laotian border into the rice-producing coastal areas. At our location the river was studded with huge, jagged rocks which churned the water and really played hell with our efforts. The banks of the Song Trau rise steeply in a series of sandy tiers covered with waving elephant grass four and five feet high in places. These tiers finally culminate in two large hills on either side of the river, and each hill has an LZ on top—LZ Karen on the east, LZ Siberia on the west. We set up our night defensive position on one of these tiers below LZ Siberia. A chopper brought a small dozer out and this enabled us to cut a makeshift road from our camp to the beach and to make a chopper landing pad so we could be resupplied.

We left LZ Baldy on the morning of July 1, and it took two choppers three trips each to get us and our gear out there. The first day was spent cutting bamboo poles for our shelters, digging foxholes and machine gun emplacements and setting up claymore mines and trip flares around our perimeter.

All of the children from Hiêp Duc flocked down to help, of course, and we put them to work carrying boxes and tools in exchange for "chop-chop" (extra cans of C-Rations). These little beggars proved in the end, however, to be almost as much of a distraction as did the village women washing their clothes and bathing at the riverbank. I was somewhat hesitant about taking to the river in the nude during our breaks, but all the guys who have been over here awhile didn't think twice about it, so I finally decided to forego American culture and join them. The Vietnamese women didn't give us a second look, and I'm still trying to figure out whether that's good or bad. At any rate, the water felt better than that damnable sun.

Toward the North and South, the river disappeared into the jungle-covered mountains. In the morning these mountains were always covered with a thin shroud of fog, and this view, together with the raging river and Hiệp Dục nestled among the palm trees was really a remarkable sight—if, as I said, you could dissociate it from the hell you know exists all around you.

Everything went fairly smooth up until the day we were supposed to leave (be extracted, as the chopper pilots say). We finished up around 4:00 that evening, and spent the next 3 hours tearing down our camp and putting away all of our tools. Well, at 7:30 we got word that extraction wouldn't take place until the next morning. Disgusted, no one felt like putting their shelters back up, so we just put our trip flares back up and threw our sleeping bags on the ground. Naturally it rained cats and dogs that night, and all of us spent most of the night huddled under wet ponchos and watched our beds float away. What a night.

To top off that thrilling trip, I lost my .45 pistol somewhere enroute back to Baldy (I think one of the door gunners on that helicopter got it), and so I'll probably have to pay for it if I don't find it. It gripes me, because I never wanted the stupid thing in the first place.

I got a nice package with cigarettes, dried fruit and magazines from Lucy, and am still anxiously awaiting the arrival of my other packages.—I hope they come soon.

Yes, I think sending things like packages by PAL instead of SAM would be best—I know it costs more, but sometimes SAM packages don't get here for a month or more.

I got two more letters that you had sent to me when I was still in Oakland and Long Birch, plus an old letter from Mrs. Skilling.

Thanks for the pictures of you, Linda and the puppy—I can't get over how much she looks like Babette did, but if I remember right, her hair is supposed to turn color, isn't it.

As to calling home from over here. I appreciate your offering to help defray the expenses by sending Lucy a check, but I think I'll wait until I can get to DaNang or Chu Lai to call. You see, I can call from Baldy, but its a relay type of affair, with hundreds of people listening in, and you have to use all that military communications lingo, like "over", after each sentence. They have regular phones in Danang, and Chu Lai.

Well, guess I'd better close and get this in the mail, or you'll really be worried about me. Take care, please, and keep writing as much as you can—I know it's hard to think of things to write about, but never the matter; any news is welcome news.

Thinking of you all, all the time.

Love,
Dail

Thursday, July 3, 69

Dear Dail,

Well, here I am late again in writing you. Planned to do it last nite, but Dad had one of his periodic impulses to go to the movies. And of course, we saw a lovely one. Something called, I think, Kakatora—something that shook the world. It was at Cinerama and almost the entire movie was one exploding volcano after another. I felt like I had witnessed my 4th of July celebration. I really wanted to see "Popi" with Alan Arkin, but when Dad decides to see a movie that's where you go. Linda has been bugging me to go with her to see Goodbye Columbus, but I've held off after Joan Seibert's views of it. If she is shocked I know I would go into a coma.

Tuesday afternoon I was out in back cleaning out the garage and this car pulled into the driveway. It was Bob Karasek. He came over about 4 PM. and it was almost 10 o'clock when he left. He and I sat out . . . talking but then Dad and Linda arrived home about 6 and he and Bob got going and I frankly never have heard either of them talk so much. He's had quite an interesting year and some of it is rather amusing to me. One expression he has picked up and which he uses almost constantly is "bloody". Everything is bloody from the war to his life to everyone's existence. This is such a British expression that it rather surprised me as he spent no time in England. He loved Sweden, but this doesn't surprise me as probably the free love interested him. He had a long Edwardian corduroy coat on which reached to his knees. He said he had had very long hair and a mustache but had to cut both when he applied for a reserve unit placement.

As far as I can gather, Bob was forced to return home even tho he would have liked to spend another year in Sweden. Upon arriving in the U.S., he made his Princeton contacts and found that there was a reserve opening in San Antonio, Texas. The only thing his induction date has been set and it is my idea that after you have your induction date you cannot get into a reserve unit. He has taken the oath in Texas, but still hasn't been sworn in by Webster Draft Board. He was telling us that he had had some correspondence with MIT and they were interested, but couldn't keep him out of the army. The bad part about tying himself down with a reserve unit in Texas is that he cannot remove himself from that area until there is an opening in some other reserve unit. But old Bob plays all the angles— he feels in a year or so there should be some openings in the east.

Unfortunately, his asthma keeps him out of the air force, navy and any officers' program, but it doesn't keep him out of the regular enlistment program.

We have had some bad storms here recently and some of the aftermaths have been rather funny. Remember the Santa Maria replica that old Cervantes brought to St. Louis. Well last Saturday night it and the Becky Thatcher (a restaurant boat) were broken loose from their moorings in a storm and floated all over the Mississippi. There were about 200 people on the Becky Thatcher having dinner. They finally were able to get this boat back to a mooring the next morning, but the Santa Maria is still grounded somewhere on the east side. It made it from Italy but can't stay parked on the riverfront.

Last Sunday Dad and Linda and Base and Vera and Barbara took Grandma for dinner at Green Parrot. Grandma gave her usual munificent gifts of a dollar to Denny and Linda and a tie for your Dad. But what floored me, was a pair of stockings she sent to me for my birthday. Linda said she even mentioned my name twice that eventing. I go to church every Sunday and pray for tolerance and understanding, but it still doesn't seem to extend to her. I would really rather not get involved with her pettiness. I would just like to keep it at the status quo it has been in. I would feel like such a hypocrite by being sweet to her, as I frankly cannot ever forget the things and accusations she made against me and my parents. I know this is wrong and this is why the world is in the shape it is in today, but I feel things will go along much more smoothly if we just have no relationship at all. Any way, during the course of the meal Vera and Base mentioned that they are thinking of going to Europe next year, which strikes me as hilarious. Your father has always felt so guilty because he received(?) the education and Base didn't. But here they are going to Europe and Vera went to Hawaii last year and we are hoping to be able to spend about 4 days in Panama City before we take the kids back to school.

Linda came home the other nite and informed us that Cindy Hodgson is getting married the 27th of December and has asked Linda to be a bridesmaid. This boy still has another year and a half at Tulsa, altho he is older than Cindy. She has graduated and is going back to Tulas to teach school. As Denny said to Linda, "always a bridesmaid, but never a bride"; which really set her off. I really get upset about her. She had a date with Mark Wissert the other nite and came home and said "what a goon". No one seems to please her and she seems more uncertain about what she wants than ever. She really thinks the ideal life would be going to Athens college the rest of her life and being a perpetual freshman. She is driving me nuts.

Denny is really funny. He has become an authority on cars in the three weeks he has been on this job. You should hear him tell us about how we should take care of our cars. He bought two wide track tires and put on the Mustang the other day and your dad almost had a miscarriage. He wasn't going to have all that "crap" on his cars. He is working tonite until midnite and I am not happy about it. He is getting a little upset about his feelings about the negros. They have a lot of Meacham park customers and Denny has trusted them in many ways and he finds out they are playing him for a fool. They come in and ask him to lend them tools and then they laugh and ride off with the equipment and he has to pay for anything missing from the shop, out of his salary. Last week he had about eight dollars taken out of his pay so he is learning they cannot be trusted. I hate this neighborhood he is working in, but of course I would worry if he was picking petunias in a lush meadow.

Talking about worry, I am sure you are well aware of how I feel about this demolition job. It was my understanding that all details of this sort were purely voluntary and I hope you won't do this. In fact, I hope this dysentary keeps you tied up for the duration. Please don't volunteer for anything. Tonite, for the first time in a long while, the news seemed encouraging. They feel that the Viet Cong are beginning to pull some of their troops back and it might be an answer to our troop pull out. God, how I pray this is so.

Your letters keep us going too and we look forward to them so much, even tho what your are going through just is beyond our understanding.

We were supposed to spend the 4th on the Reinhardt's boat but as of tonite we haven't heard anything from them and I'm just as glad. The highways to the Ozarks are bumper to bumper for miles and that boat is not much fun when the temperature is 100. Then too, Denny's birthday is Saturday and I'd rather be here, even tho he probably will be working.

We think and talk about you constantly and miss you so much.

All our love and payers.
Mom & Dad

PFC Dail W. Mullins, Jr.
488-48-0511
CoA, 26th ENGR. BN.
APO SF, 96256

9 July 1969

Dear Mom and Dad,

I wanted to get a letter off tonight before our platoon left tomorrow for LZ Ross, but it's rather late now and I may have to postpone some of this until tomorrow. You'll remember I told you that each of the three platoons here in A Company takes a turn spending about a month up at Ross, sweeping the road from that end. Well, our turn starts tomorrow. My mail situation will not be affected by the move, as they bring it up to Ross from Baldy every day. Just keep sending your letters to the same place.

I got your food package today—thanks a lot. It's really a luxury to be able to munch on pretzels and drink a Coke before bed. I still haven't received Lucy's packages—I sure hope they weren't lost in the mail.

I'm keeping my fingers crossed on the current lull in the fighting over here, though I'm afraid it will be just another repeat of past performances. While the newspapers and radio seem to be making a big deal of it, all the fellows who have been here awhile say they've seen and heard it all before. Maybe this time, though, it will be different.

Oh, I wanted to thank you for the book Catch 22—I've heard alot about it and have read several reviews. I should be able to get it read, as I find that I do have some time to devote to this small pleasure, though I have not attempted anything heavier than Isaac Asimov and Marvel Comics. Even comic books, though, help make the time pass a little quicker.

I don't know whether I've mentioned Hugh Barksdale or Larry Lemar in any of my previous letters or not, but I feel I should, as they are probably going to play a big role in helping me maintain what little sanity I have left. Hugh has a master's degree in English, is married, lives in Murray, Kentucky and has been teaching at Murray State University for the past two years. Like myself, Hugh is an OCS dropout, and is as crazy about the Army and Vietnam as I am. Lemar has a degree in civil engineering from Illinois University and was apparently doing quite well with some architectural firm before Uncle Sam grabbed him. He stuck it out in OCS at Fort Sill for 8 weeks before he "wised up". At any rate, we three get along quite well, and I think we really help each other out alot. If one of us can't think of anything to gripe about the other one usually can. This TROIKA-style attack thus enables us to maintain an almost endless list of injustices perpetrated on the soldier by the military-industrial complex.

Charlie hasn't messed with LZ Baldy for several weeks now (knock on wood), and I guess that reflects the current fighting lull. However, one of Baldy's helicopter gunships did kill 15 VC about 1/4 mile west of Baldy yesterday. We also captured a VC carrying rice for his buddies along the road on a minesweep today. He was a short, mean-looking guy, but didn't put up any kind of a struggle. Actually he couldn't with 15 rifles and my M-79 grenade launcher pointed at him. Some MP's came out in a helicopter and took him away after our radio man called in to report his capture.

I had guard last night and around midnight I found myself suddenly unable to sleep, so to occupy myself I began playing with the shortwave band on my radio. I picked Hanoi Hannah up and listened to her tell me how much money my government is spending on this war—I felt like saying, "you're telling me?"

Well, it's late, and I'd better get some sleep. Looks like I did finish after all.

Please take care and let me hear from you.

Love,
Dail

Sunday, July 6, 69

My dear son,
    Well the long week end is over and it leaves a lot of automobile accidents, boating accidents, drownings and the lesser evils of sun burns and worn tempers.
    About a month ago the Reinhardts had asked us to go down to the Ozarks on Thursday and stay on their boat over the holiday. I was not too enthusiastic about spending that much time with them on that hot boat and winding up doing all the cooking and work, but your father seemed to like the idea so I went along with it. He cancelled his appointments and then we never heard another word from them; which, to me, is so typical of them. I was really glad because the highway to the Ozarks is one continuous stream of cars and then I hated to be away for Denny's birthday, but dad was really disappointed and kept wondering what happened, not realizing they do this all the time. What I'm getting to is that because he had all this time off and nothing to do, we have seen three shows this week end. I'll probably not see another movie now for six years. Think I told you we saw that Kakatrie thing and then we saw "Popi" with Alan Arkin, which was tremendous. He is, to my thinking, the best actor to come along in years and I'll take him any day in preference to Rod Steiger. Then tonite we saw "True Grit" with old John Wayne, and he is getting old, but like old wine he seems to improve with age. This is his best picture.
    Denny has had rather a rough week end and for all the hours he is putting in you would think he would have a bigger paycheck. Friday he opened the station at 7 AM and didn't get home until midnite; Saturday, his birthday, he worked from noon until midnite, and today he went in at 7 again to open it and he still isn't home. He's really so funny as he knows everything about cars now. He bought two wide track tires and put them on the Mustang and your dad is having a fit.
    I keep wondering how your amoebic dysentery is. It's bad enough being over there without being sick on top of it. Please don't try and be stoic and if you don't feel well see that you have attention.
    We're finding it a little difficult to evaluate the news right now. All we hear at this end if it's true, is the slow down in Viet Cong activity. Why this is so seems to be rather puzzling to all and sundry. You have those who see a counter action to our pull out and then you have those who see them re grouping. I wish the hell someone knew what was going on. I'm sending you an article that was in the Post Dispatch today and it makes the whole thing even more ridiculous; it's all been such a stupid waste.
    Last night, which should have been a party for Denny, turned out to be a party of Linda's friends. She had Linda Beswick, Carole Hemphill, and Cindy and her fiancee over for dinner. He seems to be a very nice boy, but he still has a year

and a half in school and then the army so I guess Cinday will be the breadwinner. We wound up having a rather nice evening. We played Jeopardy for awhile and then the kids decided they would rather play charades and even got your father in the act and he wound up being the most avid player. It was funny to see how seriously he took the whole thing. The girls were having hysterics and he thought they were applauding his acting ability.

That Carole Hemphill is really something else again. You know she has two sets of friends; the girls she went through high school with and then the "wild ones" she met at Washington University Art School, and she never lets them intermingle. She was with two of her hippie friends the other nite riding in one of those boats that Forest Park rents and as they rode under one of those bridges and two colored boys pulled a gun on them. It was in the paper, but they saved Carol the embarrassment of having the names in the article. To hear her tell it, it was very funny.

Well it looks like the moon shot is going to come off on time. Out TV has been on the fritz, so were going to have someone out tomorrow to fix it. Dad wants to have perfect reception for this and he is even going to stay up until 1:27 to see it. These things make me so nervous that I think I'll just wait until its all over.

Thought you would be interested in the Jules Feiffer strip and "aint it the truth". Also the Steve Sees column.

Received a nice note from Lucy and she tells us that Dan left Tuesday for his summer with the Indians in Mexico. Hope it proves to be as interesting as he thinks it is going to be.

Well I hope and pray that all is well with you. The holiday messes up our mail delivery, so we haven't had any mail for awhile and of course, we can't help worrying.

You mention a friend who taught at Murray College. This is the school young Bob Paschan was enrolled in and then decided he wanted the University of Louisville. And is he sorry now.

God be with you and take care. With all our love,
Mom & Dad

———————————

PFC Dail W. Mullins, Jr.
488-48-0511
CoA, 26th ENGR. BN.
APO SF, 96256

12 July 1969

My dear Parents,
    Again I find that I must apologize for not having written in some time, but in the Army there's only 36 hours in a day, and we have beaucoup things to do. You know I promised myself that I'd answer every letter I got, and people have been awfully nice about writing, so . . . I wrote a letter to Gaye Rieschel and to Jennifer Henley, both of whom had written me. What I'm trying to say is that I'm just now getting around to writing a letter I should have written some time ago.
    Right now I'm sitting in our bunker (hooch) up at LZ Ross (I believe I mentioned that our platoon was pulling its turn up here now), listening to the pitter-patter of little feet—LZ Ross' bunkers are loaded with rats. They don't really bother me too much, except that if you get bit by one you have to go to Danang for rabies shots, and I hear those are pretty painful. You have to sleep with a net over you and a flashlight—the light will scare them away during the night in case you have to get up. There is one advantage to sleeping in bunkers, however—if there's a mortar attack you can just stay in bed.
    I'm enclosing a couple of flicks I took with the Polaroid you sent me. They're not very good, but maybe they'll be some touch of reality for you—at least you can see I still look the same except, of course, for my neat moustache. I put them in order for you, and as is my usual practice, I'll describe each picture for you.
    The first one is of your son (with moustache and bush cap) and our platoon medic, whom we fondly refer to as "Doc" Morris. Doc is a true "southerner" from North Carolina and an alcoholic (his wife had a child by another guy while he was over here, and it really hit him hard). He's a good medic, though, and, in fact, has been recommended for a bronze star for valour. However, if he gets it he's going to tell the Army to stick their medal up their ___, which is the way I feel about those pieces of tin. Consequently, we get along quite well. Can you dig my moustache, though—that's the neatest thing A company has. Also note the gold cross around my neck. It was given to me by Lân, my soda girl, as a token of my "number oneness" as a G.I. I'll have to send you a flick of Lân sometime—she's a real cute little girl.
    The second picture is of Doc, Hugh Barksdale (center) and Larry Lemar (he's shaving). I've already mentioned Hugh and Larry in my last letter. Barksdale is a

short, skinny runt, and has about as much business being over here as I do. You've heard of the dirty dozen? Well, we're the f_____ up 4!

The last picture, as you can see, is of Barksdale, me and Lemar (still shaving).

By the way, that first picture of me and Doc has a good view of the central highlands in the background. I really wish these flicks were in color—Vietnam is a beautiful country in many ways, believe it or not. Those mountains are a lush green color, and in the morning they always have a light mist on them. What brings you back down to earth, however, is when that mist turns to black smoke by noon from napalm strikes.

Well, I just wanted you to have these pictures and let you know that I'm doing OK. By the way, by the time you get this letter I will have been over here for 2 months—10 to go—hope I can make it.

Take care, all, and I'll be writing as often as I can. You keep in touch too, and let me know how you're doing. I miss you all—

from your peon first class,
Dail

Wednesday July 9,

My dear Son,

It's close to midnite, but want to get a letter off to you before I crawl in bed; but if it is a little "kooky", you'll know why. Between the hour and my inability to type, this is going to be great.

Since Linda's home and Pete is out of town, Bob in Philadelphia, and the other available males are "gross", in her estimation, she prevails upon her dad and I to keep her amused, and it is killing me. She is the only one in the world who can keep your father up past ten o'clock on a week night. She and Meacham. They were over last nite to play cards and didn't leave until 1:30. I was winning all his money and you know how sick that makes old tightwad Meacham. So he was staying around trying to recoup. Then I have to get up at 7 to get Denny off. Then tonite Linda wanted to go to Shakeys for pizza and then downtown to the Brathaus. This is a beer and sandwich place across from Busch Stadium. They have a Banjo band and everyone sits at long tables on top of each other and the noise is horrendous. When the band isn't playing they show old Laurel and Hardy movies and W.C. Fiedls. They have a door charge to get in and the people are lined up out in the street. Anyway I really am getting much too old for this stuff.

Then when I got home that stupid animal had gotten a pillow and there was cotton stuffing all over the family room. She is exactly like that dog of the Bells.

She has chewed every piece of furniture in the room and I don't think she will ever be house broken. If I had my way she be the next "Dog of the Week."

We too enjoy your descriptive letters, but intermixed with enjoyment is horror that your a part of this unholy mess. Reading your last letter describing the little children you are seeing and the utter filth seemed so shocking and then I thought of this movie "Popi", which we had seen the other nite. I don't know if you are familiar with the plot, but it is about a Puerto Rican whose wife dies and leaves him with two little boys to raise in the Spanish Harlem district of New York. This movie company was given carte blanc by Mayor Jonh Lindsday and it is all filmed in a tenement in Harlme with most of the cast people who live in this area, and it is on a par with the children you are seeing except they are at least out in the air. They show scenes in this movie of the huge rats that just take over this area and the streets are thick with garbage. It is really soul shaking to some one who lives out in the suburbs. I keep finding myself asking—"Dear God, what is it all about."

Tried to reach Bob Karasek to see if he could come for dinner but haven't been able to reach him. It could be that Webster Draft Board is going to let him take the reserve unit and if so, guess he is on his way to San Antonio. Hope he doesn't regret tying himself down to this area for 8 years.

Well we got our television all in order for the blast off to the moon next week and then the landing on the moon, which comes through here at 1:21 A.M. Dad sweres he is going to see this. What he plans to do is go to bed around 7 and set the alarm for 1. I don't want to miss this either.

Am getting another package ready for you, but I wish you'd get the first two I sent. I guess I should have insured them, but they charge so stupid much for this mailing.

Today I got a pamphlet from our senator Jim Symington with a long list of questions from the Viet Naam War to taking off college costs on income tax returns to 18 year olds voting and on and on and he has asked everyone to please answer and send back to him to a special mailing address and also send in our comments. I've already sent two letters to hime which are probably in the bottom of some waste basket, but he is going to get this one back. This seems to be the biggest frustration to friends of Bob Karaseks, whom he has spent many hours here and abroad, talking to; the inability to get anyone in command to listen and realize that our constitution and government has been outmoded and that drastic changes have to be made. As he says, what can you do and who can you get to listen. Bob seems to be worried that his actions aren't in keeping with his moral beliefs. In other words, he said if he was honest with himself he would burn his draft card, but he doesn't have the clourage to suffer the consequences.

Well they just came on TV and said there is another Tornado alert until 1:30. This is really getting to be a joke. We have had about 8 Tornado warnings in the last week and people just don't know what to do. And when you have someone like Linda around it really gets you down. As I told her I'd rather be blown away than have a pile of bricks fall in on me in the basement.

Well, I'm glad you warned us about the possibility that we might not be hearing you as often as we have been, but I'm still going to worry. God I'll be so glad when your back in the "World".

God bless and keep you and be careful and take care of yourself.

All our love and prayers,
Mom & Dad

PFC Dail W. Mullins, Jr.
488-48-0511
CoA, 26th ENGR. BN.
APO SF, 96256

15 July 1969

Dear Mom, Dad and kids

Well, another day tucked down into the duffel bag of life, never to be endured again. That's about how it is over here—even though everyone gets a little nervous when the sun goes down, knowing that's when Charlies' on the move, you're still glad to see it because it means one more day gone. If I'm not mistaken I'm about to break 300 days over here, which is generally accepted as the first milestone. Of course, the big milestone is that 100th day, after which you are said to be "short" and referred to as either a "shortimer" or a "two-digit-midget" (i.e., 99 days, 98 days, etc.). It is customary for a man on his 100th day to get up early, go outside and yell SHORT! at the top of his lungs.

I ran across two quotations I thought you might enjoy. I don't know who the first is by, but the second is by Albert Camus, author and existential philosopher:

"The Army is the uneducated, leading the unwilling, to do the unnecessary"

"I wish that it were possible to love justice, and still love my country"

I can't remember whether I mentioned it in my last letter or not, but I now have a parrot! His name is Dust Off. I assume you know what a dust off is. I bought him off some kid in Que Son, one of the villages around LZ Ross, for

$2.00—he's not too much bother, and really digs the canned fruit from our C-rations. Another guy in our company ran across a baby mongoose—I'm enclosing a picture he took with me holding it. Pretty cute little guy, isn't he?

I, too, am anxiously awaiting the moon shot. While I won't be able to see it on TV, they are planning live coverage of both the blastoff and landing on AFVN radio here out of DaNang. I hope I'm free to hear both.

Hugh Barksdale, my friend from Murray, Ky, just made an interesting comment about the Vietnam War. He said the ARVN's are fighting because that's the best job most of them can get; the VC are fighting because that's all they've ever done; the NVA are fighting because Uncle Ho has delusions of grandeur; and the Americans are fighting so they can go home and say the hell with it! And that's just about the truth.

Right now we're rather in the dark about what's going on militarily over here—it's almost as if they've censored the radio as to news of the fighting or lack of it. A few weeks ago it seemed that things were beginning to slow down some, at least that's what the radio reports said. Then—nothing. Naturally I'm curious to know whether the lull is continuing or whether its stopped up again. I do know that they're still planning to pull a few more troops out of 'Nam. Keep your fingers crossed.

Well, not much else to report. I stayed up rather late last night shooting the bull with Barksdale, so I'm pretty tired tonight. Guess I'll close. Take care everyone, and keep those cards and letters coming in.

Love,
Dail

Sunday July 13, 69

My dear Dail,

Just finished a letter to Lucy. I always start my letters with the statement "don't know what to write" and then I proceeed with four or five pages.

Well our television is all repaired ready and waiting for the blast off Wednesay morning. Again we go through this apprehension and then wait four or five days until they land on the moon. I'm a little apprehensive after what happened to the monkey they just sent up for a few days.

This young fellow they have filling the pulpit at South Webster spoke this morning on these men making a break through and how blasé everyone has become and he deplores this attitude. I have so enjoyed these two young fellows they have until they get a minister to take over. I hope they never do as having all these different personalities each Sunday is, to me, so challenging. You would so enjoy listening to these young and vibrant fellows.

Southern Illinois University campus at Edwardsville, Illinois has been having a summer music program in conjunction with the St. Louis Symphony and they have been having some very notable and controversial people. Joan Biaz, Buffy St. Marie, Van Cliburn, The Rascals and anyone else you can think of. Last Thursday I had lunch with Mrs. Bell, and Lorraine Hester and Mrs. Bell was going over to Edwarsdivlle with Joan to see the Iron Butterfly. Now they mean nothing to me, but evidently they are the THING. I talked to Mrs. Bell Friday to invite her to a luncheon I'm having Wednesday and I asked her how she liked her evening with the "way out" people. It was like turning on a rushing faucet. Never in her life had she been so shocked and amazed by the filthy language and obscene behavior of young people. This concert was evidently atteneded by every hippie within the St. Louis area and their open love-making was more than she could tolerate. So you need not feel any qualms about striding into a stream in front of native women.

We have beee n [been] a little heartened about the latest move for peace. This is the free election that Thieu and Nixon have [agreed] on. Now you know if the Vietnamese have a chance to vote they are going to go Communistic regime all the way and what the hell have we been over there for? It is so impossible to understand.

Pete is back after two hard weeks sailing on the lakes of Minnesota. He says he has written you two letters and hasn't heard from you. Did you received any main from him? I have to hear it from you before I'll believe it from him. He is a congenital liar. The more I see he an d Linda together, the more I feel they deserve each other. Bob is too nice for Linda and nobody could stand Pete, so he and Linda really ought to get together.

Took Ken Meacham and Rosemary out to the airport Saturday morning for their flight to California. Young Ken Meacham was married Friday night and it must have been rather sad. Her father and mother said they would not attend, but at the last minute the mother decided she couldn't stand her only daughter getting married without her being there, so she and the Meachams were the only ones at the ceremony. Then young Ken and his new bride had a reception at theri apartment. I hope this marriage lasts more than two months.

Talked to Mrs. Bill this morning at church and Wayne is due in next week for his final leave. He has to report to Travis the end of July and is headed for Viet Naam. I mentioned to the Emersons about David looking you up but they have no address for him at the present. His year was up in June so he took a leave that was due him and went to Japan. But he extended his time for another six months, but they don't have any idea where he will be. Mrs. Bill is going to let me know when she hears from Wayne and I'll let you know.

We were so thankful to know you had gotten back safely from your first missions and I really am living through this whole damn thing with you, and I know Lucy is too. Please take care and let us hear when you can. I have another package ready, but I'd like to know you got the first packages before I entrust this onee to them. You said you had received Lucy's package and I know she sent it about two days before mine. When I wrote her today I told her we were planning to take the kids back to school in September and we thought we'd go down to Panama City for a few days. If she could get here, we'd love to take her on down with us. I know it is not going to be like last year when you were both with us. I so enjoyed that and I am so grateful for that time when the whole family was together for a short time. I realize as you children get older this won't happen often, and that is why I look back on this week with such pleasure.

Please take care and I'll be so glad when you have this mess behind you.

With all our love and prayers.
Mom & Dad

PFC Dail W. Mullins, Jr.
488-48-0511
CoA, 26th ENGR. BN.
APO SF, 96256

20 July 1969

My dear Parents,

I fear a still greater length of time has transpired since I last wrote you, and, no doubt, you're still wondering what has happened to me. Well, nothing, actually, although I do have a few things to relate to you.

I got a letter from Don Jackson and Mary Jane the other day. Don managed to acquire his master's degree, finally, but was not accepted at medical school. It apparently came as quite a shock to him, although I was not particularly surprised. I did feel sorry for him, though, because he sounded quite depressed and at a real loss of what to do with himself. He has taken a job teaching 8th grade math in Dickson, Tenn., which will, of course, keep Uncle Sam off his back (in Tennessee, as I've told you before, teachers are draft-exempt).

Don's letter also contained some rather sad news of a different sort—Dr. Tate, Memphis State's new comparative anatomy teacher, was killed in a car wreck over the 4th of July weekend. I'm sure you don't recall my ever mentioning Dr Tate, and, in fact, I didn't know him very well at that. Nevertheless, I had heard from other students that he was an excellent teacher and a really fine man to work for. He had just gotten his PhD from LSU the year before he came to Memphis State—one of those guys whom everybody says "had everything going for him." He was young, single, wealthy and intelligent. You know, after you've been over here for awhile, you tend to lose your perspective, and its sometimes difficult to realize that people do die in other places besides Vietnam. I guess that was the reason Dr. Tate's untimely death depressed me so, even though I wasn't that well acquainted with him.

The other day, on our way back from sweeping the road, we all stopped at one of the small "shops" (I use the term loosely) in Que Sôn, which, as I may have already mentioned, is the largest village on the LZ Ross side of highway 535. These small open-air stores specialize in the wholesale distribution of junk to civilians and G.I.'s alike—for a handsome price, of course. At such a store you can purchase a variety of such necessary items as: small pillows stuffed with water buffalo hair, bottles of concentrated mint (which the Vietnamese people sprinkle on their cigarettes—a custom not unlike our menthol brands), incense, crucifixes, colored construction paper (presumably for use in shell-shock therapy), hand mirrors, marijuana (10¢ per reefer—no, I don't touch the stuff), opium, Desenex foot cream (confiscated off the medics and resold at extraordinary prices) and cold beer and sodas. Anyway, I was browsing around in all this junk while the rest of the guys were drinking beer and trying to outbid each other on some local femme fatale when I came across a small, hardbound book with a large pineapple embossed upon the cover, along with the words Hiêu Trái Thóm. Hiêu Trái Thóm, I later discovered, is Vietnamese for pineapple, which says something about the cleverness of the oriental mind. "Well", I thought, "what have we here?" Obviously, a book about pineapples. Upon closer examination, however, I discovered that the small book was, in fact, a diary, and not a text on pineapples at all. I was immediately reminded of something you had mentioned in one of your earlier letters, namely, that I keep a diary of my experiences in Vietnam. So, taking your suggestion to heart, I paid the mama-san 150 piasters and became the proud owner of a pineapple emblazoned Vietnamese diary.

Well, small-talk aside. I thought you all might be interested in hearing about one of our more exciting days out on the road—in fact, my most exciting to date.

The day started as usual—the road was crowded with people, the sun was horrendously hot and the humidity ungodly. I was working demo that day, and it was my job to place a 1/2 pound charge of C-4 explosive on every suspicious area in the road that had been circled by the sweep team, the theory being that if there was a mine present below, better if the C-4 finds it rather than the pressure-test truck. Well, we came to one area that looked particularly suspicious; so suspicious, in fact, that the detector operators had circled four areas all within a few square yards. I blew four C-4 charges but nothing happened. Nothing, that is, until the pressure-test truck ran over the area.

It wasn't a big mine, as mines go, but it did blow the rear wheels off the truck and send the driver sailing into a rice paddy on the side of the road. Fortunately, he was unhurt, although we dusted him off just to be sure.

Well, by the time we got the truck moved off the road, filled the crater and finished the sweep, it was nearly 4:00, and we still had to wait for the convoy to go through to Ross from Baldy. So, taking advantage of the local vegetation, we all sat down under the shade of a clump of palm trees and waited. In about half an hour the first truck in the convoy appeared around a bend in the road, highballing it to Ross. Three diesel tankers, two trucks loaded with lumber, a flat-bed truck carrying ammo for the Ross artillary and four security jeeps made it past us without incident. The last truck in the convoy was a converted gasoline tanker carrying a load of liquid asphalt. We stopped the truck because his battery was hanging loose. I recognized the driver because he and I had both come to Baldy the same week. As the truck was pulling away I flashed him the famous V symbol for peace, now as common in Vietnam as the salute. He smiled and returned the gesture as his truck sped by, American flag waving in the wind, the setting sun turning the letters U.S. ARMY a pale orange on the side of his tanker.

As he rounded a bend in the road about 200 yards ahead of us, we heard a terrific explosion and the rear end of his truck disappeared in a plume of black oily smoke. "Mine!" someone shouted, and we all took off running toward the truck, pieces of metal and dirt raining down on us. I was about 75 yards from the truck and going at a dead run when the main asphalt tank exploded, knocking me to the ground. At the same time I saw the driver jump from the cab of the truck and start running, his left arm a flaming torch. Doc, our medic, got to him pretty quickly and extinguished the blaze. A chopper which had been flying by saw what had happened and landed nearby to fill in as a dust off medivac. It was only after we had followed through on our natural instincts and had gotten the fellow GI on the chopper, that we noticed that there had been other casualties. Two of the soda girls had been riding alongside the tanker when it hit the mine. One was only shaken up, but the other one, who wandered out of the black smoke toward me, looked pretty bad. She was burned on her chest and arms from molten asphalt and her head was bleeding rather profusely. I figured she would go into shock at any time, as all she kept yelling was "Goddamn VC! Goddamn VC!" I scooped her up in my arms and ran over to the chopper with her, and I think it must have been her first helicopter ride, as she seemed strongly opposed to getting on the thing. Nevertheless, I succeeded in convincing her that there was nothing to worry about and that going on the chopper was the best thing for her.

Well, folks, its getting late, and since we have a long sweep tomorrow, I'd better get some sleep. Keep the letters coming, folks, they really help. Take care,

Love,
Dail

PFC Dail W. Mullins, Jr.
488-48-0511
CoA, 26th ENGR. BN.
APO SF, 96256

22 July 1969

Dear Mom and Dad,

I hate to write on unruled paper, as my sentences invariably begin to take on the appearance of roller coasters as I near the bottom of the page. This is the only type of writing paper that is enclosed in field resupply packages, however, so I'll have to make do.

I'm writing to you because I'm slightly troubled at the moment about something that has come up. Don't panic, now, it is nothing serious and, in fact, may prove to be somewhat of a break—maybe the first one that I've had since I've been in the Army. I'm not writing to you for help, as the matter will undoubtedly have been settled before this letter reaches you. Rather, I'm hoping that putting down my thoughts on paper will help me to arrive at a decision—or, at least, give me some confidence in the decision I think I have already made.

Yesterday, when we arrived back at LZ Ross after a long sweep, Reiterman, out platoon radio operator, informed me that our company CO, Cpt. Farewell, had called in from Baldy requesting that I return there on the morning reconnaissance chopper for the purpose of being interviewed for a clerical position. My first reaction was one of ecstatic jubilation, as you can well imagine. The thought of sitting back at Baldy behind a desk and typewriter, as opposed to humping highway 535 amidst exploding asphalt tankers and occasional sniper fire was, at the very worst, a comforting one. At last, thought I, the Army has come to its senses!

Well, you ask, what can possibly be troubling me? Did I not bemoan my plight as a combat soldier to you and all concerned in countless letters?

As I said above, I think I have already made my decision about this matter, although it certainly was not as easy as I once thought it would be. You see, in a combat zone, a soldier becomes very emotionally attached to his unit and the men in it. Each one becomes, truly, a brother in arms. You eat, sleep, laugh, cry, joke, curse and fight together until, one day, quite unexpectedly, you realize that you've become rather attached to this potpourri of slobs, idiots, fools and bastards that is the combat unit. You have your favourites, yes—your buddies—and, in fact, these are the men that provide the real cement between you and your unit. In my case there is Hugh Barksdale, the English professor from Murray, Larry Lemar, the civil engineer from Chicago, Bob Elliot, the Dartmouth graduate from Vermont and Doc, our platoon medic, from South Carolina, the least educated among us, but in many ways the wisest, and certainly the most worldly. He's also good for a laugh once in awhile. The five of us have been together a mere two months—but in that short span of time I have come to like and understand these men fully as well as I do Steve Thoms, Ray Henley, Don Jackson and Pete Merrill—all of whom I have known for several years. How can such be? I can answer in one word—Vietnam. Vietnam forces you to make a friend, fast—for that friend is as vital to survival as your weapon. He is a link with sanity during a mortar attack—a person to talk to when you don't get a letter from home. In short, he is your buddy. Well, enough of my demented babbling.

When I got back to Baldy this morning, I found the situation to be slightly more complex than I had originally imagined. I had reached the decision to, in fact, accept the clerical position, with the dual rationalization that, first, it would be a safer job and, hence, greatly increase my chances of making it back to Lucy and the world unscathed and, second, that I would, after all, still be in A company and in close association with my friends. I learned upon reaching Baldy, however, that the clerical job was not with A company at all, but rather back at the 26th engineers headquarters in Chu Lai, an even safer spot than Baldy. Needless to say, this information immediately brought to mind all of the sentimental rambling that you were forced to endure above.

Right now I am sitting in my hooch at Baldy, alone, awaiting some form of transportation to Chu Lai for my interview.

I do not yet have a clerical job, and, I suppose the whole thing could fall through. Nevertheless, I am going down there for the interview and to see just what kind of clerk's job they have for me. About all I can gather from people around here is that the job will probably be in some captain's office which has, as a staff, clerks with college degrees and, second, that I will probably get the job if I want it. May the God who watches over combat buddies everywhere, forgive me. I think I'll take the job if offered.

If I do get this work it will, of course, mean that I'll be going back to Chu Lai, which means my mail will be all messed up again for two or three more weeks. But, I've made it through that hurdle of depression before—I guess I can do it again.

I know you both, and Lucy, whom I have already written about this matter, will feel a great sense of relief should I get such a job. That was one of, if not the most, decisive factor in my decision. I only hope you understand how hard it was for me to leave "the crew" back on highway 535—and why.

I'll write soon to let you know how things came out—and to send my new address if need be. Take care, please, and do let me know how you feel about this.

Your loving son,
Dail

July 17, 1969

My dear Dail,
  Well, we just received your letter with the pictures, and I can't tell you how we have pored over these snaps. Every time we look at them we discover something new to comment on. It wasn't until much later we discovered Lucy on your hat. And, of course, Denny had to point out the knives in your belts and grenades hanging around your neck. His comment—"Gee Cool!". And I just gasp. You may have your title for the four of you, but all I could think of was the Wild Bunch. Linda said they are either very tan or very dirty. They look like a good bunch of guys and I am so grateful you have at least a few people you can communicate with. I imagine it helps a lot. Talking about your medic—John Custer was telling me, the day he stopped by, that this is the worst detail in the Army and the one spot he always prayed they would never tab him for.
  For some reason we hadn't received a letter from you for about ten days and believe me when I say I was beside myself. Then yesterday we received two letters you had written the 1st and 5th of July and today we received the one you had written on the 12th. I just can't understand the mailing set up, but rest assured I'm a little perturbed when I don't hear for several days. We are so very appreciative of your writing us so often especially when we talk to other parents who sometimes only hear once a month. I know To mmy Emerson said they hear very little from David. I asked her how often she wrote him and she said about once a month, and I thought—What does she expect. Anyway I'd write you even if you didn't write me, but I sure am glad you do. Talking about letters, old Pete Merrill claims he has written you twice and hasn't heard from you. All I'd like to know is—did he really write you or is this another of his tall tales. You know that guy is a congenital liar.
  This may be a little on the depressing side so if you yourself are in a low mood, put it aside. I warned you I wasn't going to keep my letters all gay and frothy, because life and events haven't changed back in the "World" and we still

have our problems. As I've told you many times, I miss you so much because you were the one person in this whole damn family I could get across to, and it gets so frustrating at times to have no one to converse with. I know Joan Seibert is a good listener, but you hesitate baring all family affairs to outsiders. We are having more trouble with Linda and I go around in circles, wondering how I can help her and what I can do for her, but this definitely is something that you have to experience yourself to evidently understand. She doesn't seem as bad as she was last summer but she has made an appointment with Dr. Emerson. She refuses to see any psychiatrist up here as this Dr. Witt finished her with St. Louis men. I'm afraid some of the things he told her have had a lasting impression on her. The young fellow she was going to in Florence Alabama seemed to be a different cup of tea. I've read more articles and opinions on problems of this type and the more I read the more I realize how little is known about the human mind and psyche. The only thing that makes any sense to me is a research scientist up east who describes Linda's symptoms to the last detail, even to a fear of some fatal illness, and he has found a sugar imbalance genetic disorder which triggers this. It's funny, but when your father had a physical shortly before he was seeing Dr. Gottshcalk, they found that the sugar content in his blood stream was not being utilized.

The thing that is most upsetting to me is her unwillingness to face anything unpleasant and how in the hell can she go through life in this semi state of euphoria. Do you know there are many times she won't even read your letters because they might upset her little world. And of course, I keep thinking "what have I done to this child". Now when it is too late I look back on things I concealed and problems I hid because I thought it was wrong to show any unpleasant relationships with their father in front of children. God, how wrong I was.

And then we have your grandmother. We have been having such brutally hot weather with typical St. Louis humidity. He went over to his mothers and he said it was unbearable. She still has that little air conditioner which she doesn't run because it makes her electric bill too high and he also noticed that her ankles are beginning to swell. Obviously she should go to a doctor and she should have something to cool that house off, but what can you do. So he comes home and thinks about her, about Linda, about you—and in the meantime has about four drinks which will not solve the problem, and then has to be at that office at 8 O'clock and listen to gripinq all day long and realize that he cannot tell them to go to hell, because he has two tuitions that have been raised 100 dollars each plus the tax situation—and it all tears your heart out.

Then we have Denny, who came home last nite and infomred us that one of the men in the station across the street from his was shot in the stomach last nite. He hasn't been able to get all the details, but when he mentioned shot and police and ambulances I just went to pieces.

So the World is pretty sick too my dear boy, and all this crap is what you are fighting for.

What makes some of this so ironic is that yesterday I had a luncheon. I do things like this to keep busy and also to be with people. I can go so long without human conversation and then I must break loose—even if it is conversation with idiots and spoiled American women. To have all these hidden problems on your mind and then spend an afternoon listening to Suzie Bell talking about Jon in Innesbruck slaying the people with his knowledge and Joan Bell whooping it up with the debutantes from Mary I, and Jean Brown talking about her eight week trip all through Europe, and Aud Hoffmeister talking about Stan, the Bank President, and their trip to Hawaii in September, and one of the women whom I had invited, talking about her classes with a Dr. Pitts, Psychiatrist at Webster College, in which she is learning all about raising children and the damage mothers do to children when they do not take courses in mental problems and rehabilitation.

It really gets to you.

But the funny thing, while they were all outdoing each other, all I could think about was the time Suzie Bell came running over to me in hysterics, claimign that Gail was at home raving that she was putting poison in his food, and Aud's drunken father and mother who died in the poor house; in fact, each one I could relate some pretty rotten situation to and I thought—how soon people forget.

I had planned to have Mrs. Kreyling at this luncheon but she was in Chicago checking into some details with the home they are buying up there. She called me today and we must have talked at least an hour. We are going to meet next week for lunch. Anyway she wanted me to be sure and tell you how very upset Ed, Debbie, and young Eddie were when they found out you were in Viet Naam. She said she has never seen young Eddie so perturbed about anything and he said to her that "Dail was always my favorite". I Belive I told you that she and Carole and Carole's little girl stopped by not too long ago and while they were here I guess I talked about Lucy quite a lot. Anyway, Mrs. Kreyling told me today that it bothered Carole that I seemed to be so fond of Lucy. Evidently she doesn't get along with her mother-in-law too well and that deep in her heart she said she still always thinks of me as her mother-in-law. I guess that is a compliment. I wrote and told Lucy they were here and that all I could think of was how glad you had married Lucy. Even Mrs. Kreyling said that Carole leads her husband a merry chase. She evidently is constantly after him about a bigger home, a newer car, better furniture, and let's go here and Let's go there. Boy are you lucky. I am still very fond of Carol but she wasn't the girl for you. Mrs. Kreyling also told me that the horse you rode was struck by lightening the other day and died. It must have been quite a session as they couldn't get anyone to take it away and after about five days they couldn't even go out the door, so they finally had to hire a bulldozer to come and bury it on their ground.

Well, I don't know how much news you get about the moon shot, but we watched every minute of the blast off and the colore this time was fantastic. Tonite they had a television program from inside the space capsule showing them doing push ups with no gravitation. It was funny to see their flashlight just suspended in mid air and then when they move it, it just spins over on end. Very eery. The Post dispatch is advertising a special deal in which for the week after the moon shot they will be printing special issues for a week and they will send them anywhere in the world. I'm going to have them send them to you. Don't know how long it will take but it shouldn't be any longer than our mail. Anyway, maybe you'll enjoy reading the paper. Let me know if you ever receive it.

Southern Illinois University, in conjunction with the St. Louis symphony orchestra, have been having these fantastic concerts on the Edwardsville campus. During the week they have artists like Joan Baez, Janis Joplin, somebody named Guthrie, Dylan Thomas, Buffy St. Marie; you name it. On week ends they have had the more serious artists such as Van Cliburn. Anyway last Monday nite they had a musical group called the Iron Butterfly and Mrs. Bell took Joan and three of her debutante friends and you should hear her tell about this evening. 15,000 hippies of all shapes and descriptions. She said she knew most of them had just taken sugar cubes and as the evening wore on the mixing of couples was evidently similar to a Roman Orgy. She said she was physically ill at the display and finally had to leave. I feel you ask for it when you go see these way out entertainers as they are going to draw the off beat audiences.

Do you remember that little doggie bed I had gotten for Babette, but which she would never use. Well Chanel has really enjoyed it. Today I went to the store and was gone for about two hours and when I came home she had ripped that bed into shreds and the stuffing was flying all over the room. She is really impossible.

She is just like a little child. When you leave her alone for more than ten minutes a light bulb goes on in her head and tells he—"lets do something." And boy does she do it. She has ruined everything in that room. I really have to stay away from her or I'd kill her.

Well this was a bitter letter and I will try not to write to many like this, but things haven't changed and we are trying to cope with a few problems over here.

I'm enclosing an article that appeared in our church bulletin which I thought you might enjoy reading. As I told you, St. Louis has been having these confrontations and this is the advice we have received.

Have another package about ready to send you. I'll mail it PAL. This gets it to you quicker and it can weigh more, but the overall size of the box cannot be much larger so I am limited as to what I can get in a box of this size.

Please take care of yourself dear boy and let us hear and our love and prayers. Don't know if I mentioned, but as of now we plan to take the kids back to school in September and we thought we would run down to Panama City for about 5 days. Told Lucy if she could get to St. Louis some way, the rest of the trip would be on us. This is when I would love to be rich so I could just send her a round trip airline ticket and say come ahead, but I just can't. All the things I'm going to do when the kids are out of school.

All our love,
Mom & Dad

PFC Dail W. Mullins, Jr.
488-48-0511
CoA, 26th ENGR. BN.
APO SF, 96256

24 July 1969

Dear Mom and Dad,
Elation, followed by depression—the story of my life. If that statement doesn't stem from heredity . . . . . !

Yesterday our 1st Sergeant informed me that the clerk's position in Chu Lai had been filled by a new guy, just arrived in country, with a clerk's MOS. This is really only fair, although you can imagine my disappointment. Strangely enough, I was not as depressed as I thought I might be, however. This is due, in part, to the fact that I no longer have to face the prospect of saying goodbye to my friends or undergo the trauma of resettlement, and also to the fact that things have really not gotten worse—they just haven't improved, that's all. I know this will come as somewhat of a letdown to both you and Lucy—I would have been wise to have kept my mouth shut about the whole matter, I guess. Well, you can't win them all, I guess. This development, of course, removes the necessity of my having to go down to Chu Lai for the interview. I shall be returning to LZ Ross on the morning reconnaissance chopper, even though my platoon only has about 5 more days out there before we all return to Baldy.

I got a real nice letter from Mrs. Reinhardt yesterday—apparently she had read the letter I sent to Gaye. I was somewhat puzzled by her remarks to the effect that I had sounded so optimistic and unburdened by bitterness about my present situation. While it is true that I do not attempt to maintain an unoptimistic attitude over here, to say that I sound optimistic is perhaps stretching the point somewhat. I am also bitter about this ridiculous war, a fact which I have not attempted to hide in my letters, although I do seem to recall not having made a point of it in my letter to Gaye. Perhaps that's just as well—I really don't want people to start thinking of me as a martyr of disillusionment; neither, of course, do I want to be regarded as a fervent patriot of American military action.

Well, I made my first major purchase over here, thus taking advantage of the serviceman's increased buying power in the Pacific Exchange area. I bought a Canon, 35 mm camera (stateside price—$65) for $40. It's an excellent camera, having an internal light meter and a wide range of exposure settings. Someday when Lucy and I can afford a screen and projector I'll begin taking slides—until then, however, I'm just having prints made, some of which I hope to be able to send you when they are developed.

I received your "gripe" letter the other day—that's fine, keep them coming, as you know I will. You are absolutely right in one respect—that is, I do not want to get letters which constantly reflect the lovely state of affairs back home. Everyone had problems before I left—why should they cease just because I'm over here. Good grief, I'll be thinking I was the cause of them all! I've heard, from more than one person, how petty and unimportant their own troubles seem when they realize what unspeakable terror I must be experiencing. This is really silly. Life in Vietnam is not 24 hours of horror. No one, not even John Wayne, could stand it if it was. I'll admit that uncertainty and tension are ever present emotions, but certainly not a feeling of impending doom. Many people back home would probably be amazed to find that we sometimes actually have fun—maybe not orgies of hilarity, but fun, nevertheless. We do see some humorous things out on that road (humorous to American eyes, anyway), and when we're back at an LZ, we cut up, shoot the bull, drink a little beer, see a movie occasionally and, generally, try to release some of the tension brought on by a rough day out on the road and the impending night. You have to, or you'd go crazy. In one respect, hearing about the continuing trials and tribulations back home serves to remind me of the fact that, in some ways, I'm lucky. Some of the little things you all worry about will never bother me again—at least not for several years.

Neither shall I ever again be troubled by heat, lumpy mattresses, mosquitoes or dirt (the latter probably much to Lucy's chagrin).

To give you some idea of how quickly the GI can snatch humour out of a situation which, back home, would fill people's minds with dread and horror (myself included), let me relate something that happened out on the road the other day. We had finished a long sweep, quite without incident, and were walking back to Ross (we always walk back instead of riding the truck, which says something about the faith we have in ourselves as mine sweepers). Barksdale, Elliot, Doc, Montaigne, Sgt. Anderson (a rather rotund, colored squad leader) and I were bunched together, talking while we walked—something we shouldn't really do, as it makes an easy target. Well, sure enough, someone, somewhere, took a shot at us. The round went over our heads—from the sound of it, probably about a foot. I, of course, was the first one down—I pride myself on my ability to begin closely inspecting dirt at a moment's notice. Lying flat on the road, I began to look around for some better cover (hopefully a 12 foot hole in the ground). Seeing only a small rise of dirt to my left and rear, I immediately put my 6 1/2 year education to work and crawled like hell—I remember saying to myself as I crawled along, "Please, God, let him be a bad shot!" I swear that's what I thought, so help me! I was no more safely down behind that beautiful pile of dirt when Doc landed right on top of me after completing an unassisted 6 foot leap. He looked at me and said, again I swear this, "What are you doing down here?" I looked back at him and said, "What are you doing here?" Meanwhile, Sgt. Anderson, whom I think hit the ground only milliseconds after I did, and whose eyes looked like Steppin' Fetchit's in a haunted house, began blasting away at the horizon with his M-16. I was almost afraid to look up for fear of seeing half of North Vietnam come charging down on us like flies. I did raise my eyes above the dirt pile, though, only to see a cow running like mad away from Sgt. Anderson's barrage of lead. Lt. Ballinger came casually strolling down the road and calmly told Sgt. Anderson to cease fire, that he thought the enemy had been routed completely. Barksdale, the fool that he is, then asked the Lieutenant if he wanted Barksdale and me—me, of all people—to go recon the area from which the shots had come. I almost shot Barksdale at that idiotic comment. Thank God the Lieutenant said no! Well, that's the story of the "ambush" of second platoon. It really was funny when we got back, although I wasn't smiling when I was crawling over toward that dirt pile. I keep thinking how amazing it is that Vietnam can actually cause you to become quite emotionally attached to something as unemotional as a dirt pile.

Well, folks, I guess I'll close. Keep writing, as I know you will, and take care, please. I hope you get things straightened out with Linda, and that Grandma is alright.

Love,
Dail

July 21, 1969

My dear Dail,

Fantastic, unbelieving, tremendous,—in fact every explitive you can think of to describe the last few days. Your father and I were glued to the television almost the entire day and I was so relieved when they moved their stepping on the moon up four hours, as our eyes were beginning to show the strain and I was so afraid we would both fall asleep by 1:30, if they had waited that long. I have been in front of the television for the last two hours and just have heard the perfect take off from the moon. They have about two hours to docking time, but everyone seems to be breathing easier now. Watching actual TV reception from the moon and the eerie pictures of these two creatures bouncing around was almost too "movie like", to believe; especially when Armstrong started running and bouncing. I thought the trip had gotten to him, but I heard Houston explain that he had been requested to do this to enable medical men to see the effects of the moon on the human. There is still a lot of guessing being done about the Russian space ship and the consensus now is that it crashed. Our only feelings of disappointment came when we thought how very much you would have enjoyed watching this history being made.

Sunday morning as I was getting ready for church CBS had a special on called "Nearer to Thee", and it was quite fascinating. It was on from 9 A.M. until 10 A.M. and consisted of a Dr. Davidson, Humanities Professor and a Philosopher, Reverend Theodore Gill, a Presbyterian minister and teacher, Edward B. Lindaman, NASA scientist, and Richard Lippold, Art Expert and Artist. They and an anchor man had cross-fire conversation on the moral, religious, aesthetic, and scientific meaning and future of the era we are now embarked upon and it was quite interesting. What surprised me most, that the two men closest in their thinking were the fellow from NASA and the minister. The Humanities fellow was the furthest out and the artist was the most articulate and caustic. If all this knowledge that is evidently in our country could only be harnessed and used in the same manner they have used in this space program. Wonder why men of this caliber cannot be encouraged to go into the Senate and Congress, where we are so lacking in intelligence and ability to get things moving in a hurry. Certainly they aren't being enticed into the space program by money or even glory (which only a few achieve). And think what men of this capability could do with the ghetto problem, if they would attack it as they do space problems.

You mention the let up in news and we seem to be going through the same thing. Evidently everyone is quite puzzled by the lull in fighting by the Viet Cong and there are all sorts of theories and I pray the one that they are ready to start talking, is correct. I see Westmoreland and a few other brass happy big mouths are all getting together again in Saigon trying to figure out what is going on.

You know what I think of the general tone of Esquire magazine, but we got this month's issue and it had an article in it that is still making me retch. I'm trying to decide whether it is the type article which would serve any purpose in sending to you at this time, but I do know I will save it. It is entitled "An American

Atrocity" and it states—"the facts of this report are available for public inspection in the office of the Judge Advocate General of the Navy in Washington, D.C." It tells about a squad from the Second Platoon and a night ambush they were sent on, and what they did to the hamlet of Xuan Ngoc in a sector of Tra Bong Township. I have no idea where this area is in Viet Naam and they give no more details. There were ten men involved in this horrendous display of animalism in the raping and point blank killing of little babies and it is beyond comprehension. This happened September 23, 1966 and I know nothing was ever mentioned in our papers about it. These men should have been turned over to these villagers to have the same treatment meted out to them, but instead seven are free in civilian life, one is a seargent in the Marine Corps and two are still in prison. And think what sentences were handed out in California, for singing.

Don't know how much news you hear over there and wonder if you heard anything on the latest Kennedy family incident. I'm sending you an article that was in the Post Dispatch. It doesn't look good and might be the end of his political future. Wouldn't you think he would use more discretion. Am also including an article on Memphis thought you'd be interested in.

Have a package all ready to mail to you but President Nixon has declared today a National Holiday so the Post Offices are all closed. I'm going to send this one Pal and it will be a chance to see if it makes it sooner than sending it SAM.

Well we have another of your fascinating letters. The one with the picture of you and the mongoose. When I first saw it I thought, "My God, he's made a pet out of one of the rats". I hear that they are good ratters, besides taking their toll in snakes.

Poor Denny wanted so much to see the Moon landing yesterday, but he worked from 7 in the morning until almost 11 last night. That poor kid has not had one night off this summer, hasn't even gone to a movie. If he were being paid commensurate with the work he is doing it wouldn't be so bad, but for 50 and 60 hours of work each week his checks average about $50 a week after everything is taken out. We had Lorraine and Ralph Hester over Saturday night to play some bridge and I wanted to show them your pictures and I couldn't find the one of you and "Doc", where you have all that weaponry hanging on you. Then I find Dennis is carrying it around in his billfold. If you would ever have a spare minute he'd really appreciate a letter to just him personally. He's really so concerned about you and reads your letters over and over. Maybe it's because he feels someday he might be in the same boat.

Well Linda goes in to see Dr. Emerson Thursday for a physical. She has done this all on her own. I'd love to talk to him first, but I feel I must keep entirely out of her affairs. Dad thinks she has been cautioned and pushed and coerced and thought for, too much. Pete was here almost every night and often took her to lunch, but I haven't seen him since last Wednesday, so I don't know what happened there. Bob called her last night and she seemed very happy after she talked to him. Probably one thing that made her ego rise was Bob's brother-in-law quitting working for Mr. DeCurtis. Bob didn't go into too much detail but evidently they must have had quite a row and now Linda feels they will realize she isn't the only one that thinks they are hard to get along with.

Don't know if I ever told you about Bob's theft while he was visiting us. He and Linda had gone to the Zoo one afternoon and parked and locked his car, in the Zoo parking lot. When they got back after about and hour someone had broken in his car and stolen his electric guitar and amplifier which he had in the back. They had just spent that morning cleaning and polishing the entire car and there were hand prints and finger prints all over the window which they had jimmied. They reported it to a park policemen and wanted him to lift the prints but he saw the Alabama license on Bob's car and said "when you come to the big city you've got to be careful." Linda and I were just furious and I was already to call Cervantes, the Chief of Police, etc. Anyway we checked with Bob's insurance company here, but they said thefts weren't covered, but that perhaps his parents' household insurance would take care of it. Well when he got home he found out it would if a complete report had been made of the incident, in the St. Louis Police Department files. I was very much afraid they had just ignored the whole thing, but surprisingly enough I received complete cooperation when I called. I told him how furious we were with the police's reaction and remarks and he explained that this happens constantly and they have no means of getting 90 percent of this equipment back as it is sent to out of town fences. He said this is a well contrived and big business. Isn't this sad, when we can send men to the moon? Anyway Bob will get his money back for the equipment.

Well I'd better quit rambling or I'll keep you up all night.

Let us hear and our prayers, needless to say, are ever present.

With all our love,
Mom & Dad

P.S. I've been forgetting about the sequence information on the back of the envelopes but will try and remember.

P.P.S. I contacted the Post Dispatch and send money to them to have a special moon issue sent to you. Don't know how long it will take to reach you, but let me know if you receive it and I hope it is something you will enjoy.

July 24, 1969

My dear Dail,

Well the splash down is over and everything is A-OK. It has been a momentous week and this was an important part of it. I'll be a little glad to get away from the television set. This was a very different setting foot on ship board as they had no red carpet and no reception committee. They transferred them to isolation immediately and even President Nixon waited until the doctor had taken blood tests and cursory physicals before he talked to them through a shield.

Sitting here waiting for Linda. She had an appointment with Dr. Emerson at 4:30 and it is now 7:30 and she still isn't home. Of course I must keep in mind that this is normal procedure for his office. She seems a little more cheerful the last few days except she is now worried about that mole on her back that I wanted to have removed 5 years ago and everyone vetoed me. I never have liked this. I really wish she could settle down a little. Your father is just amazed at the way she has taken hold at his office. She is there alone now as Christine is on her vacation. He says she is the best assistant he ever had and the patients all love her, but she has no confidence in herself.

Linda has been trying to get your father to invest in a small portable swimming pool for the last two weeks. Finally yesterday he gave in and bought one. As usual, anything done in this family is spur of the moment and no thought is ever given as to what it entails. While it is not large it needed to have all the ground under it dug up and moated to support the plastic pool. So Denny has to get out and dig all this and he's grumbling and griping as he thinks it's a stupid idea to begin with. He said "Mom, you know the neighbors are going to think you are having another baby, because they couldn't believe grown kids would put something like this in the yard." I'm a nervous wreck worrying that some little kid is going to fall in it. I made them by a cover which must be kept on it at all times, but I still worry that some child will start to investigate when I am not home.

Well, I got some welcome news yesterday. Received a letter from Wendy Paschen. She said her mother wanted me to know they would be in St. Louis the 30th of this month. They are leaving Louisville the 25th for Denton, Texas where Wendy is enrolled at Texas Women's College. They are staying at the Holiday Inn on Lindbergh Blvd, which is really bugging Mr. and Mrs. Paschen. But I can understand perfectly. I wrote Aunt Dot and told her she was welcome here but that if she wanted to loaf and have a real swimming pool, I envied her and would do the same. Anyway I'm really going to be glad to see her no matter where she stays. They didn't say a word about young Bob, so I don't know if he went ahead with his plans for enlisting or not. Mrs. Paschen told me that both Kurt and Marilee Eisleben's engagements were announced in the paper last week end. Kurt is on leave right now before going ot San Antonio for further training in how to keep medical records. He'll probably spend his entire two years being sent from one army post to another in the states.

It has been almost a week since we have received a letter from you and of course, this always stirs me up. I must realize that there are many reasons we don't receive mail, but I always think of the worst—and that is that you are in such a horrible place you can't get mail out.

Joan Seibert called to ask if I had heard from you and she wanted med to be sure and give here love. Her sister just got back from their Mediterranean cruise and evidently they had a quite marvellous time. The bridge club I belong to with Winnie Bill had to disband for the summer as three of the women are in Europe. I'm beginning to be a little sensitive about my lack of cultural background (along with the lack of educational—viz. Suzie Bell and Joan and Etc.). The funny thing I couldn't care less about seeing Europe or any place. Just let me alone and please allow my family to live with peace of mind. That's all I ask.

Anyway, I think I told you Joan is involved in a Head Start program through Webster College, in Flat River and Potosi Missouri, for which she will receive six hours credit. As Charlie says, she gets six hours and it costs me 300 dollars for her to find out there are poor people in the world, of which I will soon be one. Anyway I was describing to her your letter in which you talked about the little children you see in Viet Naam. Here comment was that you really didn't have to go to Viet Naam to see this. They are working with under poverty level children from ages 8 to 12, who have never spoken in their lives. Joan has a little girl of 8, whom she has fallen in love with and wants to bring home with her, and a 10 year old boy. This psychologist asked her if she was having any results with the children. Typically Joan, she said the little girl was coming along but that she wasn't having any luck with the boy. She told Dr. Pitts if he could ever stop masturbating for a few minutes he might be able to talk. Anyway she said the conditions of these poor whites in this area 80 miles from St. Louis is beyond belief—

Linda just walked in. Dr. Emerson took her mole off and is sending it to a lab for analysis, so she'll sweat it. My typewriter ribbon broke.

Dad's waiting to eat so must run. Our love & prayers & hope I get a letter tomorrow.

Love
Mom & Dad

———————————

July 26

My dear Dail,

Typewriter ribbon broke so back to the mighty pen.

When we don't hear from you for several days my imagination scurries back & forth imagining all types of events; then we receive your letter describing your visit to some God-forsaken village where dope is sold on the open market and the events of just one mine sweep, and I realize even my imagination doesn't portray what you are going thru. Dear God, when will it be over? Every time your father sees a picture of Nixon smiling from the doorway of a plane on his latest world tour his remarks are standard—"that horse's ass; why doesn't he stay in Washington and get that damn war over." And then the world wide television coverage of his talking to the Astronauts on board the carrier also elicits the comment—" "My God, you'd think he had something to do with their achievement." I think, also, the fact that he went against his early upbringing and voted for him, will always be a thorn in his side.

One of the men from Washington University is of the group who will be checking the moon "rocks" brought back. I frankly don't think they'll find out anything of surprising knowledge, that they weren't able to determine without the sample.

Then minister this morning was the young chaplain from Washington University and of course the moon shot was mentioned. He extolled the Astronauts but felt we had better get our heads out of the heavens and concentrate on a few of the major earth bound problems, and I quite agree. He mentioned that 90 billion dollars defense budget, which he felt was like a terminal cancer patient buying a gun to protect his life. In other words, if we don't change our values, why defend a decaying country or world.

Linda had a blind date last nite and wasn't enthusiastic about it before hand. We were at the Vermillions playing bridge and arrived home just as she did. He seemed like a nice boy but her remark was "Ugh! My last blind date. He's been back from Viet Naam just 7 days and I don't think he's had a date for a year." Anyway it seems he was in the same outfit you are, as a Lieutenant. Linda said he was a real "Hawk" in all ways. He told her you had to be on guard at all times with those "soda" girls. He said they ride bikes during the day and throw hand grenades at you during the night. The stories I hear from all sources can be something. Anyway please take care and be alert. Aren't you due for some rest period soon?

Dad just got back from Grandmas and now he will be depressed for 2 or 3 days. Why does she affect people that way? Every Sunday morning I pray for tolerance and understanding of how to heal the gap, and then I cannot make the move. When I'm honest with myself I know its because I like it this way. Of course, I may pay because I might be old myself someday.

Well, Dan Jackson would get out of the Army deal. You mention that young professor getting killed. Yes, all is not lovely back here and in a state of suspicion. I know I stopped to see Mrs. Pratt she is living on borrowed time. These arteries they tied off in her brain have developed adhesions and she doesn't have much longer. She was such a vital person and it is so sad to see her.

I can never remember what I've mentioned in one letter from the next so I don't know if I've said anything about Linda's planned trip. She, Linda Beswick & Carol Hemphil are going to Phila, New York & New Jersey leaving St. Louis the 17th of Aug. I've bitten my tongue so often to keep from saying, "no, you aren't going. But she's 22 and this trip seems to be another test she is putting herself thru. Bob is evidently going to follow her back to St. Louis & stay with us until we leave for Athens.

When I hear these girls talk about what they are going to do in New York, a cold sweat comes over me.

Then Denny is supposed to have two friends come thru town the week they are away. So I'll be busy. Denny said today "—Boy, I can't wait to get back to Athens." "I thought that town was dull, but this is worse. At least in Athens you have a lot of company when you are doing nothing." He has worked 7 nights a week since he got that job, not even one movie. But he realizes he's so lucky compared to you.

Please take care & be careful and no heroics. All our love & prayers.
Mom & Dad

The pictures should speak for themselves.

PFC Dail W. Mullins, Jr.
488-48-0511
CoA, 26th ENGR. BN.
APO SF, 96256

1 August 1969

Dear Mom, Dad, Linda and Denny,
Not having written for some few days, I'm quite sure that everyone is frantic with worry about what is going on over here. Well, I shall console you immediately by saying that nothing is going on about which you should concern yourselves. As to why I have not written—I plead exhaustion. I have only written Lucy once in the past four days!

You remember I told you that we had returned from LZ Ross, so that 1st platoon could take their turn up there. We came back Tuesday on a sweep—when we got to the half-way point between Ross and Baldy, we just kept on walking instead of turning around and going back to Ross. Well, that was a 12 mile hike. Wednesday we had a long sweep, Thursday we had a long sweep, Friday a long sweep (today), tomorrow we have a long one and Sunday, too. To compound this situation, Wednesday night I had interior guard from 1:00 until 3:30 in the morning—and 2 1/2 hours of lost time that I could be sleeping, before and after a long sweep will do you a job, believe me. Fortunately, I am being allowed to stay back from the sweep tomorrow to clean up our hooch, so I can take the time to write tonight—I do not plan to work very hard tomorrow.

We had some excitement on the way back from Ross Tuesday, though, really, all of the excitement was over by the time we arrived on the scene. You'll recall that I've mentioned the fact that the Seabees (the Navy's counterpart to the Army's Corps of Engineers) have been working out on the road we sweep, Vietnam highway 535. They're staying at Baldy, following the sweep team from Baldy out every morning. On this particular day (our last day at Ross), 1st platoon was sweeping the road from the Baldy side, and were to meet our platoon, coming from Ross, at a place called triple culverts, which is approximately the half-way point. Apparently what happened is this. About 2 hours before 1st platoon and the Seabees were to arrive at triple culverts, 70 VC moved to within 400 yards of the road, apparently with the intent of ambushing either the Seabees or 1st platoon. Well, unfortunately for them, but fortunately for 1st platoon and the Seabees, some PFs (the Vietnamese equivalent to our national guard) walked right into the ambush ahead of the sweep team and Seabees. We could hear the firefight which resulted from this encounter 2 miles down the road, but when we got there it was all over. One VC, a woman about 25 years old, had been killed by the PFs and we found her lying in the road. She had been shot in the back with an M-16, and when the bullet came out it took half her chest with her. I did get some pictures of her and someday I will show you why just hearing about the horror of war cannot really serve to bring home its true disgust. Yes, she was a VC—but she was a human being, too. Further on down the road were two PFs who had been wounded, one in the lower leg, the other in the hip. They were awaiting a dustoff back to the medical center at Baldy. Still further down, in the next village, were two PFs who had not been so lucky—one had been shot through the heart, the other through the neck. Both of them were stretched out on the ground, awaiting the arrival of their wives and a vehicle to take them back to Baldy and an autopsy. I wish I had not been around when their wives arrived, but I was. It was horrible—something I don't want to see again for some time.

I'm awfully sorry to have depressed you with this description of just one day and place in this damn war, but I'm sure you do want to know what's going on, just as I do about home, good news or bad.

I am often amused by what you've been told by the few Vietnam veterans you've come in contact with—Seibert, that other friend of his and the Lieutenant Linda had a date with recently. Of course, I must remember that they were over here for a year (compared to say 2 1/2 months), and also that the war is different to different people. For example, you said you were told by somebody that the medic's job was the worst over here. In what way? While it is true that a medic over here, especially one assigned to the infantry, does see, close up, how horrible the effects of war really are, I would imagine that the work would, in many ways, be very satisfying, to the extent that any job over here is—saving lives instead of trying to kill them, and all that. I've also observed that a medic is one of the most respected guys in any unit. They sometimes have more pull, as a PFC, than a Lieutenant or a Captain. If a medic thinks a man is too bad off to do something under orders from an officer, the medic's word is law—and it will be backed up by the Defense Department all the way up! As an example, our platoon sergeant had ordered this guy in our squad to go out on a sweep one day. He complained of having a bad blister on his foot and said he didn't think he could make the 12 mile hike. Our sergeant, being a typical sergeant (IQ of about 35), of course thought he was faking. Doc looked at him and told Sergeant Williams that the man was staying behind. Sergeant Williams had no choice but to comply with his decision, and the guy did stay back.

I also enjoyed the Lieutenant's comments on the soda girls. I think if that Lieutenant had to get out and hump the road like us peons he'd soon learn that some of these girls can be the best friends a soldier has out there. Now, I'm not talking about all of them—in fact, when a strange one shows up on the road, everyone is particularly suspicious and our infantry security watches her like a hawk. But as for the ones who come out with us everyday, rain or shine, and go the entire 12 miles, day after day—they can be trusted completely. They really can. They have, in the past, found mines for us, pointed out VC riding bikes and hauling rice for other VC and, in two cases, been killed by trucks hitting a mine. I'm afraid that our regular soda girls, Dolly and Linda, are the last two people we have to worry about hitting us with a hand grenade.

Well, I guess that's about it for now. Thanks for the letter, the pictures and the special issues of the Post-Dispatch—all arrived today, intact. Take care, write again soon and pray for peace.

Love,
Dail

———————————

1 August 1969

Dear Mom, Dad, Linda and Denny,

Not having written for some few days, I'm quite sure that everyone is frantic with worry about what is going on over here. Well, I shall console you immediately by saying that nothing is going on about which you should concern yourselves. As to why I have not written — I plead exhaustion. I have only written Lucy once in the past four days!

You remember I told you that we had returned from LZ Ross, so that 1st platoon could take their turn up there. We came back Tuesday on a sweep — when we got to the half-way point between Ross and Baldy, we just kept on walking instead of turning around and going back to Ross. Well, that was a 12 mile hike. Wednesday we had a long sweep, Thursday we had a long sweep, Friday a long sweep (today), tomorrow we have a long one and Sunday, too. To compound the situation, Wednesday night I had interior guard from 1:00 until 3:30 in the morning — and 2½ hours of lost time that I could be sleeping, before and after a long sweep will do you a job, believe me. Fortunately, I am being allowed to stay back from the sweep tomorrow to clean up our hooch, so I can take the time to write tonight — I do not plan to work very hard tomorrow.

We had some excitement on the way back from Ross Tuesday, though, really, all of the excitement was over by the time we arrived on the scene. You'll recall that I've mentioned the fact that the Seabees (the Navy's counterpart to the Army's Corps of Engineers) have been working out on the road we sweep, Vietnam highway 535. They're staying at Baldy, following the sweep team from Baldy out every morning. On this particular day (our last day at Ross), 1st platoon was sweeping the road from the Baldy side, and were to meet our platoon, coming from Ross, at a place called triple culverts, which is approximately the half-way point. Apparently what happened is this. About 2 hours before 1st platoon and the Seabees were to arrive at triple culverts, 70 VC moved to within 400 yards of the road, apparently with the intent of ambushing either the Seabees or 1st platoon. Well, unfortunately for them, but fortunately for 1st platoon and the Seabees, some PFs (the Vietnamese equivalent to our national guard) walked right into the ambush ahead of the sweep team and Seabees. We could hear the firefight which resulted from this encounter 2 miles down the road, but when we got there it was all over. One VC, a woman about 25 years old, had been killed by the PFs and we found her lying in the road. She had been shot in the back with an M-16, and when the bullet came out it took half her chest with her. I did get some pictures of her and someday I will show you why just hearing about the horror of war cannot really serve to bring home its true disgust. Yes, she was a VC — but she was a human being, too. Further on down the road were two PFs who had been wounded, one in the lower leg, the other in the hip. They were awaiting a dustoff back to the medical center at Baldy. Still further down, in the next village, were two PFs who had not been so lucky — one had been shot through the heart, the other through the neck. Both of them were stretched out on the ground, awaiting the arrival of their wives and a vehicle to take them back to Baldy and an autopsy. I wish I had not been around when their wives arrived, but I was. It was horrible — something I don't want to see again for some time.

    I'm awfully sorry to have depressed you with this description of just one day and place in this damn war, but I'm sure you do want to know what's going on, just as I do about home, good news or bad.

I am often amused by what you've been told by the few Vietnam veterans you've come in contact with — Seibert, that other friend of his and the Lieutenant Linda had a date with recently. Of course, I must remember that they were over here for a year (compared to my 2½ months), and also that the war is different to different people. For example, you said you were told by somebody that the medic's job was the worst one here. In what way? While it is true that a medic over here, especially one assigned to the infantry, does see, close up, how horrible the effects of war really are, I would imagine that the work would, in many ways, be very satisfying, to the extent that any job over here is — saving lives instead of trying to kill them, and all that. I've also observed that a medic is one of the most respected guys in any unit. They sometimes have more pull, as a PFC, than a Lieutenant or a Captain. If a medic thinks a man is too bad off to do something under orders from an officer, the medic's word is law — and it will be backed up by the Defense Department all the way up! As an example, our platoon sergeant had ordered this guy in our squad to go out on a sweep one day. He complained of having a bad blister on his foot and said he didn't think he could make the 12 mile hike. Our sergeant, being a typical sergeant (IQ of about 35), of course thought he was faking. Doc looked at him and told Sergeant Williams that the man was staying behind. Sergeant William had no choice but to comply with his decision, and the guy did stay back.

I also enjoyed the Lieutenant's comments on the soda girls. I think if that Lieutenant had to get out and hump the road like us peons he'd soon learn that some of these girls can be the best friends a soldier has out there. Now, I'm not talking about all of them — in fact, when a strange one shows up on the road, everyone is particularly suspicious and our infantry security watches her like a hawk. But as for the ones who come out with us everyday, rain or shine, and go the entire 12 miles, day after day — they can be trusted completely. They really can. They have, in the past, found mines for us, pointed out VC riding bikes and hauling rice for other VC and, in two cases, been killed by trucks hitting a mine. I'm afraid that our regular soda girls, Dolly and Linda, are the last two people we have to worry about hitting us with a hand grenade.

Well, I guess that's about it for now. Thanks for the letter, the pictures and the special issues of the Post-Dispatch — all arrived today, intact. Take care, write again soon and pray for peace.

Love,
Dail

July 28, 1969

My dear Son,

This will be short, but I did want to answer your letter which we received today.

Thought maybe the exigencies of your decision might be bothering you & just want you to know we sure feel you did the proper thing. After your letter about that mine sweeping incidence, this seems to be an answer to my prayers.

We also are very much aware of what this decision is costing you. You know, it's funny, but I have often thought the camaraderie of war is one of its contributing attractions. Why else is the Veterans of Foreign Wars such a popular pastime. Men find a relationship with other men, which they can never quite reach in a normal, peaceful day to day existence. Of course, this exists, among all people in trouble, in the same boat. It was remarkable while I was at Mayos Clinic, to hear (& be a part of) patients reaching deep friendships with people whom they would never have been a part of away from the hospital.

These men you have met will be remembered by you always, for what they have shared with you. I would very much like to have their addresses as I had planned to fix up a box for all of them.

I know you'll hear glad reception from Lucy and we all thinking of you constantly—

I'm glad—

Love
Mom

PFC Dail W. Mullins, Jr.
488-48-0511
CoA, 26th ENGR. BN.
APO SF, 96256

3 August 1969

Dear Mom and Dad, Linda and Denny,

Yes, its me again. I remember in one of your letters that you remarked how grateful you were that I took the time to write you as often as I do. At first I thought this was rather silly, but in checking around I found that Dr. And Mrs. Emerson are apparently not the only parents who don't hear regularly from their sons over here. There's one guy in our platoon who hasn't written his folks in over 9 months! I really think this is terrible! All of these guys gripe about being over here away from their loved ones, and they can't even take the time to assure them that they're still doing OK. And they're always the first to gripe about not getting any letters from home. I try and write Lucy at least every other day and you folks about two or three times a week. Of course, the number of letters that I write will depend upon what's going on at any one time, so that sometimes, like when we're out in the field, I may not get any off for a week or so. I hope you understand. One thing wives and parents never have to worry about, though, and which seems to trouble you all a lot, is not being notified if anything should happen to me. The Army automatically and immediately notifies all concerned should a boy be killed, wounded (even slightly) or found missing in action. If you don't hear from me for several days, it just means I haven't found the time to get a letter together—please don't worry.

As usual, not much has happened in the last few days, so this letter won't contain anything of outstanding interest. Knowing you, you're probably relieved to hear that.

I got your letter lauding my decision to accept that clerk's job in Chu Lai yesterday, and I really felt bad about even having informed anyone about that whole mess. I should have just kept my mouth shut until I was sure one way or the other. As luck would have it, the job fell through, as you already know. What can I say except that I'm sorry everyone was so disappointed.

Barksdale is sitting here with me writing a letter to his parents. I had to laugh because he was answering a question his mother had asked him in one of her letters, to wit, "How are the sanitation conditions over there?" Obviously a question any normal mother would ask. Barksdale's answer—"What sanitary conditions?" His poor mother will die.

I have been looking for that letter you sent me in which expressed disgust and astonishment—and rightly so—at the action of a unit of Marines in some village up in the northern I Corps area. From what I've been able to gather, which, I'll admit, isn't much, this type of thing apparently happens more than the American public realizes. I have heard about and seen one "atrocity", if you can call them that, since I've been here. 3rd platoon, which is, at present, out on some island in the S. China Sea, clearing it for allied use, captured a VC woman last week. They ran into red tape trying to get her sent back to the POW camp here at Baldy, so the platoon leader told three guys to take her into the jungle and shoot her.

You'll remember that dead VC woman I told you we saw out on the road after that firefight? Well, when we got to her, some ARVN (S. Vietnamese) politely cut her left ear off and gave it to our Lieutenant as a souvenir—neat, huh! I think its repulsive!

Most GIs will excuse actions of this type by saying that it is an involuntary response to the heat and excitement of battle. I say it is a graphic representation of the true nature of the naked ape—Cain killed Abel and forgot to stop there, while the American soldier certainly does not have a monopoly on atrocities of war, neither is he immune from perpetrating same.

Well, I have apparently run out of things to say, so I guess I'll close. Please keep writing, though; your letters, and Lucy's, are always welcome and read, re-read and re-reread, again and again. Take care, all—only 9 1/2 months to go!

Love,
Dail

P.S. I am enclosing a page from the latest issue of UPTIGHT, a quarterly published for and by U.S. Troops serving in Nam. It may help you understand some of my language a little better.

PFC Dail W. Mullins, Jr.
488-48-0511
CoA, 26th ENGR. BN.
APO SF, 96256

6 August 1969

Dear Mom and Dad, Linda and Denny,
Well, here's another letter to keep you posted on what's happening to your own personal military representative to that sun and fun capital of Southeast Asia, Vietnam.

I heard on the radio yesterday that Nixon will soon announce the withdrawal of 50,000 more troops by January. These, together with the 25,000 which have already left, will not leave many combat and combat support troops in Vietnam. The key unit to watch for is the 196th light infantry brigade, Americal Division, since that's the infantry unit to which A Company, 26th engineer battalion is attached. I keep hoping against hope that we'll all be able to go home soon.

Incidentally, all of your middle class friends, staunch anti-communists and tax-payers that they are, might be interested in knowing that as of June, 1969, Vietnam has cost the American government $83,000,000,000—that's 83 thousand million dollars. Perhaps people would be more impressed with monetary figures than they are by the casualty lists.

Well, in just 8 days I will have been in Vietnam for 3 months—1/4 of my total time.

I'm still planning on meeting Lucy in Hawaii for R&R—sometime in December, preferably during Christmas, although this may be hard to arrange. One good thing about waiting until December, I feel, is that I will, at that time, be on the downhill side of my tour with but 4 1/2 months remaining.

You asked me in one of your recent letters if I wasn't due for a rest soon. Well, no I'm not, really. After you have been in Vietnam for 3 months you are entitled to one 5 day out-of-country R&R, one 7 day out-of-country leave and one 4 day in-country leave—that is all. Now, I suppose you're wondering why I don't meet Lucy in Hawaii on my 7 day leave rather than my 5 day R&R, since the former is 2 days longer. That would be possible but for one small factor—you can't always plan the city in which you take your leave, whereas you can with your R&R. You see, when you go on 7 day leave you take a chopper down to Cam Ranh Bay and sit and wait until a plane leaves for one of the places you've chosen. For example, on my 7 day leave I plan to go to either Tokyo, Hong Kong or Bangkok—but I won't know which one until I get to Cam Ranh. If the first plane that leaves is going to Hong Kong, I'll go to Hong Kong; if it's going to Bangkok, I'll go to Bangkok. I want to go to Hong Kong—I know a guy from Webster Groves that is teaching there and I might be able to stay with him, thus saving beaucoup money.

Well, as you can see, I'll go to December without a "rest", unless, of course, I'm granted a 4 day leave in country to Danang or Saigon, which I most probably will sometime.

I know for a fact that many people back home are curious about just what Vietnam is like for the GI over here—I know I was, though, of course, my reasons for wanting to know were perhaps more immediate than some peoples. So, I thought I'd tell you all about some of the things that we have or receive to make this existence just a little more bearable—luxuries you might call them, and for a war zone I guess they are just that.

First, we have a radio and TV station over here—AFVN and AFVN-TV, both of which have their stations located in Danang. We get most of the popular stateside TV shows and sports events, even though they may be several months late; Johnny Carson, for example. I believe I've mentioned AFVN Radio before. They play nearly all types of music, but mostly hard rock and country & western, as these seem to be the most popular types with the troops. The station has some pretty good disc jockeys and they carry on pretty much like the DJ's do back home—we even get Chicken Man over here!

Reading material. We get a newspaper, the Pacific Stars and Stripes, everyday with our mail. It's free, but is always at least two days late. Still, its better than nothing. Once a week we get a supply of Time, Life, Newsweek, Sports Illustrated, etc., which we share with one another. Also, we get tons of paperback books, donated by the various publishing companies. They put these up in the orderly room for anyone to come and get to read. There are all types of books, from Micky Spillane to Shakespeare, and I do have plenty to read.

Every 10 days each squad gets what is called an SP pack. These things are vital. Each SP pack contains 10 cartons of cigarettes, a box of matches, chewing tobacco (for the sergeants), pipe tobacco, snuff, flints, pipe cleaners, bathing soap, laundry soap, shaving cream, tooth paste, tooth brushes, razors, razor blades, sewing kits, shoe laces, and a big case of candy, including Chuckles, M&M's, chewing gum, life savers, tootsie rolls and a box of Hershey's tropical chocolate bars, which are so hard that GI's have to call them John Wayne bars.

Well, I guess I'll close now. I'm hoping this letter finds all of you well and in good spirits. I'm fine, keeping myself occupied by counting the days. Please take care of yourselves, and do keep writing.

Love,
Dail

P.S. No, I have not gotten any letters from Pete.

P.P.S.—You remember my pet parrot, Dust Off!? Well, he went AWOL and I haven't seen him since. I now, however, have a baby ocelot that some guy gave me. I haven't named him yet—any suggestions?

Aug. 1, 1969

To our dear "Demo Dail,"

Please just forget my letter #28. As the mailman dropped your letter in the mailbox telling us that the clerical job had fallen thru, he picked up my letter—so they criss-crossed. You know how we felt so there is no need to "slaver in sorrow" and just make you feel worse. Just another low blow that life keeps handing out and you learn to take. You'll probably wind up "punch drunk" like your mother—but so what!

Well, Aunt Dotty & Uncle Bob got in with the "personality kid". I swear I've never seen anyone as sour as that girl. Nothing ever pleases her. They are staying at the Holiday Inn because she wanted to be near a pool and this she even gripes about. Had them all for dinner Wednesday nite and then Aunt Dot & I (& Wendy) went out for lunch Thursday & then last nite Dad took Bob & Dot & me down town to make the rounds of some of these new places in town. The Mansion House Complex on Broadway has at least 5 nite spots, each one with a different theme and different music. We just made 2 there, as we'd have been "stoned" trying to make all. The first stopped at "L'Apartment" which is way out with a loud, young band and garish lights & mod art. Above, the bar they have a screen on which films are shown of poses of famous people, or news events, war pictures; but on each picture from one mouth is a cartoonist's balloon and always saying the same thing—I thot I saw a putty cat.

After a couple of drinks seeing this come out of the mouth of a beautiful picture of Jackie Kennedy, or Richard Nixon, or even a shot of a huge lion yawning—becomes quite hilarious. Then we went to the "River House". This was nicer; quieter, more elegant & they played music we could understand. We wound up at the "Brathaus" which is Pete Merrills hang out; a beer, banjo place where everyone gets into the act and I'm sure youcan picture Uncle Bob singing. Just as I started to sit down I heard someone yell "Ginny" and it was Mildred Zeigler. She was with a rather young looking fellow and a group of people. She looks terrific—real short platinum blond hair. Couldn't talk much but we are going to get together for lunch.

Last nite we all went out to Roland & Alice Eislebens for dinner. They have quite a lovely new home and it was a nice evening. Marilee just announced her engagement to a young boy who graduated from Veterinary school at Missouri U. He is an ROTC boy and is leaving for Viet Naam as a Captain in Sept. Of course, he's connected with some animal procedure. Kurt announced his engagement last week & he's getting married in Nov. He is at present in San Antonio getting some training in medical records. Grandma & Grandpa Paschen were there and it's funny to watch your father with her. He can't stand her & says she's the worst bigot and nag he's ever met. Funny thing is, she's a twin of Grandma Mullins.

Bob was in the office today & was telling your father the FAA really was on his neck. His instructor's licence ran out a couple of month's ago and like a Mullins—he kept putting off getting it renewed. He had a young girl he was teaching to fly & he soloed her & checked her out. She got one of these wind up planes & the first time she was going to take it up she had the throttle in full speed & gets out and cranks up the propeller and it takes off across the field & runs into several planes, one a $30,000 job. Of course, the FAA swarmed down & wanted to know all the details, including who taught her—which brought out his expired instructor's licence. They slapped him with a stiff fine.

Stopped in Crestwood to purchases a wedding gift for Nancy Emerson who is being married Aug. 16. David has 1 year gone and his 6 month extension has started. He had a month's leave and went to Australia and Tokyo. They now have him in Saigon teaching English to natives. Dr. Emerson told Dad that Timmy Emerson, who graduated from Webster High in June got married last night to a little girl 17. He's leaving for the Navy Sept 1 for 4 years. That poor guy takes one low blow after another and I don't know how he stays on his feet.

I haven't been commenting too much on your episodes of ambush, mortar attacks, mines blowing up, etc.; but I just can't. I get a letter like this and I pace from the kitchen thru the dining room, and a couple of turns thru the living room and I keep repeating—"G-D, what is this all about, he's never done anything to anyone and he doesn't even know any Viet Cong". I'm bitter, very bitter.

Just got back from saying Goodbye to Dotty & this is a sad time. I would so love to have her closer so that we could be together just once in a while. After the kids are back in school, I've made up my mind I'm going to drive down to see her. Nothing more could happen to me on the road than happens sitting at home. They are in a quandary about young Bob. He's 17, but his grades were a "B" average & they were all set to take a chance on starting him back at school when they received a letter from the school stating they felt he'd be happier at some other school. It came as such a shock & of course they hopped on young Bob wanting to know if anything had happened they didn't know about. Of course, he said no & the only thing they could come up with was his school newspaper work. He got on the staff as assistant editor. They were having some discontentment among the students & a few demonstrations had been planned, but Bob felt the paper was the proper place to air their gripes so he wrote some articles. This is a small methodist school under the control of a Dr. Horton—who also owns most of the town. They feel this was behind the letter so Uncle Bob has to go down and see if something can be done. I really don't know how Aunt Dot will stand it if Bob has to go in the Army.

Bob Karasek evidently got his reserve detail in San Antonio and is now doing his 6 month stint at Fort Bliss, Texas.

Stay alert and let us hear. Tomorrow is Sunday and my big prayer of the week will be winging your way.

With constant bewilderment but all the love—
Mom & Dad

PFC Dail W. Mullins, Jr.
488-48-0511
CoA, 26th ENGR. BN.
APO SF, 96256

8 August 1969

My dear Parents, Linda and Denny,

Well, our vacation is over. For the past 10 days our platoon leader, Lieutenant Ballinger, has been on R&R in Hawaii, and we've had it relatively easy—afternoon off after a sweep, etc. He got back today, though, so I guess things will get back to normal—darn it. Oh, well, he goes home in October, so we've only got three more months under him. Of course, the new Lieutenant could be just as bad.

Yesterday, just as my despair over my mail had reached a pinnacle, I received six—count them—six letters, one from you all, two from Lucy, one from Ray Henley, one from his wife, Jennifer, and one from the bank. Needless to say I enjoyed every one of them, with the possible exception of the one from the bank, very much.

I was glad to hear that you and Aunt Dotty were able to get together for a few hours and do whatever separated sisters do when they are briefly reunited. Please do make yourself go down and visit her after the kids are back in school—if you drive, be careful, but I don't see why you don't fly Ozark. Surely it can't be all that expensive.

Speaking of travelling, I tried to encourage Lucy to accompany you and Dad down to Florida after you take the kids to school, and she was fairly receptive toward the idea. She was a little worried, though, that if you and she got together and started bemoaning my present situation, it would only serve to depress her still more—and you too. So, if she goes, try and keep it a happy trip and have some fun, instead of sitting around talking about me and Vietnam. Also, Dad, stay out of the sun!

We got word tonight that the 196th light infantry brigade and all of its support units, to include, of course, A Company, 26th Engineer Battalion, will soon be leaving LZ Baldy for good, probably around the middle of this month. We will be moving 10 miles South, near the city of Tam Ky, just off Vietnam highway 1, on Hill 29. I can't give you anymore information than that, really, except that our company will have to build 42—count them—42 bunkers! What this move means I don't know. I do know that LZ Ross, Baldy's sister LZ, is being turned completely over to the ARVNs, and that LZ Baldy itself is being given to the Marines. Barksdale has suggested that the move represents the beginning of the disengagement for the 196th, since, in some respects, our new locale can be considered to be somewhat more secure than is LZ Baldy. Who knows? Perhaps the 196th is being pulled out soon. Let's hope so. I will, of course, keep you posted on developments.

Tomorrow on the sweep we will be trying something new—an experiment in mine detecting, really. Let me explain. The VC get most of their mines from us. You're aware, of course, that one of the most powerful weapons that the United States has over here are the B-52 raids. Well, sometimes a few of the bombs that these things drop won't go off—they are referred to as duds. The main explosive in these 500 and 1,000 lb. bombs is a substance called Composition B, which can be removed from duds, melted down and formed into mine-size blocks. Well, some guy down in Chu Lai has trained three German shepard dogs to smell and respond to melted composition B. In controlled tests these dogs were able to detect captured VC mines that had been buried as much as three feet in the ground. One of the dogs will be going along with us tomorrow, so we'll see how he does.

It's very late now, folks, and while I did want to discuss something you had remarked on in an earlier letter, namely, marijuana smoking over here, I'm afraid it will have to wait until another day. Please take care, keep writing, and I'll let you know what comes up about our move.

Love,
Dail

Aug 5, 69

My dear,

Well, it's over a week since we've heard from you and I can't help it, but I become a little uneasy. I pray everything is as well as can be expected.

Talked to Winnie Bill after church Sunday and she was feeling the way I did your last week at Fort Leonard Wood. Wayne was leaving Wednesday from the coast. He feels with the equipment going with them, they should be somewhere around Saigon, but this is a guess. Anyway Winnie is giving him your location in case you are in any area he might wind up in, & a possibility of meeting you.

Bill Colbert finishes OCS in September and he doesn't think he will be going over, as most of the Officer graduates are staying here. What use they will have for a "chopper" spotter in the states, I can't imagine.

Went to—oops! Just a minute while I get that stupid dog!

You can't believe what that animal can do in five minutes. She makes the Beels "Sam" look like "Mr Goody-goody." We've had to replace that plywood board I used for Babette, with a heavy, heavy dungeon like affair and she still manages to move and maneuver it. Then she races around the dining room, upstairs & down. Yesterday she pulled the cord on one of my good lamps in the living room and "crash," in pieces. If I could have caught up with her I really think she'd have been the third breathing object on the moon.

As I started to say—went to dinner last nite with Meachams and then they came back to play cards. They just returned from their vacation which was 3 weeks alternated between San Francisco, San Diego, & Los Angeles—and evidently topless restaurants. In between descriptions of scenic beauty and comments on the land slide problems he'd bring in the topless restaurants and the topless pool halls. And, of course the long haired hippies and and homosexuals. Not realizing he has as bad a "hang up" as the flower children. I must watch it as

I'm getting as critical as an aged recluse and find myself beginning to dislike most people more and more.

Can't remember if I've mentioned Nancy Emerson and her wedding this month. It is evidently going to be quite an affair. In the midst of all this preparation, Timmy, their third child—who just graduated from Webster High School—informed them that he had gotten married last week. He is the son who signed up for 4 years in the Navy instead of going on to school. Poor Dr. Emerson—I really don't know how this man manages to keep his sanity. The little girl Timmy married is just 17 and, of course, the comments which are rife—is the shotgun marriage.

Well, poor Dennis got taken Sunday and it makes me feel so sorry for him and also angry that someone does this to my child. What happened was Dennis opened up the station Sunday and was alone the entire day until 11:30 that nite. There happens to be another boy (or man, as he's 24) working at the station, colored, named Don. Dennis received a phone call stating "Dennis this is Don. Smitty (the owner) just called & wants me to take a customer's car to _____ (some garage—I can't remember this detail) so he wants you to make out a cash register ticket for $47 & I'll send my brother up for it. Of course Smitty & Don both knew nothing of this transaction so Denny has to make up the loss—which means working for a full week for nothing. He went to the Kirkwood police station and they just laughed at him. It has made him bitter and he says he will never trust, or turn his back again, on another colored human being. He says they are all "liars, cheats, & thiefs." It's been an unfortunate education for him—working in that area.

He sees these fellows from Meacham Park get paid good money on Friday & he completely broke Sunday morning—while their wives and hordes of children—spend the rest of the week stealing to live. And he's amazed at the complete lack of morality regarding the marriage "status quo." I tried to tell him that these characteristics are not just found among the blacks, but that hordes of white married men are running around with other women, & also cheating their friends—but he is very bitter. As he said—"Mom, the longer I work and the harder, the more in debt I get." Of course, what bothers him too is his pride—that he could be stupid enough to fall for this "pigeon drop."

Well, I've really missed Aunt Dot. The 3 days having someone to really talk to—just spoils things. I so wish we were closer—at least where I could see her maybe once a month.

Well, what I expected to happen with your father and Linda working together, has. She came in last nite & said she'd had it and was quitting as of right now. I told her she just had 3 more weeks & could put up with it. She disclaimed this with a vehement "No." "In fact," she commented, "Christine and Beverly (the hygienist) have both told me they cannot imagine how my mother has stayed with him for over 20 years. It's beyond them." They resent he's always accepting a patients word against theirs and his dictatorial, and to them, utterly ridiculous policies regarding the "nazi like" regime which that office must operate under. And then his moodiness is the last straw. I'll really be glad when school starts. As Mrs. Bartges says—"a time is reached when children must leave the nest. We are too old to change and put up with it and they can't tolerate it."

Well, I really hope & pray everytime I hear about another "pull out" of American troops—that you'll be included. Wish that "horses ---" Nixon would stay home & concentrate on getting this war over—

With much much love—
Mom & Dad

PFC Dail W. Mullins, Jr.
488-48-0511
CoA, 26th ENGR. BN.
APO SF, 96256

11 August 1969

Dear Mom and Dad, kids—

I'm enclosing two shots of myself that I thought you might enjoy. The close-up, taken outside my hooch at Baldy, is horrible, isn't it? Elliot said that same expression must have been on the face of George Washington as he crossed the Delaware. Barksdale said that if you looked very closely at my eyes, you could see two small American flags. Actually, at the precise moment that that picture was taken, I was thinking to myself, "What in the hell am I doing over here!"

The second flick, which is a candid shot of sorts, was taken inside one of the village hooches out on highway 535. Not very exciting pictures, I'll admit, but they are of your conscripted son, so I thought you'd like them.

Did I mention that I had gone down to Chu Lai again yesterday? You remember that I was promoted to PFC back in April at Leonard Wood. Well, somehow, Finance never received a copy of my promotion orders, so I have never gotten PFC pay. I had to go down to Chu Lai and get a Xerox copy made of these orders and give it to the people at Finance. They said that all of that back pay would be made up on my August check, so I should be getting a nice tidy sum at the end of this month.

When I came back to Baldy this morning on the chopper, I discovered that my squad had left for Hawk Hill the previous afternoon. You remember I mentioned that the 196th and all of its support units would soon be leaving Baldy for the Tam Ky-Chu Lai area. Well, our platoon is going down early, along with most of the 17th armored cavalry, to build bunkers for the rest of the brigade when they come down.

I got a letter from Wintker yesterday. He is getting his master's degree at Vanderbilt, you know, in psychology, and is apparently doing pretty well, except that he is being forced to hold down two jobs in order to pay for his schooling. These, in addition to a scholarship and money he gets from Uncle Sam on the GI bill.

I was surprised to hear that Bill Colbert was going to finish OCS—I had thought that he had been somewhat distressed at the prospect of being a forward artillery observer in Vietnam. I'm afraid that Bill is in for a rude awakening if he thinks he won't be coming to 'Nam. No newly-graduated OCS Lieutenant comes straight to the war zone. They are always given a four to six month stateside tour of duty first, to "build their confidence as a leader of men." Unless, as we all hope it does, the war comes to a close soon, Bill can look to be Vietnam-bound around February.

I was sorry to hear that Denny had been taken for all that money at the service station. Live and learn, I guess, is about the only attitude you can take when something like this happens. I do hope, though, that he realizes that he has been made the victim of an irresponsible individual and not an irresponsible race. I am tempted to give you another one of my emotional "lectures" on pride and prejudice, but you already know how I feel about these matters. Moreover, Vietnam, and the many different types of men and boys that it has forced me to live with and get to know, does not make it easy for me to sympathize with your feelings toward the black people.

I'll be leaving with the rest of the second platoon for Hawk Hill tomorrow, so I guess my future letters will be from there. I'll keep you posted on developments—please take care, keep writing, and please continue to let me know how everything is going back "in the world." Think peace.

Love,
Dail

P.S. I did get your last package, and I thank you very much. If you do send any in the future, please enclose some Superman, Batman and Marvel comics—no, I'm not crazy—we just dig reading those things over here, and when we're through with them, we give them to some of the kids—they go wild over them. You once mentioned that you would get me a watch if I wanted—is the offer still open? Mine conked out! If you do get one, make sure it is waterproof—the Monsoon season will be here next month.

PFC Dail W. Mullins, Jr.
488-48-0511
CoA, 26th ENGR. BN.
APO SF, 96256

13 August 1969

Dear Mom and Dad, Linda and Denny,

You remember I told you that when I got back from Chu Lai last Monday morning, I discovered that my squad had already left for Hawk Hill to begin work on the bunkers for the rest of the brigade. Sgt. Williams, our platoon sergeant, told me that I would just go down that afternoon with the first and second squads on the convoy. Before we had a chance to get rolling, though, something happened. The Vietnam finance center in Saigon to order a currency conversion operation, effective immediately. I'll try and explain what this means.

In Vietnam we don't use the same type of money that you do back in the world. As soon as you arrive "in country" over here, all of your American cash is converted to MPC (military payment certificates). About every two years or so, everyone turns in their MPC for a new series. This, of course, comes as quite a shock to many Vietnamese civilians who have been hoarding the old MPC, since they are not allowed to participate in the conversion. Two years ago, the army was unable to account for $6,500,000 worth of old MPC—this meant that $6,500,000 in MPC, which had originally been paid to GIs, was now in the possession of Vietnamese civilians.

Well, whenever Uncle Sam pulls a currency conversion, he closes all LZs down—no civilian laborers come on, no GI's leave—until the conversion is complete. While combat support, food, water and medical lines are, of course, kept open, other things—like mail—are not. Thus, no mail came in or went out for the two days that we were restricted to Baldy—and, of course, we were not able to go down to Hawk Hill on the day planned. We had to wait until Tuesday evening. Which was just as well, as we learned upon waking up Tuesday morning that Hawk Hill had been hit pretty hard that night.

Nobody in my squad had been hurt, thank goodness, but 7 GIs were killed and 65 wounded from the other units already there. They found 12 dead VC in the barbed wire the next morning.

Let me tell you a little about this particular attack, at least from what I was able to gather from Barksdale and Doc, since you once expressed shock at what some Marines had done to a village. Keep in mind, now, that people are not at their most reasonable best when the VC hit.

At about 2:45 AM, mortars started coming in—about 30 of them, all in the space of about a half hour. In addition, the VC sent in one or two rockets. Just as the mortar and rocket barrage was about to lift, about 30 sappers came in through the wire. What is a sapper? A sapper is a VC trained to get through barbed wire, blow up as much equipment and kill as many people as he can before he's killed himself. All sappers take opium or smoke marijuana before a mission, and none ever expects to get off of an LZ alive. They are the suicide squads of the VC. They always wear only a pair of underpants, and carry leather cases loaded with explosives (satchel charges), rifles and hand grenades.

Well, as I said, about 30 came through the wire. They scattered once inside the LZ, and went from bunker (sleeping quarters) to bunker throwing satchel charges in. One laid a hand grenade right next to a sleeping Lieutenant's head. They killed, as I said, 7 GI's and wounded about 50—the rest of the wounded were from the rockets and mortars. We killed (I say we—remember, I wasn't here) 12 of them, but the rest got away. Now, some guy up in artillery said that he thought he saw some flashes from enemy mortar tubes down in this village right near the LZ. All villages near an American LZ are considered to be friendly—and most, if not all, are—that's why they live there, for the "security". However, sometimes the VC use these villages to launch their attacks from, thinking we won't shoot back for fear of killing innocent civilians. This time, however, they did shoot back. Barksdale said the artillery unit here at Hawk Hill fired about 360 high explosive rounds point blank at the village, killing about 70 Vietnamese—probably 4 or 5 of these were VC, maybe a few more. Many, though, were innocent women and children, caught in just one more battle for a lousy piece of real estate.

What really got me was the next day on the radio when they said that "last night the Communists launched 45 attacks against allied bases and civilian towns, but none were significant!" This war is crazy!

This morning Sgt. Alexander, my squad leader, called me aside and asked me if I wanted to go down to Chu Lai for the Leadership Course. This is a two week (or maybe a four-week) course which trains you to, in effect, become a squad leader. The biggest advantage of it is that you graduate as an E-5 (buck sergeant), which means, of course, more money.

Well, I told him I wanted time to think about it. I need to think about it because I must make sure that I am capable of assuming responsibility in a combat situation. I've never been really wary of accepting responsibility before, contrary to what my actions may have suggested. I got married, never really doubting that we could make a go of it, and I've never really felt that I couldn't do a fairly decent job of raising some kids. But this situation has me bewildered. Do you have any suggestion?

I guess I'll close now. Please take care, as will I, and please continue writing. My address here at Hawk Hill will remain the same as it was at Baldy unless I write and tell you otherwise.

Love,
Dail

PFC Dail W. Mullins, Jr.
488-48-0511
CoA, 26th ENGR. BN.
APO SF, 96256

16 August 1969

Dear Mom and Dad,

I think they're trying to see how far they can push us around here before we drop. Yesterday we started work at 6:30 in the morning and didn't quit until 5:30 that evening—11 hours of building bunkers in 105° temperatures will wear you out. Then, when we got in, we discovered that we had to pull guard that night until Charley Company, 17th Armored Cavalry got back from an operation. Well, they rolled in about 10:30, so by the time we got to bed it was 11:00. Today was pretty much the same—no guard tonight, thank goodness, so I can get a few letters off.

I am doing fine, although I must admit that I am a bit jumpy—all of us are. This new offensive is such a contrast to the peacefulness of the lull. Baldy got hit last night, and Ross tonight. Intelligence says Hawk Hill is supposed to get hit sometime during the next 5 days. We are the reactionary force at night (we go to the part of the bunker line that's being hit, or, if the VC get inside, we defend the colonel's hooch), so we have to sleep with our pants on and be ready to go in an instant. Needless to say, I do not like these offensives, and I will be glad when it is over.

Not much else very exciting has happened around here, thank goodness—we build bunkers everyday and all day, which is a fairly safe job. It's just the night's that are so terrifying, but I guess I'll get used to it.

Well, just a short note to let you know that I'm OK. As I said, we've been so busy lately that I just haven't had the time to write as much as I should, I know. You will forgive me, I hope, and understand that it's not because I'm not thinking of you.

Love,
Dail

SP/4 Dail W. Mullins, Jr.
488-48-0511
CoA, 26th ENGR. BN.
APO SF, 96374

19 August 1969

Dear Mom and Dad,
    I'll start off this letter with two small bits of information. First, since our unit is no longer at Baldy, we have an APO change—the new APO is 96374, which, you'll remember, was my APO number when I was in Chu Lai for two weeks in May. Don't worry about the letters you may have sent to the old number, they will still get to me.

The second bit of news is that I am now a specialist fourth class instead of a PFC—so you can address the letters to SP/4 DAIL W. MULLINS. Big deal! I don't know, yet, just what I'm supposed to be a specialist in, except possibly working my tail off.

You can't believe how hard they're pushing us! We now are working until 6:30 instead of 5:30, because, in addition to building all of the bunkers around the perimeter here at Hawk Hill, we now have to start work on the construction of our own living quarters. Right now most of my squad and a few other guys are living in a bunker that belongs to some infantry guys in the 196th—they're not down here from Baldy yet, but when they come, we'll have to move, and unless we have a squad hooch built, I don't know where we'll sleep.

Well, the new Communist offensive certainly has Hawk Hill jumping. Last night they hit us awfully early, around 9:30 at night. They threw in about 6 mortar rounds and knocked out an armored personnel carrier that was parked on the bunker line with an RPG round, wounding two men. They really pinpointed the location of the VC mortar tubes fast, because we began throwing mortars back on them, plus communications headquarters here at Hawk Hill called in artillery from Baldy right on them. The mortars were coming from behind this small hill about 1/4 mile outside our perimeter, and within 10 minutes after the alert siren went on, that hill was a flaming hell, with willy peter (white phosphorus) and HE (high explosive) rounds going off all over it. I think the VC got a little more than they bargained for.

Our platoon is the reactionary force here at the Hill, which means if there is a strong ground attack, we have to go to the enemy's penetration point or the command bunker to help fight them off. Fortunately, such was not the case last night. We just grabbed our weapons, ammo, flak jackets and helmets and ran up to the center of the company area, where we sat, behind a mound of dirt, until it was all over.

This morning, at 9:30, in broad daylight, they sent in four 122 millimeter rockets, one of which fell short of Hawk Hill, and the other three going over the base and landing in the local villagers' rice paddies—you should have seen those farmers out there run. None of us heard the first rocket come in as they travel faster than sound, and it hit in front of us. When it exploded, I thought it was just some guys blowing up some dud rounds outside the perimeter. But when the second, third and fourth rockets came whistling in over our heads, you better believe I did some running.

I really can't say that there's much more to write about at the present time (as if the above wasn't enough, I guess you're saying). Oh, I did get a real interesting letter from Karasek yesterday. He described his stay in Sweden (I guess he told you about it, because he mentioned that he had spent some time visiting with you and "debating" the war, etc.) I thought his comments about the deserters over there were particularly interesting. I know you don't agree with Bob's and my philosophy on the matter, but that's really beside the point. You must admit that his experiences and impressions were most interesting.

Well, I guess I'll close now. Please take care, folks, and keep writing. Think peace.

Love,
Dail

Sunday Aug 10, 69

My dear,

Now—I have to stop and think what has happened since I wrote you last. Really, not much but I store up all little incidentals, so pages can at least be filled.

Don't know if I went into details on Pete & Linda's relationship (whatever it is—and sometimes I'm afraid it might become more than we'd want). He's been hanging around all summer—lunches, night clubs, dinners—the works for Pete. About a month ago he stopped all communication for about 2 weeks and now it's started again. Speak of the devil—he just walked in and said he'd stay for dinner! Anyway, he and a bunch of his buddies have formed a club, I think they call it the "Last Survivors", which doesn't pertain to war but marriage. These are all fellows who graduated with you and they get together constantly—at Aspen, the Ozarks, and in town. When one of them gets married—they allow the wives to tag along—if they stay by themselves and keep quiet.

Friday nite, Tom George had their big monthly get together at his apartment and Pete took Linda. She said it seemed like your whole class was there. Buckie Clement, Steve Parson, Jim Patterson, Craig Eaton, Tom & Pete Brown,—anyway about 20 fellows. They don't, as a rule, invite a special girl but ask any girl they might meet during the month & they come alone. It's really a take off on the "singles" parties that are so attractive in California.

Anyway, Tom Brown is leaving for Viet Naam for a 3 year deal with this orphanage and refugee deal, which he hopes will keep him from Army duty. He'll do anything to keep from carrying a gun. He has your address & thinks he will be in your general area & will try and contact you.

Wayne Bill left Fort Lewis Thursday and also has your general location. I know you sent a letter stating exactly what specific outfit you were with, but I sure haven't been able to find it so I've just been giving out the LZ Baldy and 26th Engr. details.

Last nite the New York jets and the Cardinal Football team played a benefit football game in St. Louis and, of course, Joe Namath, drew the crowd. That big jerk; he's terrific playing football but his knee prevents him serving his Army time. Anyway we went out with Seiberts for dinner and as every place in St. Louis was packed, we ate at the Stockyard in East St. Louis & then came back to St. Louis & parked our car in the Mansion House & walked over to the Spanish Pavilion for an after dinner drink on their Patio. It's simply unbelievable what this arc has done for St. Louis. You sit on this outdoor terrace and the Old Courthouse is on one side and a new parkway in front and the Arch visible from all areas—it's really quite a sight and I can't wait to take you & Lucy down there some evening. We are going to do it—just hold on to that thought. As we sat there the football crowd began to spill out and to see 53,000 people thronging St. Louis, is quite a sight. By the way, St. Louis won 13-6.

Have been thinking what a year this is proving to be for 3 children, whom all I wished for was a placid, happy, carefree existence. You, and your complete "limbo" existence, in which you are questioning all humanity; Linda and her complete irritation with her father and the disappointing realization that "patients and the office" come first if she is to be kept in a private college and have the access to a very special existence; and poor Denny "who will never trust anyone again—especially if he is black". It truly makes my heart ache and wonder how I could have made things turn out differently.

This young minister from Washington University talked this morning about what has happened to joy in the world. As he stated throughout the Bible God tells us to be joyous and he mentioned his 6 year old son who wakes up each morning bursting with love and exuberance. I talked to him after church and couldn't help but ask him what he would do with this 6 year old when he was 20 or older and found out he had to enter the Army or prison, face mental confusion which might overwhelm him, or practice trust & love with his black brother & be stabbed in the back. How do you keep a childlike faith through this?

Want to get a letter off to Lucy tonite so won't make this much longer. Linda and Pete just left for a carnival. (In the meantime, Bob keeps calling & writing & is supposed to go to Florida with us) Sometimes I feel Linda & Pete deserve each other and she can spend her evenings waiting for him to come home "from his nights out with the boys." I'm still trying to find out what he does to earn a living! Denny left for work—he'll be home around midnite, if someone doesn't stick a gun in his ribs—

Be careful, pray, & know you are loved & missed beyond belief—
Mom & Dad

Remember you have an anniversary this month! Hah! Just keep thanking the 3rd will be with Lucy—

Received a letter from Dr. Wick & he and his wife are coming down to see us after the kids go back to school. He mentioned that Woody's 6 year old has spinal meningitis but is pulling thru & as far as can be determined will just have a hearing loss.

———————————

Thursday Aug 14

My dear son,

Well, I'm certain you are more aware that the so called "lull" is over, than we can ever know. Reading the newspaper or looking at television can drive you straight up the wall. I just get sick hearing the infiltration of Viet Cong. Just watching the TV coverage all day yesterday on the parades in New York & Chicago and the dinner last nite for the Astronauts, burned me up. Not the three Appollo 11 men, but the two-faced, corpulent, stupid politicians; & Mayor Dailey was a perfect prototype, getting up & all making the same statements about paving the way for peace. All I could keep repeating was "shit"—My language is getting very gutterish, but lady like prose cannot handle my feelings any more.

Am about ready to have Dennis and Linda return to school. My worrying is spread too thin when they are home. That stupid job Denny has is getting me down. Two of his other helpers (the owner) have quit so Dennis is working all shifts. Some of the things he has heard and seen are unbelievable—to me. The thing that bugs me is he has had several chances to take other jobs & he won't. He seems to be trying to prove something and then he feels sorry for the owner. And you can only tolerate Linda's moods for so long and then you too become a subject for the psychiatrist couch. She's got this thing for Pete, but then she has the school year so we must keep Bob at bay. I never could stand girls dangling affections & boys—line charms for a bracelet.

She and Pete went to Bill McLean's wedding Sat nite and Steve Parsons was one of the groomsmen. As usual, he upset the whole affair by being almost 30 minutes late. In fact, they had decided to go on with the wedding when he comes running down the aisle.

Went to a shower Monday for Nancy Emerson and among the guests was a lovely woman, whom I spent the afternoon talking to. A Mrs. Roberts whose husband owns Roberts Boys Shop. Her daughter Barbara graduated either 1 year before you or with you and then she had a boy graduate with Linda, a boy with Denny and a boy this year. Her daughter married a boy she met at K.U. & he was just sent home from Viet Naam wounded, and as Mrs. Roberts said—this changes your earlier viewpoint. This fellow was a 2nd Lt. and he said his life was saved by a colored medic in his outfit—whom he said spend most of his time scared to death, but performed some of the most unselfish courageous acts he's ever seen.

Interruption: had a phone call from a woman whom I haven't seen for 28 years. This old friend of mine, Dorothy Johnson, lives in New Orleans and is visiting her daughter who went to nursing school here & married a St. Louis fellow.

Dorothy was such an attractive, blond, popular girl; in fact she was the gal who was engaged to Dick Hofmeister for so long and then took off and married Alan.

Her oldest son is at Yale on a fellowship in the theology school. He started out to be a Jesuit priest, then got married & decided to teach his religion. Her third child who is 23, also spent 6 years in the seminary then decided against the cloistered life & is teaching at a girl's finishing school. She still has 2 children home—one 13 and one 8. It was so good to hear from her. Dorothy was another girl who had a rather unhappy childhood—and, as she said, always felt so close to my parents and thought so much of them. I was amused when she asked me—"what ever happened to that couple who sponged off your parents for so long?" At first I didn't know who she was talking about, but then realized it was Aud & Stan. When I told her what a pillar of society he was & how far he'd gone, she was floored.

She said—"I thought he'd just wind up a no good bum." Of course, when I related this to your father, he wasn't amused.

Talking of Stan—he called Dad & asked him to lunch to talk about Kent again. He said a little girl has her "claws" out for Kent & they are just sick for fear she will make some headway. The reason he wanted Dad's advice was the fact that they (her parents) had been neighbors of ours & perhaps we knew something conclusive about them which they could present to Kent. It's that little Mikey Donovan girl who lived on Grant Road. Her mother was that blonde model whose husband walked out with some other gal who was also married. Stan said they just couldn't have a boy with Kent's potential involved with this trashy background. How they forget! I don't know anyone whose background was trashier than Auds. Anyway they've decided to send him to Colorado until SMU starts, to keep him away from her.

They had quite an interesting documentary on TV the other nite entitled "Fathers & Sons"—which again dealt with the "old hat" cliché of generation gap. These were su pposedly representative sons & fathers: a policeman and his hippie son; a colored student at Cornell & his father; an executive and his establishment son; and a small businessman and his son who is head of the draft resistant movement at the graduate school in Minnesota and who has just received wife a 5 year prison sentence. Next week it is "Mother's & daughters" and that should be an eyebrow raiser.

Am reading a book entitled "In Touch", by John Steinbeck IV. He's definitely a renegade, trying to live down his father's fame, but it is a revealing insight behind the scenes in Viet Naam. He went over when he was 17 and, was arrested and acquitted on a charge of possession of marijuana. He was also called up before a Senate sub-committee on the use of marijuana in the Army. It's a shocking story of what goes on in Saigon especially, with other locales—behind the news we get.

A package is on its way via PAL. Please don't open it until Aug. 26. Am sending same money to Lucy for your anniversary to put in your R&R fund. Not much—but have 1 celebration on us.

Well, Pete is here watching TV and I'll relate his story of the evening. It's about this hill billy who was drafted and for the first time in his life became aware of inside plumbing. When he was mustered out, he made up his mind he was taking home a toilet as a surprise, to replace the "outhouse". He installed it when he thought everyone was away from the house & then decided the only way to get rid of the old accommodation was to put a charge of dynamite & get a block away & blow it. Just as he pushed the plunger down he saw "Grandpaw" running to the outhouse. He rushed back & saw him lying on the ground, really shaken from the explosion. The young one said "Grampaw are you all right?" And the old man said—"Yup, but am sure glad I didn't let go of that fart in the kitchen."

He's really impossible. Had asked him when he was going to get a wig and he said he was going to wait for you, so you both could get a price on 2. As he said one wig & you could cut a hole in the top & use this part & he'd use the front—

Well, take care dear boy and don't you think the danger is enough without having an ocelot sneak attacking. Where in the world do they find these pets—Do they run around loose? How about "Ossie" the Ocelot—

With all our love & prayers for peace—
Mom & Dad

Monday Aug 18

My dear Son,

Received your letter today about the bombardment of Hawk Hill and it just confirmed suspicions I had. I listen and read the news with great concentration and while they never referred to Hawk Hill, this general area has been outlined on all the maps as being heavily hit. As you say—"this is the damndest war"— Amen!! Am not going into detail how I feel (and I know Lucy) but believe me when I say we are living every minute with you. It colors everything I do or say.

Am supposed to have bridge club here Wednesday & I just talked to Wayne Bill's father. Wayne has a ham operator in Texas he got in touch with to let them know he arrived in Viet Naam. Mr. Bill doesn't have the exact address but he said Winnie did and I'm waiting for her to call me as she wants you to have it.

Had a note from Lucy and I was so darn glad to hear that she might be able to be with us. She wants us to meet her in Nashville, which is a 1 day drive for her, and which we can do. The only snag we might run into is the time she can take off. I'm writing her tonite and then I'm going to call her next week end, to see if things can be worked out. I'm trying to learn not to get too enthused or excited about anything, but I do so hope we can work something out. I not only miss you but Lucy. We'll cry a little but this is good as I'm tired of keeping a stiff upper lip in front of your father & Dennis. I know I'll remember the picture of you in that Indian Jock strap with the flippers and the snorkel, every time I look at the ocean or walk along the beach.

Well, Linda left this morning. Did I tell you they were planning to go to New York? That was changed to the Ozarks—Thank God! The thought of those 3 going to Greenwich Village & to see "Hair", made me lose my hair but they thought twice & decided they were just brave enough for a drive to Lake of the Ozarks. Denny was so hoping he'd make enough money to get to California, but all his loss deductions just keep him above the red. Now he's trying to get your father to agree to his buying a "52 Chevrolet that he wants to rebuild & take to school. He can get it for $45. Now you know what type deal this is and I'm sure you can recite your father's remarks "verbatim". "Have you got the money? What about Insurance? What about gas & on & on."

Speaking of cars, Pete picked Linda up Friday nite and he has bought himself a new Grand Prix. Even Linda thinks he needs mental help more than she did. She said as they were driving down the street he kept saying—"Well here he is driving a Grand Prix—but he's still the same Old Pete." These parties he and his buddies throw are ridiculous to me for I feel I can see behind them. They call them "singles" parties and all these fellows rent these new apartments with pools & try and pretend they are swingers emulating the California jet set. They invite any girls they might meet during the week and, as Linda says "Wouldn't you know Pete always has the most girls show up." She will only go as a date (which is really taboo), but I think she had it the other nite. Pete takes her but disappears to keep his other females happy. She was sitting talking to Pete & Tom Brown and she looked up and here was a guy standing in the middle of the room taking off his clothes—down to his shorts. He was hot! So she hunted up Pete & made him bring her home. She gets furious with him and is very well aware of what anyone would put up with living with him—but she wishes she could put the fun of Pete in with the steadfastness and gentlemanness of Bob into 1 person; then she'd have something.

Just talked to Winnie Bill and each time she renews my faith. Wayne's 1st anniversary was today & his wife is staying with Winnie & so she's kept her busy all day. They got a call from a ham operator in Texas stating that Wayne had arrived safely and his address was Lt. Wayne R. Bill, C. Battery, 1st Bn, 44th Artillery APO 96269. Winnie mentioned another boy who graduated with you that is at Long Binh—James Kuhl. Also Gordon Yost is a Captain in the infantry about 45 miles from Da Nang. He spent such a terrific year in Germany with his wife, he extended his time and presto—they sent him to Viet Naam.

Am sitting watching that fool Woody Allen. Remember him. He's the hottest thing on Broadway with his new play and his movie previewed today to raves.

They were asking him if all this had changed his way of living and he said "No, I still live in a sleazy, filthy apartment in the Bronx." He said he hadn't moved because he has "this strange lust for filth."

Speaking of movies. Linda insisted I go with her Sunday afternoon to see "The Midnite Cowboy" with Dustin Hoffman. Now I'm not advocating the new trend (or maybe I'm getting used to the new scene) but to see the switch in characters from the graduate to this sleazy TB victim he plays in this new picture is something. And the guy who plays the Texas Cowboy Stud whose going to make a fortune satisfying all the rich New York women, is perfect. It's sad, funny, sickening—but a superb acting job.

Remember Phil Miller? He stopped by to visit. He was married in June and is waiting for Uncle Sam while his wife is waiting for the stork.

Saturday was Nancy Emersons wedding and it was quite an affair. She looked beautiful and it was very formal with a sit down dinner at Algonquin Country Club. We sat at a table with some patients of your fathers. Two men & their wives. The men were brothers named Maloney—as Irish as you could get—1 a lawyer and the other in public relations. The dinner was over at 9 and I made the mistake of saying "come by for an after dinner drink." This was after glasses & glasses of champagne. They went through beer, scotch, bourbon and left at 3 in the morning. Naturally they were Catholics & for some reason we got on religion & scripture and your father got on a tangent about his fundamental training & the lawyer was most interested & wanted to challenge your grandmother. He kept insisting on wanting to know when your Dad visited your grandmother. By gosh, if he didn't show up Sunday around noon & insist on going over to your Grandmothers. I haven't heard & I haven't asked what happened on this visit.

Pam Banks, Ellen Winkler, Nancy Devlin were all married last Saturday. The churches in Webster installed revolving doors.

About this new assignment! I can't advise you, because all I think of is safety, safety—If it could possibly mean anything more dangerous than you have—TURN IT DOWN.

Am looking for a watch and will try to get it soon. Hope you got my package before your anniversary.

With all the love—
Mom & Dad

SP/4 Dail W. Mullins, Jr.
488-48-0511
CoA, 26th ENGR. BN.
APO SF, 96374

26 August 1969

Dear Mom and Dad,
    Well, I finally got some mail today. Since neither you folks nor Lucy probably have my new APO number at this writing, my mail is taking somewhat longer, since its still going through LZ Baldy. I suspect, though, that by the time you get this letter, you will have sent a letter to 96374 instead of my old APO, 96256.
    I did receive your package today, by the way, and I thank you very much. Barksdale and I promptly put the champagne in an icebox and, after it had chilled down, polished it off. Unfortunately, however, we had to drink it out of paper cups, as the plastic champagne glasses you sent were smashed to splinters—I don't know why they broke and the bottle didn't, but they did. Somehow, though, drinking champagne out of paper cups seemed quite appropriate in Vietnam.
    Hawk Hill, growing bigger everyday, thanks to the engineers, has been spared the agony of attack for several days, now and I hope it keeps up. The heaviest action in Vietnam right now, however, is being fought not far from here—elements of the 196th light infantry brigade are engaged with an NVA force near Hiep Duc, which, you'll remember, is that new refugee village near where we put in that raft. According to reports that we have, about 25 Americans have been killed, while over 600 Communists have died in about a week and a half of fighting near Hiep Duc.
    We heard on the news today that Secretary of Defense Laird (bless his little militant mind) said that if there is no appreciable lull in the fighting, or if there is no substantial progress in the Paris peace talks, the U.S. forces in Vietnam may be reduced to 250,000 volunteers. Barksdale and I have been asking around as to the whereabouts of the place where one would go about volunteering for Vietnam— we don't want to make the mistake of going near that door! Somebody suggested that our CO draw a line along the dirt in the company area with a sword and ask anybody who wants to volunteer for duty in Nam to step across it—at which point Barksdale and I would begin running in the opposite direction and begin packing.
    There is a rumor going around here—and it is just that, a rumor—that after we have completed our construction work toward helping to build up Hawk Hill, we will be moving to Chu Lai, and from there to Japan! Now Japan I could dig. I hope this is one rumor that proves to come true.

We have completed work on the bunker line around here—34 bunkers built in 5 days (that must be some kind of record; at least my arms and hands would seem to think so)—and we are now starting on our own living quarters and some living bunkers for the grunts in the 196th. Our CO has said that we'll be busy doing mostly construction work here at Hawk Hill at least until the middle of October (then, if the rumor about our moving to Chu Lai and then to Japan is, in fact, true, it certainly won't come until after that time).

I'm so glad Lucy may be able to go to Florida with you all—I really think the trip will do her some good, as I know it will you. I only wish I could join you. I am planning on going down to Tan-Tara with you and Lucy when I get back, though—remember, you promised! Please tell Lucy to drive carefully, though, and you do the same. Will she be leaving the car in Nashville with Wintker or the Strohms, or will she just follow you down? You all drive carefully too.

Needless to say, this was not a very joyous anniversary. All married men in Vietnam have to endure this day, though, so that helps some—no matter what you do over here, you are not alone. As you said, I just keep thinking ahead to our third—at which time we will celebrate enough to take care of that one and this. I thank you again for the package and your nice note—Lucy wrote and said that she had sent a package, too, but it hasn't arrived yet. Nevertheless, the packages will help brighten up a gray time.

Well, I guess I will close now. Please take care, continue writing and I'll let you know how everything is going as often as I can. Think peace.

Love,
Dail

Thursday—21st—69

My dear,

This is going to be a sleepless nite; but that in itself is probably foolish to even mention to you. The newspaper came today and of course the news of the 2196th Light Infantry companys being completely surrounded by VC's. I just don't know what to do! I found myself in the front yard with a rake, crying and raking. When your poor Dad drove up I know I scared the hell out of him. People going by just stared at me. And poor Denny—you just don't know how this gets to him. Of course, Linda is down in the Ozarks swinging it. But, I shouldn't begrudge her this little time to have fun. God knows, we get so little of it!

Well, another of your friends will be joining you. Frank Currier called & he's home for his first 10 days. He has orders for individual replacement out of Long

Binh. He has your complete dossier & is going to make an effort to contact you some way.

Last night I had the women from my bridge club over and its funny just in this group watching what V. Naam does. Jay Eichhorn, Letitia Janis & another woman whom you haven't met were filled with exhullation about their European travels thru the Continent & England & Ireland. Of course this was natural & I'm sure most of them thoroughly enjoyed their pictures & tales of events, but Winnie Bill & I spent the evening talking about you & Wayne and the other boys. I did come alert when they talked about going into Yugoslavia and how horrible these people have it and the complete deadness of expression on the faces they saw and how they were searched going in & coming out & how wonderful it was that America was keeping Communism from spreading and I almost shouted "Bullshit." See how my expressions have become gutterized, But this is the only term, Why did they have to go into Yugoslavia in the first place? Who needs it? Why not stay home & clear up our own back yard. Have they ever looked at the deadness in the faces in Appalachia, Mississippi, Alabama, etc., etc. How do we have the nerve!!

I'm sure you've had news of the hurricane Camille and its devastation. It has been quite bad; in fact the worst natural disaster this country has ever experienced. But even this moves me not. Tuesday nite, we had dinner with the Meachams and for 4 hours straight he talked about this horrible catastrophe & how places they knew had been leveled & on & on. I finally said "Meacham, how the hell can you get so shook up about this when we are doing the same thing in Viet Naam, but you term it Patriotism." Ken I think, is sick & needs care and I've about had my bellyful of him but I hate to really sever all ties because your Dad still counts him A-1, and I'll never understand why. Probably because they are 2 of a kind.

Did I tell you Denny had to join the teamster's union? Which also chokes me up—in fact, I'm turning into an embittered old hag—but I could care less. I told him to forget it that they just wanted the 18 dollars for dues. But he felt he should in order to get the type job he's doing; so he joined, and now they have contacted him because he hasn't attended any of their meetings. So Monday nite he goes down to the council house for a benefit for old Hoffa—with Harold Gibbons the protector. This should be interesting.

Wrote Lucy & I'm going to call her Sunday to see what can be worked out regarding Florida. We'll probably spend most of the times crying—

Well, life goes on—Denny is expecting two of his fraternity brothers for the week end and Bob called wondering why Linda didn't go up east. Frankly, I'm glad they didn't. Do you know what changed their minds? Not the horrors of N York or girls travelling alone; the fact that none of them would drive the

Pennsylvania turnpike or drive their car into New York—so they wound up at Lake of the Ozarks.

What can I say Dail—I pray and pray & pray & hope & hope and love and beseech. Take care—

With love
Mom & Dad

———————————

SP/4 Dail W. Mullins, Jr.
488-48-0511
CoA, 26th ENGR. BN.
APO SF, 96374

28 August 1969

Dear Mom and Dad,

Well, three more days and it will be September! The monsoon season will soon be upon us over here, and I understand that it will rain cats and dogs for two and a half solid months, literally! That should be fun—for a while, I guess, it should be a nice change from all of this dust and heat, but I imagine, also, that it will get pretty old itself.

I am terribly sorry that the Post-Dispatch got you so upset the other day. While all of the action that you have been reading about did, in fact, take place very close to Que Son, that village on highway 535, we here at Hawk Hill have so far been quite unaffected by it all. Two demo men from the first platoon were sent out to Hill 201 to blow up some enemy bunkers, but they saw no action—only beaucoup dead NVA.

No, things have been remarkably quiet here at Hawk Hill for quite awhile, despite the unusual amount of action in the 196th's AO. They did spot 185 VC 2000 meters to our west today, and they have been dropping artillery on them all day. Also some PF's and RF's went out to meet them, but they haven't reported back yet. General Powell, the assistant Division Commander, was at Hawk Hill the other day, though, and he did say that this LZ has the best bunker line he's seen since he's been in Vietnam, so I doubt whether Charlie can get in very easily. Please don't get upset about what you read in the paper, folks—when they say that the 196th is surrounded by VC, they mean that maybe 2 or 3 infantry platoons (not engineers) have made contact with the enemy somewhere out in the boonies, not here at Hawk Hill. Pray for those poor kids and their worrying parents, not me—those infantry dudes are the ones that have to go out and find the enemy and kill him. I am glad I am not in the infantry—I see enough action as an engineer, thank you.

Barksdale would like me to remind you, as he did his parents, to be sure and send a large jar of instant coffee (preferably the freeze dried type) in your next food package. Also, if you get the time, could you send some of that good sausage, cheese, hot mustard and rye bread? We would really dig some sandwiches of that stuff!

I have been taking many slides with my new camera, and after I get them back, I'll send them all to you. Look at them, show them to all your friends, but please don't lose them—I do want to keep them!

Well, I guess I'll close. Please take care of yourselves and have a real nice time on your trip to Florida—Take care; think peace.

Love,
Dail

Tuesday Aug 24

My dear,

Just returned from church and while my feeling of peace & hope lasts, felt I'd like to write. I really wish this nirvana would last, when every problem is in someone else's hands. But around 4 or 5 it will gradually pass and I'll be in my normal frenetic state. We had the young fellow from Washington University today and for the first time I found out what his position there is. He explained that for many years it was the policy of the church to separate itself from learning and intelligence, but that this was one of the more important things the reformation changed. In the beginning of our country he mentioned that the basic institutions for intelligent questioning & learning were purely schools for training ministers—Yale, Princeton & Harvard. Then we entered into the dynamic changing world where man began questioning all aspects of life. As he stated, "be glad when your children come home that first year of college and throw the bomb at you that they are agnostics. This is such a good word. It means that they are questioning their parents old beliefs and will soon find their own answers. Maybe not yours, but theirs" He, the interim minister, and thru other men of the cloth, have 10 institutions of higher learning where they stand by to try & answer this period of agnosticism. He had been at Rice University before Washington U, where he was instrumental in setting up their first psychiatric clinic after 12 suicides in one year. As he says "Man does not live by bread alone and neither can he exist in a world where academics hold complete sway without food & answers for the soul."

He seemed to feel this was such a tremendous era in the scope of man and, as he mentioned, the field of biology and genetics alone were beyond the human scope.

God knows I needed some word of hope today that this whole world isn't going to dissolve into one puff of hate of all kinds—family, neighbor and countries.

The Bills just received their first letter from Wayne and he is right in your area, about 40 or so miles south of Da Nang.

Saw Jane Lake the other nite and Russell is due home the 6th of Sept. He said not to get too hopeful as he can't seem to get them moving on his final papers getting him home. I told Jane if that was my kid I'd be parked on some military doorstep. She also mentioned that her daughter Nancy was married the end of July, pregnant. As she explains, she'd been going with this Jewish fellow for 2 years and this seemed to be the only way to get a marriage contract out of him. Isn't this sad? These are the stories I hear that make me sick, when I realize you are supposedly fighting to maintain this way of life.

Suppose you are aware by now of the death of Lucy's grandmother. I found out about this by a round about way. Bob De Curtis called Friday nite inquiring about when Linda would be back from the Ozarks and he said he'd had dinner with Lucy Thursday nite, and had enjoyed the evening so much and that Lucy looks wonderful & seems fine. Evidently her grandmother's death was rather sudden. I wrote a note to Lena & Clyde.

Well, I've avoided the 196th Light Infantry episodes as long as I can. My entire knowledge of what you are going thru is from the newspaper and I run out every 5 minutes after 3 PM and then cry for 2 hours. I look like I have a chronic sinus condition. I can see where Winnie Bill and I are going to be hanging on to each other. I felt so sorry for her this morning and especially when she said—"Today is Wayne and Betty's first anniversary." It is really Hell!!

Am calling Lucy tonite & we'll probably let you know what evolves. In the meantime God be with you, take care and hope, hope,

With all our love (and tears)
Mom & Dad

Wednesday 27th [August 1969]

My dear,

Am writing this in the car on our way down to the ball game, so forgive the shakiness. We find we are better when we get out anywhere than sitting home looking at each other. And Linda is with us because she's liked waiting for Pete to call. If she could only realize that that this is all anyone will ever do with Pete—WAIT!.

This is the longest we've gone without hearing from you and I won't go into detail about our feelings. It's hell and the enclosed clippings will partly explain why. We are so aware of what you are going thru & what can I say.

Talked to Lucy Sunday and I think we both got rid of some of our pent up feelings. She is planning on spending a few days with us and I'm so glad. We really miss her so. We're going to meet her at Henleys, Sept 7.

Well the bachelor draft dodger reserve boys had a party the other nite for one of their friends who couldn't get in a reserve unit—Mike Jenniswin—his going in! Pete was also telling Linda about Bob Trotter the other nite at one of their "singles" parties. He's evidently on LSD and got a little wild. I'll be so glad to have Denny & Linda back at school where I feel they will be a little safe. This new freedom of the sexes just isn't my cup of tea.

Guess who came and spent the day. Old Nina. She wanted me to be sure and tell you "oh ah misses that boy and ah's sure prayin for him." She is still the same and had to give everyone a big wet kiss. She was telling me that she's been converted to a new religion called the Spiritual and she can heal. She wants me to call her if I ever feel badly and she'll take care of me. First she must rub salt over her hands and pass them over the heat of a flame. Then she was washes them; this prevents her from acquiring the disease she casts out of you. Can you believe it! Products of the great "World" which is spending its youth, money, and future supposedly saving the "superstitious" peoples of the globe, from ignorance. I laugh with tears in my eyes.

Well, the Cards lost. I have rarely seen them win when I've been there. Last nite was Family nite and 2 & 3 year olds were running all over the place. Three young fellows sat in back of us and struck up a conversation with us. They were 3rd year students on their way back to Missouri U. Their main objective, of course, was Linda. As I told her—from listening to them talk to one another—the one word they've learned very well in 3 years of schooling was "shit". Anyway, they expect to be called up soon and insisted I enclose their names & "scratchings" in my letter to you. This was written by them—after about 10 beers apiece.

Have the "Today" show on while I finish this and when I see that "Tricky Dickie" Nixon grinning like a jackass, dedicating parks and cornerstones and other trivia, I swear a shoe is going to go thru this set one day.

Thought you would be interested in the picture of Frank Currier.

Well, must quit rambling & get this in an envelope so I can give it to Mr. Mailman.

Dail—you are never out of our thoughts one minute and as parents—it's Hell. Up to this point; we could hold your hand, talk to you—but this thought transference is something else again. As I go from room to room in a daily routine, which you know so well, dusting, making beds, cooking—my constant plea is "Dear

God—get this stupid war over—please, Dear God!" These are the times that try men's souls & when you must have something outside yourself to call on.

With so much love, prayer and thought
Mom & Dad

SP/4 Dail W. Mullins, Jr.
488-48-0511
CoA, 26th ENGR. BN.
APO SF, 96374

Sept 3

Dear folks, kids—

I can't even remember how long its been since I've written, but I fear it has been quite some time. We have been working very hard, and although we still have our evenings free, I'm afraid that at the end of some of our days, I'm just too tired to write.

Yes, I was aware of the sudden death of Lucy's grandmother. She wrote and told me that her grandmother had had a heart attack and was not expected to live, and then a few days later I heard that she had, indeed, passed away. As you know, Lucy was not, what you'd call, overly fond of her grandmother. Nevertheless, having to attend the funeral and put up with all of the concomitant family mournings apparently put some strain upon her, and I did write as sympathetic a letter as was possible under the circumstances.

We were informed the other day that all of the demo men in A Company, plus 20 demo men from headquarters company in Chu Lai, would soon be leaving on a mission to the Que Son Valley where the 196th has been so heavily engaged for the past week and a half. As you may have read in the paper, the infantrymen out there have discovered some 900 odd bunkers—our mission was to destroy them with explosives. At first I was very frightened at the prospect of going out there where all the action is, but after mulling over the situation for a few days I calmed down a little. The senior demo man in the company, Sgt. Benson, a young married guy from Nebraska, was apparently not too perturbed at the thought of going out there. Benson is a college graduate, quite smart, and does know what he's doing when he's working with demolitions. I think his calm, almost anticipatory attitude about the mission did settle my nerves considerably. However, tonight Benson told me that there's a possibility we may not go—he said that there aren't enough experienced demo men in the company for such a heavy mission. Benson said it was as good a place as any to get experience, but know one knows yet just what will come of it. I'll let you know just as soon as I find out what is going on.

The rumors to the effect that we are moving to Chu Lai on or about the 15th of October still persist. We have a guy living in our hooch who was transferred up here from headquarters company in Chu Lai—he's working in supply, not with us, but living space is scarce, so they put him in with us. Anyway, he said he heard down in Chu Lai that we were moving, first to Chu Lai, then to Duc Pho and finally, out of Vietnam sometime in January. Duc Pho, incidentally, is a base about as far south of Chu Lai as Baldy is north. We'd be going down there for a few months to, I presume, build that place up in much the same way as we are Hawk Hill now. Bolten, another guy in our hooch, said he was shooting the bull with our CO last night after supper, and Capt. Jacoda said that we were going to Chu Lai for a "stand-down" on October 15—stand-down is the military term for a 3-day rest and fun period at the S. China Sea beach. It will be sort of a reward for our efforts here at Hawk Hill. The CO also apparently confirmed the Duc Pho move, although nothing was mentioned of the withdrawal from 'Nam. Not that the Captain would say anything even if it were true—the military cannot really afford to give out information like that to all the troops, security leaks being what they are. Keep your fingers crossed and, of course, think peace.

I'm sending you a few pictures that were taken with my new 35 mm camera—I think it takes pretty good pictures, don't you? I wrote a short explanation on the back of each flick. As I told you in my last letter, I'm now taking slides with the camera, and since neither I nor Lucy has a slide projector, I'll send them all to you—enjoy them (?), but please take care of them—I did work hard for some of those flicks.

I got your letter dated August 27 today, the one with the Post-Dispatch clipping enclosed. Yes, it was a heart-rendering piece of writing. I showed it to Barksdale and he said, after reading it in silence, that every American soldier in Vietnam should sit down some morning and say, "That's all—we're through!" Of course, this is wishful thinking and will, unfortunately, never happen. All the "battle-hardened, flag wavers" back home would go into cardiac arrest and, no doubt, America would crumble before the Asian hordes within a week. When will we learn that the VC don't want to invade the U.S.—they just want us out of their country, and frankly I can't blame them. I really don't like to reflect too much on the horrors of battle and what some of these kids around here have to go through, so I will say no more about the matter. It takes a tremendous amount of courage to follow some idiot, violence-hungry XYY sergeant into a terror-filled gun battle—but its going to take, I think, just as much, if not more, courage to tell that same sergeant, and the whole military establishment, to go to hell and that the United States will have to look elsewhere for young men to spill blood for her.

Well, I've rattled on enough, I guess. Please keep writing, as will I, and do take care. Think peace.

Love,
Dail

SP/4 Dail W. Mullins, Jr.
488-48-0511
CoA, 26th ENGR. BN.
APO SF, 96374

10 September 1969

Dear Mom and Dad,
    I know that by the time this letter reaches you, you will have been to Florida and returned. I do hope you had a good time, and that that Florida sun helped relax all of you. We'll all have to go back there again sometime soon—together.
    I have guard tonight with Barksdale, so from 10:30 until 1:00, he and I will be walking around the company area, doing very little guarding and a great deal of talking. The other good thing about guard duty, of course, is that we get off until 10:00 in the morning.
    Well, we're still building bunkers around here, and I understand we'll be doing it for some time yet. After that—?
    As you may have read in the newspaper or seen on the news, the monsoon season has started in Vietnam. This, of course, is my first monsoon, and, hopefully, my last. It is something else. Technically, the monsoon is supposed to start in September—well, when we went to bed on the night of August 31 it was as clear as a bell out—when we awoke the next morning, however, it was pouring, and today, 10 days later, it stopped. And when I say it poured, it really poured—so hard you can sometimes barely see your hand in front of your face. And mud! I don't even want to talk about the mud.
    Our platoon sergeant said tonight that the 196th was "still" scheduled to pull out in November! Needless to say this boosted my morale considerably. I only hope our sergeant knows what he's talking about.
    I know this letter wasn't very informative, folks, but it's main purpose was just to let you know that I'm still OK. A little tired of war already, I'm afraid, but then I guess everyone is pretty tired of hearing about Vietnam.
    Oh, I did finally get a letter from Dr. Fattig. He's doing fine—you might be interested to know that he and Dr. Finley have become quite involved in draft

counselling—encouraging and advising young men to resist the draft. I think this is wonderful—I hope they can use a veteran in their program.

Take care, please, and think peace. Love,
Dail

SP/4 Dail W. Mullins, Jr.
488-48-0511
CoA, 26th ENGR. BN.
APO SF, 96374

Sept. 10 (2)

Dear Mom and Dad,

I fear I am really getting behind in my writing, folks, to you and everyone. I owe you, Wintker and the Strohms all at least one letter apiece. Nevertheless, I have managed to write to Lucy at least every other night, which I feel I must do—I hope you understand.

Since you are all apparently leaving for Athens and Florida soon, I doubt whether this letter will reach you before you have, in fact, left. Well, I hope you all had a good time and that the sun was relaxing—I only wish I could have been there to join you. Well, there will be years and years of fun to come.

I am enclosing an editorial clipping that Lucy sent to me in her last letter. It's from the Richmond Times-Dispatch and is in reference to the combat "mutiny" incident of Company A, 196th light infantry brigade. God, that it would happen more often! You may be interested to know that up until I received your article and Lucy's, nobody around here had heard about the incident—nothing appeared in our paper, the Stars and Stripes—I guess Uncle Sugar doesn't want to rock the boat that all of his troopies are in. The political shenanigans that have accompanied this war—the only war, of course, about which I can speak—in addition to the tremendous influence that such authors as Robert Audrey and Desmond Morris have had upon my thinking have left me, I'm afraid, completely devoid of any patriotic feelings whatsoever. America, once, in my naive mind, a bastion of freedom and liberty, has become for me a land mass containing a few more social and materialistic conveniences than other land masses, and nothing more. I doubt, seriously, whether I will ever participate in any of her governmental functions again—I will pay my taxes and bleed her of what I can for my own personal, selfish interests. Whereas before and during this war I was encouraged to stay and fulfill my military "obligation", they'll probably be asking me and telling me to "leave if I don't like it" after I get home. America the dead—God rest her blood-stained soul!

Nothing else of great importance has occurred recently—we continue to work on the construction of living bunkers for the infantrymen in the 196th. Kids are dying out in the jungle, entire villages succumb to Napalm, hairy anthropoids with sergeant's stripes and U.S. Army tatoos keep getting their combat thrills, and Nixon plays golf—day after day.

Excuse this letter—I'm tired tonight, I guess. Take care, keep writing and do think peace.

Love,
Dail

P.S. We have been told to ask our wives and parents to start putting "2ND platoon" in the lower left hand corner of the envelope.

Sunday, Aug 31

My dear Dail,

You'll never know with what relief we viewed your letter dated Aug 26, which we received August 30. This is the quickest delivery we've ever had on your mail and perhaps even the stupid military organization is aware of the apprehension we at home are having with the news about your area. It was such a blessing to hear from you.

Sat with Winnie Bill today in church and we really use each other for sounding boards. She just received word from Wayne and he is 7 kilometers (whatever this means) south of the DMZ line near Dong Ha. He's operating a "duster "(anti-aircraft artillery) defending marines & seabees (rockpile) who are asphalting roads & crushing rocks. Winnie & my translation of all this leaves something to be desired. Winnie said when she tries to picture a "duster" all she can see is some huge tank affair.

The minister today was Dr. Mickle, who has been teaching the Jesuits at St Louis Univ., and terrific. He hasn't been at church since the last week in July and he is sporting a full beard. When he walked over to the pulpit to give his sermon, he mentioned that perhaps some would want an explanation. As he had said to his wife before he left for church "I'll have 2 definite camps in the congregation today. Those over 40 will go home and vehemently discuss my beard and wonder what has happened to that fool—those under 40 will dig it." He and his wife & children have been camping for a month and this was an ambition of his & his wife he said was patient, even tho she hasn't spoken to him for 2 weeks. He said the last week he was out alone hiking and when he got back to their tent his wife erected a sign which read—"Children, If you see something woolly, hairy and big crawl into our tent, don't step on it, it may be your father." As I left church I said to him I had a difficult time separating Paul Newman, Charlton Heston, or you.

Do you remember the Lees from Seattle & Fort Bliss? Sat. morning I received a phone call & it was their oldest son Randy. He was at Lake of the Ozarks at a "Teke" convention and stopped in St Louis so I had him for dinner. He seemed to enjoy it so much that he's decided to stay over until Tuesday and I said he'd be welcome to stay here. Denny said to me later "Well, there goes the neighborhood." He's a very poised, intelligent young man and quite ambitious. He's planning on Harvard for graduate work. We talked to his parents last nite & and they are coming east next month (Oct) and might make a few days with us on their trip back. I'd love to have them here when the Wicks come down & then we could have a reunion.

Talked to Joan and she sends her love & and prayers. She's been having some heartaches. Kimmy decided she'd like to go into nurse's training so didn't send in her housing request at Missouri U. She flunked the test for St. Lukes and now is stalemated. Joan went down to M.U but all housing is taken. Normandy will not accept her because she has only a 1.9 average. This friend of Joans, Phil, is a principal in Ladue & also has a special school for extremely slow young students. He tested Kimmie and said her reading skills are extremely low and so now they start the devious road of "Why". He wants her eyes thoroughly tested and if this checks out OK, he's going to put her in a "cram" speed reading course. But he also wants a battery of psychological tests run (similar to what Linda went thru), which he said gives an intelligence basis but also would indicate emotional problems, which he feels could be the problem. Joan said here I am "farting"(her word) around with all this education and I'd give my life if Kim could get some training to enable her to fit herself for the future as she doesn't think marriage for her can be counted on.

Well, must get dressed as we have been invited to the Bells for barbecue—along with the Seiberts.

Bob DeCurtis is coming in tomorrow to stay until we leave for Florida and this is going to be ticklish, as Linda does not want to get involved with him. Then getting trunks packed & clothes ready—it will be a full interesting week.

Lucy is meeting us in Memphis and wants to drive down as she plans to leave Panama City before we do. She is going to return home thru S. Carolina & stay with relatives. You should have heard your father talking to her over the phone about driving that VW all over the country—She finally said, "Pop, I've got 4 brand new tires and Dail is over there doing what he has to—so why should I worry about something like this." Don't you worry & Dad will make her stay right behind us & will probably drive 30 miles per hr. Then we'll have Bob & his car and Linda's roommate Suzi Lonigan is also driving her car down with us. They'll think we are a parade for George Wallace—

You take care and how we pray the Japan deal comes thru. As Dad says—"Once in a while, something good has to happen."

Hang on Tiger!

With much much love and hope and Peace—
Mom & Dad

Wednesday 9/3

My dear Son,

Am still trying to get over the week end. Not a riotous one but hectic. Randy Lee was having so much fun that he stayed over (with us) until Tuesday. Bob came in Sunday nite, so the beds have been full.

The party at Bells turned into an Establishment Group discussion (all WASPs) against me. Guess the smart thing to do would be to just keep still because you really can't change people of this order.

Linda & Randy went down to a Peace Power March of Young People, but it didn't evolve into any significance as they had arranged to gather under the Arch, and this being under the auspices of National Parks & Landmarks, they were forced to leave.

The Wunderlichs came by Monday nite to see Randy and then we all went over to their home to swim. Dick was telling us that Jim still has 2 more years in the Navy. His was a 6 year hitch. He is on a nuclear submarine based out of Spain and he spends 3 months submerged & 3 months at home base. During this 3 months he hears nothing from his family and they have no contact with him. Young Dick is working at Chrysler.

Well, this is Denny's last day at the gas station and I don't think he's unhappy altho Mr. Schmidt told him anytime he's home he'll take him back. Denny was telling us that they found evidence of a form of life on the moon. They found ticks in the moon samples "Lunaticks". As he explained, that's a service station joke. More & more I'm realizing how fortunate it is that school is starting. Now some of the colored boys who are temporary help are trying to get Dennis to date some of their friends. And I still have some prejudice I haven't handled yet.

Bob DeCurtis has grown a mustache over the summer and he really looks good with it. It's not a bushy adornment but rather on the Oriental type. You know [drawing]. I'm sure you can hear your father's remarks. We went down with Bob & Linda to the "Brathaus" last nite. This is the beer place which has been a fantastic success. They have a Banjo band and everyone sits at long tables & sings along. In between music breaks you see old Charlie Chaplin movies, WC Fields Laurel & Hardy, etc!

Well, it's been a week since we've heard from you and we can well imagine the strain you are under. Hope you are at least getting your mail. Last nite they announced the death of Ho Chi Minh and of course the TV & newspapers and politicians are rampant with speculations as to the effect of his death on the policies in Viet Naam. I'm getting like you, I don't believe anything I hear anymore. Thought I'd enclose some of the clippings which have been appearing in our paper.

I'm sure you have heard the following story about the new inductee from the hills, who went AWOL after 3 days. When they picked him up this typical seargeant questioned him and wanted to know why he'd do a stupid thing like this. The backward boy replied "Well the first day they gave me a comb and then cut off all my hair. The second day they hand me a toothbrush and some guy pulls out all my teeth, so when they handed me an athletic supporter the third day I said—Man! I'm getting out of here."

Take care, let us hear & think & pray peace.

With so much love
Mom & Dad

Mon— September. 8—

My dear,

Thought I'd be able to get this written yesterday but getting everyone packed up & trying to get the house in reasonable order just about does me in. Denny & I took 3 trunks to the airport Sat nite for shipping off to Athens and even with this you couldn't believe the luggage for those two, that still had to go in the car. Bob was no help as he had a portable TV, a big new stereo outfit, his tank with his gerbils and enough clothes for 5 people & a new 12 string guitar.

Well, we made it to Memphis and Lucy was at the Henleys so they all came over to the motel for a drink. The Henleys baby is a doll and I just sit in wonderment looking at her & thinking "how can a child who looks so much like Ray, be so cute." Don Jackson & his wife came in SO Lucy saw them & and then last nite Mauria & her husband & baby were coming over to the Henleys last nite. Lucy looks wonderful and seems fine, altho I thought she'd lost weight—which didn't make her feel badly. I'll let Lucy tell you about the Jacksons & the Henleys.

They did get to talking last nite about different times you had all gotten together and they mentioned a "strip poker" game, at which Lucy said you embarrassed her. Dail!!

Denny is driving your VW with Lucy and as Ray gave Dad a new route to take we expect to be in Panama City tonite. We are really seeing the back roads of Mississippi & Alabama. We met Denny & Lucy in Meridian for lunch & next in Panama City. They can't stand following us so they went on ahead.

Sure wished I'd brought some flash bulbs so I could have taken a picture of Jennifer's little girl and the dog. They really took to each other. She'd keep calling "goggie-goggie" & then Chanel would jump up & lick her face and Andrea would squeal & shut her eyes, & fall on the floor—then get up and & repeat it.

Bob & Linda went right on to Athens as he wanted to drop his stuff before going on to Florida. Linda would have preferred going with us, but Bob looked a little hurt so she went on. She is sure having trouble making up her mind whether it should be someone like Pete or someone like Bob. Your Dad told her this is her last year in school he's paying for and I think it shook her. She said—"well guess I have no choice but to get married." But to whom.

Am enclosing a picture of Debbie Kreyling. Isn't she lovely & doesn't she look like her mother?

This is going to be hard to read as I've been writing in the car with the dog breathing down my neck.

Next letter I'll enclose some pictures I'll take. You just don't know how I wish you were with us and I almost hate to write and tell you what we are doing—except I know you are too big to begrudge this.

Our love and thoughts
Peace
Mom & Dad

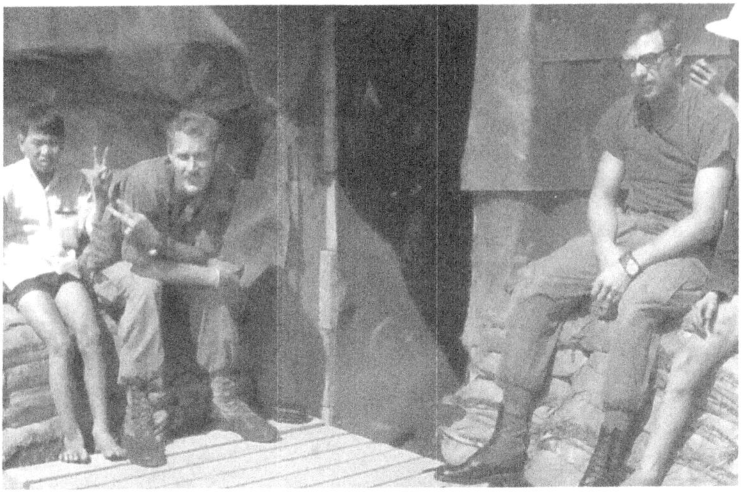

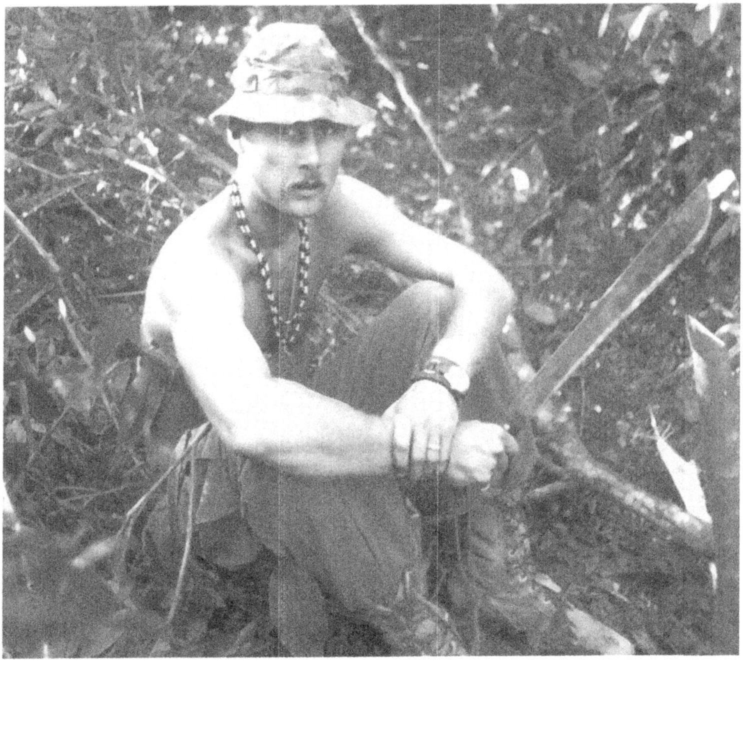

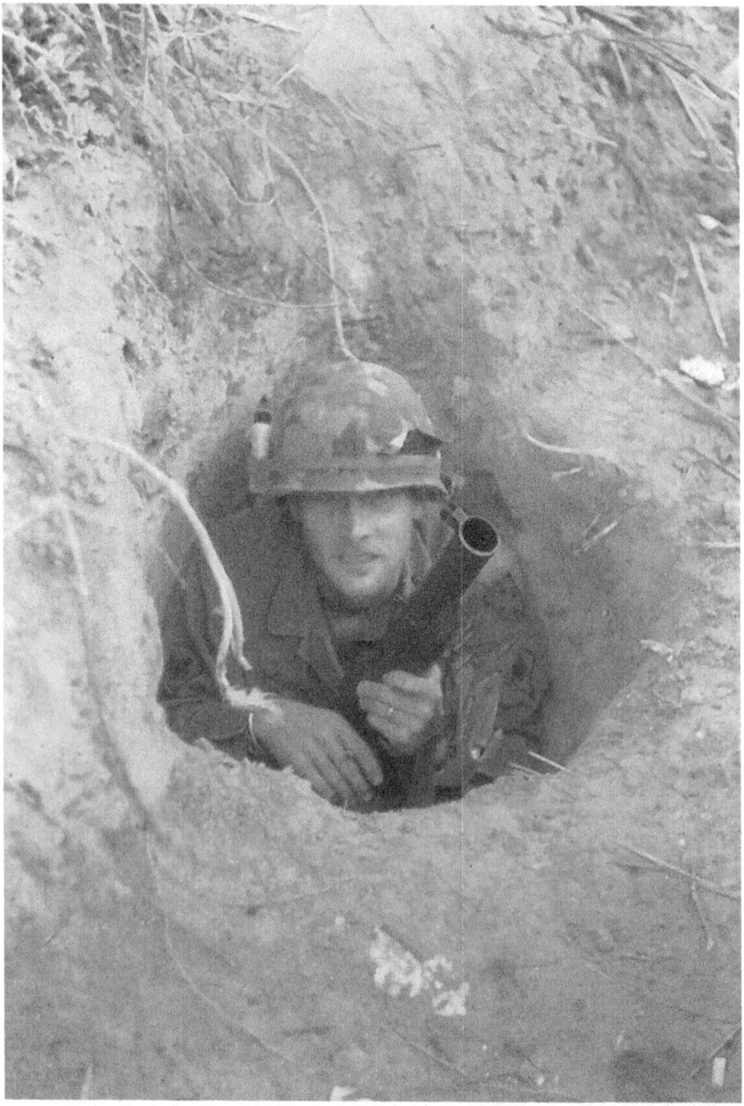

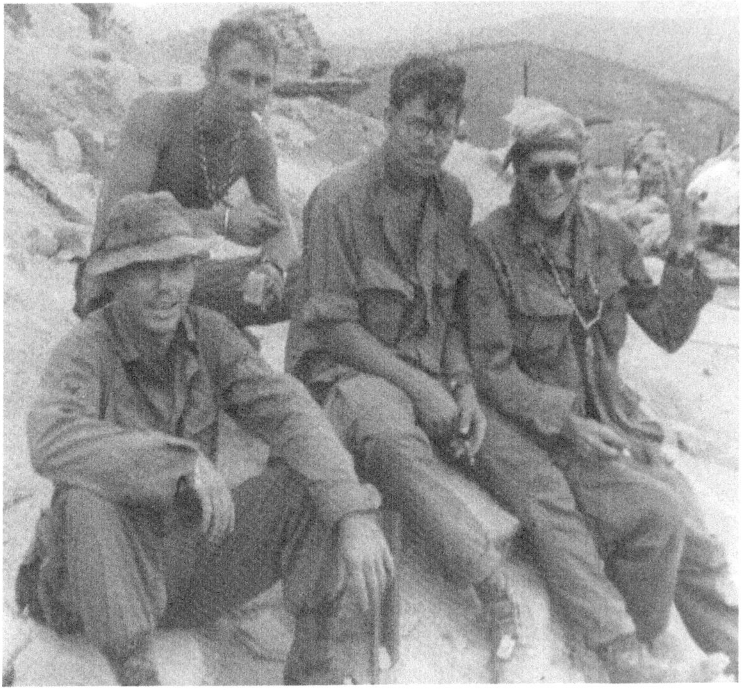

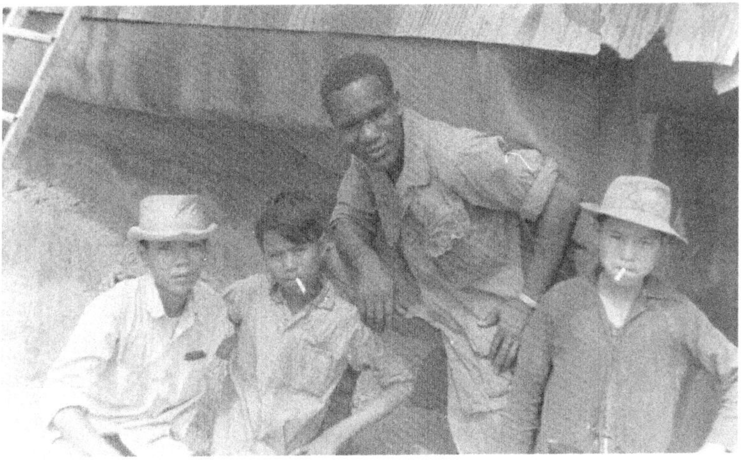

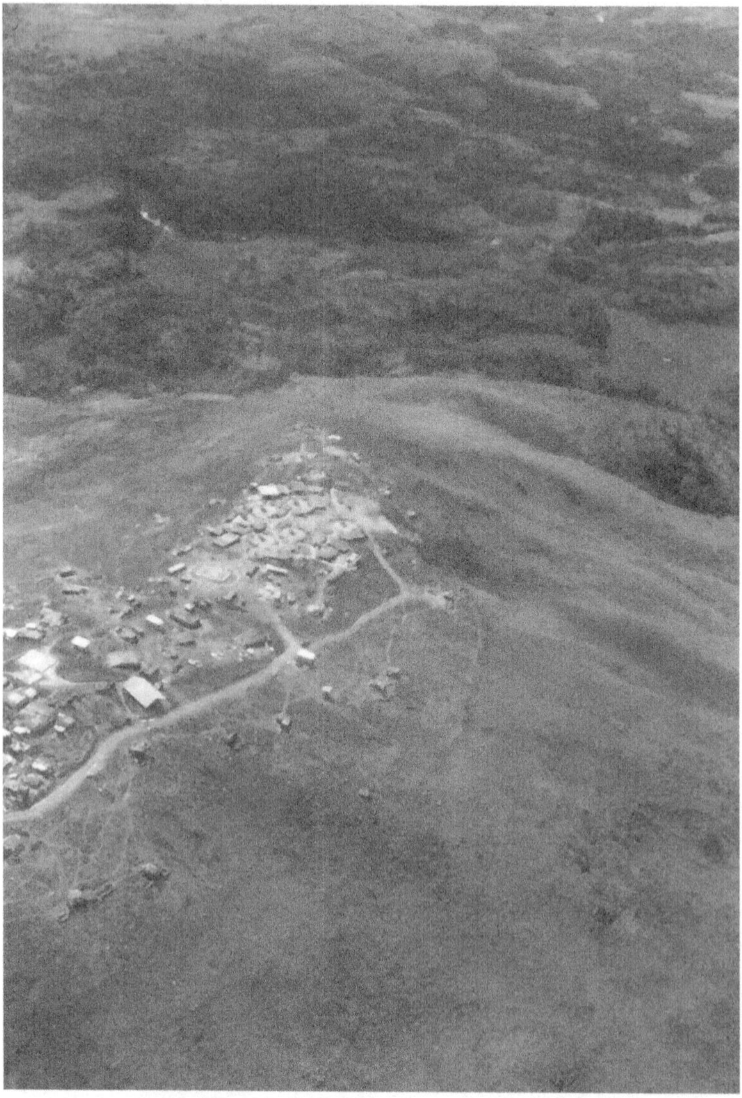

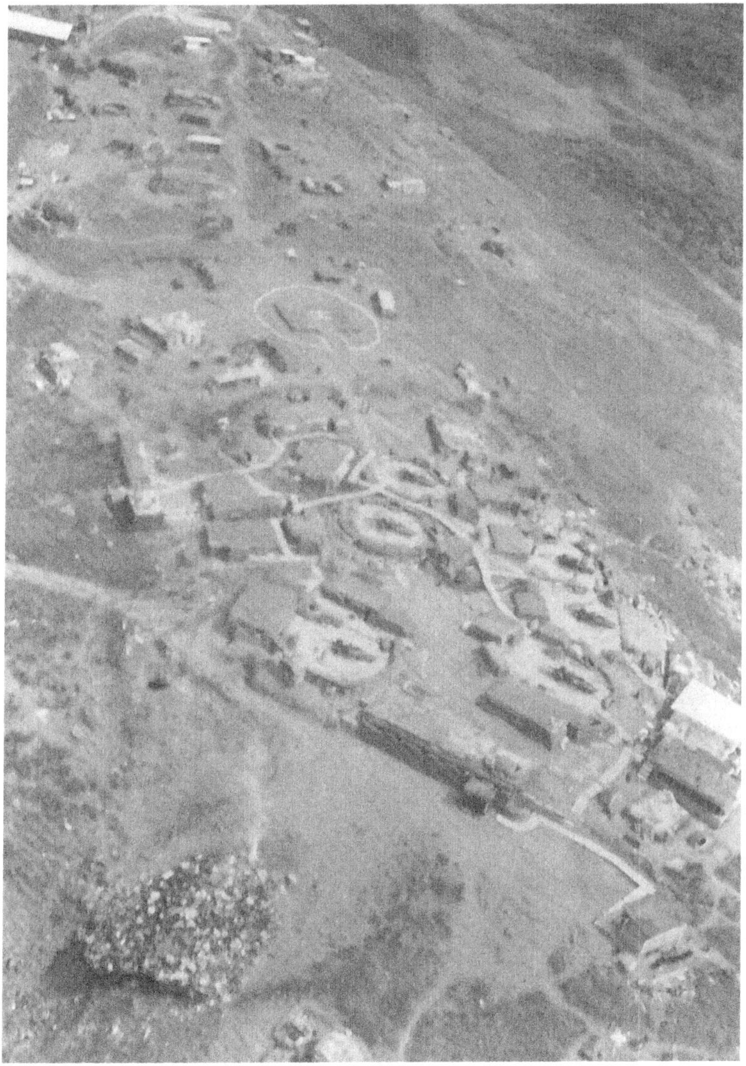

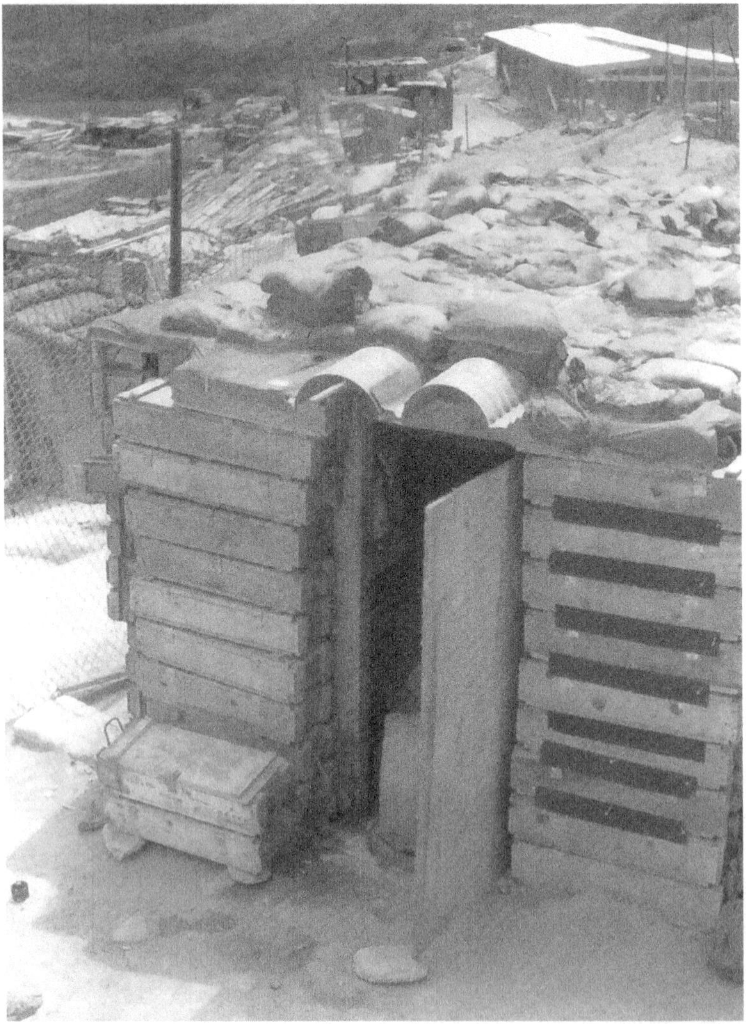

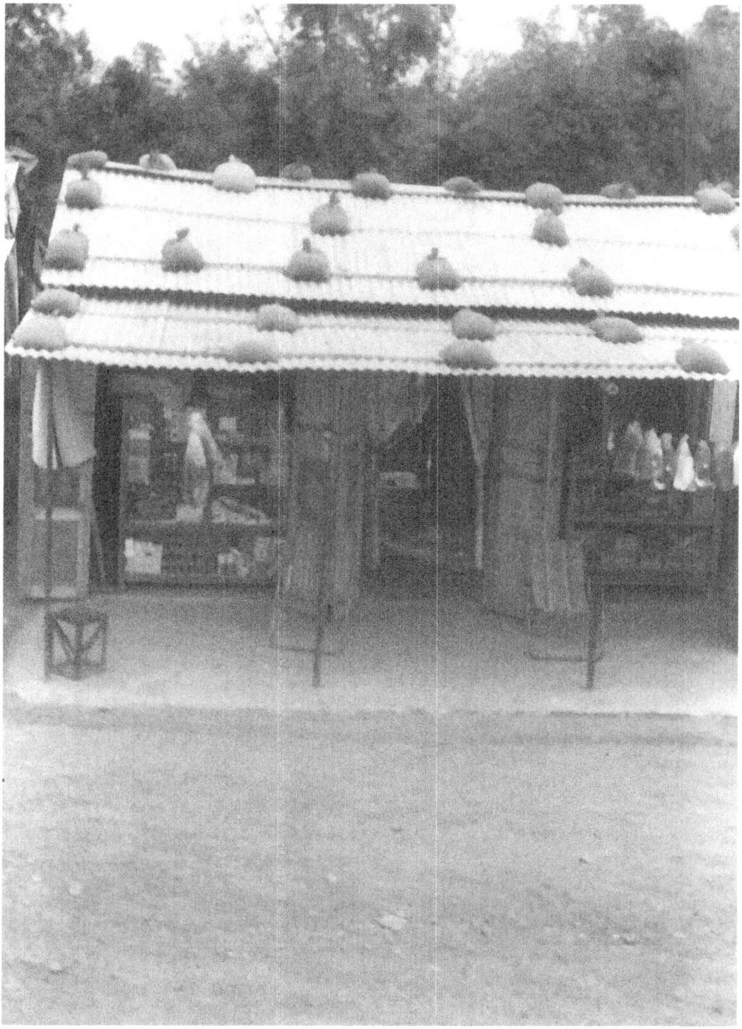

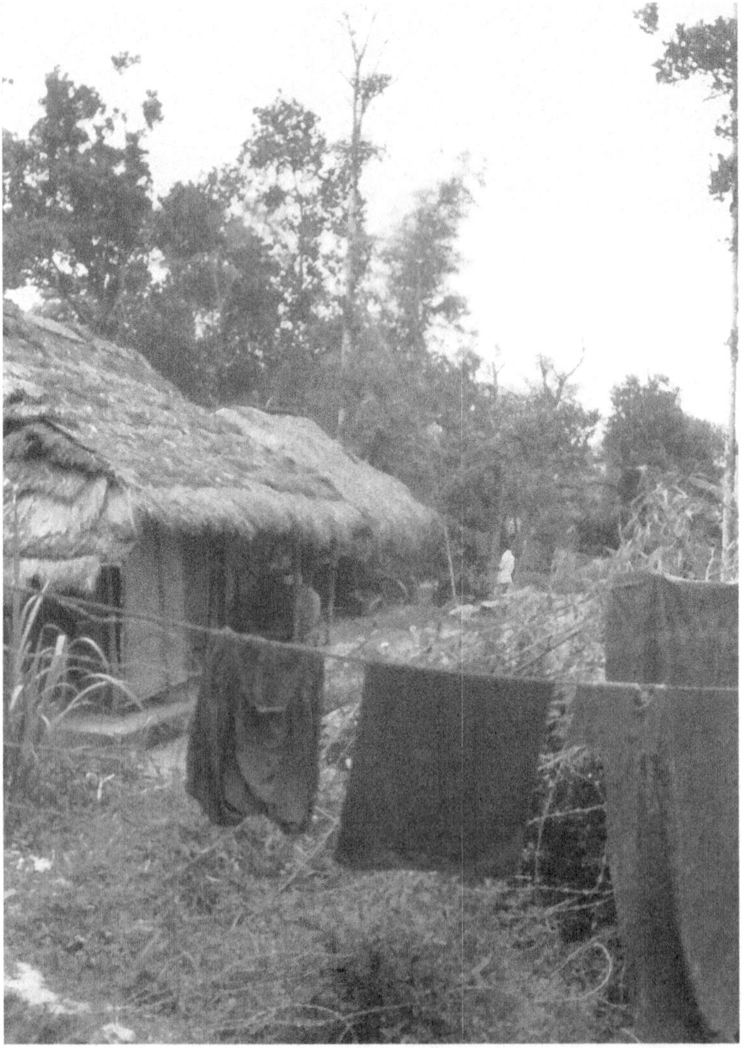

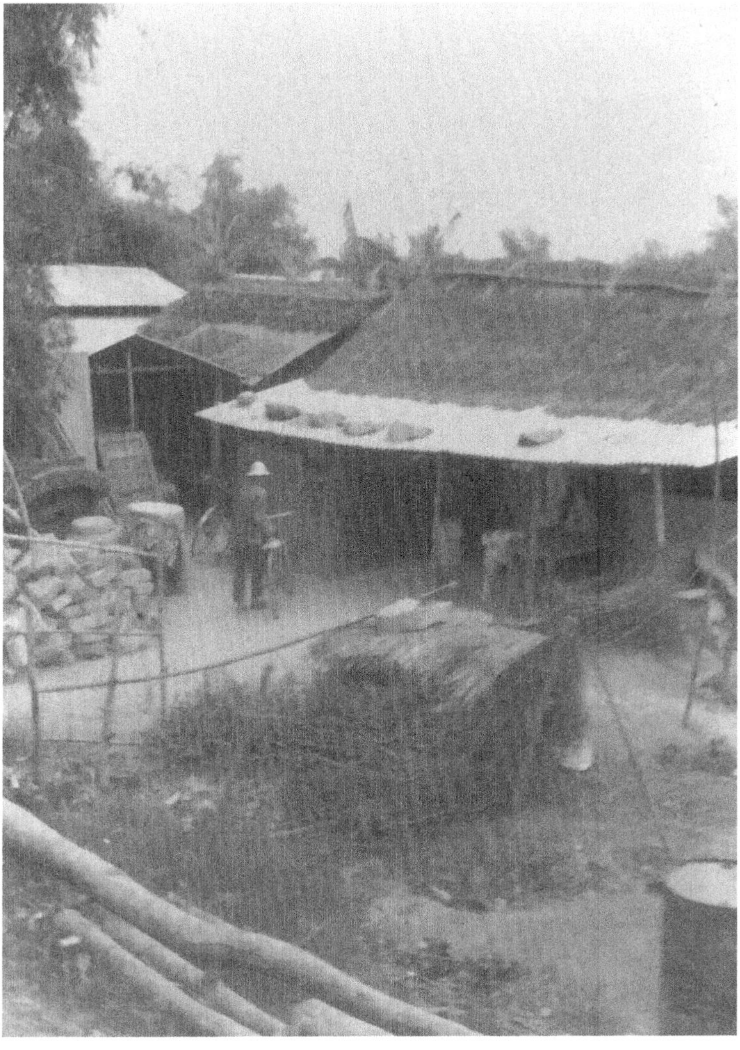

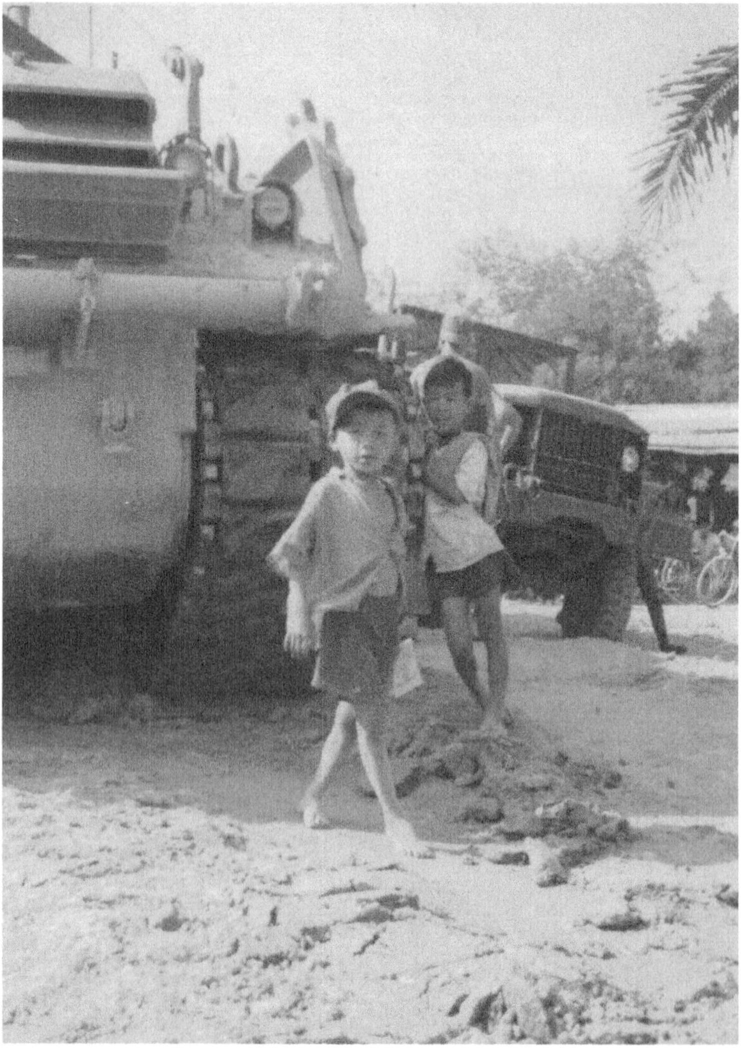

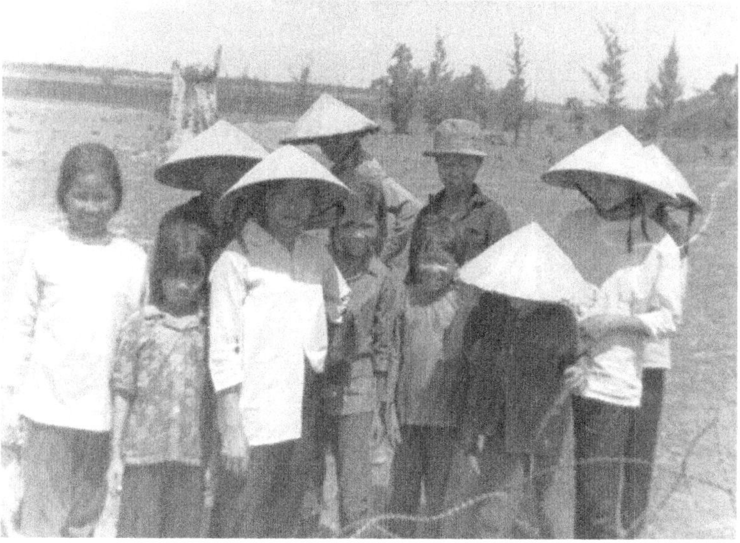

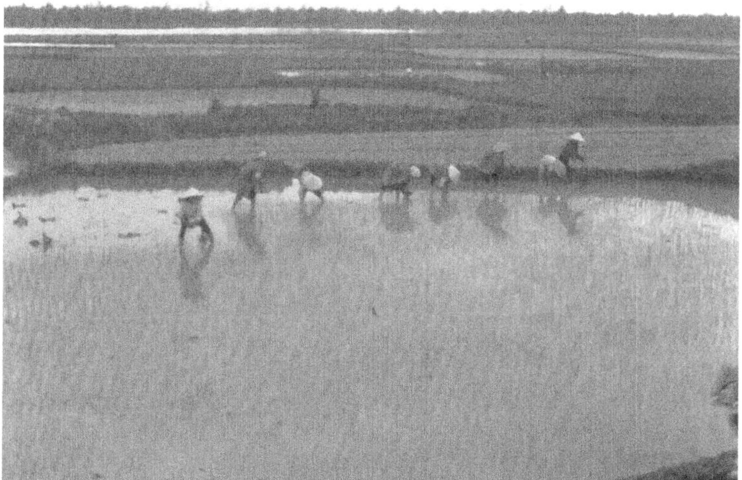

The Overseas Weekly

THE GI NEWSPAPER THE BRASS CAN'T KILL!

For those of you who missed the OVERSEAS WEEKLY story in the July issue of TRUE magazine ......

The kids were selling an item so hard to get in Viet Nam, Laos, Thailand, Korea, Formosa and Japan that, although it was only an 11-by-16-inch tabloid with a scrambled scattering of unmatched type and contained but 18 pages, they were demanding, and receiving, up to $1.50 for a single copy. Within minutes the GI's on the spot bought them all.

It was a case of buy quick, or not at all. For this was the long-awaited arrival and first distribution in the Far East of the *Overseas Weekly*.

Whompingly independent, *Overseas Weekly* is written and edited for the ordinary, in-the-ranks serviceman. Put out by a staff of former GI's, the paper crusades in defense of the soldier's rights.

OW calls itself "the enlisted man's court of last resort." Its targets are autocratic generals, sadistic junior officers, courtmartial boards too quick with dishonorable discharges, war profiteers in uniform, civilian crooks operating post exchanges, brutal MP's, unfit combat commanders and any others who need the clear light of publicity.

Although the embattled tabloid's weekly pressrun amounts to less than 60,000 dogeared copies pass from man to man and reach some 200,000 troops in 12 countries, from Iceland to Germany, England to Turkey, Spain to the Philippines.

If not for the Weekly's inquiries in Germany, the public quite possibly wouldn't have learned, in 1966, that tons of brand new Seventh Army tires, tools and motor parts were secretly dumped and bulldozed out of sight. Or what went on in Mainz and Hanau, where commanders disciplined GI's who had gone AWOL or otherwise goofed up by shaving their heads, binding them with ropes and handcuffs and having them beaten with sawed-off pool cues. As a result of *OW's* stories, the responsible officers were either courtmartialed or transferred from their posts.

In the past few years the paper has exposed a colonel who made men walk 90 miles under full pack as punishment; an insurance company which fleeced GI's; and a group of officers who paraded around in Ku Klux Klan sheets.

Editor Curt Daniell and his staff barged into Viet Nam in the only way open to them.

First they set up a Saigon news bureau. Next they rented printing facilities in Hong Kong, where they ran off the Pacific edition. Having been refused the use of government aircraft, they hired the expensive services of two private concerns, and flew their newspaper into Saigon. Then they employed a few dozen native kids to peddle *OW* on the streets and outside the barracks. Along with a few Saigon book stalls and hotel stands, this was their only outlet.

"They won't let us get to you," advertised *OW*, "so it's up to you men to find us."

One man who knows very well the perils of getting stories for *OW* is reporter Bob Stokes, a husky, handsome ex-military-intelligence-agent who handled German beats before moving to the Saigon bureau. Stokes was wearing his arm in a sling this past winter, the result of a wound he received from the Viet Cong in January while covering a Marine helicopter mission. "In Europe," Stokes said, "in the cold war, local government censors don't bother us much. Our main problem there is U.S. Seventh Army brass, which thinks it is holy and above criticism."

Many of the questions about *OW*'s remarkable ability to tell hot tales can be answered by a visit to an old stone building at 19 Schillerstrasse, in Frankfurt. There the paper is put together in a drafty, cavernous newsroom by a group of young men, mostly in their early 30's, who could have stepped out of a Ben Hecht yarn of the wild, wacky, Chicago yellow-press days of the 1920's.

"The joint may look like hell," says six-feet-four-inch, 220-pound Charlie Barr, a 28-year-old former student at Cornell University, who took an Army discharge five years ago to join *OW* as a reporter.

"But we work much harder here than we'd ever work on a Stateside newspaper. Call it responsibility to the guys we left behind in the Army. Or call it using *OW* as our training ground for a newspaper job back home some day. Whatever it is, we enjoy a job where we can write anything that's honest, without political interference, knowing that it helps give the GI some sort of even break in a world he didn't ask for and which works strictly to his disadvantage."

Phones ring from midmorning to 3 a.m. at 19 Schillerstrasse. Dozens of enlisted men appeal to *OW* each week, and the majority of "big" stories — cruelty to or harassment of the ranks — reach the office as tips from victimized GI's, or their pals or wives. "Every goddam soldier in Europe seems to be a spy for your sheet!" a major bitterly told Charlie Barr recently. "No, only one in about every two or three," he replied.

"Our theory was," says Marion Rospach, who today, at 39, remains *OW*'s publisher-owner, "that servicemen in Europe would welcome a free press. There seemed to be a large vacuum in that department. But with creditors howling and nobody buying us, I began to think we'd been crazy to try it." Carrying on alone, the stubby, stubborn Marion concluded that what *OW* needed was more dynamism. She looked around.

OW always protects its sources. The Army, for instance, is still trying to learn how *OW* blew the lid off a private officers'-club party at Darmstadt, Germany, in March, 1965. Sixteen officers, dressed in white Ku Klux Klan sheets and carrying burning crosses paraded about, drinking and chanting.

"And while that went on," angrily exploded the *Weekly*, "Negro GI's were forced to serve food and drink to these people."

In spite of heavy pressure, *OW* never revealed the names of its informants. In the end, admitting the story was true, the Army punished the KKK demonstrators.

OW will undoubtedly keep right on demanding — the tabloid has one very big incentive. The troops are there, waiting for their newspaper. Bob Stokes saw this firsthand in Viet Nam during the action in which he received his wound. In the bullet-riddled helicopter with him were four badly-wounded Marines. "After they got a bandage on me," he wrote back to the editors in Frankfurt, "I looked around and two of those Marines, who had caught shrapnel and escaped by the skin of their teeth, were leaning back in that chopper and they were reading copies of *Overseas Weekly* which I'd brought along. Hell of a good thing to see. They'd never read us before. They told me they wanted to become subscribers."

Subscribe now and read about what's really going on in Army, Navy, Air Force and Marines

SP/4 Dail W. Mullins, Jr.
488-48-0511
CoA, 26th ENGR. BN.
APO SF, 96374
2ND PLATOON

15 September 1969

Dear Folks,
    I got two letters the other day, one from Lucy and one from you all, both written enroute to Florida. I'm, frankly, a little relieved that everyone must be home by now, safe and sound, I presume. I do hope you had a good time, really, and that you are relaxed after enjoying that (hopefully) warm Florida sun.
    The letter I got from Lucy was written in Nashville, so I haven't had a chance to hear about her visit with the Henleys and Jacksons. I'm anxious to hear about how she and Don got along.
    I was so happy to hear that Roy and Jennifer's baby is doing so well—Andy is cute, isn't she? So she's talking now, huh? Jennifer had written some time ago and said that she was walking, but this is the first I've heard about talking.
    I heard on the news this morning that President Nixon has definitely decided to go ahead with further troop withdrawals, specific units and numbers of troops to be announced sometime tonight. Here's hoping.
    Last year around this time, A Company got a great many new men through the replacement center here in Vietnam. This, of course, means that we're now losing all of them as they bring their tours to a close and head home. Right now, I think our platoon is down to 12 men—this would be OK if it weren't for the fact that it leaves we who must remain with a still larger workload. However, I suspect that we'll be getting some more people in before too long—when they come, they'll all come at once.
    Two or three days ago I passed the 1/3 mark of my tour—8 months to go (in Vietnam it helps to say 7 months and days). Sometime near the end of this month we begin signing up for R&Rs in December. I'm still hoping that I can get my R&R to fall over Christmas, but I suppose that may be expecting too much. Barksdale and I are both going in December, and while, as I've told you, they are very reluctant to let two men from the same Company have coinciding R&Rs, much less the same platoon and squad, we're both hoping that they overlap by one or two days. At any rate, I'm certainly looking forward to December, as you can imagine.
    Well, I guess that's about all I have to say right now. We're still building bunkers right and left, although this weekend we do have a short sweep and clear operation somewhere out West of here—not my favorite pastime, but I suppose it will be a change.

Please take care of yourselves. I guess now that Linda and Denny are in school, the house will be somewhat quieter. It sounds from some of your previous letters, though, that Channel will be more than enough to keep you busy. Write often. Think peace.

Love,
Dail

SP/4 Dail W. Mullins, Jr.
488-48-0511
CoA, 26th ENGR. BN.
APO SF, 96374
2ND PLATOON

22 September 1969

My dear Parents,
 You'll have to excuse this rather outlandish paper, but at the moment, it's all that is available. While USO's are actually a far cry from being a "Home Away from Home", they are, nevertheless, something which every serviceman does learn to appreciate, even though much fun is made of them.
 You'll remember I told you awhile ago that our new CO, Captain Jacoda, had made arrangements for our company to come down to Chu Lai for standown (rest), one squad at a time. Well, yesterday my squad left Hawk Hill for its three days of relaxation, and right now I'm sitting here in the Chu Lai Beach USO writing a couple of letters on their free stationary. Ed Ames is singing "My Cup Runneth Over" on the stereo tape recorder here; the Vietnamese USO workers here are dispensing free coffee for anyone who asks; and before me, through the huge windows facing east, I can see the white sandy beach running down to the sparkling blue water of the South China Sea. Anchored about a half mile out is a huge oil tanker, surrounded by hundreds of small fishing sampans, rocking crazily in the gently rolling waves. It doesn't sound much like the Vietnam you read about back home, does it. I guess all but the most hard-core soldiers over here are grateful for places like this—places which offer a brief respite from the constant sound of cannons going off, of flares at night, of sirens going off in the middle of the night. Of course, all I have to do is turn around and look out the window to my rear to see the mountains, and be reminded again of the war (I hope when I return home that mountains don't remind me then of what they do now—danger).

At any rate, it was nice to sleep late this morning; to sit over a cup of coffee and read—in short, to do what I wanted for a change instead of what the Army wanted.

I would really dread the arrival of Wednesday and the signal that we must return back to Hawk Hill were it not for another piece of good fortune that came my way the other day. Barksdale and I were both granted a 3-day in-country R&R for October 2–5 in Danang, at the China Beach USO facilities! One reason we're so anxious to get up to Danang is because they have stateside telephone facilities there, which will, hopefully, enable us to call our wives and parents. However, upon our arrival here at Chu Lai for Standown, we were surprised to discover that the Red Cross has such facilities here, also. So, a little later on today, we're going to go up there and try our luck—should we fail, of course, we will still have an opportunity to call from Danang next month. One word of warning, though. While should we get through today, I realize all of this will be so many wasted words, you can consider them if we have to call later on from Danang. First, we have to call collect, since there are no payment facilities here in Vietnam. Second, the waiting lines are very long, such that by the time I get to a phone, it may be very late (or very early) in St. Louis—I hope being awakened at 4:00 or 5:00 in the morning won't frighten you unduly. As they say in Vietnam, this is a "hardship tour", and I guess that expression refers to wives and parents too.

Well, unless you hear from me today, look for a call around the 3rd or 4th of October—if you don't hear, though, don't panic—it just means I never was able to get to a phone. Please take care, keep writing and I'll do same—

Love,
Dail

———————————

Sept 11 1969

My dear son,

Have your ears been ringing! We've talked about you constantly and if you cannot be here physically, you are here in spirits.

Right now Lucy & Bob are serenading all of us with singing and his guitar and we've laughed about your impersonations of Ray Charles last year. But there will be another time.

Even tho this seems like another world, no matter where I am or what I am doing I run in to get the news and right now I'm keeping my fingers crossed that this high conference meeting Nixon is holding about Vietnaam will amount to something. For some reason I think Ho Chi Minh's death has them thinking a change will be in the picture.

The weather has been so beautiful, but we do have one problem. Flies! This is the hatching season and today they absolutely ran us off the beach. Dad hasn't ventured out during the hot sun and then he gets everything set to spend 10 minutes on the beach and the flies eat him up so he runs back in the motel. Denny says " — "Jeez—38 dollars a day and all he does is sleep." You know Dad, 2 days & he can't wait to get back filling teeth. It really is sad when you cannot relax for 2 days. What I must learn is to ignore him in his perplexities instead of raring up.

The enclosed pictures are the latest members of the Hell's Angels. Bob rented a motorcycle & he & Linda peeled around. I think your Dad would have taken off on it if we would have encouraged him.

I've been getting sunburned, but have about decided that I'm getting too old for a sunburn as it just shrinks up my skin and I'm looking like an old prune while Linda & Lucy just look tremendous.

We've really enjoyed being with Lucy and she has managed to keep herself busy and useful and just keeps planning for the time when you'll be back. I'm so glad you have her to come home to.

Lucy & and I have talked about Linda and of course she can be more impartial and feels more sorry for Bob than Linda. I really do too, but I still feel it's up to Bob to tell Linda—"I've had it. I'm calling it quits." But he doesn't do this & with Linda its all fun & games

The dolphins haven't been around too much & I think the flies have driven them off. And you don't even see the shells on the beach that we were finding last year. But the people remain the same

We're going out to dinner so I'll have to get ready & will write you tomorrow or Friday.

We miss you much & send Love & Peace and Remembrances—
Mom and Dad

Saturday September 13

My dear Dail,

Just bid adieu to Lucy and we hated to see her go. I think she had a good time, at least I hope so, although there are many times I know she is utterly confused by all the loudness and confusion. Even our dogs take on these characteristics and add to the bedlam. This puppy will not go into the ocean unless pushed but she will sit on the rubber rafts waiting to be rowed around. This she loves.

I had lift a special delivery envelope with Eloise to mail any of your letters that might arrive home while we were gone & right after Lucy left I received a letter from you. You sounded so bitter and depressed and, perhaps I'm wrong, I can't help but think that knowing Lucy and all of us were down here probably gets to you. I know it has been a pall on my mood. In fact, I was against sending any pictures—but Dad couldn't see this. He'd have been snapping the shutter day and nite. I do think the picture of Bob, Linda & Lucy was especially good. Just cherish them, my dear, and look ahead.

You know in many ways the periods of mental depression you are having are closely akin to what many people who are getting old—are going through. But instead of wondering "What's it all about "—(in re Vietnaam), they look back on a whole lifetime & ponder the same question. Please, please don't be too bitter. Part of your personality & dearness to me (and others) was your enthusiasm and enthrallment in everything and anything. Sometimes this bothered me when you would go off on tangents, but rather this than a stoic embittered attitude of disillusionment.

Dennis bothers me so much in this respect. At 20 he seems so caustic about everything, and I feel personally responsible in some ways. Your father too has changed and you'll probably be more aware than any of us, having been away for a year. It becomes so noticeable on a vacation when he cannot relax one minute. I don't mean sleep—because this is all he does—but just relax and enjoy his family for just a short period without looking at them and thinking—"well, Denny's going to cost me about $4000 this year & next, and Linda the same, and then I've got income tax to pay and then I must mail a check tomorrow to pay salaries and on and on." It's so sad and then I see him also becoming a typical old Mullins with no ability to show or allow anyone to see emotion. And, of course, his hearing is so bad and he refuses to do a thing about it.

Funny thing he encouraged Basil to go see Dr. Tindall, the ear specialist and of course, this just made your father more dogmatic in diagnosing this impairment—as Tindall told Base there was nothing he could do as most of it was caused by the noise in the factory & he should just wear ear plugs. To your Dad this means his hi-speed equipment & how could he wear ear plugs in his office.

So being home isn't Paradise—just the same old '76.

I'm ready to sell the house, cars, & and take the kids out of school—if it would mean one smile out of him. And, of course, your being in Viet Naam just adds to the list of insurmountable problems he has.

This isn't just us—I hear it from so many. The Skillings, Sieberts, Bells etc etc, and all you can think of is "How sad, how horribly sad." This is why prolonging and experimenting on extension of life seems so utterly ridiculous to me and why I have such loving nostalgia thinking of my parents who bowed out of this picture fast and young & remained interested and interesting. I find I so enjoy being with Denny & Bob & Linda & Lucy so much more than my peers and I truly am trying so hard to understand the thinking of the young. I'll never entirely, as certain patterns cannot be erased. The utter disregard of discipline (and by this I am referring to all aspects—discipline with sex, family, fellow man, etc.) bothers me and I cannot see anything but complete chaos when everyone keeps saying "Do your own thing." Have you ever thought how different your life would have been if your Dad & I had practiced this? Remember how you always say one of the most upsetting moments in your life was one time when you were little and I walked out the front door & you all thought I'd left. If I had done "my own thing" that nite—I probably wouldn't have come back. This is discipline and I knew I had to walk back in and do what I had committed myself to—even tho I might have done it wrong.

Didn't mean to sermonize and as Lucy said "You write like you talk." But I really feel your present predicament with my soul today—because you are part of it and I pray & pray this won't scar you too much.

You are loved & missed & thought about constantly and don't you ever forget it.

This is way out—but what can we start accumulating for Xmas? I'd like to remember some of your buddies but all I know is Barksdale & Doc. Give me a list of those you'd like me to remember.

Peace & Love—
Mom & Dad

Lucy is trying to get her parents to take a trip West and I hope & have asked them to spend a few days with us. Told Lucy I'd take her Dad to the Brathaus to hear Dixieland Jazz and drink beer. She said "That's really an incentive".

SP/4 Dail W. Mullins, Jr.
488-48-0511
CoA, 26th ENGR. BN.
APO SF, 96374
2ND PLATOON

27 September 1969

Dear Mom and Dad,

Well, I guess you're both wondering what in the world happened to me—well, nothing, except that our deadline here at Hawk Hill is rapidly approaching and they're pushing us pretty hard. For example, our platoon (21 men) just completed building another five 20' x 32' living bunkers in six days—tomorrow we start again on four more! To tell you the truth, I've just been so tired at the end of the day that I haven't felt like writing anybody. That's terrible, I know, and, although I have somehow managed to keep up my letters to Lucy, I'm afraid you folks have been neglected for several days.

You'll be happy to hear that Hawk Hill has, for several weeks, been free of Charlie's harassment (knock on wood). Every once in awhile we get the word from intelligence that we're supposed to get hit, but we never do.

I told myself that when I wrote this letter I would have the last one I received from you before me so that I might refer to it—unfortunately that particular letter is now tucked somewhere down among the miles of my other mail, and it would take me the rest of my tour to find it. I do remember, though, that reference was made to my apparent growing discontent and bitterness with this war, the army and my country. I believe you expressed the opinion that this viewpoint of mine was causing you no little anguish, since you had always thought my attitude about things to be more vibrant, more tolerant and more "young at heart", if you will. Well, I hardly think things are quite that serious—at least I hope not. I should hate to think that this, my own personal war experience, had done so much to alter my basic character. Certainly it will effect changes in my thinking—if a single book can do it to some people, then you wouldn't expect a year in a combat zone to have any less of an effect. My interests in just about everything have remained the same, and in many cases, may have even grown somewhat. There is a saying in Vietnam that you really don't love and appreciate life until you have had to fight for it—this is true in many ways. Nevertheless, while I hate to say I have lost considerable respect for my country, I will say that my attitude toward her has been made considerably more objective. I am now, and probably will be until I die, very suspicious of patriotism and patriotic people. Patriotism, as Thomas Jefferson said, is the last refuge of a coward. If I had to sum up my feelings about America and her self-appointed role as world policeman. I would refer you to something that Jean Paul Sartre, the great French existentialist, once said, namely, that "I wish I could love justice and still love my country."

Oh, by the way; we have been told to inform our families back home that there has been a rash of crank calls to people back in the States who have relatives serving in Vietnam to the effect that such and such relative has been killed, captured, etc. Should by some slim chance, heaven forbid, you ever receive such a call, ignore its content and report it to the police. Be advised that the Department of the Army always notifies relatives of someone who has suffered such a misfortune by personal representative (usually an officer) or by a U.S. Army telegram.

Well, not the most "newsy" letter you've ever received, but at least you know now that your son is alive and well somewhere in Vietnam. Keep writing, your faithfulness is a tremendous help—take care of yourself, and give peace a chance.

Love,
Dail

SP/4 Dail W. Mullins, Jr.
488-48-0511
CoA, 26th ENGR. BN.
APO SF, 96374

30 September

Dear Mom and Dad,

Yesterday we finished building living quarters for the MP detachment here at Hawk Hill, and while we were over in their company area I had a chance to go to church a few times, since the chapel is situated just adjacent to their POW compound (that certainly says something about religion in the military doesn't it?) Anyway, every time a chaplin began a service he had to come out and ask us to quit hammering and turn off our chain saws—so, instead of just sitting out in the hot sun, we all decided to attend church. In this way I managed to avoid two hours of work and attend both the Protestant and Catholic services, something I don't even do back in the world.

Anyway, as I was leaving the little chapel after the second service I happened to notice a Catholic religious publication lying on the literature table near the rear of place. What caught my eye was the title of an article in the magazine entitled "The Joys of War". I asked the priest if I might borrow the magazine over the weekend, but he told me to go ahead and keep it, saying that he had plenty. Later that evening, while browsing through the thing, I came across another article of great interest entitled "The Old and the Young—Two Different Worlds?" Both this article and the one on "The Joys of War" were excellent, and if I had extra copies I'd send them to you. I may yet.

I remember in one of your more recent letters that you said something to the effect that you were interested in the youth of today, in their interests and opinions, but that the so-called generation gap prevented you from completely agreeing with all of their ways, particularly as regards sexual and racial matters. This was one of the reasons why I read the article about the generation gap.

Rather than attempt to paraphrase the article, which is rather long, I thought I'd just quote a few of the more interesting passages for your enjoyment and edification.

"The problem that the words 'Generation Gap' describes is as old as the human race. It is a breakdown in communications between parent and offspring. It is youth refusing to see eye to eye with their elders, shocking them, trying to change the world. It is the new generation rebelling against the old traditions, rejecting timeworn values and institutions, forcing change upon the times."

"Ten years ago American adults were complaining about the apathetic, do-nothing crop of college kids. Today they are saying college kids are doing too much."

"Youth has always revolted; but the reason for our concern with the present rebellion is its extent and leadership."

"Admittedly the vocal ones are few. The mass of kids still give 'correct answers'. But they're involved; there's not a kid on any campus who's indifferent, for instance, to the sexual revolution. Whether they approve or not, they're caught up in it."

"Evidence seems to show that a glacier of tradition is breaking up. All the old sureties, organized religion, family life, patriotism, God, mother, country seem to be losing their force. And these enormous historical rifts come at a time that coincides with the coming-of-age of half the nation's population. The median age in the United States is now 26."

"Today's revolution is led by the highly intelligent, highly motivated kids. This wasn't true before."

"This may be the first time a sensitive younger generation has risen above the survival struggle and has had the guts to tell their elders: 'We don't want your world'".

"Kids see their elders preaching hollow words, extolling honesty but cheating on their income tax, talking about 'causes' and 'allegiance' to high principles yet 'selling out' when faced with the choice between idealism and self-interest."

"Asked by a research sociologist during a peace demonstration how his parents felt about the anti-war movement, one young man said: 'my parents are for the same ideas but against doing anything about them.'"

"Today many young people are turning their backs on capitalism's goods, competition and consumption. Competition, the rat race, the scramble for money and prestige, brutalizes humans, they say."

"And many don't buy the puritan ethic idea that pain is better for you than pleasure, that work is virtue and leisure sin."

"Parents who struggled, scrimped, fought, and sacrificed for their children now find these 'ungrateful' recipients condemning everything they valued. Parents are hurt, baffled, angry. Yet, ironically, parents' struggles made the changes that now influence their offspring. The machines, products, knowledge and technology that their labors produced have brought on the Generation Gap by shaping a new breed."

"The generation that has never known depression feels little compunction to save or put off for tomorrow what can be had today. In 1970 teens will spend $30,000,000,000. The generation that has had everything by age 15 sets out on an early search for new challenges."

"Bridging the Generation Gap requires that both sides understand both the society-wide upheaval and the dynamics of adolescence. Despite thousands of years of experience, most adults still don't seem to understand what growing up is all about."

Well, enough is enough—I'm afraid if I went on I'd bore you. As you can see, the article is an excellent one, as was 'The Joys of War'. Incidentally, the magazine in question is called the "U.S. Catholic and Jubilee", just in case you want to check it out at the library.

Well, Barksdale and I leave for Danang tomorrow morning for our 3 day in-country R&R. We sure are looking forward to the rest. I'll try and get off a few letters to you while I'm gone, and, of course, try to make that phone call.

Take care, all, keep writing and, of course, think peace.

Love,
Dail

Sept. 16,

My dear Son,

Well, we arrived in Decatur and the kids will register and Dad will "plunk" out $23.00 & we will head home. At this point I feel I've been a nomad for months. Dad doesn't have any appointments until next Monday, but he sent in in his $1500 quarterly donation to the Pentagon the 15th, and $200 to Governor Hearnes, and tuition, plus the motels etc.—so we'll live on beans until we recuperate—then it will be time for the next donation. We sometimes get discouraged when we find we are on a sort of treadmill, just keeping our heads above water; and at our age this gets a little frightening.

We've tried to get thru to Denny & Linda that they must knuckle down and get the credits needed to graduate—as we are really looking ahead to the point where we can start saving some money again. Linda says she cannot graduate with one more year—so we are going to check into this. She might have to earn her credits "piece meal" at a state extension University.

Before I forget again,]. Dad had one of his patients, about a month ago, ask about you. For some reason, a lot of people back here think you poor weary souls are constantly getting chances to go to exotic and far out places it's rather difficult to explain that you spend all your time in bunkers & rice paddies. Anyway, these patients lived in Bangkok for three years. Their names are Mr. & Mrs. Young & he is with the Sverdrup & Parcel Consulting Engineers firm, and if by some fluke you get to Bangkok they insist you look up an importer there who has a large store and is very well known. His name is Johnny Gems (for real) and you tell him they sent you supposedly he will really show you around. Well, I've passed on this message. If you could hear some o on his head f the requests we get to tell you.

Don't know whether Lucy mentioned, but Denny and Bob both decided to buy a hair preparation which, when squirted on your hair, under the sun turned it blonde. Well Denny's isn't too bad—he's what I'd call a honey blonde right now. Bob's hair actually turned Orange. So Linda had to go with him and get a dye & dye his hair. Wish I'd been able to get a picture of him with this goop on his head with a plastic cap over it, sitting for 45 minutes while it took. I developed a rash from the sun, and Dennis has blisters on top of blisters. The only ones not affected were Lucy, Linda and of course Dad, and he spent so much time inside he's been bored to tears. This is when not liking to read can really be sad.

Well, word has been coming thru about the new pull out of 40,000 more troops and our ears prick up—but from what we can gather most of these troops will be from around Saigon. Why in the he—can't they train the U.N. to protect their area around the DM zone, instead of the Pretty Boy's City. I wish someone would plant a hand grenade right on top of Thieu. We got rid of Ho Chi, now let's get the other side & maybe something will happen.

Dad & I drove over to Huntsville today & this is our first visit to the area. It's fantastic when you read before 1960 it had 17,000 people & now (or in 1964) had 150,000. Didn't you visit someone there? One thing we had wanted was some liquor. You should have seen & heard your father following various directions to find a state liquor store. Everyone & everybody was a horse's ass and he was about to go to someone & tell them what he thought of the whole set up—but he didn't know where to start.

Well it seems like Dad & Linda might be off again. He wants her to give up the representation of Denny's frat & a few other things & she refuses because her goals are still fun-fun-fun. Don't know if I'm sorry as spending the last 3 weeks with him makes me so glad they called off their serious plans. He's a nice boy— but in many ways he's as young as Linda. The only thing that bugs me is the financial cost to your father in finding out if her swains are going to be taken seriously. It gets a little expensive finding & rooming these characters so this is it—no more vacations where she invites all her friends.

Well, I'll be most anxious to get home to see if we have any news from you and we hope everything has been as well as could be in that hell hole. Those 2 larger colored pictures of you Lucy wanted and if I would have been generous I'd have given them to her; but I did say I'd have 2 larger ones made. One of these is the picture where if we look closely we can see the American Flag in your eyes—

Take care my dear and keep your spirits up & think Peace

Much much love—
Mom & Dad

P/4 Dail W. Mullins, Jr.
488-48-0511
CoA, 26th ENGR. BN.
APO SF, 96374

4 October 1969

Dear Mom and Dad,

Again, you'll have to excuse this atrocious paper, but it's all that is available at the moment.

You remember I told you several days ago that Barksdale and I had been granted a three day in-country R&R to Danang over October 2-5—well, that's where we are now, although at times I would have been willing to bet that we weren't going to make it!

On the morning of the second we were to get up at 6:30 and catch the morning recon chopper to Chu Lai, and then on to Danang by plane. Well, as luck would have it, it was raining cats and dogs that morning and the chopper, we were informed, wouldn't be coming in. So, rather than waste a day of our R&R and catch a chopper the following morning, we chose to ride convoy down, in the rain, with no cover. Needless to say, both of us were quite wet upon arrival in Chu Lai.

After drying out for a few hours at the Chu Lai USO, Barksdale and I then hitchhiked down to the air terminal and waited for a standby flight to Danang. Surprisingly enough, we managed to get one within an hour and a half—on a Marine corvair parachute assault plane! That was an interesting trip.

We landed in Danang at around 5:00 PM, and by the time we got our bearings, found a bus and made it to the R&R center it was too late to check in! Where to sleep? Fortunately, we made friends with this Navy post taxi driver (nice job) who, obviously a good Samaritan at heart, sneaked us a bed at Camp Tien Shan, the Navy's main barracks center here in Danang. We spent a pleasant night talking with some Navy personnel, getting their views of the war and giving them ours. Quite a contrast. The next morning we took the bus to the China Beach USO here, then to the PX, and finally back to the R&R center, where we were allowed to register this time.

Danang is quite a place. The extent of the military involvement in Southeast Asia can best be seen in a place like this, I think. Danang, believe it or not, reminds me a lot of Birmingham, Alabama—not, of course, because of the people or buildings, but rather because of the way its vastness seems to nestle in among the surrounding mountains—Marble Mountain, Freedom Hill, Monkey Mountain. At night, when the lights from the barracks, radar installations and bunkers spread all over the mountains are twinkling, you couldn't recognize it from any of a dozen Appalacian towns. But then you see a flare, a helicopter gunship pulling out or hear the distant thump! of artillery falling, and you remember.

The eastern perimeter of Danang, like Chu Lai's, is bordered by the beautiful South China Sea, blue as an emerald when its sunny, but gray and sinister-looking during this, the monsoon.

By the time you get this letter, of course, we will both be back at Hawk Hill, beginning the long stretch to December and R&R in Hawaii with Lucy. You might be interested to know that, as of this morning, I have 217 days left over here. In 10 days, I shall pass the 5 month mark. In some ways the time has gone remarkably fast—in other ways, though, the ways that count, it has gone unbearingly slow. It still seems like an eternity until May.

I got a kick out of a comment you made in your last letter to the effect that some of your friends thought it just wonderful that I had this opportunity to see such exciting and mysterious parts of the world. Do these people really, seriously believe that Vietnam is a pleasure excursion? Jeez! Granted, a 7 day leave in Hawaii with Lucy won't exactly be hell, but when it's over I'll have 5 more months of living underground and dodging mortars. Fun? Hardly.

Well, keep your chin up in front of these flag-wavers and let them keep thinking what they will. I'll straighten them out with some slides and pictures when I get home. Ken Meacham will love the picture I have of a "dirty communist's gook's" legs hanging from a piece of barbed wire—they couldn't find the rest of him.

Take care, keep writing and keep me posted on the news from back home.

Love,
Dail

[No Envelope]

5 October 1969

Dear Mom and Dad,
    Came across this map in one of the service papers here—thought you'd like it.
    On the large colored map I have pinpointed some of the LZ's that you have heard me talk about—LZ's Baldy, Ross and Hawk Hill. Look way up by the DMZ and you will see the Rockpile, where Wayne Bill is stationed.
    Well, just thought you'd like this. Take care and I'll write again soon.

Love,
Dail

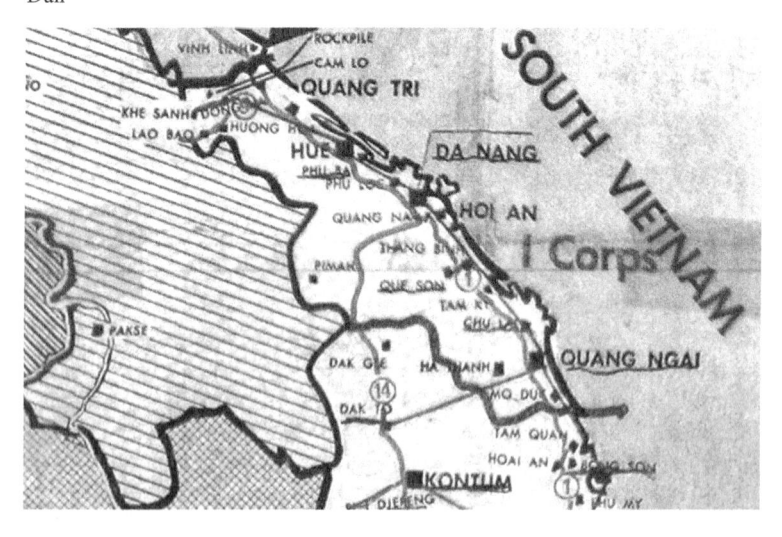

Sept 21, 1969

My dear Son,
    Well, we arrived home safely. Came via Nashville and thought of calling Ray Wintkert but knew he'd be in class. Lucy was saying how well he's doing and I'm so glad he seems to have found himself, altho I'm wondering if we need any more psychologists.
    Felt so relieved when we arrived home and had a note from Lucy stating she'd had a good & safe trip home. She mentioned Dan's arrival home and his little Mexican girl friend and her mother's concern over it all. Guess she should just thank heaven he didn't spend the summer in Nigeria & acquired one of their natives.

Talked to Judy Colbert and she was telling me that Bill Colbert has orders for Vietnaam for Nov. 1. He should have graduated but they felt he was lacking in leadership ability & sent him back for 6 weeks further training. He plans to then drop his commission. Judy thinks he's under the miscomprehension that this well countermand the Viet naam orders.

Claire Veith, one of my bridge friends, has a daughter married to a medical student & he has just received his orders for Vietnaam. All these orders make you wonder what the pull out is all about.

Saw Winnie Bill in church this morning and what empathy we now have. Wayne is on what is called the "Rockpile" and they & his wife have only received 1 letter since he arrived in V.N. & they are so concerned. This stupid damn war is doing such horrible things to all people.

Spent last nite with the Meachams and he's still the same old WASP. One half the evening was spent bemoaning the sons of prominent & influential business men who are patients of his. They are coming into his office with hair to their waists, beards, and the gold rimmed eye glasses. Now it has become just funny to me watching & listening to him stutter & turn red, white and blue.

It was also amusing at church this morning to listen to the changed views about Dr. Nickle's full beard. The first Sunday it was a condescending point of view, excusing his facial adornment as a temporary lapse. Now that he still has it, more bushy than ever, the comments are changing.

Well so much for the pithy views.

Saw a television show with Woody Allen last nite & this guy is such a character. He is in the process of divorcing his wife and he mentioned that he ran into her at a dinner party the other nite and being a civilized human being asked her if she wouldn't like to make love for old times sake. She just looked at him and said "Over my dead body." And he said—"O that's always the way it was when we were living together."

Have you heard anymore about moving out to Japan? Oh how I pray something will evolve out of this rumour. Did you ever get my last package with sausage and Superman comics?

I'm finding it difficult to get back into the routine of house work, but I must get busy & get things in order for the Wicks & Lees visit. Since I arrived home I've spent most of my time shaking sand out of everything we own.

Well must drop a short line to Linda & Dennis and take care, God speed & you are always in our thoughts,

Love and Peace
Mom & Dad

———————

9/23

My dear,

Well, how glad I was to receive a letter from you today! This was your letter in which you mentioned you had gotten Lucy & my notes from our trip enroute to Florida. It always surprises me when you mention receiving something that seems to have occurred eons ago. Of course, this too adds to my apprehension—wondering what has happened between the date of your letter and the date I receive it which brings up something I've wanted to find out! How many days does it take you to get our letters? Sometimes yours arrive in 4 days and then it could be 8 or 9.

Had a letter from the Wicks when we got home telling us that they could make it the week-end the Lees would be here so you know how I am. Today I have been sewing like mad to make new slip covers for my family room and I feel the bed rooms they will have should be spotless so I'm busy. And the yard demands so much attention at this time. I really want to get some paying job, but I'm always doing something around this house. Of course, I'm not too stupid to realize that I invent these chores to keep me from doing something more lucrative. I was born 50 years too late, as I am very content being a housewife when I should be out helping to earn some money. It's really too much now-a-days for one person to earn the living for a family.

Had (or went) to my bridge club last nite and I picked up Winnie Bill. When I drove her home we sat in front of her house talking for about an hour. She was always one of my favorite people but now that we have Wayne and you in common—I feel she's more terrific. We both spent a good part of the time talking about the wonderful girls our sons were married to and how sad it was you both had to be apart. Wayne's wife, named Betty, is so loved by Winnie, but who wouldn't love a mother-in-law like Winnie

Haven't heard from the kids since we got back but know we will as soon as they need money. Caustic, but true.

Funny what money does. Your grandmother is quite alert & on the ball since she found out she might have a 10% increase in social security. It gives her an impetus. Do you know, she still doesn't realize you are in Viet Naam. Isn't this sad & sickening. God forbid!

You don't know how I'm praying & hoping for your R&R and how I wish I could write Lucy & tell her "I'll pay for it." This is all I've ever wanted money for and when I think of how easily your grandmother could do this, I just want less to do with her.

Sending some clippings you might enjoy.

Take care, we love you & we miss you so much!

Peace
Mom & Dad

September 26,

My dear Dail,
    Well now that my letter writing has increased again I felt I had better get the old typewriter fixed so I could really turn out the words. It seems to take me forever when I hand write. Typing lets me flow along. In fact, Lucy mentioned that my letters were just like my talking—now I don't know if that is a compliment or a tongue in cheek remark.

    Yesterday was Dad and my 29th anniversary and when you have lived together that many years you just take it in your stride and celebrate casually. We went out for dinner and then to bed by 9:30 (and believe me not for sex, but just because we were tired). Alas! and also Alack—and that can be two words. Dad gave me an electric wristwatch—which he really shouldn't have, because we are really strapped for money right now. But I know I would hurt his feelings if I took it back.

    Had a letter from Linda and she seems adjusted and very pleased with her schedule and all her professors. She is pretty busy right now being the Sweetheart of Denny's fraternity during all the rush events—but this she likes. Evidently she and Bob see very little of each other and he is rushing some gal off her feet. Glad this all worked out, but it gets rather expensive for us boarding and rooming all her friends until she makes up her mind. A dentist has built a very attractive office right across from the campus and she is contacting him to see about the possibility of working for him Saturdays and during his evening hours. This would be good as it would give her some extra money, but I don't want her to take on too much. I just keep thinking of the old adage "give it to the busy man and he'll get it done."

    She tells me Denny is the talk of the campus. They evidently had a dance the first week of school as a sort of get together. They had Poo Nanny and the Stormers (never heard of them). The Stormers are four Negro girls. Well, guess who got up on the stage to dance with all these "chocolate" drops. That's right = Denny. I sure hope the repercussions aren't bad.

    Talking about schools and trouble. Did I tell you that Dot and Bob had gotten a letter from the school which young Bob had gone to, telling them that while he was an excellent student they felt he would be happier at another school. You must keep in mind this is a Methodist college of about 500 students and is completely dominated by a Dr. Horton who is chairman of the board and also owns the whole town. Bob had been doing so well and had become very active on the paper—in fact, he was asked to be editor; so this came as a complete surprise. Well, I finally heard from Aunt Dot and I am going to quote verbatim. It's long, but I think you will get a kick out of some of the things going on in the "World."

Quoting—

"Now, back at "Good Ole' Lindsey-Wilson" and it's outsdtanding student— Bob Paschen. Feeling we had nothing to lose and also that we were due and had the right to a more explicit explanation than we had received from the Administration's decision that Bobby would be happier elsewhere, we contacted them and set up a hearing before the so called "Administrative Board." Found out that in talking to a few of the individual members before the meeting—they knew nothing about the fact that we had been so notified or why. Evidently this was done by Dr. Horton and Mr. Gaddy—(the boy's housemother(?)) alone. We were not present at the conference = just Bobby—which was alright, but as I told Bob—if the decision was against him I was going to find out why and have the opportunity to speak my piece one way or the other. I told young Bob before he went in to be polite, use his head a little but not to crawl for any of them. This would make it miserable for any future at this school.

After about an hour he came out to get us and told us before we went in that their decision had been reversed. When we got seated Dr. Horton proceeded to tell us that he thought things had been straightened out to every one's satisfaction. He was sure Bob understood their view point better and that they now understood him a lot better. Of course, in my opinion this should have been done before all the fuss instead of after, but I was diplomatic.

Now the reasons for this mess: basing everything on the posters he drew for the other students who asked him to, they were typical psychadelic posters with Love and Peace themes. Dr. Horton and Mr. Gaddy arrived at the conclusion that—hold onto your seat—Bob was planted on the campus by the S.D.S. to organize the students. They were sure he was the instigator of the protest march, such as it was, and that the peace symbol is the sign for an internationals students protest groups for the violent overthrow of colleges as they are set up today. This is the kid who just finished a mural—psychedelic—on the M.Y.F. room at the Middletown Methodist Church—and is also considered the biggest square in the world by his sister's friends because he can't stand to see a bug hurt, much less people. How off-base can you be.

The painting of the Water Tower was also mentioned. On this point I agreed that it should not have been done—mainly, because the fool tower is at least 160 feet hight and is reached by climbing up a two foot wide ladder and the platform around it is to say the least, ver-r-ry narrow. If he had stepped back to admire his work things would really have happened. He painted this about 3 A.M. one morning when his allergy kept him from sleeping. In other words, it was a stupid thing to do from my point of view for his safety, as well as anything else.

Dr. Horton and Gaddy again were really off base in the meaning they put on this. Bobby had painted the background of the tower white and then had the word KISS printed in large Black letters on it. He had intended to paint some lips in red next to the word kiss, but had to come down for more paint and in the meantime the sun came up and he didn't want to be seen so he was unable to finish it. Gaddy and Horton arrived at the conclusion that the finished product was to be a nasty remark directed at the school. This really threw Bobby. He didn't even realize what they were talking about and when it finally dawned on him, I think he came closer to walking out than he had at any time during the whole meeting. As he said—for being such supposedly pious Christians they sure had dirty minds. I really think the two of them were finally embarrassed."

Shades of Southwestern! The sad thing is that they either leave him in an institution like this or the damn Army gets him. As Dot said, he made this whole mess when he didn't apply himself at the University of Louisville, and now he's got to put up with this crap until his grades prove he can transfer to another school. This is really, more or less, what happened to Denny. He says he hates it down there, but that it is too late to transfer now as they wouldn't accept all his credits and it would probably mean longer than fours years and Dad and I are really getting tired of tuitions. We have to call quits to it someday.

This seems to be the time of the year when so many things need taking care of. Worked in the yard all day yesterday (with the help of little Trent next door) and I really ached in every muscle. Of course, age doesn't help. And then almost every room in this house needs painting. If I didn't think Dad would really be miserable, I'd sure force the idea of an apartment. I can't possibly get a job and keep up this house. We are not allowed to burn leaves any more and Webster has purchased some kind of suction machine and we all rake our leaves into the street and they take certain areas for the month of October. Can't you see Berry Road filled with tons of leaves. Wait until no cars can get by. They really pushed this anti-pollution measure through full force but haven't given one thought to birth control.

Speaking of birth—we have a nice little scandal in Kirkwood. Some emminent Internist—Dr. Burnside, performed an abortion and she is quite ill. All his altruistic reasons don't quite come across, when she said he charged her $350 and a diamond ring that she was wearing. It's the ring bit that sort of gets you.

Well it's late and must get to bed. We are going out to dinner tomorrow night with the Reinhardts.

Listened to Nixon's speech this morning and all I want to do is put my foot through the TV screen. The same old foot deep crap—excuse my language.

Be of good cheer, we miss you so much and think of you always and let us hear.
Mom & Dad

Thursday, October 2,

My dear Dail,

Well we received your letter from Chu Lai and A Navy Marine Corp Mars Radio Message from someone in Waukegan, Illinois (which, by the way, scared the pants off me) and as a result we are about to become nervous wrecks. I, of course, don't want to leave the house and your father just keeps telling me "don't be ridiculous".

Called Lucy Tuesday night and we spent 10 minutes figuring when it was October 2 to October 5th in DaNang, what the time and date would be over here. Think we finally got it pretty well straightened out. She is fine and working hard and it was good to talk to her. She was telling me about Dan's little Mexican girl friend and Mrs. Bartges has reached the stage where she goes around saying "Well, one good thing, she isn't catholic". This is on a par with her being so glad you are light skinned.

Went to a bridge luncheon at Mrs. DuBois today and even with Terry being in the service they are still having their problems. He borrowed his father's staff car and completely demolished it. He had been transferred from Langley to Scot Air Force Base. The night he wrecked the car he and four other fellows decided to drive to Champagne, Illinois. The Army insurance will not handle it as he was not on official business and their private insurance won't fool with it, because he is in the service. The car is the least of the problems, as two of the boys with him needed orthopedic specialists and one extensive plastic surgery. As Ruth said, the only thing good about it was that Terry's outfit was shipped to Viet Naam while he was in the hospital—and she doesn't know if that is good or not at this point.

Dad is at Grandmas tonite and it is really sad to see how he dreads going. He went over about a week ago and he said it was like walking into a cage of tigers. He keeps telling me how I must have patience with people who have mental problems (referring to Linda), but he has not one ounce of patience with his mother and if she isn't a mental case I don't know what is.

Speaking of Linda, received a letter from her today which upset me a little. Finished a letter to her before I started typing this to you, but don't know if I'll mail it. Might try putting through a telephone call. She just can't seem to make up her mind about Bob. When he issues the ultimatum that it is him or nothing she wants no part of this. But then when he starts dating all these different girls at school it makes her furious and very depressed, even tho she is turning down seven dates for one night. Now what the hell do you do about someone like this. Dad just keeps saying "Patience, you must have patience—I know what she is going through", and all I want to say is "For God's sake, quit acting like a spoiled brat". I know the other night in talking to Lucy she thinks Bob is entirely in the right and much too good for Linda. She and Bob seem to hit it off, which surprises me as I really always felt, with all his good points, he was a light weight in the brain department. And I really feel that in many ways he has as much growing up to do as Linda.

While I'm writing this Dean Martin's program is on and he has Bob Newhart as a guest and those two are nuts. In one of their little vignettes a girl goes to her doctor and wanted to know what was in the birth control pills he had given her. He said he was doing some experimenting and had combined hormones with mexican jumping beans and then asked her why she wanted to know, and she said—because I just had a bouncing baby boy.

Well this is rather a typical civilian letter but I really am so thinking about the possibility you might get through to talk to us, that I am really not making much sense.

It looks like there might be a few men in our country who are going to force Nixon to put up or shut up on his Viet Naam policy and the sooner the better as far as I'm concerned. Were you surprised regarding the Green Beret decision? I frankly wasn't and had mentioned some time ago to old Meacham, that they wouldn't dare bring them to trial.

Well take care of yourself and along with all the other prayers I'm saying for you I have added one that your R and R will work out exactly as you want it.

With all our love,

P.S. Dad just walked in and the grown up thing to do would be just to ignore the latest, but to me, it's rather hilarious along with being sad. You know Grandma keeps harping on two facts—one, that I was going to put her in a home and two—that I told her to go to Hell one day when she called here. She just keeps repeating these two things over and over to your Dad. Last night she wanted him to set up an appointment at the police station for me to take a Lie Detector test. I had just about reached the point where I was going over on my own and visit her and something like this comes up and I just think "how useless". I guess this is the aging of certain people. Mrs. DuBois was telling about the problems they are having with General DuBois' mother. She called him about two weeks ago at midnite to tell him that she wanted him to go to the cemetery where his father was buried and purchase a third grave lot. She knows she is going to be buried with him but she wants the grave next to her to remain empty because their could be the possibility that some man would be interred there and she didn't want him reaching across and patting her knee. Isn't this sad!

Take care, with all the kooks in the world we desperately need you young people.

Love,
Mom & Dad

SP/4 Dail W. Mullins, Jr.
488-48-0511
CoA, 26th ENGR. BN.
APO SF, 96374
2ND PLATOON

7 October 1969

Dear Mom and Dad,

Well, Barksdale and I made it back from Danang yesterday, safe and sound, but we're still stranded in Chu Lai, unable to get back up to Hawk Hill. Actually we left Danang on the 5th, but the plane's landing gear wouldn't go up, so the pilot turned back—as I said to him, I'm glad it stuck in the "down" position, rather than in the "up". Well, there were no more flights scheduled for Chu Lai that day, so we had to wait until the next morning—the 6th. That night the monsoon really hit hard, and it was still raining cats and dogs when we left Danang airport the next day. We made it, though; and then hitchhiked up to the USO (naturally!) to dry off and get a cup of their free coffee—our first of the day. Last night, then, we stayed in the transit hooch at the 26th Engineer's headquarters, in the hopes of then catching a chopper or a convoy back to Hawk Hill today. Well, the monsoon kept up in full force, washing out a bridge on highway one and grounding all choppers. So, we're going to have to stay here in Chu Lai another night—this, in itself, is not so bad; we are both, however, a little on the dirty side, not having changed clothes for about 5 days. We're scheduled to leave tomorrow morning at 7:00 on the recon chopper, but if it's grounded or already full, I guess we'll have to stay still another night down here.

We had a pretty good time up in Danang—nothing special, just sleeping, reading, writing and doing a little sightseeing. As you already know, we weren't able to make the phone calls that we had wanted to make. Personnel are restricted to the in-country R&R center there until 6:00 AM, and by that time the line at the stateside telephone facility is already 6 blocks long. I guess I'll just have to settle on talking to you by MARS radio-telephone. I think I can do that from Hawk Hill.

By the way—I believe I wrote and asked you all, not too long ago, to go ahead and send me a watch. Well, I hope you haven't already done that, because I managed to pick up a nice Omega watch at the big PX in Danang. If you were planning on sending me one for Christmas, I'm afraid you'll have to think of something else.

That reminds me—you asked me to give you some suggestions about what to send me for Christmas. Well, fortunately (or unfortunately, as the case may be), Uncle Sam provides me with just about everything I really need (not want, but need). Really, it's not necessary to go to all that bother. If you really want to send me something, though, you might try and find a used pair of rubber hip boots for me—about a size 13 (so they'll fit over my combat boots). You know, the kind that come up to your knees or higher. If you go to an army surplus store, ask for Navy assault boots—those are the kind that, when you roll the tops down look like the kind of boots Errol Flynn wore as Captain Blood. I'm not getting them to look like either Errol Flynn or Captain Blood, but just to keep my feet dry in this damnable rain.

Rain, rain, rain—I've never seen so much. And just 2 weeks ago it was like the Sahara desert around here. What I've seen of Vietnam, it would serve the VC right if we did pull out and give it to them!

Well, that's about all the news I have right now, folks. Nothing much, as you can see. How is everything back home—I'm anxious to get back to H.H. and see how much mail I have waiting—a letter from you all, I hope. Take care, keep me informed, and don't worry about me—

I'm doing OK. ☮ and love,
Dail

P.S. Confucius say, "Child conceived in back seat of car with automatic transmission grow up to be shiftless bastard!" That's to get you back for the last joke you sent me!

October 8

My dear soldier,

It doesn't quite make sense to be answering your letter written just before you left for Da Nang, and know that it, your brief leave, is over and you are back in the bunkers. We were disappointed, as I'm sure you were, that no telephone contact was made. I really pray that you got through to Lucy.

Frankly, I was pleased to hear that you had been attending church services. In fact, this past Sunday was World Wide Communion and the young minister for college students, who has been filling in at Southwebster, mentioned the fact that this partaking of communion was being done in every corner of the world and specifically mentioned Viet Naam, which he felt should make parents of young men over there close to them at this moment. And it is true, there are fleeting moments such as this when you almost feel a physical nearness—at least I do. Course it could be my emotional mind taking over my common sense, but then once in a while we have to have this sense of meta-physical.

Went to dinner last night with the Meachams and they came back here and, as it seems to happen lately everytime we are with them, wound up in a big fat argument. Dad read your letter to Ken about the generation gap arguments which you had quoted from the catholic publication and even tho your father and Meacham think exactly alike on this and any other subject, your father took the side of the young—I think just to get Meacham stuttering. Then they got on (or we—because I'm always in the thick of these arguments while Rosemary nods her head sleepily—) what Man is doing to his World and how little time is left for him. I will say I have to agree with Meacham on this point of over-population, or as he terms it "screwing himself to death"—but now he uses another word beginning with "f". Now your father cannot see this—or as he said last nite—maybe he doesn't want to see it, because he feels that if he had a part in contributing to this completely horrendous possibility, he can't bear it and would not want to live another day—or wouldn't want any of you kids to live. In listening to them, to me, it was so obvious which one still—maybe naiively—believe in a Supreme Being and which was a complete Atheist. (Could be that word is too strong—Agnostic?)

Anyway Ken mentioned that he would love to have had you here to argue some of the points in question regarding the generation gap; (does he think we wouldn't). But in listening to all of us last night, it made me realize how very ineffectual people are who become too emotional in their arguments; which you have had a tendency to do and I have always been guilty of and of course Meacham just becomes a stuttering hulk of sheer Hysteria. This was also brought home to me recently by two events that have happened in the news media—television. A renegade priest from Milwaukee, Wisconsin named Father Groppi has been the black man's advocate for that area. Recently he made the news again when he was arrested and put in jail for instigating a march on the capitol of Wisconsin with several hundred mothers on ADC, white and black, who were rebelling against a recent cut in their funds. They interviewed him in prison and it was the most calm, powerful, heartbreaking, impassioned plea I have ever listened to in regard to help for these youngsters. I've always been a little cynical regarding mothers with all these children and not evident male sperm around, but listening to this priest's very quiet unemotional explanation of why we must be concerned for these children made more of an explosive impact than all the screaming and crying anyone could do. The very next scene on TV showed the Southern Conference for Christians, Dr. Martin Luther King's old group, meeting somewhere in South Carolina, and a young militant black speaking—really not speaking, but literally screaming and vomiting forth a tirade of words that you immediately closed your mind and ears to. What all his hodge podge of words I've just put down is trying to say is, if you believe truly in what you are saying, learn to step outside of your emotions and present your arguments calmly and quietly and you will be listened to and heard.

It really is so hard to remain calm about some of the issues today. One I am referring to is that group of Mess Seargeants that Congress has on the carpet right now. I don't know how much of this type news is allowed to filter into the bunkers of Viet Naam, but it is the nastiest piece of "Khaki Costra Nostra" (Senator Percy's words) ever brought to light. And the ramifications of it are still being brought to light. This Master Seargeant General Turner (he holds the highest rank ever given a non-commissioned man) has bilked the Army, country and young men and had a chain of command with other regular army seargeants that was fantastic. They even find out he was now visiting various police chiefs of big cities throughout the country confiscating guns and all types of ammunition and weapons, under the Army's name, and then selling them to undercover groups.

Well Dennis called us Monday night and everything seems fine down on the Alabama front. He said he didn't want me to get up tight about dancing with that black girl because she asked him. Then he said—"she was really a knockout Mom, and I just kept wishing she wasn't so black." Well, I've lived too long. Asked him how Linda was faring and he said she seemed to be doing fine and was taking over as Sweetheart of his fraternity with a will and a way. (this probably all seems so ridiculous to you.)

He mentioned that he had a good schedule lined up and felt one of the hardest subjects he was taking was going to be Religion because he didn't know Adam from Eve. This really made me feel like H--, to think a very important aspect of his growing up training, had been so very neglected.

Nell McCulloch came by and we had a real nice talk. Here again, is a perfect example of a guy who really walked out on life. His children, Dr. McCulloch's, finally had to put him in a state institution as it was ruining all their lives, financially and emotionally. They would get calls from the police at three o'clock in the morning telling them to get down and pick up their father—who had been found in some gutter. And then they were paying for a room and his clothes and food and the trouble he would get into. So they went before a Welfare Board who agreed with them heartily that they had all done more than their duty—so he was put in this state nursing home where he is fed and watched closely. In talking to Nell, you realize that a little good can sometimes come out of the service. Here third son, Bob, who graduated just after you, couldn't go on to college so he enlisted in the Navy right after hight school graduation and was trained in electronics and radar installations. He is now out and is evidently finding this training invaluable in helping hime have the kind of life he wants, that would not have been possible otherwise. He wants to travel and see everything possible in this world before he settles down so he contacts private concerns who need experts in this radar field and he signes up for short term contracts. Right now he is in England for six months with a company, before that it was somewhere in the Far East, and he is dickering with an outfit in Australia after his England job is up. You should hear Nell talk about her boyfriend. It's funny and sad, but it is good to see her having some love and pleasure after all the years of Hell she had.

She also has a new male poodle puppy which she is hinting about mating with this mop of hair running around our house, but I said emphatically NO SOAP. Never have I had anything around the house that is a complete pest. She will not leave my side for one minute—I can't even go to the bathroom alone. It really is worse than having a baby around.

Thought you would enjoy the enclosed clipping. When Jules Feiffer is at his best—he is hard to beat.

Hope you had a good R and R in DaNang and, take care write when you can and know that we are loving you and thinking PEACE.

With so much love,
Mom & Dad

P.S. Never did get your slide pictures. Should we start inquiring? Also, I am sending a box of homemade cookies and candy. Have hesitated doing this before—so let me know how they took the trip.

SP/4 Dail W. Mullins, Jr.
488-48-0511
CoA, 26th ENGR. BN.
APO SF, 96374

17 October

My dear Parents,

I'm sorry that you haven't heard from me in so long, but I just haven't felt up to writing. My finger has been hurting so at night that I haven't been able to get as much sleep as I'd like. Consequently, I'm so tired at the end of the day, it's all I can do to just and write a letter to Lucy. Last night, however, was better, and this morning my finger doesn't hurt at all—just a little stiff.

On the 14th of the month I marked my fifth month here in the Republic. No great cause for celebration, but at least it served to remind me that there is one thing the army can't do—slow down the time. The seconds, hours, days and months keep ticking by, slowly but surely.

We all anxiously awaited the arrival of the 15th and news from home on the nationwide anti-war moratorium, and were gratified to hear that it was so successful. I notice that the organizers have stated that, should this demonstration prove ineffective, they will have a second on the 15th of next month. Excellent. Several of us wore a black armband that day as a sign of support for the movement. We suffered a few cat-calls and mumbled obscenities, but nothing serious. Our first sergeant, a tatooed, hairy-armed, anthropoid-type professional killer for the United States stopped me and asked what the armband was for. When I told him that it was a silent protest against the war, you should have seen his face. He was so taken aback that he didn't know what to say. An even more amazing incident occurred out at the job site we were working at. We were working on an FDC (fire direction center) for the 3/82 artillery unit here at Hawk Hill, when the assistant commander of the LZ, a major, drove up in his jeep to check it out. He walked around, looking at our work, nodding and smiling—like brass does. After awhile he called me—why, I don' know—over and said we were doing a pretty good job. Then he lowered his voice and asked me why everybody was wearing a black armband. I told him it was in support of the anti-war demonstrations back home that day. He smiled, patted me on the shoulder and said, "Good! If I thought I wouldn't be court-martialed, I'd wear one myself!" It was my turn to be taken aback.

Did you all participate in any of the local anti-war activities, or were you just sympathetic bystanders? The tone of some of your recent letters has led me to believe that perhaps you have become less passive in your views—more willing to take an active role in such goings on. Like most citizens who feel that they are too old to join the marches, though, I imagine that you are in somewhat of a quandry as to just what you can do to express the feelings you seem to have about Vietnam, overpopulation and the generation gap. May I suggest that you both act through the most powerful medium at your disposal—your friends. Let them know how you feel—don't be afraid to "step on their toes" a little. It will do them good. The sooner people like Meacham are made aware of the fact that things aren't going to be like they were, the less painful it will be for them when the time actually comes.

Well, as they say in the military, "be advised that all is well here." I'm working hard—yes, I know, that won't hurt me—and doing little else. Thanks for the brownies, fudge and cookie crumbs. Very good. When I get to Hawaii I'm going to send you a postcard of Waikiki beach and the message, "Eat your heart out!" Take care and let me hear—

Love,
Dail

October 12

My dear boy,

Received both your letters written from DaNang and so darn glad the rest period came through for you, but we were certainly a little "up tight" about the methods of transportation you have to arrange to get away for a couple of days. Also, what happened to the possibility of a telephone call—you didn't mention this and we wondered what happened?

Had dinner with the Seiberts Friday nite and I always enjoy being with Joan, even tho she irritates the hell out of your father—now that she is almost a psychology major graduate. She is student teaching at Kirkwood High and so involved that this has been the first time I've talked or seen her since we got back from Florida. She is taking this whole thing seriously, very seriously, and your dad's only comment is "by God, as mixed up as she is, she'd never teach my kids".

Last night we went to the OPti-Mrs. annual card party with the Vermillions, and again, your father had quite a few comments to make about the people who get so excited and involved in affairs like this. I enjoyed it as we played bridge and I walked off with the table prize—but as far as your sire was concerned—it was a stupid week end.

Last Wednesday night we received a call from Linda. Could she please use some of her money to buy a new formal—as she was going to be a maid at the

Founder's Day Ball and just had to have a new dress. We had told the kids that the money they earned this summer was going to have to be their spending money and not to spend it foolishly; but as usual—your father told her to go ahead. Then we received a letter from Dennis Saturday and he stated he was pretty sure Linda would be the Queen as he was on the committee counting the votes and three out of five were for her. Well today we got another phone call and she was Queen. She was walking on air—it was the most wonderful affair and she got a crown and a silver charm bracelet and flowers and wore a robe and the whole bit. And then she said—"Guess what—Denny came up and kissed me in front of everyone." I think this pleased her as much as anything.

Am looking forward with anticipation to Wednesday which is to be a national moratorium day. As you can tell by the enclosed editorial in the paper, this thing has snowballed beyond anyone's expectations and I really think the young are finally beginning to be heard. They are getting the support of all the churches, colleges, a great many business men and their companies, and men in the Senate and Congress. I trully hope it can be carried off with dignity and purpose and that a few hopped up individuals don't turn it into a window breaking melee. They have asked we, who are too old to participate actively, to fly our flags at half-mast and You can bet mine will be. People are really beginning to be extremely concerned with Nixon—old tricky Dicky—and the old Republican Guard are being very quiet at this time. I just pray it is not all too late to save this country. I truly think, that whether we like it or not, we are really going to have to get back to some of the basic tenets of the ten commandments—and how you do this after years of rot and decay—I don't know.

Do you remember old "Hail Mary" from Southwebster church. Well they do not attend any more, but this morning I met their daughter-in-law, Henry Hale's wife, and she is a very attractive young girl. Anyway, Henry Hale is also in Viet Naam; I didn't really get to much into details with her—as I figured this is one guy you probably wouldn't want to run into. Took the map you sent me to church to show Winnie and Don Bill as they, like myself, know just about where Don is, but it really isn't listed on a map—so they enjoyed poring over the area with me.

Well, a two hour lapse. I had started to get dinner ready when I sat down to write this letter—with barbecued pork chops and french fries. Dad though he would help and turned on the grease for the french fries and then forgot about it. By the time I got out there to look into things it was pretty bad—in fact, so bad we had to turn on all the vent fans, exhausts and then leave and have a sandwich at steak and shake, and wait until the house cleared out. Thank heavens it didn't catch on fire or we really would have had a mess.

Don't know if I mentioned it or not, but Larry and Judy Colbert just got back last Wednesday after eight days in Hawaii—courtesy of the Banker's convention (this is the same group that paid the way for Stan and Aud Hofmeister—they just got back). In fact the entire island was one huge group of Wasp bankers —most of them Stan's age with their chests slipped down around their waists. Can't you just picture this entire group of superannuated 8 percenters, doing the hula and trying to surf. Anyway—Judy said it is really lovely over there, but to try and stay on one of the smaller islands as they are nicer than Honolulu or Oohau (or whatever it's called). If you get this R and R, keep this in mind—if you have a choice. Judy also said that the only thing worn by the women over there, day and night, are muu-muus. So I thought I'd get busy and try and make one for Lucy to take with her.

Must get letters off to the rest of the progeny so will close with our everlasting love and peace—

Mom & Dad

SP/4 Dail W. Mullins, Jr.
488-48-0511
CoA, 26th ENGR. BN.
APO SF, 96256

19 October 1969

Dear Mom and Dad,

Well, how is everyone? Fine and well, I hope. I trust that the office and Chanel are keeping you both busy. I was happy to hear that you and the Bills got some use out of the map I sent you. It wasn't very detailed, I know, but if I sent you one showing the location of every road and LZ, the army would probably accuse me of sending out classified information.

I found out something rather interesting today. Hawk Hill, when its finished, is supposed to be a model LZ—in fact, THE LZ in Vietnam. It will eventually have over $2,000,000 worth of underground bunkers, a $180,000 computerized artillery fire direction center and paved roads. While all of this may impress the brass no end, about all it means as far as most of us are concerned is more work. Incidentally, they're going to change the name from Hawk Hill to LZ Charger—that has a nice blood-and-guts ring to it, don't you think?

Oh, before I forget. My APO has changed once again. Now its back to 96256, the same that it was at Baldy. Vietnam is nuts! Back in the world, your address changes when you move—over here, your mailbox moves!

I really don't have a great deal to tell you, as usual. People back home, I think, are always rather amazed to hear that one can have a rather uneventful week over here. Aside from the fact that there exists, always, that potential for danger, I'm glad to say that most weeks are as quiet as, I guess, weeks can be over here.

I do want to let you know that I am fine—working much to hard for my own good—but nothing serious. Keep in touch, please, and I'll do the same. Take care and think peace.

Love,
Dail

P.S.—on the slides—no, don't start checking—I haven't sent them yet. I'll probably just take them to Hawaii and give them to Lucy—it's just so hard to mail packages out of here.

P.P.S.—Received your CARE package. Many, many thanks—the cookie (crumbs) and fudge were delicious.

Enclosed find picture taken on Moratorium Day. The short runt beside me is Barksdale—we're defending freedom!?

October 16

My dear Dail,
 Did you hear about the little boy who drank three bottles of Fresca and snowed in his pants? (that's to take care of the Confucius joke you related—I've got a good one I'll tell you later in this letter.)
 Just realized it has been over four days since you received a letter from me. Now that the kids are back in school I get a little tied up in my letter writing. I try and get one letter a week off to them and at least two to you, but sometimes things get ahead of me. I've been housecleaning and you know what that entails. As your Dad says—"Now what cleaning is this, fall, pre-Thanksgiving, pre-Christmas of just pre-pre." I've got so much painting that should be done around here and fixing of furniture, that I feel like I'll never get finished. I just don't know how people work and keep house.
 Went over to Webster Bank Monday to put some money in Denny's account and ran into that friend of mine Annabell Rennick. Do you remember that family. They had a son named Kyle, who was a little younger than you and then they had three other children. Anyway she was telling me that Kyle is taking his last year at Oxford College in England. He has always been extremely talented musically but he is planning to be a music and drama critic. Their second child is in her second year at Monmouth College, which is a very expensive school and a

very good school, in Illinois, studying Theology. She showed me a picture of all her youngsters and the third child, a girl of 16, is simply beautiful. It's funny to hear about these youngsters whom you haven't seen for years and years.

Sitting here watching the celebration going on in New York over the Mets victory today in the World Series. They really surprised everyone—not only by winning the Series, but by winning it in four straight. That town is completely wild.

Hope you got back to your "little home away from home" without any further problems. When I read all the mess and trouble you have to go through to get a lousy three day leave—it just makes me boil and so I go and call Winnie Bill— she's my new sounding board. I imagine that rain must be pretty horrible—especially when the five days rain we've had here has everyone griping.

Thought you might be interested in the comments about the nationwide moratorium held yesterday. Your father, for some reason, felt that this whole thing would be terribly upsetting to the fellows over in VietNaam. How did the men feel about this whole set up. Received a letter from Dennis and we had wondering how far some of these smaller schools would allow the students to go. Dennis said they had been told that their would be no cutting of classes but that the chapel would be open the entire day with someone of all faiths there speaking and that they felt the best way the students could participate in a peace movement would be to go in and pray.

Dennis said he had written you. Don't know what has happened to that youngster. Last year I don't think I received five letters from him the whole semester—and this year I've been getting two a week. He also tells me he is dating a freshman from New Jersey—and he says "Now, Mome don't get excited—she's just someone to take out once in a while." Last week Dennis and Linda had an invitation from the young priest, who has charge of the at haletic program at the college and whom Dennis has become very fond of to go to Huntsville for cocktails. I'd like to have listened in on that evening's conversation.

Thought you would also like to read the articles about the latest Nobel prize winners, and also the article that appeared in the issue of Time that came today.

Went to dinner Tuesday night with the Meachams and went over to their house afterwards and Rosemary gave (or lent) me a dress to send to Lucy to wear in Hawaii. It is one she bought when they were over there two years ago and is just darling and typically hawaiian. She would like it back when Lucy comes home as she wants to keep it for keepsake. Have you heard anymore about your R. and R.? Boy, I'm praying.

Now would you like to hear another joke. Dad came home with this one and I thought it was funny—It seems there was this young priest who had been assisting an older priest in a large parish. Finally the old priest told him that the next Sunday he wanted him to give the sermon. Of course he was quite excited and nervous and afterwards he went up to the old priest and said "Father, how did I do?". The old priest said "Not too bad, just a few mistakes." "For instance, there are only ten commandments, not fifteen; and Jonah did not swallow the whale, the whale swallowed Jonah; and it is not a Peter's pull at St. Taffys, it's a taffy pull at St. Peters."

Well, on that I'll close. Dad has a cold and I'm doing everything I can to avoid getting it. It really upsets me when he comes down with colds. First it isn't good for him and I don't want to get them. I've been trying to get him to wear surgical masks when these patients come in who are sick but he always thinks that's ridiculous.

All our love, and Peace—
Mom and Dad

SP/4 Dail W. Mullins, Jr.
488-48-0511
CoA, 26th ENGR. BN.
APO SF, 96256

24 October 1969

My dear Parents,

The day before yesterday was a bad day. I had to pull guard all day out at the sanitary fill (that's Pentagonese for trash dump) here at Hawk Hill. There were two other fellows with me, and we were supposed to sit out at the fill, which is located about 1/4 mile outside the perimeter, and keep the local Vietnamese from rummaging through it for food and other items that they apparently find valuable. I suppose this is mainly for health reasons; nevertheless, it is very sad to sit out there with loaded weapons and have to listen to those hungry, hollow-eyed children beg for food. We were instructed to keep them outside the wire surrounding the dump by firing tear gas grenades at them, something we managed to avoid until the end of the day. As I told Lucy, it was weird in one sense—almost like being somewhere in the future, in some authoritarian state, guarding a food stock that must be rationed out to an overpopulated world.

As I said, we avoided having to fire any tear gas until almost 4:30 in the afternoon, a half-hour before we were to go off guard. At that time, however, the crowd grew to almost 100 people, and when several of them tried to break open a section of the wire to get in, we were forced to fire one round of tear gas at them. A guy from the motor pool, Hanshue, actually fired the round. Now, the tear-gas rounds we use, which are made to be fired from the kind of weapon I carry, an

M-79 grenade launcher, is about 4 inches long and made of aluminum. They don't explode when they hit the ground—they're only supposed to bounce around and spew tear gas. Anyway, Hanshue fired a tear-gas round which bounced once and then hit a small boy in the right side of his forehead. Another boy grabbed the youngster, who, of course, was unconscious and bleeding quite badly, and carried him over to us, crying. I grabbed my first aid packet, but Herrin the other guy with us, yelled that the boy was already dead. I put my bandage back into its packet, but when they brought the youngster over and layed him down on a flak jacket we had, it seemed to me that he might be alive. I checked his pulse and put my ear against his chest—sure enough, he was still alive. His wound was awfully bad, however, and I was afraid to put a bandage on it. A good part of his skull had been blown away, and there was a great deal of brain tissue exposed—some of which was slowly being exuded from the wound. I pushed what I could back in, and then told Hanshue to go for help. He looked awfully scared, though, and when no help arrived after 15 minutes, I decided to go myself and leave Herrin to stay. By this time, the boy's poor mother arrived, near hysteria—you can imagine what she must have gone through seeing her son lying there with half his head blown away. We had almost as much trouble trying to keep the boy's mama-san from crushing her son as we did helping the boy. Anyway, I took off and ran all the way to our orderly room where I had the first sergeant call a medivac. By the time I returned, the child and his mother had both been dusted off, so I just came on back. I later learned that the doctors expected him to live, but they said he would have brain damage. Nothing will happen to Hanshue—the boy's injury was "merely" an unfortunate accident which resulted from his following through on his orders—that is, to fire tear gas grenades to keep the people away. Nevertheless, seeing the poor child laying there is something that's hard to pass off as "merely an unfortunate accident." I hope he recovers quickly and without too many detrimental effects. I'll try and follow up on his development and keep you informed. As is always the case, the children are the real victims of this war.

Not a very pleasant letter, I know, but it's what's happening around here, and you did want me to let you know what's going on. Other than having been saddened and somewhat depressed by this incident, everything else is still the same. Bunkers, more bunkers and still more bunkers—day, after day, after day.

The myth that seems to be going around to the effect that the October Moratorium has a detrimental effect on the boys in Vietnam is, to a great extent, just that—myth. Most of the men, at least those I have any contact with, are either completely unaware of what's going on or, if they do know, they don't care. I don't think disapproval of the war, no matter how widespread, really has a depressing effect on the soldiers. Most of them realize that dislike for the war doesn't mean that they are disliked—we hope most Americans don't think that the majority of us are over here by choice. There are, of course, those few who think war protestors are godless communist pigs, but these, fortunately, are fairly rare. Most of them are career men with lots of body hair, thick burly necks and small, beady, hate-filled eyes, not to mention almost non-existent minds. It's fairly obvious, at least to me, that those men with upper-lower and lower-middle class upbringings usually direct their hostilities toward the anti-war demonstrators themselves, while the soldiers from middle-middle and upper-middle class backgrounds tend to direct their's toward the army itself. This phenomenon, of course, is not directly the result of the social class, but rather, the educational levels usually attained by those from the different social backgrounds. And so we go back to money. Even so, I often wonder whether 4 years of higher education could overcome the damage done by 18 years of the kind of crap that the parents of children raised in lower class families put out to them—all that nonsense about any non-democratic country being godless and a constant threat to the lily-white purity of Christian America! To sum it all up—if the anti-war demonstrations back home upset anybody over here, its only those people who deserve to be upset—the sick ones—the real reason almost 40,000 young Americans are dead today.

Take care, both of you—let me know how everyone is, the kids, the dog, and be sure and let me know if you have any snow—I'm really going to miss that this year. If you can, send me some pictures of the snow—I'd like that.

Love,
Dail

195 days left—my, how time flies when you're having fun!

Wednesday,
10/22

My dear,

Sitting here watching the 10 o'clock news and an interview with that "horses ass," Spiro Agnew. Wouldn't it be wonderful if they reversed the entire Pentagon scheme and sent every male past 50 to U. N., including the entire Senate & Congress. What a botched up mess. Have you heard that Luice, one of the Nobel Prize Winners, is on the H E W's unwanted list?

It's been over two weeks since we've received any mail from you and your father keeps telling me "Patience". Almost called Lucy tonite but I'm so afraid of upsetting her, but I can't help worrying.

I'm really thankful I've been so busy lately or I'd

spend my days walking from one room to the other wringing my hands. Don't think I'd be so upset if your last letter hadn't stated you were stuck in Chu Lai — and of course I envision you in some detention cell because you were AWOL.

Went to dinner last nite with Meachams and they came back here to play cards — but we got into heated discussions instead. Have perused the evening and realize how impossible it is to change the views of older people who have had certain fixed ideas implanted in their minds from childhood. Ken Meacham, who is supposed to be an intelligent, educated man will never in this world feel anything but antagonism for any negro who tries to step into his world. It's really sad! I know I still have some prejudices but I'm a complete militant compared to him.

Well the Young Lees arrive tomorrow night via Easter airlines and then the Wicks come in Friday nite so we've got a big week end. I've been cooking all week so I won't have too much to do while they are here. The Wunderlichs will be here too.

We got together with the Wunderlichs Monday to plan the week end and I was telling him how "up-tight" I became when I didn't hear from you and he said "how would you like to have him on a submarine like Jim where we have no contact for 3 months". So guess I should keep still.

I'm enclosing a picture that appeared in the St Louis paper. We have no idea how they got the picture or information. Anyway, I think you know how I feel about these "queen" affairs. As I said I'd rather she would make Phi Beta Kappa as this lasts longer than the "beauty" bit. However, I received a letter from Linda yesterday and maybe some good comes from this. She said she has always felt shy and inferior, but since she knows that by a personal election the student body felt she was capable of this position she feels so much differently about herself. Even in her classes she speaks out and doesn't hesitate in participating in oral discussion, where before she was always

5

hesitant about speaking out. The scroll she received did not stress the physical attributes but said she was selected because "she typified the ideas, honor, traditions & was considered an exceptional woman." In this day & age I guess this is far fetched — but it seems to have answered a need for Linda, and for this I am most grateful.

I pray everything is alright with you and let us hear when you can. You know you are on our minds and in our hearts always. Sometimes I'm busy & happy, cheerfully talking to someone and I stop in mid sentence and get such a sickness and I say "how can I laugh", but life goes on —

Peace, love, & prayers
Mom & Dad

Wednesday 10/22

My dear,

Sitting here watching the 10 o'clock news and an interview with that "horse's ass" Spiro Agnew. Wouldn't it be wonderful if they reversed the entire Pentagon scheme and sent every male past 50 to V.N., including the entire Senate & Congress. What a botched up mess. Have you heard that Lurie, one of the Noble Price Winners, is on the HEW's unwanted list?

It's been over two weeks since we've received any mail from you and your father keeps telling me "Patience". Almost called Lucy tonite but I'm so afraid of upsetting her; but I can't help worrying.

I'm really thankful I've been so busy lately or I'd spend my days walking from one room to the other wringing my hands. Don't think I'd be so upset if your last letter hadn't stated you were stuck in Chu Lai—and of course I envision you in some detention cell because you were AWOL.

Went to dinner last nite with Meachams and they came back here to play cards—but we got into heated discussions instead. Have recoursed the evening and realize how impossible it is to change the views of older people who have had certain fixed ideas implanted in their minds from childhood. Ken Meacham, who is supposed to be an intelligent, educated man, will never in this world feel anything but antagonism for any negro who tries to step into his world. It's really sad! I know I still have some prejudices but I'm a complete militant compared to him.

Well, the Young Lees arrive tomorrow night via Easter Airlines and then the Wicks come in Friday nite, so we've got a big weekend. I've been cooking all week so I won't have too much to do while they are here. The Wunderlichs will be here too.

We got together with the Wunderlichs Monday to plan the week end and I was telling him how "up tight" I become when I don't hear from you and be said "how would you like to have him on a submarine like Jim where we have no contact for 3 months." So guess I should keep still.

I'm enclosing a picture that appeared in the St. Louis paper. We have no idea how they got the picture or information. Anyway I think you know how I feel about these "queen" affairs. As I said I'd rather she would make Phi Beta Kappa as this lasts longer than the "beauty" bit. However, I received a letter from Linda yesterday and may be some good comes from this. She said she has always felt shy and inferior, but since she knows that by a personal election the student body felt she was capable of this position she feels so much differently about herself. Even in her classes she speaks out and doesn't hesitate in participating in oral discussions, where before she was always hesitant about speaking out. The scroll she received did not stress the physical attributes but said she was selected because "she typified the ideas, honor, traditions & was considered an exceptional woman." In this day & age I guess this is farfetched—but it seems to have answered a need for Linda, and for this I am most grateful.

I pray everything is alright with you and let us hear when you can. You know you are on our minds and in our hearts always. Sometimes I'm busy & happy, cheerfully talking to someone and I stop in mid sentence and get such a sickness and I say "how can I laugh," but life goes on—

Peace, love, and prayers
Mom & Dad

SP/4 Dail W. Mullins, Jr.
488-48-0511
CoA, 26th ENGR. BN.
APO SF, 96256

29 October 1969

Dear Mom and Dad,

I got your letter dated October 22 today (number 53), and was a little dismayed to learn that at its writing you hadn't received a letter from me in two weeks. I really don't understand this, because I know I write at least twice a week, if not more. It's bad enough not receiving mail here for days on end because of postal inadequacies, but you'd think they'd make a special effort to let the wives and parents of men over here get some word. Bombarded with the constant TV, radio and newspaper coverages of the war as you are, I can imagine how much these letters help. I'll try and make an effort to write more frequently.

No special changes to report, at least as far as this war affects me. I guess that's good to hear. Charlie hasn't hit in several weeks, now, although nothing relevant can really be concluded about the war in general from the battle reports from a single LZ. You folks know as much, or more, than I do about what's happening over here. NBC News, I'm sure, has far better coverage of the war than either the Pacific Stars and Stripes or AFVN Radio.

I am anxiously awaiting the arrival of Nov. 3 and Nixon's "big" speech on Vietnam. While I'm not too optimistic, I do hope a change, or the hint of one, will be indicated.

We are still working on living bunkers here at Hawk Hill (LZ Charger), and will be up until around the 10th of November. At that time our entire company is scheduled to go on a 5-day standown in Chu Lai. When we return—who knows? Since LZ Charger is eventually supposed to be the LZ in Vietnam, I suppose that there will always be work to do around here. In addition, we'll probably be going out in platoon or squad size units to various other LZs and fire support bases around the Americal Division's AO to build, repair, destroy and sweep. Sergeant Hileman, our new platoon sergeant, still seems to think we'll all be pulled out sometime in January or February, but, for the most part, those rumors have died down considerably. A premature pullout being rather unlikely at this point, you both may be interested to know that as of today, the 29th of October, I have 190 days left over here in this hole. On the 22nd of next month, I will officially be "getting short". I think I've already explained to you the significance of that expression. So, keep the home fires burning—I'll be home shortly after that last snowfall melts.

I guess the word "monsoon" is one which people back home are familiar with, mainly from Pearl Buck's writings and the TV news coverage of the war, but which they probably know very little about. It is, of course, Southeast Asia's equivalent of winter, but instead of snow, they have rain, rain and more rain. I have seen some heavy, lengthy rains back in the states, but this is unreal. You can't believe how much water falls in a 24 hour period. How much rain does Missouri have in a year—10 inches, 15? During the past 48 hours here at Hawk Hill, we have had 46 inches of rain—46 inches—nearly 4 feet! In 2 days! In low spots the water will not infrequently reach a depth of 10 feet—and this is compounded by the fact that the whole LZ has become, literally, a sea of mud. There is no place where the mud is not at least 2 feet deep. Everyday a jeep has to be called out to pull some poor hapless soul out of mud that is shoulder deep. Dry clothes is a joke—I have seen two men come to blows over a pair of dry pants. Your hands and feet are constantly wrinkled from exposure. Nobody bothers to walk down to the shower anymore—we just take a bar of soap and step outside the bunker. Yesterday I stood in waist deep water nailing boards onto the side of a bunker! And this is just the beginning—we still have 5 more months to go. I'd like to take some pictures, but I don't dare take my camera outside. Well enough of Vietnam.

I agree with you completely about Linda and the queen contest. Beauty and personality contests were never my cup of tea, either; I particularly dislike the Miss American pageant. Nevertheless, if such has helped Linda to overcome her self-consciousness and shyness, then, indeed, perhaps it was a good thing. I hope so.

I have gotten two letters from Denny—and I feel terrible because I haven't returned them. I will, though, I promise—until then, please let him know that I appreciate the letters and am glad to hear that he is apparently doing pretty well. I was especially glad to hear that he has at least begun to think about social and political problems a little less "blue-collarly". He also seemed to be somewhat in favor of the Moratorium. This is good—very good.

Your story about Ken Meacham reminded me of something I heard on the radio today about a mob of teamsters that rioted somewhere up East, killing two and wounding several others. Aren't these the same star-spangled, hairy chested, red-blooded Americans who jump at the chance to condemn the Yippies and Black People for rioting. So now the tables have turned, and the law and order boys take to the streets.

Well, I guess I'll close. Happy Halloween. Needless to say, I won't make it out trick-or-treating this year, but next year.... I should be getting my R&R orders fairly soon, now—I do hope its for the time I asked, but I'll just be thankful to see Lucy at anytime. Take care and keep writing—you don't know how much your letters help.

Love,
Dail
☮

Sunday October 26

My dear boy,

This isn't going to be long, but I did want to get a line off to you before I dropped into bed from sheer exhaustion.

Well our big week end is over and while it was so much fun, I couldn't do this very often. This is about the only good the Army, or any other type service does; it enables you to make some friends who you never forget and who you get together with once in a while, and have a ball.

You just can't know how relieved we were to finally get a letter from you and know that you are alright. One thing, you mentioned a hand injury that was giving you trouble but we have no idea what kind of an injury it was or how it happened. And isn't it possible to get any kind of medical treatment in that hole of Hades? Also enjoyed the picture of the "two lost sheep" with your silent protest emblems. Dad was a little worried that the seargeant who approached you about the arm band, will now go out of his way to make things unbearable for you but I pray this won't be so.

You were so right in stating older people have a little difficulty in coming out of their rigid molds of past behavior in trying to let others know they are changing their minds. And I also find my best way is as you suggested—just to keep talking. Better yet, I find reading some of the paragraphs in certain letters you have written to us, even more effective.

Well Marge and Young Lee came in Thursday night from Washington, D.C, where they had been guests at a big party at the Chinese Embassy. They had been in Boston visiting Young's brother who is chief of surgery at Boston General Hospital. It's funny, they have such exceptional backgrounds but are so sensitive to slights. And you find that bigotry is not one sided with just the caucasians. Young and Marge are both in a complete state of collapse because their daughter Cheryl is getting quite serious with a "white" boy. Funny.

Ashton and his wife Helen got in Friday and that night I had a dinner for all of them, with the Wunderlichs. We had such a good time reminiscing and talking about all our children and they all said to to tell you hello and God Speed and send their very best to you.

It seems, when you get together, that everyone has had many problems with their personal lives over the years, and it seems to make your father feel a little better when he finds that the other fellows have had their share of health problems too. Young Lee has a serious high blood pressure problem, Dick Wunderlich has arthritis so bad he lives on aspirin and he loves to play golf but in order to do so every time he goes out to tee off he has to dope himself on aspirin, and Ashton Wick is having trouble with his diabetes and also a high cholesterol count. Then Dick is having serious problems with young Dick and his family. Evidently Dick, Jr. is starting on the same path that his mother took and is periodically walking out on his wife and two little children and Dick has to take over this responsibility until he shapes up. I don't think Ashton will ever really get over his wife's death, and I feel rather sorry for the woman he married. I had a long talk with Ashton. He came down early one morning when I was starting breakfast for everyone, to give me a beautiful sterling bracelet, ring, and earring which he had bought for Dorothy in Juarez. He said he thought she would want me to have it—and I tried to tell him you couldn't live in the past and that maybe Dorothy was a lot happier living just as long as she did—actively, than have more years just being an invalid. Sounds like it was a morose week end, but it wasn't. Saturday nite we all went out on the town to the Brathus which is a Banjo Dixie, sing along place, and then to several other night spots in town. The Wicks drove down so they left today around noon, and then we took the Lees to the airport and also the Wunderlichs who were leaving for three weeks in Florida. And then back home to collapse.

Thought we might get a phone call from the kids tonight as this was Denny's fraternity's big fall week end. Heard from Linda and she was excited about this. She also mentioned that Bob had bought himself a new motorcycle and had gotten her a helmet for a present. Now I have something else to worry about—you in Viet Naam and Linda riding around on a motorcycle.

Keep your chin up, don't aggravate anymore seargeants, and think peace as we do constantly. We miss you always, take care of yourself, and let us hear when you can.

With all our love,
Mom & Dad

I certainly don't understand this changing of APO numbers but it is typical of the Army.

SP/4 Dail W. Mullins, Jr.
488-48-0511
CoA, 26th ENGR. BN.
APO SF, 96256

1 November 1969

Dear Mom and Dad,
   Well, I see by the old scratches on the bunker wall that another month has rolled around—and, in just a few short days, I'll pass the 6 month point and will be "getting short". Surprisingly, when I look back on it, that 6 months did seem to go fairly fast—I hope this second six passes just as quickly.
   I was so glad to hear that your weekend was successful. I would have enjoyed seeing the Lee's again. I don't know whether I've mentioned it before or not, but all Americal Division troops in Vietnam return to the United States through Ft. Lewis in Seattle, Wash., rather than through Oakland. Maybe, if I have any free time at all there, I can see them then.
   I did manage to get a letter off to Denny the other day—he has written me twice since returning to school. I know you mentioned that he seems to be writing much more often than he used to. I also received a letter from Bobby Paschen, which I will answer just as soon as I figure out what in the hell it's all about. He certainly is a different person, isn't he?
   I suppose Lucy has either written or called to inform you of the latest escapades of the Bartges family's answer to Errol Flynn—Dan. He ran off to Mexico with two other buddies from school, presumably, to see that little chiquita he met there last summer. I only heard that he had reached the border—not whether he had chosen to go on or return. For his poor mother's sake, I hope its the latter.
   As you can see, I really don't have much news to relate. I did want to let you know that I'm fine—healthwise, that is—if I don't lose my mind before my tour is up. Do me a favor, please. If you see anything lying around the house that is OD in color, destroy it before I get home, OK?

Love,
Dail

Thursday morning, Oct. 30

Our dear Son,

Yesterday morning we received your letter describing one of your bad days and the injury to a child—who probably since the day he was born was fated to die before he ever really lived—either thru starvation, war or some other form of man's inhumanity to man. I just sat for an hour thinking of you, the child, the mother—thinking of most women and their feelings of inexpressible joy and amazement when they find they are carrying a child within them. How you say to yourself—"things are going to be different with this baby, he's not going to suffer, he's going to be happy, good, loved and protected". But the really sad thing is that not all children conceived are wanted—and maybe this would be the answer to overpopulation. If all women all over the world could band together and be able to say—"I will only bear the children I want." In other words sex in one sphere, but the actual fruits of sex entirely separate. Of course, this is Utopia and Shangri-La, and it will never happen to the "Naked Ape". (By the way his new book the "Human Zoo" is now out and I have the Library saving it for me).

What I'm trying to say is how sick and sorry inside I feel, knowing the soul tearing things you are having to witness and partake of. Never for one moment, did I think any of you children would have to endure anything of this nature and so I become a little more tired, a little more bitter, a little harder to live with, a great deal more puzzled trying to find the answer, and an inexplicable amount of fear as the days grow short. The title of Peggy Lee's new hit song keeps running through my mind—"If That's All There Is My Friend, Well Bring Out the Booze." Maybe you've heard it.

Anyway, last night I had bridge club at Lucille Monroe's house, and while I realized we get together just once a month for enjoyment, I took your letter with me. As you say, it's my only chance to capture some kind of an audience and have them hear the horrors of war from someone they know. Anyway, believe me when I say there was shock, horror, and incredulousness—which maybe they have forgotten this morning but a little seed was sowed. The sad part is that while you are trying to get to the "don't care" and the "super-patriots", you also are hurting people like Winnie Bill and Clair Vieth—whose son-in-law just finished his internship and has his orders for Viet Naam Thanksgiving Day. His wife and two little children are returning to St. Louis to wait.

Don't know if you are aware of all the hub-bub going on back in "the world", about monsodium glutamate and the chemical element in diet sodas and foods. Anyway the other nite your father came home from the office just exhausted and we sat and watched the six o'clock news. It started out with the war, and then the involvement we seem to be in in Laos, the Arabs and the Israeleans, the trial going on in Chicago between the SDS and the Police, Margaret Meade speaking before a joint committee in Washington on marijuana, earthquake in Yugoslavia, and then a fright commercial on smoking. In other words a half hour filled with sickness and fear and more fear. Dad sat there and looked at me and said "after a day like I've had with 25 patients when you can only properly handle 8 in a day, working like a dog—knowing that over nine-tenths of what I made will go to inflated prices, taxes to support a war that no one wants, and then a half hour of news, I really don't want to live—it's just not worth it."

With all this, I have Camille next door. Eloise is going in to the hospital today for tests and all week long she has had me running to the store, to the library for books, etc., while she plays Camille. I don't think there is a damn thing wrong with her except stagnation and brittle bones from lack of movement. When you talk about the upper-lower and lower-middle class attitudes toward the war, the moratorium, the other social problems it strikes me as odd, because back here I am confronted with the truly upper-middle, well educated, well raised humans who think exactly like the uneducated you are in contact with. The people like the Skillings, Seiberts, Meachams, to name a few, and especially Suzie Bell who sees a commie lurking behind every tree and is always telling people—"I know the Russians and we must live in mortal fear of this beast." I have never wanted any boy to have to go into the service, but I wish Jon Bell were older and serving in Viet Naam. Wonder what her comments would be?

Haven't heard from Dennis and Linda this week but I know that they are in the midst of mid-terms and trying to make up for all the hours they spent having fun. I'll probably get two letters this weekend, both stating—"Now Mom, such and such grade is not going to be what I expected, but now I know what is wrong and next term it will go up." And then next term I'll get the same kind of a letter.

You ask about the dog—now that is something else again. She is completely and hopelessly retarded as far as I am concerned. Around six o'clock every morning she starts barking, yapping, and howling in the family room—to let us know that it is another day and let's get going. Really, it's more trouble than having a baby around. I've never seen a dog that likes people more than she does. When the doorbell rings she runs to the front hall and literally turns inside out waiting to see who is coming in. When our weekend guests were here we finally had to lock her in our bedroom as she will not leave people alone. And as far as being any kind of a watch dog—forget it.

Guess this is not the up-lift letter you are told to write to loved ones, but you are too intelligent to know that we are not living in "God's Country" back here, but it's a hell of a lot better than what you have. Again, we think of you always and follow every bit of news avidly and fearfully,

Love and PEACE,
Mom & Dad

SP/4 Dail W. Mullins, Jr.
488-48-0511
CoA, 26th ENGR. BN.
APO SF, 96256

7 November 1969

Dear Mom and Dad,

I received your letter dated October 30th today—the one written in response to my having described the incident out at the trash dump. While I hesitate to say that it upset me, it did, nevertheless, serve to remind me to be more careful about what I write home about. I'm sorry.

I remember that you once told me, when I was very young and still liked to play at war, that those men who had really seen, firsthand, the horrors of combat talked little about their experiences. This was always difficult for me to understand, as I think it may be for anyone who has not lived in a combat zone. Why is this? You would think that most people would have enough common sense and compassion to realize war's ugliness and horror without having to experience them. Apparently, however, this is not the case—and so, after every war, the combatants return, proud, but hollow-eyed and silent, while those who remained behind clamor for stories of valor and heroism.

What, then, is the origin of this glamorization of war? There are, I think, two main reasons. First, mankind has been forced to make war, its primary means of settling differences, seem less horrible than it is, else suffer some form of mass neurosis in the face of war's true atrociousness. We came close to this at Buchenwald, at Bergen-Belsen, at Dachau and at Hiroshima. But mankind escaped self-condemnation and guilt by putting the blame, not on itself, but on one man, Hitler, in the case of the Jewish slaughter, and, as fantastic as it may seem, on the saving of American lives in the case of Hiroshima. Leonard Cohen has recognized the ridiculousness of such shenanigans—here is something he wrote that I like:

All There is to Know about Adolf Eichmann
Eyes: Medium
Hair: Medium
Weight: Medium
Height: Medium

Distinguishing Features: None
Intelligence: Medium
What did you expect? Talons? Oversize Incisors? Green Saliva? Madness?

The second reason that mankind, nations, must glamorize war is so to make it seem inviting to the young, the only members of the warring factions physically capable of undergoing its hardships. Seventeen, eighteen and nineteen year-old boys are particularly susceptible to shiny medals, patriotic drivel, the words "heroic" and "brave" and being referred to as "men doing a man's job!" With visions of John Wayne charging a machine gun nest and a flashy green beret setting girls' souls aflame, these same young boys are made to forget that they are also susceptible to bullets and bombs.

I bring all of this up because, frankly, I was amazed to discover that some of the women in your bridge club appeared shocked and surprised by my account of the shooting of that small child out at the trash dump. What can these people think it is like over here to be shocked by something like that? Are they that naïve; have they erected so strong a mental block against what a war is like? I will join the ranks of the hollow-eyed and silent, and refuse to stoop to telling war—stories. Nevertheless, it is, oddly, a little self-satisfying to know that I could probably really upset these fools by describing all I've seen, which, to be quite honest, is probably not all that much—compared, for example, to an infantryman. I have seen enough, however, to last me a lifetime.

Enough of my dribbling—I sound like Eric Hoffer! Before I close, though, there are three things I must mention.

First—the MPs, in making a routine patrol of one of the many small villages which surround Hawk Hill, came across an entire government bag of mail destined for A Company, 26th Engineers. How it got there, nobody knows—a team of CID men will probably be up here to investigate. Nevertheless, it was there, so we have been asked to respond accordingly. If any VC got ahold of your address or Lucy's from the mail that was in that bag, be prepared to receive some interesting mail. You will probably be informed that I have been killed or captured in action, or that I am a dirty capitalistic aggressor and I am going to be killed. I know this sounds ridiculous, but the VC and NVA do this, so we can't take any chances. Take the letter, if you get one, to any military installation and report the incident. Above all, ignore the contents—it is terror propaganda. The letters are true in one sense—we are capitalistic aggressors; I am not going to be killed, however!

Second. Someone broke into my foot locker last week and stole my new Omega watch and watchband. We think we know who did it and what happened to the watch—probably used to pay for drugs or prostitutes in the village—but can't prove it. So, it looks like I'm just out $100. Anyway, I recall you mentioning onetime that you would buy me a watch if I wanted one. Is the offer still open. If so, make it gold instead of silver, and make sure the watchband is one of those wide, thick leather ones that buckle—not an expansion band. Do you know what kind I mean? Thanks.

Finally—and you're going to think I've flipped—could you get out to Central Hardware and buy a cheap doorbell (bell and button) and a 5 volt battery for me. This is not important—just a novelty I'll explain later.

Take care all—ignore the beginning of this letter; I was just blowing off steam. Keep writing and I'll do the same.

Love,
Dail

P.S. Thought you might enjoy the enclosed pictures.

———————————

Sunday, November 2

My dear Patriot,

Know you just love that salutation. But actually there are many uglier words than that; bigotry, fanaticism, greed, hate—of course these can all be encompassed in patriotism. It was funny when we had all our company we got in to some very interesting discussions and how irrational men can be in their thinking. All without question believed that you should be proud to go the defense of your country when she calls you and try and abide by the laws of the land—but then get on the question of the Supreme Court telling you you must accept colored as patients and their patriotism disappears. This all came about by a notice they all received from the American Dental Association stating they cannot turn down a patient because of race, creed or color. They still have a right to dictate what patients they may accept—but not for the above reasons and evidently cases are being brought to court against dentists. Outside of Young Lee, your father was the only one who will accept colored patients (with discrimination that he uses on his white patients too) and Dick and Ashton were amazed. Dick simply refuses and Ashton doesn't run into this situation in Sheboygan. The Human Zoo.

Friday night was Trick or Treat and you should have seen this stupid dog. She had more fun than anyone. After the first few youngsters came she wouldn't leave the front door and just sat there waiting for the bell to ring.

Speaking of Halloween night—around five o'clock I had the strangest phone call. I answered and a young girl's voice answered and said "Happy Halloween", guess who this is. I immediately thought it was Linda calling but after a little more conversation I knew it wasn't Sis. We kept up the guessing, with my calling out names. She said she was in her twenties and I knew her. Finally I said Carole (thinking it was Hemphill) and she said yes, but not Carole Hemphill—and then I said Carole Kreyling Knight and she said yes—although I still didn't think it sounded like her. Anyway it was the most disturbing conversation. She said they had been transferred to St. Louis and she was living near Telegraph Road and Broadway in Mehlville and she was so frightened of the neighborhood and the people were so odd. Several times I would say I must go and she would say "Oh, God, please don't hang up, please." I could hear a doorbell ringing quite often but she said no one was ever there. I asked her about her mother and she said I'll never see her again; I said where was her husband and she said he wasn't coming home; then she said she was expecting another baby; then she would again repeat "God, please don't hang up". Your father was sitting listening to all this and went in to the kitchen to listen in on the other phone. He came back and said that woman is either doped, sick or drunk—so hang up. I said I must go and again it was please don't hang up. I asked her if she had a phone number and address to give me and she rattled off this phone number and said the address was 416 Kingston. Dad then came over and hung the phone up and said it was ridiculous to go on with the conversation. I don't think it was Carole and I don't think it was a crank call—but someone who really needed help. I just couldn't get it off my mind so I finally called the operator and explained to her what had happened and gave her the phone number which had been given me. She said to stay on the line and she would do some checking. She called the number and some fellow answered, named Stahlhut. It was his number but he said the address wasn't right and no one named Carol lived there. She said she would give the address to the police and let them see what they could find out. I haven't heard any more and as the operator said—I had done all I could. Do think I will write Mary Kreyling and see if Carole has moved back to St. Louis.

This morning was Stewardship Sunday in church and while this is a necessary evil, it usually is as boring to listen to discussions about money in church as it is anywhere else. The Sermon "The Shrinking Dollar and The Shrinking Church" and as I told him afterward the Shrinking Dollar in the Home. Dad's accountant called him the other day to inform him that his social security and the payments he makes for the girls who work for him, had gone up again and now the money he must deposit in the bank to the Federal Government has gone up to $150 a month. This is in addition to the $500 a month he pays for Income Taxes, so we can have 500,000 men in Viet Naam and allow a bunch of S.O.B. seargeants bilk the G.I.'s and the government in the canteens. Dad's accountant told him four days he works for the government, his help and his landlord, the fifth day he might get to keep to live on and pay tuitions and the rest of the struggle. I know we live well compared to what you are seeing over there, but when I see what it is doing to your father and inevitably what it does to the people over there—it really makes you wonder what it is all about. The other night he was so discouraged he said he though he'd just convert everything, declare bankruptcy, let the kids get Government loans then, and take off for Mexico or someplace where he could just hole up and rest. Of course, you know he wouldn't do this but he has to explode once in a while. And all of this is what you are trying to protect for us. That's the biggest joke. Of course, it is still one of the few countries where we can sound off at the mouth.

Thought you would be interested in the plans for the next moratorium day in St. Louis. Please don't antagonize anyone over there too much—you just can't buck the army. Dad still feels this is why you had to stand guard the day the little fellow was hurt.

God bless you, and again our love and prayers for Peace.
Mom & Dad

P.S. Did you know the Italians have had the Pill for years and no one knew about it—it's called Garlic.

Wednesday, Nov. 5

My dear,

Received your letter in which I upset you by telling you we hadn't heard from you for a while, and I think this had better be one of the things I shouldn't mention to you. First of all I must learn not to get upset when I run to the mail slot everyday to see what is there. It even bothers me if I don't hear from the younger ones for a while.

Well the Big Speech is over and he didn't say a damn thing. We had dinner with the Meachams last night—which we shouldn't have. I told your dad not to bring up the war, religion, over-population and just talk about sex—which is the only thing he and Ken agree on. I really feel I sometimes malign Ken simply because we see more of him than any of our friends and that is because your Dad and he really have empathy—even tho they are always screaming at each other. And Rosemary just sits and quietly falls asleep. Anyway, Ken made the mistake of saying "what did you think of Nixon's speech" and the war was on. But this isn't all bad—because everything is aired and basically everyone really feels we have got to get out of this damn situation—the only thing we seem to have trouble getting together on is how to do it. Look magazine has an excellent article on the

Viet Naam situation and I will send it to you after I have perused it thoroughly. Last night Ken called your father ambivalent and it was so funny to see your dad trying to raise umbrage to this but failing, because he didn't know what the word meant. And then on the way home he got mad at me because I told him if he read a little more he would know what it meant.

I'm sure you can imagine my reaction to a letter I received from Lucy in which she told me about her brother Dan. She mentioned that she thought her parents were bearing up pretty well but she wondered how I would feel if it were Denny. And this shook me. I can remember my father telling me how many times he had run away from home and it seeemed to be a way of life with young boys of his era and I really can understand Dan and his desire to get away from it all and "do his thing", but if it were one of mine I would be absolutely heartsick. Not that he wanted to go to the hinterlands, but that I wouldn't know where he was and could envision him with his head banged in by some "kook". And what does he do when the Army finds out he left school and can't find him?

Halleluiah! Denny wrote home today and asked if he could bring a girl home for Thanksgiving. He asked me to get him two tickets for the Kirkwood-Webster football game so she must be someone he wants to show off or he wouldn't dare parade her in front of his friends. I think she is from New Jersey and I am most anxious to meet her. I have already started warning your father not to make any remarks and to be very much the quiet father because Danny doesn't go for the type kidding some of your girls took. It really "bugs" Dennis. Don't worry about not writing to him as he had told us he was going to write to you but was going to depend on us to keep him informed about you. Denny's extreme concern about you is another facet of his character that I am finding out. He has always been the most difficult of all three of you for me to understand and get close to, but we never have received a letter from him or a telephone call that he doesn't want to know everything about you and begs us to let him know what we hear from you. Linda is so much like your father and I've always felt you were an O'Donnel and a Hetherington in feeling, emotion and personality; altho you do have a lot of your father in you.

We got some slides back that we took in Florida and I took them to Deering today to have some prints made as I thought there were some of Lucy that you would like to have. I also had a picture of you that you sent me, which Lucy saw and wanted, blown up to put in a frame she has.

Yesterday I started going to the Women's Circle at church. It is a service group and I felt I would be doing something more worthwhile in this than some "talk" group. We have two families in Webster which we take care of during the entire year instead of at Christmas and Thanksgiving. We spent yesterday sewing and mending and pressing clothes for a woman with 9 (too many) children whose husband died this summer. The other woman has four children and has evidently never had a husband. Of course, they are colored (any why did I say this—doesn't it happen to white woman?). Blanche Robertson was there and while I know you never thought too much of her, she was so concerned about you and begged me to mention her to you and that you are mentioned in her daily prayers. We must be forgiving.

Went up to St. Luke's today to visit Eloise Skilling. Dr. Skilling was over this morning and I am convinced that most people do things for her because of him. He was so appreciative of what I had done for her and he was extremely concerned when he put her in the hospital as he thought there was the possibility of cancer. Her blood count had gone down so rapidly and when they put her in they gave her four transfusions in two days. But all they can find is a hiatus hernia and diverticulitis, which could cause the blood count. Anyway he asked if I would go up and see her as I always seemed to do her so much good. He is one of the few persons who asks about you and truly seems interested in everything I can tell him about you and wants to know all the details. She is something else again. She sits up there in a room reserved for the elite and really pushes the fact that she is Dr. Skilling's wife. And the nurses, of course, knowing his influence, don't dare say one word.

Yesterday we received a letter from Linda and she really shook your father. She said she had been giving this matter serious consideration ever since school started and she had about made up her mind that she wanted to go on to graduate school. He really turned pale. He's been looking forward to two years from now when he will be out from under the load and she pulls this. She has a Dr. McCasling teaching her socially this year and he has her snowed. He just received his PhD from Vanderbilt and knew Ray Wintkert. Anyway a friend of his who heads the Sociology Department at Alabama U. is coming down to Athens this week end to talk to Linda. And they talk about parental influence. Your father said—"why the hell doesn't she find some nice boy and get married like the rest of the girls". I think he would feel so relieved if she would settle down and be a submissive housewife and the funny thing is I feel just the opposite; I don't think girls have to use marriage as the only way of life anymore—of course Linda doesn't fit this picture to me. Again I quote your Aunt Dot—"raise chickens instead of children."

In my last letter I talked about the odd phone call I had. Well I finally called Mrs. Moulder to really find out whether Carol could have moved back to St. Louis. She said no—so it was some disturbed young person. Anyway, Mrs. Moulder told me that they had just gotten back from visiting the Kreylings in Chicago and that they had a beautiful home and that they were a little happier because they had been able to convince Carol's husband to quit a job he had been trained for, and come to Chicago and work for the railroad company that Ed is with so Carole could be with her mother. Aren't you glad you didn't get into this situation.

Thought you would enjoy the enclosed clippings about the controversy regarding sex education—especially the one about genes (jeans).

This is Ken Meacham's joke, which he thought was funny but I, frankly, didn't get—"Confucius say—Girl who sit on jelly roll, get ass in jam."". I thought the one about the fellow whose wife got her diet pills and birth control pills mixed up and it was Trick or Treat for awhile, was much funnier.

Received letters from both the Lees and the Wicks and they simply raved about the weekend—I didn't think it was that fantastic—quoting Ashton—"you are both capable of putting us in another world—we are different people—happier—after being with you." I am taking this as an extreme compliment.

We love you, we miss you, and we think of you constantly—

PEACE—
Mom & Dad

SP/4 Dail W. Mullins, Jr.
488-48-0511
CoA, 26th ENGR. BN.
APO SF, 96256

8 November 1969

My dear Parents,

It's amazing, really, how a little thing like a letter can make one realize how lucky he is to have such wonderful parents. Your fine letters, and the changing attitudes toward so many things that they have lately begun to reflect, are, next to Lucy's faithful correspondence, the biggest morale booster I have in Vietnam. If my tour over here serves no other purpose than it has, namely, to encourage you and some of your contemporaries to reflect upon matters more serious than you had in the past, then I will consider it to have been worth every miserable day. Yes, I look forward to your letters very much.

A year ago, had I been present at the discussion you described in your last letter, the one in which you relate the conversation you had with the Wicks, the Lees and the Wunderlichs, I no doubt would have found myself quite alone in my opinions about many of the topics you discussed. Now, however, I feel as though I might have allies in such a confrontation of views. Of course, I do recognize full well that your current pacifistic outlook is the result of your eldest son's current situation. Nevertheless, I am grateful for the fact that you view my servitude, not with laudations of patriotic sacrifice and flag-waving frivolity, but with genuine concern, not only for me, which, of course, is to be expected, but for us—all of us—the human race. I cannot begin to describe how relieved and pleased I am—how proud—to find that you now recognize the hypocrisy and two-facedness of people like Dr. Meacham who, on the one hand, are such strong advocates of democratic principles of freedom, justice and liberty, but who, in the same light, cannot bring themselves to accept a person for what he is, rather than on the basis of skin color, hair texture and lip size.

Have you, by chance, seen the new movie with Peter Fonda, Easy Rider? Probably not, since I know you're not fond of movies starring people who have been arrested for such heinous crimes as possession of marijuana. I, of course, have not seen it either. But Lucy did, and she wrote me about it the other day. I also read Cavalier Magazine's review of the movie. Anyway, I wish you'd see it. While the development of the plot (it concerns a trip made by two "hippies" on motorcycles from California, across the American southwest, into the deep south, ending up in New Orleans at the Mardi Gras) is not too terribly exciting, the movie does have some interesting things to say about America, her people and her ethos. The two principal characters in the story, Peter Fonda and his friend, are supposed to represent ideal hippies—that is, they are two very free souls—free of responsibility and problems, true, but also free of hate and prejudice (impossible, I know, but they are just imaginary ideals—you have to accept that). Anyway, the movie deals with the nature of the relationships that they establish with all of the people they meet on their trip—migrant farm workers, gas station attendants, rednecks and the like. Anti-Southern in its treatment, Easy Rider plainly depicts the fact that the further south they go, the more hostile do the people become, until finally, in New Orleans, they are killed by a band of rednecks who simply don't like "nigger-lovers" with long hair and beads and pot. Why? Well, Easy Rider purports to explain that the most freedom-conscious people in the world, the Americans, are actually terribly afraid of freedom—true freedom—so much so that when confronted with those who, in fact, are really free, they can do little else except strike out in fear and distrust. Thus, the freedoms that all Americans are supposed to enjoy—freedom of speech, freedom of the press, freedom to worship, etc.—are only freedoms of conveniency—they make life more bearable. But real freedom—freedom from prejudice, hate, superstition, fear—these are the true freedoms; the ones that will not determine whether man lives conveniently, but whether he lives at all. In the closing scene of the movie, as they lie broken and bleeding under the lead pipes and chains of a New Orleans motorcycle gang, Peter Fonda says to his friend, "Man, we blew it!" And he was not talking about just them—he was talking about America. I am convinced that the new American

Revolution, the one now in progress, for all its faults and falsities, is still the only hope for our nation. Martin Luther King lying in a pool of blood on a Memphis hotel balcony; the Chicago police and Mayor Daley; Spiro Agnew's idiotic drivel; the Mississippi school system; Detroit afire—these are the things which show America to be not what we had been taught in Sunday school that it was. Appolo XI; a black man as mayor of Cleveland; the Peace Corps; Vietnam Moratorium Day—these are the things which show America as it could be. If we don't blow it. I only hope Dr. Meacham is around to see the outcome, whatever it may be.

Love,
Dail

Peace

SP/4 Dail W. Mullins, Jr.
488-48-0511
CoA, 26th ENGR. BN.
APO SF, 96256

10 November 1969

Dear Mom and Dad,

Just a short note to tell you the good news. I got my R&R in Hawaii over Christmas! I'll leave Danang on December 19th, and spend the 20th, 21st, 22nd, 23rd, 24th, 25th and 26th with Lucy—isn't that wonderful? Likewise, Barksdale and his wife will be there too, one day later, from the 21st to the 27th. I know Lucy will be thrilled to know that we'll at least be together on Christmas—of course, my joy is doubled! Christmas with Lucy and without Vietnam. I, of course, will call you from Hawaii.

Love,
Dail

SP/4 Dail W. Mullins, Jr.
488-48-0511
CoA, 26th ENGR. BN.
APO SF, 96256

13 November 1969

Dear Mom and Dad,
    I am still, as you might guess, walking on the proverbial cloud nine as a result of having been granted an R&R over Christmas. Why isn't it December yet? I think I probably neglected to mention in that rather hastily inscribed note that Barksdale and his wife, Marilyn, will also be in Hawaii over Christmas, although his R&R begins one day later than mine. Hopefully, the four of us will be able to get together at least one night for dinner. I'll be leaving Hawk Hill on the 17th of next month for Chu Lai and then Danang, and arrive in Honolulu, as I said, on the 20th. I will, of course, call you from Hawaii—at least there are enough phones there where I won't have to wait in line for eight hours and then find that it's too late to call.
    I meant to write sooner than I have, folks, but my pattern of correspondence was interrupted the other day by a demo mission to the field. Sgt. Hileman, Barksdale, "Pigpen" Hogan, Allen, Cullen and I were CA'd out to LZ Center on Tuesday morning at around 9:30. After about a twenty-minute information stop there, we left again by chopper for a captured VC village in the Que Son Valley. Two platoons of infantry pulled security for us while we blew up six NVA bunkers—these, incidentally, were part of the same complex of bunkers that made the news not too long ago, and which involved that case of battlefield "mutiny" by an element of the 196th. Anyway, for about four hours, the six of us played tunnel rat, crawling in and out of bunkers and tunnels, searching for booby traps and setting charges.
    The village that these bunkers were situated in and around was, as I said, a suspected VC village—at any rate, there was a conspicuous absence of men; none in fact. The only people we saw were two old women, two young girls and two small boys—all of whom were scared to death. Whether because of our presence or for fear of what the VC might do to them when they returned and found their bunkers destroyed, I don't know.
    While the day was not exactly enjoyable, it was, nevertheless, interesting. If you can detach yourself from the situation (nearly always impossible), most things over here are interesting.
    Well, just a short letter to let you know how I'm doing. Our whole company will be in Chu Lai over Thanksgiving for standdown—that's something, anyway.

I'll write soon and, of course, keep you posted on any and all developments. You do the same.

Love,
Dail

Wednesday night—Nov. 12

My dear,

Well this is the longest I have ever gone without getting a letter off to you but things have been happening. It upsets me when this happens because I think the least any of us can do is keep mailing rolling to you. But I hope you will understand.

The Missouri Dental Association had their convention in town beginning last Sunday and running through today and your father had marked off his books, but he came home Friday night and said he was "sick unto death" of teeth and he said get ready I'm going to take a ride down and see the kids at Athens; so we left Saturday around 2:30 and stopped in Memphis Saturday night. We stayed at the new Medical Center Holiday Inn (the only place we could get reservations) and I told your father I felt like I was back at Mayo's. It was a beautiful room on the 18th floor with a picture window over-looking the city of Memphis but it evidently has some connection with the hospitals near by as the halls are filled with patients in their robes waiting to find out what is wrong with them.

We arrived in Athens Sunday afternoon and took a few of the young people out to dinner. Dennis had informed a friend of his, John Lynch, we were coming down and he insisted we come out to his place after dinner for a few drinks. This fellow just graduated from Athens last year even tho he is around 29. He had been in the service, married with two children, divorced and back to school. He was President of Denny's fraternity and quite active on campus. He is now teaching school to some of the Nasa people's children in a semi-private school outside of Huntsville. Anyway, he and a bachelor physician, who evidently owns the whole town of Decatur, live in a new home they have built and it is really something to behold. It's back off the highway and is simply beautiful and huge. I counted about 10 rooms and then gave up; and I mean big rooms with a beautiful baby grand piano in the living room, bedrooms that look like harem nights, a huge swimming pool with brick walls and patios. They have parties for the fraternity and have 50 boys at a time with their dates and provide the food and liquor. It's rather an odd set-up and I don't quite understand it—but then I am always circumspect.

You know Bob and Lennie have their own place, which the school doesn't (?) know about. Athens doesn't allow any student who isn't married to live off campus so both their parents are paying for their dorm rooms to the tune of 900 dollars and then they rent this 3 bedroom home for 100 a month. I wish you could see it. This Lenny is something when it comes to decorating and the place is fantastic. Dad and I bought the food and we went over there Monday night and cooked for the kids. It is immaculate and when I look at Lenny and Bob all I can think of is the "Odd Couple", with Lenny being the guy who is constantly following you around with a mop. He is much worse than I am believe it or not.

Bob is growing a beard and I'll say he looks good. Dennis still has his streaked blonde hair from Florida and it is long and on him (or is it because he is my son) I don't like it. I tried to get him a haircut the whole time he was with us—but no luck. We were going to leave early Tuesday morning to get home that night so Dad could have one day to rest but Monday night as we're all sitting around he says "I thought I'd go through Louisville and you could spend one night with your sister". Well I'm sure you know how really elated I was with this. We didn't get away until around 10 as Linda just insisted we come back to school to meet this Professor McCaslin who has really stirred her up. I was really expecting a real "kook" but he is a very fascinating, disturbing, thought provoking young man and he felt Linda had so much potential and he said she was a very promising young lady and we shouldn't squelch her ups and downs. We also met her physcology teacher and the minister who teacher her "old testament" and everyone spoke so highly of her. She seems to be well liked and of course, this makes her like the school.

Denny is another cup of tea! His fraternity kicked him out of the lounge because he was too noisy so he retaliated by telling them he was not going to play football for them in the remaining games. We had gone to a game Monday afternoon only to see Dennis play and he refused. I took him aside and said sometimes by being stubborn he only hurt himself, but he was adamant—he said I said no and I'm sticking to it. The thing is that he is their best player and they are due to win the inter-fraternity cup—but don't think they can do it without him. Some of his friends told me they are going to buy a baby-rattle and give it to him for Xmas. He's just like your father. Also, the girl coming home for Thanksgiving is all off. I met her and she is a very nice little girl and is crazy about hime, but I think Denny was so hurt by Lisa Lambert that he has made up his stubborn mind never to get involved with anyone again. I hate to say it—but I don't think he has ever gotten over Lisa.

Linda told me she was out one night and when she came back they told her she had had a call from "Mike Steele"—old Pete Merrill. They don't know if he was in town or what. She said she has gotten a few letters from him. I still don't understand what the deal is between she and Bob. She doesn't want to be engaged to him but she gets furious when any other girl tries to get him—and pletnty are trying.

Well we arrived in Louisville around 4 PM and we really had such a nice visit with Bob and Dot. Maybe it was because their kids weren't around and just the four of us spent the evening talking about everything and anything. They are fine and wanted to know all about you and if I didn't have some pictures of you. I had taken the picture of you and Barksdale with your arm bands on to show Denny and Linda, but Dennis nabbed it and begged me to let him have it, so I didn't have anything to show Aunt Dot. They are going to Wheaton Illinois this month to Kurt Eisleben's wedding. He is being sent to the Medical Record Department at West Point. The luck of the Irish. They have decided they will just send Lucy a little money this Xmas—it won't be much, but they want you and Lucy to have a couple of drinks in Hawaii on them.

Your letter about apologizing for upsetting us was waiting for us. PLEASE, never feel that we don't want to hear these things. Of course, they upset us—as they would any parent who has a son over ther, but this is the only way I can stir people up. Please remember we are thousands of miles away from this damn war, with no restrictions on buying, no rationing—only huge taxes—and we must be told and others must be told—so keep up the information. We must have it. You have to realize that most of the women I come in contact with lead very sheltered lives—myself included—and their main concern is with their children and their husbands—who for the most part have been very successful. This is the story of a great part of America and the saddest thing is that none of them are aware that this is going to change.

But then I get another disturbing picture when I talk to Dennis. He has a history professor—Dr. Jenner who blatantly is informing them that Russia is going to insidiously take over within ten years. He is not a John Bircher—in fact, the reverse. He is informing his students they deserve to take over—and he goes into great detail with them showing the progress and the desirability of the Communistic state. It was rather disturbing and I'm quite surprised a southern, church orientated school would allow this. I really do have some patriotism; and it upsets me that our country is being torn apart by this Vietnaamese war; financially and mentally. Never have I seen people so divided—and this is not good. I really am praying that this second moratorium can be kept in the peaceful vein that the first one was—but I am worried. If violence breaks out among this group it will be finished. We have men like McGovern and Fulbright who will be finished if it turns into a riot. I know some drastic changes have to be made, but I truly do not think any of you young people would truly like living under a communistic state—where you would be told exactly on what job you would spend the rest of your life—and this is part of it.

I realized this more than ever when I received a package from Memphis State last week. It was a bound copy of your Thesis which was sent to us. Needless to say, your father and I were so proud; even tho dad said—well some concrete evidence of all the money I spent. But you might not have been able to have had this book published in Russia. I really do not know what the answer is, and perhaps we must just resign ourselves to the fact that man is an inhuman creature and we can't change it. Just read a book about Alexander the Great and it was quite challenging. We really haven't progressed at all.

Am going out tomorrow and get a watch for you. It is not going to be an expensive one as evidently you must have some lovely characters fighting with you. This just made your father furious—that boys in the same hell would do this to one another. Also, I didn't forget about the Navy combat boots, but I cannot find one place that knows what I am talking about. Will still try.

Well I'm beginning to get invitations to showers from friends of Cindy Hodgson. She is going to be home Thanksgiving and wants to get together with Linda about the wedding. The dresses are ordered and Linda wants to give her a shower at Xmas. This means I'll have to do it. Also received an invitation to Kurt's wedding—which we won't make—and an invitation to Letitia Janis's son's wedding. This is another Catholic mass wedding on the 28th. I don't understand how he can be married in a catholic wedding as he has been married, has a child, and was divorced. Oh well!

Am enclosing a picture we took of Dennis and Linda at school. We bought a $6.00 roll of Polaroid film to take 8 picture to sens to you and this is the result. Your father just doesn't know how to load this camera and the rest of the pictures were all ruined.

We, of course, took the dog with us and about 50 miles out of St. Louis she proceeded to get car sick. Every 50 miles we were stopping to clean up the back of the car. This was it! Either she goes or I go, but never the two of us. I will say she had a ball after we got to Athens and she could run around the school having everyone pet her and make over her. But when we got to Aunt Dot's it was a different story. She and their cat just didn't hit it off—so we had to lock them up in different rooms. Chanel loved Puttyshwa, but it certainly wasn't returned.

You take care of yourself and inform the U.S. Army and the Government of Hanoi that if one hair of your head is touched they will have a whirling dervish on their hands.

Talked to Judy Colbert just before we left and Bill graduated and then turned down his commission.. They are sending him to Radar school for a month, a month's leave and then Viet Naam in January. But he still feels he comes out ahead moneywise and term wise. He is due to be released from service October 1-1970, so he will spend about 9 months in Viet Naam. That's figuring the angles.

Let us hear everything and I loved the pictures but I see such sadness in your eyes. Please don't let all of this horror get to you too much.

With all our love—
Mom & Dad

SP/4 Dail W. Mullins, Jr.
488-48-0511
CoA, 26th ENGR. BN.
APO SF, 96256

20 November 1969

Dear Mom and Dad,

Well, I got your Christmas package today—thank you so much for the watch. It's really nice, but I hope you didn't spend too much for it. Barksdale and I also want to thank you for the doorbell apparatus—I know you think we're both over the hill, but perhaps it will satisfy you somewhat to know that we are probably the only enlisted men in the Americal Division, and perhaps Vietnam, who have a doorbell in their hooch. Lennie and Bob, with their $1000 a month apartment, have nothing on us. As a matter of fact, we're hopeful of making next month's issue of "Better Bunkers and Gardens"! Ah, the humor of the American G.I. I am going insane.

In addition to the package, I also received your letter today—the long one, written after your return from Athens and Louisville. The day before I had gotten a letter from Denny, telling me that you had been down to see the kids, but, of course, he made no mention of the fact that you were able to see Aunt Dottie and Uncle Bob. I was so glad to hear that you were able to visit with them.

It was really refreshing to hear you describe your visit with Linda, Denny and the rest of the Athens avant-garde. I was especially impressed, of course, by your description of some of their professors. Professor McCaslin sounded particularly interesting. This is probably because the only disturbing, thought-provoking people around here are the VC—and I don't ever want to take any courses under them.

I, too, was somewhat surprised to hear that Athens College had on its faculty a man like Dr. Jenner who, apparently, is an unabashed procommunist. If George Wallace ever found out about him, he'd probably have the Alabama Highway Patrol firebomb him out of the state. While I do have to admire the school for having the courage to allow such opinions and viewpoints to be aired so openly, I, like you, am far from being an advocate of Sino/Soviet-style communism. I suppose that the closest thing to a communistic dictatorial state that the United States has is its armed forces—and if this is anything like a nation under communism, then I don't want any part of it. Is that patriotism? Or fear? Are they the same?

I fear I must admit that, I too, am governed somewhat by the principle of the Territorial Imperative and, subsequently, have some patriotism left in me. I would hope, however, that I could keep this "flag-waving instinct" to a rational minimum and not succumb to misty-eyed emotionalism.

I am of two minds, really, about the division of thought in the United States as a result of Vietnam. I suppose, from a purely political standpoint, that it is not a good thing. On the other hand, I cannot help but feel, somehow, that it is a good thing from a "moral" (I hate that word) point of view.

I wanted to quote you part of a letter that Barksdale received from an old friend of his from Murray State University, Dr. R. B. Parsons. Dr. Parsons, incidentally, is about 75 years old.

"This polarization of points of view concerning the Vietnam War is becoming almost brutal. It is becoming almost dangerous to dissent. Every effort is being made to discount the Mobilization for Peace. According to news reports, over 40,000 troops are in Washington right now to control the demonstration which is set for tomorrow. Again, according to reports, the F.B.I. is urging bus companies not to charter buses to Washington. Nobody knows whether participation in Mobilization activities will jeopardize government positions in the future. News correspondents say that returning veterans are being urged and admonished before leaving Vietnam not to participate in anti-war activities after they are discharged. They now have selected and trained commissioned officers, home from Vietnam, going over the country making speeches and showing slides in support of the war. According to them, our mission in Vietnam is noble; our success in attaining objectives is assured—if war dissenters can be quieted, and the appearance of national unity can be maintained.

"Nixon seems to be using Agnew as a hatchet man to fell dissenters from policy set by Nixon. A very neat arrangement; Agnew says the things "the old Nixon" would have said when he was Senator Joe McCarthy's most ardent supporter; President Nixon neither endorses nor disavows what his vice-president says, but he says he thinks Agnew is doing a fine job as vice-president.

"Paul Newman says this war has caused the mass of Americans no sorrow, no pain. There is no rationing. Many Americans are right now becoming rich, and then richer. Except for the armed servicemen in and around Vietnam, and their loved ones and concerned friends, and, of course, young men who fear they may have to go to Vietnam and their families, the war is too far away to be of more than marginal concern. Paul Newman, therefore, is in favor of moratoriums, boycotts and other non-violent means of causing pain, inconvenience, discomfort in the vast majority of the unconcerned."

What can I say? Peace?
Dail

SP/4 Dail W. Mullins, Jr.
488-48-0511
CoA, 26th ENGR. BN.
APO SF, 96256

23 November 1969

My dear Parents,

Yesterday I received a wonderful letter from Lucy in response to my informing her that we would be together in Hawaii over Christmas—she was certainly as happy and thrilled about the prospect as I had hoped she'd be; indeed, as I am. Only about 22 more days until I leave—and, believe me, I'll be counting every one.

On the 26th of this month, as I think I told you, our whole company will be going down to Chu Lai for a few days of standdown (modified R&R). We'll be returning on the afternoon of the 29th. It should be nice to get away from Hawk Hill for a change. Shortly after we return, however, 2nd and 3rd platoons are scheduled to go out into the field (for as long as 2 weeks, I've heard). As far as I can determine, we'll be heading south, down near Tam Ky to a #10 spot called the Pineapple Forest. This area used to be called an NVA R&R Center, I presume because of the fact that the enemy used to exist in and around the place largely unchallenged. Now, however, they have apparently been run out, leaving behind a good many bunkers, mines and booby traps. Our job, I guess, will be to go in, along with the infantry, and destroy these things. We're supposed to be accompanied in this mission by 4 CEV's (combat engineer vehicles), which are nothing more than huge tanks which have attached to them, dozer blades. While not exactly looking forward to this little jaunt, it ought to be a good chance to get some interesting flicks. As I told Sgt. Hileman, it's getting too close to my R&R for me to be carrying on like that! If we're out there for as long as I've heard we will be, they may have to send out a special chopper to pick Barksdale and me up!

You asked about some of the other fellows I used to mention. Well, Doc has gone home. He came down on levy orders for Vietnam near the end of his two year hitch, so he only had to spend 8 months over here. Lemar, that architectural engineer from Chicago, apparently couldn't take it in a line platoon, so he managed to secure a rather easy job in the orderly room as company architect and assistant operation's sergeant. While I'm no more fond of going out into the field as Lemar was, I feel that if these kids can, so can I. Besides, I feel that if I'm going to carry on an active program of criticism of the American Vietnam policy when I get home, I should know what I'm talking about. While some of the things I see and experience are most unpleasant as a result of this, I also feel that criticism of Vietnam would be unjust if I had spent all of my time behind a desk. Maybe, though, when I really get short, and hence, more nervous, I will start trying to get a little less hazardous job.

Elliot, the other friend I have over here, is presently on R&R, although he should be back soon. He's another one who dropped his demo duty and hazardous duty pay because "it made him too nervous", although he is still in a line platoon. As a matter of fact, he's an assistant squad leader, as I am.

Five months and days, folks—five months and days. Pretty soon I'll be so short I'll be skydiving off a dime!

Remember when I first came over here, and you wanted to get me a pistol? Well, the other day all demo men were issued a .45 calibre pistol to accompany their grenade launcher. So, now I have a pistol. About the only thing its really good for, though, is taking to morning formation—needless to say, its a lot lighter than my M-79! Take care, all, and please continue to write. Your letters are Godsends.

Love,
Dail

SP/4 Dail W. Mullins, Jr.
488-48-0511
CoA, 26th ENGR. BN.
APO SF, 96256

1 December 1969

Chu Lai

Dear Mom and Dad,
Well, as you can see from the above date, our standdown was postponed for a few days—infantry units, of course, have first priority over other front line troops (artillery, armor, engineers), so we had to wait another three days while some grunts had their standdown. It was for the best, I think—yesterday, our first in Chu Lai, was the first time in almost two weeks that the monsoon broke—right now it's fairly cool out, and quite nice; beautiful weather, really, it reminds me

of early fall back home. I miss the colored leaves, though—palm trees and rice sprouts don't turn in the fall.

I won't be doing anything special down here—I bought a small suitcase to take to Hawaii and deposited some money in the bank; other than that, I just plan to take it easy, read a little and, if the weather stays nice, perhaps swim.

I have just finished reading a couple of short, interesting books that you might enjoy. One is "America vs. America: the Revolt Against Middle Class Values" by James A. Michener. I think you both would find this book fairly easy to empathize with. It's a short study—I should say, personal commentary—by a middle-aged, middle-class man on many of the current trends which are so frightening and puzzling to the middle-aged and middle-class people of America—the generation-gap, Vietnam, the peace movement, campus riots, the "new" morality, etc.). Naivé in its depth, the book, nevertheless, may help a little to bridge the gap.

The other book, which you must read is called "The Bitter Heritage". It's by Arthur M. Schlesinger, whom I must say, certainly knows how to use the English language. The book, of course, deals with Vietnam—why, where, how, when and what will be. It is excellent.

Here's an interesting little tidbit of news. You are aware, I'm sure, of the Vietnam massacre scandal that broke the other day. Well, if you've paid any attention to the details, you will have observed that the incident did occur in the Americal Division, specifically in the 196th lib. AO, my own. Well, as a result of this story, the 196th AO is presently being invaded by a hoarde of newsman, mainly, I understand, from CBS. Anyway, just before we came down here, our company commander gave us all a briefing. While in the standdown area, he said, we were not to speak to any newsmen who approached us until we had first been cleared by him. He said that newsmen were only interested in selling papers, and that anything we said to them, no matter how sincere or innocent, would be blown up all out of proportion back home, bringing dishonor both to the men of the U.S. Army and to our country itself. After the formation I went up to Sgt. Hileman, our platoon sergeant, and jokingly said, "Boy, I wish a CBS reporter would get a hold of me!" Hileman almost turned pale and said "My God, don't you do it! If anybody in 2nd platoon says anything to a newsman, the captain will have us all out in the field on a demo mission!" I thought it was interesting to learn how the army goes about assigning men for various missions—don't you.

Well, only 16 more days until I leave LZ Hawk Hill enroute to my own Hawaiian love-in! I'll be calling you long distance from there, so be prepared! Lucy, I understand, has made reservations at the Hilton Hawaiian Village—and from talking to Sgt. Neroda, who was stationed in Hawaii for awhile, the place is really up-tight.

In many ways I feel kind of guilty about going to Hawaii—I know how much you both would love to go, but can't because of other financial commitments. Here I am getting to go, and I don't even have a steady job—haven't even finished school! I hope you understand why I'm going to spend the money to do it—everybody over here has got to get away once, even if just for a week. And, too, I think Lucy may need an "R&R" too—I suppose a war is just as hard on the people back home as it is on those who are fighting it. Please don't think we're throwing the money away.

Well, take it easy, maintain, and think peace. Always.

Love,
Dail

P.S. Thanks ever-so-much for the second and third Christmas packages. The tree is up and standing tall in our bunker. We got a great many laughs over cards and book—some of the cards have been put on our Wall of Respect. Thank you, again—really. Oh, the simple things. . . . .

SP/4 Dail W. Mullins, Jr.
488-48-0511
CoA, 26th ENGR. BN.
APO SF, 96256
2ND PLATOON

6 December 1969

Dear Mom and Dad,

Thank you for your nice Thanksgiving message—yes, I did get my stomach filled, if not my heart. The cooks (two of them) had stayed up all night cooking us a remarkably good turkey dinner. The CO did say something intelligent (for once!) in his Thanksgiving message to us. "What do most of you have to be thankful for here in Vietnam?" Pause. "Well, it will be your last Thanksgiving over here!" That brightened up my whole day.

I do hope you folks had a pleasant (by that I mean noisy and frollicsome) holiday—I know you're worried about me, and that that distracts from the joyousness of your special days—not altogether, though, I hope.

I got a letter from Lucy yesterday—in it she mentioned that you and she had had a long talk on Thanksgiving Day. She said that your main complaint about our correspondence was the fact that I never answer the questions you ask of me (?) Specifically, she said, I had failed to give you an answer about whether we were allowed to send tape recordings home. This puzzled me, since I wasn't able to recall having received such a request. I guess it just slipped my mind. Anyway, to answer your question. Yes, I can. I believe all of the Vietnam USO's, in conjunction with the ARC, have such facilities, including Chu Lai. Many of the fellas that do send taped letters and events home, however, have their own small, cartridge-playing recorders, much like Bob has. Their parents, of course, have one too, and they just keep two or three recordings going back and forth. Why? Did you want me to send a tape home? I can always borrow someone's recorder and possibly a cartridge, but what would you play it on?

Here's an interesting news item that probably won't make it back to the world—except by me. Two men from Hawk Hill—specifically, from the 523rd Signal Battalion, have recently deserted to the enemy around here. An infantry unit working this AO spotted one of them, a tall blonde-headed kid, with some VC—he, too, was carrying an AK-47 rifle. I could possibly understand deserting to an enemy that had it as good (relative term) as we do—but to want to go out and live with the VC in the jungles and rice paddies! I don't understand that at all. I really don't.

After today, only 9 more days until I leave Hawk Hill for R&R. Boy, I'm getting so excited! You were right, of course, about what you said in your letter regarding the depression that is sure to follow when our togetherness ends. All of us are well aware of the "Post-R&R blues"—everybody gets them. Nevertheless, knowing I'll have but 4 1/2 months left when I return will not make my letdown reach the depths that it did upon first arriving in 'Nam—talk about depressed! That's one reason why I wanted to wait as long as possible for my R&R—I at least wanted to be "over the hill", so to speak.

Well, enough of my chatter. I'll probably write once or twice more before I leave (unless we go out into the field as planned), and, of course, I'll call you from Hawaii. Take care, keep writing—and I'll see you in the merry month of May.

Peace.
Dail

Monday, December 1,

My dear,

The start of another month. At our age you hate to tear off any day on the calendar, but this year I'd like to tear off 5 months in one fell swoop.

Writing this with the typewrite on top of Denny's bed, the television going and my right foot stuck in a pail of hot water. Saturday night we went out with the children and when we came home the two dogs bear down on you. As I walked into the dining room I tried to avoid them, slipped on the floor and broke one of my toes. Nothing they can really do, but Emerson said to soak the foot in hot water. Your father said if I wasn't waxing the damned floors so much I wouldn't have slipped.

Well everyone has left and the calm after the storm is deafening. Poor Chanel just roams from room to room looking for her buddy. It was a rushed weekend as several things came up. Friday Mrs. Sperber (steve's mother) had a luncheon for Cindy Hodgson and it was a massed room full of the establishment. They have moved out among the wealth and the home and its furnishings would feed a dozen families of ten each for the rest of their lives. Amusing to contemplate how they accept their new son-in-law Nathan Lipscomb, whom Sue Sperber just married. Don't think they are too thrilled. Then Friday night Ronald Janis was married in an hour long Catholic Mass wedding and I was ready to throttle your father. He mumbled through the whole ceremony and I am afraid many people heard him as he muttered constantly "My God, this is an insult to intelligence—and Good Lord, it's like a carnival." I had to agree with him, but again we must respect the rights of all—Catholic, black, bigot, etc. After the wedding they had a typical Irish catholic reception at the Knights of Columbus hall on Lindell Blvd. They had an open bar and your father came back after getting us a couple of drinks and said to me "I wish you would learn to drink something besides a Presbyterian, especially in a K.C. hall; the bartender looked at him a little oddly."

263

Called Frank Currier's mother to get his address for Lucy (incidentally, it is the same) and almost wished I hadn't as I think she will be another person who will definitely count me off her list. We got into quite a heated discussion over the moratorium, especially when she called all the people who participated "parasites", and thought it was the most sacrilegious thing she had ever seen when they read off the names of the dead. Well, it takes all kinds to make up the mixed up mass of humanity. Evidently Frank shares these feelings and it again shows the spread between enlisted men and officers. Frank writes and tells her that the upper command is quite worried about these displays as they claim it would be mass slaughter of all our men if immediate withdrawal of all troops were pronounced. They claim there is no possible way to get them all on carriers within six months and they are afraid that all South Vietnaamese would immediately turn on us and it would be impossible to protect the men waiting to get on transportation vehicles. He claims that right now Saigon is off limits to all men for fear of sporadic fighting between our men and civilians.

And then Saturday night we went with Bob and our Linda to the Brathaus and met Linda Beswick and her "new" fiancée. I say new because this is her third go round. Anyway this young boy just got back from a year in Viet Naam with the 9th Infantry. I didn't want to pry as so many of them do not want to talk about their experiences, but Linda was asking him about the prevalence of smoking "pot" and the use of other drugs over there, and he said one incident he was a small part of, swore him off any form of it for life. He said he saw a large group of our infantry wiped out because the fellows manning the artillery were all high on marijuana. Really, the more I hear from both hawks, doves, and veterans, the more I'd like to find a hole and hibernate.

Needless to say, your father and I will be watching with baited breath the pulling of the first capsule with birth date, from the fish bowl tonite. As Denny said—"I've never won anything in my life, and my name has never been picked for anything, but watch July 5th be the date pulled out." Or, Bob says, January 6. From my interpretation of the whole bit, any date near Denny's birthday could mean he would be pulled in any time.

Am not going into the massacre the 196th pulled in April of 1968 as it really to me rivals Hitler's Daschau. Our country and it's people seem to be acting entirely with utter confusion and frustration and no one seems to know what to do.

Received your Christmas Card, picture, and two nice letters. BUT, we sure are not a bit happy about the detail you are going on and I think you have more than proved your manly characteristics and it's time you put in for a desk job. I mean it. Enough is enough. Whatever happened to the re-assignment in Japan. How come none of the good rumours come to pass.

Just finished a letter to Lucy and I don't know if it is entirely out of the question, but I sure wish she could stop in St. Louis on the way home from Hawaii, if even for one day.

Yesterday after the children left Dad said "let's just leave the mess and take a ride." He's got a wild idea of wanting a place out in the country and we drove out to Warrenton to see some "A" frame places they are putting up for people, on 3 acres of ground. We can't take care of the 50 feet we have her—and what he would do with 3 acres I can't imagine. Anyway, on the way out as we neared Weldon Springs we could see a large crowd of people and several police cars on the opposite side of the road and we assumed it had been an accident. On the way back, we were slowed by about 100 men and police evidently scouring the roadside looking for something. When we arrived home we find that a hired gunman from Florida had killed a witness in a narcotics investigation and thrown him on the roadside. Then he was evidently stopped for either a speeding offense or routine investigation, and he killed the highway patrol man who had stopped him. You just can't get away from violence anymore. Told Dad I'll just crawl in a hole on Berry Road and take my chances.

Am enclosing a couple of pictures we took over the holiday that thought you might enjoy. Notice the beard on young Bob DeCturis.

I'm sure you know your father's comments every time he looks at him. The first thing poor Denny had to do when he came home was get his hair cut. I will say I promoted it too, as it was dangerous the way he was going around. It isn't so long in back, but it seems to grow long in front and doesn't stay back and he literally can't see—so we did make him get the front cut or he'd be going blind. His dad says part of his poor grades is probably because he couldn't see his books. Bob does the most perfect imitation of the Fire Island boys—or the queens—and he does it whenever we say anything about the beard. "My", he drawls, "since I have this beard I just constantly fight everyone off—as they can't believe I am not Paul Newman". Funny thing, he does look a little like him with it.

You be careful and let us hear when you can.

Do you remember Mary Witte's brother, John? He spent a year in Viet Naam and got back the 2nd week in October. A week after he arrived home he was killed while riding a motor cycle. What horrible irony.

With love and more love and PEACE,

P.S. When we went over to Dr. Emerson's last night to have him look at my foot, they were telling us that David will be home for Christmas. He has spent the last month in the hospital—as he evidently had a very severe case of mononucleosis. Also their 18 year old Timmy who is in the Navy up at Great Lakes, and his wife who is 17—are expecting a baby. Think everyone knew this was the reason for the hurry-up wedding, but the Emersons are accepting it so well. Her parents have evidently completely disowned her so it is now up to the Emersons. They really have more things happen to them.

SP/4 Dail W. Mullins, Jr.
488-48-0511
CoA, 26th ENGR. BN.
APO SF, 96256

7 December 1969

My dear parents,

I received your letter of December 1 this evening—as usual I couldn't wait to open it. Your typed letters, even if they just contain silly news about Chanel or Mrs. Schilling, are always such fun to read. I suppose my favorite tales are those describing confrontations you have with various-and-sundry members of the "establishment." I can well imagine the emotional dilemma they must put you in, the role of social activist being such a new one for you—nevertheless they are funny. Keep up the good work.

The pictures you enclosed were wonderful. You all look very fine, as does Bob (I dig that beard). John (John?) is sure a cute dog. What kind of twisted mind would name a dog John?

I can certainly sympathize with you, Dad, at the Catholic wedding, and I agree with you completely in that such goings-on are an insult to one's intelligence.

I got a letter from Ray and Jennifer today. It had apparently been written some time ago and mailed later, because most of the news that it contained had already been related to me by Lucy. Jennifer, as I'm sure you know, is "with child" again, this one being due in April. Ray said that they'd be two ahead of us then, but I didn't even know we were racing.

As usual, you seem to have been misinformed about the exact nature of the new draft system. Consequently, I am enclosing the article that the Pacific Stars and Stripes had on the matter, in the hopes that it will clear things up. I have underlined those sections pertaining specifically to Bob and Denny.

That was a very interesting story you related about what Linda Beswick's fiancée told Linda concerning the marijuana incident in Vietnam. I do get a little sick and tired, however, of everyone picking on the potheads—how come nothing is ever said about the men who are killed or injured as a result of alcohol, which is a much more serious problem than marijuana will ever be in Vietnam. But, since the consumption of alcoholic beverages is a socially acceptable form of tension release and marijuana smoking is not, the latter are, of course, always criticized. One day in the not too distant future, though, marijuana will be legalized (you cannot legislate morality—witness the Prohibition), and it will be interesting to see what the Army does then—whether it will supply its troops with grass just as it does now with beer.

I'm not sure whether your comments about my "trying to prove my manhood" were meant to be taken seriously or not. I was not a little upset about them, though. Do you think I enjoy going out to places like that? Do you think I wouldn't get a desk job if I could? If you're an infantryman, though, you just don't tell the CO after 4 or 5 months, "Well, I'm tired of being a grunt—I think I'd like to get a little easier job now!" Unfortunately, things just don't work that way. I'm afraid I'll be a combat engineer for the whole 12 months.

You asked about the Japan rumor? Well, the rumors are still around, but, of course, everyone hesitates to get too excited for fear of being let down. Sgt. Hileman, our platoon sergeant, said that the 196th light infantry brigade is definitely being pulled out in February, but that this is desperately trying to be kept hush-hush. Apparently, we will be sent back to the States rather than to Japan, however. I don't know to take this news—Sgt. Hileman hates Vietnam as much as I do, so his remark might have to be taken as so much wishful thinking. As far as I'm concerned, I'll be here until May 14—anything less will be a pleasant surprise.

Well, take care, all, keep the faith and think peace.

Love,
Dail

December 6, 1969

My dear,

Haven't heard since your two letters from Chu Lai and your Christmas card, but we know you are on a stupid duty—so I try not to get too concerned (Ha!).

Finally went into see Dr. Mortenson—after an absence of a year in September. Of course he wanted to know what the deal was, and I told him that after the mess with Linda and a few other things, I had had my bellyful of the medical profession and that I was there only under the duress of your father. Anyway he did blood tests, urine, the works. I was mainly concerned with the eye hemmorage but he didn't make anything of that—said it was an injury and that my blood pressure was fine. I insisted that I had not injured the eye, but he said I did—so who's to argue. He didn't like the swollen foot and asked me if I had had it x-rayed. I said no and he said if it wasn't broken then the swelling and discoloration could possibly mean a blood clot and he didn't like that. So he xrayed it and luckily the middle toe is cracked up high. There is nothing in the world they can do about and you just limp around like an old lady—which I am anyway.

Went out to dinner with the Seiberts last night. His father is still fighting tooth and nail to live. As charlie said, any young person would be dead by now. It has been hard on all of them. They have a night nurse who comes in at 11 PM and stays until 7 AM and then Dr. Seibert's step-mother comes in and stays until Charlie goes in at 6 PM. Charlies stays until the night nurse comes. He's been doing this for almost two weeks now and he looks so tired. He (or Joan) finally asked his brother Bill if they would mind staying last night until around 10 so that Charlie and Joan could at least go out to dinner one night.

Anyway, around the middle of the soup course Charlie and your father got into the Viet Naam situation and it was hell bent for leather from there on. It really is so foolish because it just upsets both of them to no avail—Charlie is not going to be changed and your father will never believe that Nixon is anything but a "bastard", which is what he calls him now. Charlie told your Dad he is just talking about all problems now with parental hysteria. This was like waving a flag in front of your father. We had everyone in the restaurant looking at us.

Mike Seibert has quit the Wellston police force and has taken a job as Deputy Sheriff in Cedar Rapids, Iowa. Joan, of course, makes her usual caustic remarks about the cowboy sheriff and that he'll never be satisfied anywhere for very long—but I told her I think she might be wrong. I think the type thing he is going to now will be just up his alley. He wants so badly to be a "big shot" and deputy in a town this size may give him a feeling of importance. He has gotten very bitter about some of the things he has seen and done in Wellston—which is really a ghetto now with serious problems of dope rings, fences, burglary rings, and the works. And as Mike says—no cooperation from anyone—just dirty foul mouthed words thrown at them. If they do their job they are maligned and if they don't, they are jumped on. Being in police work is extremely difficult these days.

As I was sitting up in the bedroom typing this the mailman came and EUREKA, a letter from you.

PLEASE, PLEASE, don't think we are anything but ecstatic about your Hawaiian trip—our only regret is that we cannot offer to pay for the entire trip. This week I am sending Lucy $50.00 as a Xmas gift. I hate gifts like this, but I am sure she could use this better than some trinket. Next year we'll get back to the gifts. The only thing that really bothers us is knowing how hard it is going to be when you have to say goodbye after a few wonderful days—but chin up, we really can take more than we think we can. I did write and ask Lucy that, if it were at all possible, to stop in St. Louis for even one day on her way home. We'd all love to see her so much.

One of my stops today will be the library and I plan to get both the books you mentioned. I'll say right now I am not a fan of Arthur Schlesinger as I firmly believe he is a rank opportunist and talks out of both sides of his mouth. He is one of Jackie Kennedy Onnassis! favorite consorts and personally is so unappealing. I'll grant his rhetoric is hypnotic, and whenever I listen to him I cannot curb the feeling that he is not particularly interested in the words that are flowing from him—but the beautiful resonant music they make. But I've been wrong before.

After reading your letter describing the "Easy Rider" Dennis made it a point to go see it while he was home. Linda and Bob had both seen it in Huntsville. Dennis came home most enthused, especially as he said "living in Athens, the armpit of the South". He was a little up-tight about the comments from the viewers as they left the theatre, in stating that it was just another bit of propaganda about the southern people. Dennis said he almost got into a few knock-downs when very loudly he let everyone know that it was typical of the south and that you never fail to see trucks with their guns racked up behind them, every time you get out on a highway.

Yes, we are well aware of the massacre bit, and as I wrote you before—I'm just amazed that people are shocked. At first all the news was about the Lt. Calley—but now we have his senior officer Capt Medina (a typical Army product) being put in the limelight. Were you aware that Capt Medina has procured the services of F. Lee Bailey as his attorney. Now it has become a real side-show and just the type situation that Bailey revels in. He has begun his tirade of his client "being tried by the news media", before being proven guilty in the court and will probably convince everyone that he could never have a fair trial now and it will be dropped—like the Green Berets.

[obviously something missing here]

———————————

SP/4 Dail W. Mullins, Jr.
488-48-0511
CoA, 26th ENGR. BN.
APO SF, 96256

11 December 1969

Dear Mom and Dad,

Well, our field mission to Pineapple Forest has apparently been cancelled, whether permanently or only temporarily, know one yet knows. I'm sure this news is as much a relief to you as it was to me—for the first time since learning of my R&R, I have been able to relax and think about what good times Lucy and I are going to have. Only 9 more days and I'll be landing in Hawaii!

I've received two nice Christmas cards so far—one from Barbara Fattig and one from Mrs. Seibert. Both wrote very nice notes, and I must answer them as soon as possible. Barbara said that she and Don are really enjoying Birmingham this year, much more so than last; Don has a brand new office-lab combination, and has been able to do a little research in addition to his teaching commitments.

I received two letters from you today—one postmarked the 4th [no letter dated Dec. 4] the other the 6th. That's never happened before.

That's two bad about your toe, Mom. I know from experience how painful a cracked bone can be—you'll remember I did the same thing to my finger a while back when I clobbered it with that stupid hammer. I remember the night it happened—I took 4 Darvons in the space of a few hours and the damn thing still hurt so much I couldn't sleep. I was relieved, however, to hear that, except for your foot, Dr. Mortenson gave you a fairly clean bill of health.

Although Mrs. Seibert made no mention of Mike's new job, neither did she make any of her expected caustic remarks about him—I agree with you in one respect; I think his position as deputy sheriff may be just what he needs. Then too, the separation may be good for both of them. I can imagine how frustrating police work must be these days—it probably always has been, to a certain extent, but with the new element that was added by Mayor Daley's storm troopers, I imagine things are much worse. While I certainly think that our nation's police forces should be closely watched at all times, and their mistakes remedied, I see no reason for some of the unfair burdens that they must often be made to bear. To be a policeman is probably not all that hard—but to be a good one—well, there's the rub.

Our company just yesterday received the issue of Time with the cover story on Lt. William Calley and the My Lai massacre—I thought the coverage quite interesting and, as is usually the case with Time, rather damning. I particularly thought that the essay on the inescapable fact of evil's existence was quite good. Having been over here for some seven-odd months now, I, too, was somewhat surprised at the open-mouthed shock which you say has run through the country, and which I gather, from Time's article and others, is indeed the case. While I certainly have not witnessed anything to compare with what apparently took place at My Lai, and, indeed, have no desire to, I have seen and heard other things, by themselves perhaps rather small and insignificant, which when viewed collectively tend to support the growing realization that America, for all her self-piety, is really no more immune from such acts as this as are those "other" countries at which we are so often quick to point the finger of injustice and shout "J'accuse!" I suspect you rather hit the nail on the head, Mom, when you asked what is to be expected when you give 18 and 19 year-olds weapons and train them to kill, although I certainly wouldn't limit such acts to specific age groups. While the evidence is certainly not overwhelming, it is rapidly becoming clear that the some one and three quarter million years that separate today's "civilized" human being and Leakey's African veldt ape is not so vast as we once thought. Unfortunately, man's psycho-biological development has not managed to keep pace with his power of environmental alteration. That is why you still find people bludgeoned to death in the heart of vast, marvellous and beautiful cities.

I'm afraid I do not share your views of Mr. F. Lee Baily—I think he's fantastic.

Have a nice Christmas—don't worry about me, please, and I'll call you all from Hawaii. As Mrs. Seibert said, this will be a bittersweet Christmas for Lucy and I, but it will sure be better than not seeing her at all.

Take care—peace and love,
Dail

SP/4 Dail W. Mullins, Jr.
488-48-0511
CoA, 26th ENGR. BN.
APO SF, 96256

28 December 1969

Chu Lai

Dear Mom and Dad,
    Well, R&R is over—Lucy is home now and I'm back in Chu Lai, tired, a little depressed but knowing, too, that I've only got a little less than 4 1/2 months to go. It's a better feeling than I had when I arrived over here the first time.
    Thank you for the Christmas card—believe it or not, it arrived on Christmas Day. Pretty good timing.
    I enjoyed talking to all of you on the phone—you all sounded fine. I only hope it didn't cost too much.
    Hawaii, needless to say, was just fantastic—outasite, as Esquire Magazine says. Perhaps we tried to do too much, as Lucy and I were both pretty tired when we left, but the time seems to go so fast and, in fact, there is so much to do.
    Lucy was waiting for me at Fort Derussy when I arrived there by bus from the airport—bless her heart, she had been there with all the other wives since 4:00 that morning, waiting, and listening to the chaplain as he tried to keep them busy and relaxed.
    Our hotel room was just beautiful—right on the beach, 8 floors up, with a beautiful view of Honolulu, especially at night. We had our own little patio and we enjoyed sitting out there with a couple of Hawaiian drinks just looking.
    I, of course, got to take a "real" bath, lie on a "real" mattress and drive a "real" car—tremendous—I had almost forgotten what it was like.
    Although we didn't do any surfing as such, we did go down to one of the windward beaches and romp around in some of those 10' waves—that's really fun. We drove around the island, through Dole's pineapple fields, visited the University's Sea Life Park, shopped at Ala Moana (the world's largest shopping center), went sightseeing, looked at the rich people's houses (and I do mean rich people), drank and ate alot and, in general, just had a real good time.
    Lucy, of course, being a "tropical" person, fell in love with the whole place and started figuring out how we could live there. While I must admit that that would certainly be nice, Hawaii is an awfully expensive place, and I'm afraid I would not be able to make it there as a student—I'd almost certainly have to have a job as a teacher or something, and even then it would be difficult. I also understand that the University of Hawaii is not really all that good.

Hawaii is certainly not what I would call, as you have said, a young people's place. There were people there of all ages, tiny babies to old grandparents—and everybody has a tremendous time because there's something for everyone to do. Carl Reiner stayed at our hotel—he and his wife are really funny; they went in swimming a few times when we did. I think you said you always liked him.

Well, I guess I'll close, now. Please take care, write soon, and I'll see you in May—or sooner.

Love,
Dail

SP/4 Dail W. Mullins, Jr.
488-48-0511
CoA, 26th ENGR. BN.
APO SF, 96256

January 1, 1970

Dear Mom and Dad,

I suppose that by the time this letter reaches you, the kids will have packed up and gone back to school—leaving the house, I'm sure, in a veritable shambles (would you have wanted it any other way?) I hope your holiday was as happy as mine—Lucy and I, as I told you, had a tremendous time. We didn't do anything special on Christmas (as a matter of fact, we ate dinner in a Chinese restaurant, of all places!), but it was enough, believe me, just being together.

Barksdale and I spent a couple of days loafing in Chu Lai when we got back (on the army's time!), but we finally decided that if we stayed away from Hawk Hill any longer, somebody up there would start to miss us, so we got a ride up in a jeep on the 30th. Last night we had a company new year's eve party, which culminated in a fantastic display of flares and machine-gun fire from the bunker line at midnight. Most of the fellows around here (including the first sergeant) got fairly drunk, but all Barksdale and I had was one drink—we each shot one flare out of our grenade launchers and then went to bed. I was awakened, however about a half-hour later for guard—yes, one hour after 1970 began I was on guard! Wow! Well, anyway, I go home in 1970, so the year can't be all bad.

While in Hawaii, Lucy and I decided that it is about time I started making plans for school. Although I haven't heard for sure, I assume that the opening at Alabama still holds. However, since I have the time to look around, I thought it probably wouldn't hurt to apply at a few places just to see. I am going to take advantage of the army's early out for school, that's for sure. Accordingly, I would like to ask a favor of you. When you get the time, I'd appreciate your sending me the address of the graduate school at Washington U—I have been giving some serious consideration to going there in lieu of there new genetics building. Of course, I'm not sure if they offer just what I want, but I'd certainly like to check into the matter. I'll tell you what. If you could give the graduate school a call, explain the situation (I'd want to start in September) and ask them to send me a catalogue and an application form. Be sure and specify the fact that I'll be going for the Doctorate in Genetics or Molecular Biology. Thanks much.

Well, since I really don't have much news to relate, I guess I'll close. I haven't received that package you sent yet, but I expect it will arrive any day now. By the way, we have an electric percolator now, and it sure would be nice if you could send some ground Yuban coffee sometime. Thanks.

Take care, all—it was really good to hear your voices in Hawaii. I hope that call didn't cost too much. Write soon, and I'll do the same—

Peace, love,
Dail

P.S. Thought you might enjoy the enclosed Shorttimers calendar I got from one of the ARC girls—you can mark off the days after 100 right along with me!

December 11

My dear son,

Well, 'tis the season to be jolly and you know what that means. It just means that I am, as usual, behind in everything. Shopping, cooking, writing—everything and I'm beginning to get those holiday jitters. Shopping this year is a pain in the neck because everything is so expensive. I go out to shop for Linda and I decide I'm not going to spend that kind of money on a dress that doesn't even cover her rear end and so I decide I'll make them, which is just putting me further behind.

Talked to Mrs. Paschen, Sr. today and she was telling me that your Aunt Dot was the big hit at Kurt Eisleben's wedding in Wheaton, Illinois. Guess she hit this crowd the same way she did at your wedding. I think Uncle Bob ought to see that she has a more active life as she seems to go completely beserk when she does have a real swinging week end—especially when their is champagne involved. And, of course, Mrs. Paschen was quite upset when someone at the wedding asked young Bob what religion they were and he answered—"I can't speak for my family, but I am an agnostic." She doesn't understand her son allowing his child to think in this manner. She claims that Kurt and Marilee have not been ruined by education and still are nice establishment children.

Just think, 8 more days and you'll be having a lei placed around your neck by your bride. We'll be thinking of you every minute.

Our bridge club had their Christmas party last night and Winnie had just received a tape from Wayne and he was mentioning the odd feeling he gets when he looks through his binoculars across the DMZ and sees the VC going about their business, knowing many of them are looking at him through their glasses. Claire Vieths son-in-law left the day before Thanksgiving and they received their first letter and she thinks his destination was Chu Lai, with the 2nd Medical Division. He says the only treatment he has handed out so far, has been medication for diarrhoea—which he says is evidently rampant. Well the massacre and the whole bloody war is still attention getting—but our home front is almost becoming as bad. Two young girls were murdered in St. Louis the day before yesterday by some nut who wrote the peace symbol in lipstick on a mirror. The girl who owned the home was the wife of a Viet Naam boy, who had another young girl living with her while her husband was away. Then the sniping is still a nightly occurrence down at Pruitt-Igoe housing development. They have put on foot patrol policemen on down there and these poor young fellows are scared to death. Then last night your father's friend, Dr. Walter Eckert and his family were over-powered by 5 guys in ski masks and terrorized for about five hours. He's the fellow Dad would have had remove your wisdom teeth, and he had a heart attack about two years ago. Wonder what this experience will do to his heart. And the young affluent teen-agers in the country are being picked up right and left for LSD. It's a great world and I'm really afraid the pendulum is going to swing completely back to the rigid Victorian era and more people are beginning to like what Spiro Agnew is saying. People are really frightened, and I'm sure you wonder more and more what in the hell you are doing in Viet Naam. And to make it all funnier St. Louis and Tacoma Washington, have a big feud going on as to which city has the largest Xmas Tree. Yoicks.

Talked to Dennis tonight as neither he nor Linda have written since they went back to school and we must get their tickets. They will be arriving home the 20th. He says everything was fine but that they were just busy with studies and social activities and weren't needing money right now. Well, he's honest.

Getting involved in church puts another load at Xmas and it seems every time I turn around there is some event going on or something to do for our three families—which encompass 27 children. And, of course, the sore point with me and which I keep constantly bringing up, is where are the fathers? And I just get shrugs.

Your dad has a bad cold right now. At the beginning of the winter season I really get on his neck about wearing a mask at the office. Now that he has the cold he wears the mask so he won't pass it on to anyone—not realizing that I wanted him to wear it when these jerks come in for dental work, sneezing and coughing all over the place. Speaking of dental work—he has a real weirdo patient. This fellow about 30 came in a week ago begging for a temporary repair of two partials he was wearing. He claimed he was a Chemistry major and was working on his PhD at Columbia University. He was in St. Louis as he had married a local girl. Anyway he talked your father into spending one night and an entire Wednesday trying to get a horrible mouth in some kind of condition and pulled out this wallet just stuffed with $100 bills and said he'd pay anything. Dad said "no, he would charge him just what he would normally get." Anyway this has really been something. He called yesterday and your father must have spent an hour talking to him; in fact, I was getting a little frightened. Dad finally told him that he would not go up there on a Wednesday and to come in today. He came in around noon and your father finally said—let's just terminate the whole deal and I'll write you a check for the money you have given me. He absolutely refused to take a check and said he would only take cash. Dad said he did not carry money like that around with him and so the fellow is to come in tomorrow. Anyway, after he left your dad began to think how peculiar the whole thing was, so he called the Brentwood police and in about five minutes the Captain of the plain clothes squad was in his office and was very interested, so he is going to be in the office tomorrow when this jerk shows up and is going to follow him and pick him up on a traffic charge. He assures your father his name will not be mentioned—but don't think I'm not worrying. The Captain definitely feels something is very screwy, even tho your father assured him that he was not making any accusations other than that the entire transaction was so out of the ordinary.

This sure has been a sad sack letter—but sometimes it seems this is all I have to say. We are getting some nice greetings from all our friends and it's good to hear from everyone. You take care and don't day dream too much about your R. and R. Stay alert and we are so looking forward to hearing your voice.

Much much love, prayers, and PEACE
Mom and Dad

[probably written around December 15]

My dear Dail,
This will be a little short as I have been writing Xmas cards for three days straight and I'm getting a little slap happy.

Dad had to take Chanel to the vet yesterday and when he came home I asked him what was the matter and he said "she is just full of crap." Literally. He said we must keep here clipped as the hair grows around her rear end and packs the stool around her rectum and then she is afraid to have a B.M. She is much better now and is on some kind of medicine. Really, pets can get to be quite a pain.

Then last night we had to get tickets for the kids. They will arrive home next Saturday morning and when we called Linda to tell her—she said "let me warn you that I'm going to be drunk when I get on that plane." And she probably will.

I am hoping that you will get this before you take off for beautiful Hawaii. We want you and Lucy to have a glorious time and we hope you will be able to get through to call us. We will be thinking of you both and praying that God gives you courage when you have to say Goodbye. Our prayers are always with you.

Have started reading the Bitter Heritage and will let you know what I think the next time I write.

We are having several events during the Holiday at church and I didn't realize how involved you can get if you allow it. I don't see how Lucy's mother can work as the wife of a minister and also hold a job outside of her church duties. It would drive me nuts. I sure hope Dan will be home with them for Xmas. Told Lucy I really wish they could get up here to spend the holidays with us, but I know this is his busy time.

You take care and let us hear and have a wonderful time and store up lots of memories to keep you going the four months you will have left in that foreign land.

With all the love in the world and PEACE,
Mom & Dad

———————————

Christmas night—10 o'clock

My dear,

You both have been on our minds this entire day, even with all the coming and going of neighbors and friends. We know the parting must have been hell, but you must think constantly of the goodness of this whole reunion. I, personally, am so grateful to Lucy for saving and making your Xmas such a good one, because it made our Xmas too.

Just keep in mind that you are now downhill and soon you will be home for good. I got the nicest card and note from Wayne Bill and he said he was so glad you were able to get your R. and R. and that it was the loneliest Christmas he had ever spent and he too, thought so much of little things—that when he was home, never impressed him.

We, as usual, had a good Christmas. I'm enclosing a picture which I am not too proud of, but it shows my expression when I opened a present from your Dad, which was a wig. He said I act like a kid with a train set—in other words, I've been fooling with the damn thing all day. I though the extreme accolade was Denny's remark when I first put it on—"Mom, it doesn't look bad—you look like a rich Jew." Now how would you take that.

Hope Lucy showed you one of the Xmas cards she had made up. We have had more comments about it. We are really having a problem with Dennis and Linda. They think it is the greatest card they ever saw and they both want to take it back to school with them. I do hope Lucy has a few extras.

From one of the pictures enclosed you can see that Pete is in evidence. He comes around during the holidays and during the summer. Linda has spent two entire evenings with him at the Chatter Box and comes home and tells us what a ball it is. She see most of your entire class there. She had a long talk with Harold Zeabold and he was floored to learn that you were in Viet Naam as he said no one had told him. I asked Pete what Harold was doing and he said he hadn't worked for two years and was doing nothing—living on a small inheritance he had received from one of his grandmothers. What an existence.

The Skillings just left and Pete was here and it is so funny to see him in operation (when he wants to.) He is leaving tonight with Zorumski, Steve Parsons, Pete Brown and a lot of other "junior executives" for Vail Colorado for skiing. He wanted Linda to go with him, but Bob had asked her to come up to Pennsylvania and then go to Maryland to her roommates's for New Year's Eve, but I told her she is spending the time in the Midwest. Pete gave her his New Grand Prix to use while he is gone. That guy is absolutely nuts and I think it gets your father down when she comes home and Pete makes her undecided again about Bob. Simply, because Bob is definitely more appealing to fathers than Pete—and mothers too. Pete is good for the short run but I don't think he'd wear too well. I can see Linda tied down to someone like Pete and having to compete with the chatter box.

Just finished talking to Aunt Dot and she said to be sure and give you and Lucy all their love and they talk about you constantly and think of you always. Got the funniest letter from her just before Christmas. In my next letter I'll quote some of it. I just love to get her letters and I wish she would write more often.

Joan Seibert called the other day and she was crying. I was a little upset, thinking that old Dr. Seibert had again taken a turn for the worse, but she said it was nothing like that. She said I just had to call and tell you about the most wonderful letter I received from your son. She asked me if I truly appreciated receiving letters such as yours. As she was reading it she said she couldn't help recollecting about the letters she used to get from Charlie in War 2, and from Mike in Viet Naam. Charlies, she thinks, were mimeographed and Mike's were usually only two lines—"I am fine, how are you." I tried to tell her that some people enjoy letter writing and have the ability to put their thoughts on paper with ease. I was thinking of your father. He would so love to be able to write you once-in-awhile and I always enjoyed his letters, but it is sheer agony for your dad to put himself and his thoughts on paper. It's funny, but people like that have trouble in even getting their emotions across verbally.

To make a case in point. He was so excited and so "up-tight" about your calling Sunday that he couldn't relax one minute. He kept coming in and giving all of us instructions as to what we were to say and be sure and find out this and tell you that. Then when you finally called he sputtered like an idiot and all he could keep asking you was when you left DaNang, when you got in Hawaii and how long it took you. When we hung up, he said "Did anyone let him know how much we miss him and did we ask him this or what about that." I finally convinced him that you knew you were missed.

Well, Grandma and I are speaking again. She called about a week ago asking for your father. When I told her he wasn't home she started talking and it went on for an hour and I heard all the fun and up-lifting news; Jim Mullins is in the hospital real bad, Oscar Mullins isn't expected to live, the man from the Mason's organizations that always called on her at Xmas had died, somebody from her church was carrying on with some woman and on and on. Remember—these are all people in their late 70's and 80's. Then she called the next day and I went through the whole routine again. Your father is glad we are speaking, but I told him I almost wished we weren't—if I get phone calls like this every day. Must remember if I get or live to be old, that there are more interesting things to talk about. Anyway, thought I would try and get everyone together this Sunday.

The next two days are going to be taken up with Linda's involvement with Cindy's wedding. Tonight is the rehearsal and dinner and tomorrow the wedding (Saturday), with the reception at Alquonquin. Don't think Cindy is too happy about the way it has mushroomed from a simple wedding into an "affair". His people just declared bankruptcy and neither the mother or father of Cindy's fiancee can afford to make the trip from Buffalo, New York to St Louis for the wedding. Think she would rather have had her father cut down on the wedding and offer to pay their way down here—but they might not have accepted.

Anyway, God Bless you, keep busy, and be grateful you have so many people that love you dearly. Am saving some of the cookies and cakes and candy I baked and am going to try and pack them so they arrive intact. Wish I knew some way to get a piece of our Turkey over to you.

With all our love and prayers—PEACE,
Mom and Dad

———————————

SP/4 Dail W. Mullins, Jr.
488-48-0511
CoA, 26th ENGR. BN.
APO SF, 96256

January 4, 1970

Dear Mom and Dad,

I received your letter yesterday, and it was sure good to hear from someone back home after returning to "Fun City".

I can well imagine what a dismal Christmas it was for Wayne Bill over here. I don't think he's been in Vietnam long enough to take an R&R yet, but other than that, I can understand his wanting to wait anyway. It was nice (using the term quite liberally, of course) to be able to come back here with only 4 1/2 months remaining. Tell Mrs. Bill that if there is any way she can possibly talk her daughter-in-law into changing her mind about meeting Wayne in Hawaii to do so—Lucy and I certainly didn't regret it, and I can't think of anything, other than going home, that helps the married men over here more. Even hairy, gorilla-like first sergeants start acting human when they're getting ready to see their wives over there. It's expensive and the time goes by fast—but money is to spend and time is for living, and I wouldn't have changed a thing.

Thanks for all the pictures—your wig is out of sight! Are you really going to wear it, or is it just going to sit on the closet shelf. I hope you do make use of it. Did it come with, or without, a mini-skirt?

Lucy told me about the Christmas cards she had made up, but she didn't bring one with her so, of course, I didn't get a chance to see it yet. Save yours so I can see it when I get home.

Somehow, in some strange way, it's reassuring to learn that Pete is still hanging around. Like going back to the old house you lived in as a child and seeing that the "old oak tree" you used to play in is still standing. Because Pete is still there, I somehow know that Webster is still the same. I don't at all envy all of my former classmates having the usual good times down at the Chatterbox—but it's nice to know they, and it, are still around.

I received a nice card and note from Aunt Dot, but I still haven't returned the same. I must write to her—I am glad to hear that they're all OK.

The feminine mind never ceases to amaze me—I can recall fairly well what I said in my letter to Mrs. Seibert, but, for the life of me, I cannot remember what I said that would have caused the apparent emotional outpouring which you said occurred. Why anyone would breakdown and cry upon learning that tight jockey shorts do not, in fact, cause chromosome breakage is beyond me. The tears notwithstanding, I am glad she enjoyed (?) the letter. Tell her I'd be more than happy to correspond with her more often—her letters, as you know, are quite interesting.

Don't feel bad about not being able to think of anything on the phone—I couldn't either, for that matter. But after 7 months, what can one say in 4 or 5 minutes. It was just good to hear all of your voices. And yes, I know I'm missed. Isn't every mother's son over here?

Well, I was glad to hear that you and grandma have apparently ended your feud. Being on speaking terms with her, however, may prove to require more patience and understanding than were needed when you weren't talking to one another, but I don't think you'll regret it. It's not good for two people to exist as silent enemies—even though, as I say, it may seem to require more inner strength to be friends.

Well, I guess I'll close. Not much has been happening around here—I managed to talk Sgt. Hileman into letting me make some signs for the ammo dump (AUTHORIZED PERSONNEL ONLY—NO SMOKING WITHIN 50 FEET), so that allows me to stay inside instead of working out in that damnable rain! In case you're keeping track, the latest rumor is that the Americal Division is pulling out April 15—provided the Tet Offensive isn't too offensive. Tet comes on my birthday, by the way—isn't that nice!? I'm still considering that I leave on May 14—that way I won't be disappointed if we don't get pulled out, and pleasantly surprised if we do.

Take care of yourselves—keep smiling and work for peace.
Dail

[probably written Tuesday, December 30]

My dear Dail,

This was started Sunday nite and here it is Tuesday and just being typed, but I was so teed off Sunday that I felt I musn't write to you feeling this way. Then I thought; you were always the one I spouted off to whenever things got too much, why stop now. And perhaps it may make you forget for one minute, leaving Lucy for a few more months.

Settle back and have a little extra time before you start this venomous torrent of words held back for two days.

Christmas is always the time, I know, for maudlin saccahrine remembrances; but how could we live without the looking back to happy moments and joys. Certainly not by thinking of all the rotten things that have happened to us. Anyway, at this time of the year I do go overboard in thinking of my parents and my sister and of the fun, joy, good conversation, and many laughs—and perhaps some tears—that we always had at Christmas. And I always think of the year my father almost broke his neck climbing on a two story house roof to plant footprints so that he could take a 3 year old (you) out and show him Santa Claus's footprints. And the look on your face when you came in and said "Son of a gun, Santa was here." As you will remember your Hawaiian trip, I remember this.

Anyway, being in this mood, and having your grandmother talk to me, made me decide to have a family evening. I spent the whole day cooking and fixing the table and having everything just as nice as I could. Well things were fine about an hour after they arrived. I called them all in to the table and I wish I would have had a tape recorder of the dinner conversation. First Icy (I can't give her the name of grandmother even) was having heart palpitations and little strokes as she consumed two heaping plates of food topped off with two pieces of pie with whip cream (her diagnosis). Then we heard about Earl Mullins who died because his bowels wouldn't function and the rest of the 80 year olds who God is seeing fit to want to take. (Not worrying about the 20 year olds who could perhaps do some good in this sick world, that are dying in Viet Naam). Then we heard from Basil about all the niggers on Television and how it is all out of proportion to the number of them in the world. About midway through the meal your grandmother announced how all the women from the church were coming up to her thanking God that Mayo's had cured me from being an alcoholic, for which they had had prayer meetings for over two years. There was complete silence for about one minute and then they all started shoveling food into their mouths again. Linda is the only one who could not tolerate any more and she left the table furious with your father for not saying something in my behalf. I finally said—"Oh, they have that all wrong, it was dope addiction not alcoholism. And I really do wish you would set them straight." Then your father says—"lets talk about something else."

If ever anyone ever berates Lucy in front of you and you let it go by, I personally will kick you clear across the room.

All day yesterday, I kept going around quoting scripture; such as, "Forgive them Father, for they know not what they do," "blessed are the meek," "a soft answer turneth away wrath," "let he who is without sin cast the first stone." Can't say it has helped. And the old cliche that she is getting old isn't working either, as she has been a b------ ever since I've known her. But I really am beginning to laugh (albeit hysterically). There is so much hate in this world that I really cannot be more of a part of it than I am. And hate consumes you so—that it really can make you physically ill.

Now that is off my chest.

Received your post card yesterday and you and Lucy being together those few days made my Xmas and warmed me all through the holidays. Dennis started working at the gas station the day he got home and hasn't had one day off since. He even worked Christmas day and I worry about that stupid job as gas stations are being robbed almost every minute of the hour here. Linda was to go up East but the snow, flying alone, and Pete have changed her mind. In fact, she just hung up the phone after talking to Pete from Colorado. This is the second time he has called her from there. It really worries me, but keep your mouth shut. Just cannot see Pete as anything but a perpetual bachelor—even if he shoudl get married. But she is over 21 and must make her own decisions.

Talked to Steve Thoms today. He had written you a short note and had lost your address. He said the baby was growing fast and that they really enjoyed this Xmas with him, altho they couldn't bribe him to sit on Santa Claus's lap. His mother made a trip to Europe this summer he was telling me. Wonder what they would charge me for a one way ticket to Nome, Alaska.

Last night I was sewing for Linda and listened to Woody Allen on Dick Cavetts program. They asked him what New Year's Resolution he was making and he said the only one he was really seriously considering was sleeping through Nixon's administration. They also asked him how he would handle the Viet Naam war and he said he would just send over the Chicago Police Force. They mentioned Bob Hope entertaining the troops and he said he did his part too; he entertained the deserters in Canada. That guy is so clever he is prophetic and very true.

Also read something the other day that made me think! Quoting—"it isn't the hungry or defeated people that change the world. It is the idle men, restless and discontented and envious and bored; men of education and philosophy. Men who had nothing to do and nothing to worry about and so could harbour pains in their souls. Those who scream the loudest about justice to the workingman, despise him the most and it is and was the abolitionist of the North who was most vociferous to end slavery and then used the Negro." Quite true.

The most bigoted people I know are the Christian fundamentalists who quote scripture after scripture. Even with education, people with this background have a very difficult time really believing that the world must change. I know that I still have so much further to go and I do try, but many things I'll never be able to accept. I know your father feels he should sit down and write you because he thinks you have swung too far left in some of your thinking and people who have had to work for every bit of their education and work for every possession they own are really the most frightened about an upset in the status quo.

I truly hope that some of the love that everyone seems to be talking about constantly starts flowing through everyone, but I am old, cynical, and I have a mother-in-law. (See how she keeps popping into my sub-conscious.)

David Emerson arrived home about two days before Xmas and the Emersons are having an open house New Years day, I imagine partly for David. Think I will rent an aeroplane the day you come home and have him do skywriting.

Sent Lucy 20$ which Base and Vera gave me for the two of you. I also gave her their address and I do hope she will write and thank them for it.

Talked to Aunt Dot Christmas day and that is always a joy. She is a complete nut and so is her son.

Again, we had a tragedy on the holiday. John, that little dog you saw on the pictures we sent Thanksgiving, died right after Bob got home. He had been quite ill in Athens and Linda and Bob had been taking him in to the vet every other day and they thought he was better. But Bob took him to their vet in Phila. and he took one look at him and said he had "Grand Paw"(seriously) and that there was absolutely no cure and they must put him to sleep as it was hight contagious. Of course, you know how this shook up Linda.

Am enclosing Mr. Merrill's Xmas card, which I thought you might get a kick out of. He sent this to all his friends and its just like Pete.

Excuse the griping but what a relief to rid yourself of inner poison. You do the same.

Be brave, have hope, keep your head up and pray and know that we think about you always. Let us hear—

LOVE AND PEACE
Mom & Dad

SP/4 Dail W. Mullins, Jr.
488-48-0511
CoA, 26th ENGR. BN.
APO SF, 96256

January 7, 1970

Dear Mom and Dad,

I meant to answer your letter of December 30 last night, but when I came in from work I found that I had to pull bunker guard. So, of course, that pleasure had to be postponed a day in the interest of Hawk Hill's security. And, since long letters necessarily require long replys, I may have to finish tomorrow night. I want to get a little more sleep tonight than I got last night, which was none—I'm pretty tired.

What a night last night! I was scheduled to pull the second shift—2:00 AM until 6:00 AM, which is supposed to allow me time to sleep between 10:00 PM and 2:00 AM. However, I had just fallen asleep when the other guards woke me to tell me that we were on 100% alert (everybody awake—trouble expected). It seems that the guards in the bunker next to ours had spotted, or thought they'd seen, two sappers lying next to this village schoolhouse located about 300 meters to our front (we are currently experiencing the "second phase of the enemy's Winter-Spring offensive", and everybody is pretty uptight). So, after getting up and preparing for an all out assault—the idiots call off the 100% alert as a false report. After I've got 3 quarts of adrenalin in my body and can't even go back to sleep. Finally, around 12:30, I started to drift off again when the damned artillery opened up and shook me 6 feet into the air. Well, that finished it—I couldn't go back to sleep then, so I just said the hell with it, put my helmet and flak jacket on and sat down to defend freedom and democracy for the whole damn hill. And I did, too, until 6:00 this morning.

I enjoyed your letter, as I do all of them, wrath and all. "Hell hath no fury . . . . !" and all of that. Seriously though—you know how often I use this medium to air my complaints and grievances—no reason, at all, why you shouldn't do the same.

Your remarks about Christmas being a time to sit back and just remember reminded me of a quotation from Bergerson that I'm fond of, and which I sent to Lucy shortly after I returned from Hawaii—

"And yet, how many of our present pleasures, were we to examine them closely, would shrink into nothing more than memories of past ones! What would there be left of many of our emotions, were we to reduce them to the exact quantum of pure feeling they contain by subtracting from them all that is merely reminiscence?"

I, too, am fond of reminiscing—I do it quite a bit over here, as you can imagine. I abhor people, however, who travel into the past and choose to stay there. They always get buried under that pile of sand that collects in the bottom of the hourglass. It is far better, as you do, to stand outside the glass and watch the sand as it trickles down, finding pleasure in those grains at the bottom that have a special sparkle. Don't you think?

Thanks for enclosing Pete's Christmas message. Even though I've seen that joke a thousand times, I still got a kick out of it. What really makes it funny, though, is the sudden realization, upon reading it, that Pete might actually do something like that.

Your description of your family holiday dinner was fantastic. That's really the only word I can think to use to describe the potpourri of emotions that it brought forth—humor, anger, pity, disgust and, yes, even a kind of patient understanding. I only wish I had been there.

I was glad to hear that Steve and Mary Thoms are both OK—so little Christopher is growing like a weed, is he. I'll bet he's running his parents ragged. I wanted to send them a Christmas card, but I too, have lost their address. Could you send it to me.

Although Mao Tse-Tung and Ho Chi Minh might beg to differ with the thoughts contained within the quotation you sent me, I suspect, like you, that much of it is true.

As long as we're quoting—how do you like this poem by Rod McHuen?

"Who made those wars romantic in the first place?
Who led us down the line in patriotism's name,
filling us with King and Country, Fatherland and Flag,
Telling us to die was beautiful?
Who told us that as huddled masses yearning to break free
we'd have to kill a man for every foot of ground we gained?
The path we've cleared is now a freeway.
Passing through so many ill-kept fields.
Guns make lousy plowshares
But oh they rust so beautifully,
Think of how they'd look
With snap beans crawling over them."

What do you mean when you say that I have swung too far to the left? Those political expressions of doctrinal locality, left and right, are, and always have been, totally confusing to me. They always seem to connote extremism to me—left as something evil left over from the Third Reich, right as the choleric aftertaste of the McCarthy Era. I certainly don't consider myself as falling into either one of these labels. I do know this though; that these times are too exciting, to full of promise, too fraught with peril, to be nothing more than a fence-sitter. If becoming involved and having opinions is unpopular among some folks nowadays, then I'm afraid that's just the way it's going to be. Bob Dylan said it—"The times they are achanging"—for better, I hope, or for worse; nevertheless, how can anybody just sit back and refuse to participate. The frightened people—uncommonly frightened, I mean—are the ones who are too tired of life to want to change again.

Well, I guess I'll close now. I must get some sleep. Take care, keep busy and keep marking off that Shorttimers calendar for me—you should be able to start sometime around my birthday. I'll let you know when I become a double-digit midget.

Love and peace—
Dail

Jan. 4, 1969 [actually 1970]

My dear,

Happy New Year! Or is that too incongruous?

Since writing my poison pen letter about the Last Supper, I've regretted sending it, but how it helped to vent my spleen. My New Year's Resolution is tolerance.

What was going to be a very quiet uncomplicated Holiday season turned out to be a hectic, frantic, tired two weeks. Cindy's wedding and Denny's odd hours didn't help. After my attempt at a family dinner I had decided that New Year's Eve would be an "in bed by 9" deal. That morning Joan Seibert called and wanted to know what we were doing. While I'm talking to her, Ken Meacham calls your father & asks the same thing. So its a party at the Mullins'. While running out for food to feed the horde I ran into Dr. Vermillion & his first remark is "What are you doing tonite?" We wound up playing poker until 2:30 AM, but it was fun watching Meacham turn pale as he sat next to Joan betting against her with a full house in 5 card draw & have her turn over 4 natural 5's. He literally gets ill losing money.

Then New Years Day one of the gals in this group I play bridge with, had a southern open house with Ham, black-eyed peas, & corn bread. She's the woman whose son is a career officer—a captain—about 25—product of the Citadel; leaving Jan 2 for his second tour of Viet Naam. A great many of the people there were retired Army or Navy men and I'm sure you know how we fit. Then we left to go to an open house at Dr. & Mrs. Emersons. It was interesting getting David's viewpoint—which is similar to yours. Didn't know until talking to him that he wasn't an officer over there. He flunked out of OCS and was a SP/5. He seems rather lost and has no idea what he wants to do.

Friday morning after all this the phone rings and it is Edith Davis from El Paso. She had written that she'd be in town but frankly, I forgot about it until she called. She must get together with us and the Wunderlichs—so guess has the party? They all came for dinner last nite. Edith had met some friend earlier and she had a little glow on when she got here. Then she and your father & Dick started arguing about military men, especially dentists and the evening went on and on. She was staying at the Ramada Inn near the airport and Dad & I had to take her back. We got to bed at 3 AM & then had to be up at 5:30 AM to get Linda & Dennis on their plane back to school—which left at 7AM. Needless to say, we are walking around like 2 zombies. We just can't stand this.

Time out while I watched Walter Cronkite and the "21st Century Mystery of Life". Perhaps it was a re-run but it was a fascinating document on genetics and the good & horrible things it has in the future showed the fetology branch and an actual RH abdominal transfusion. Also interviewed a biologist from Scotland who seems a little frightened at what his colleagues are doing with regard to DNA. He feels if they keep it under the secrecy "wraps" which they did with Atomic energy, it will be horrendous. As he remarked "it is the diversity of man which is stimulating—not conformity" And he wonders how we can tolerate a specialized group of scientists having control of the genetic process of individual. Now he's not referring to genetic disease which can be changed—but the breeding of men like animals.

Also, just finished reading latest issue of Time in which they salute the Man & Woman of the Year: The Middle Americans (or the "Silent Majority") Read it if you can & try & understand why we have this group. Most of it is fright. As I read recently (and it's so true of your father's mother)—"We crucify ourselves between two thieves; regret for yesterday, and fear of tomorrow."

Well, Pete cut his Colorado vacation short—I guess for Linda. I don't ask any questions and just hope..

Actually, they probably both deserve each other. Both afraid of marriage, both afraid of responsibilities, and both wanting fun-fun-fun. And then Bob is waiting for her when she gets off the plane.

Well, old Nina came by New Year's Eve day to visit "Miss Virginia & her children" (& also to get her Xmas present). She wanted me to be sure & tell "mah boy" hello. It was, in a way, a wonderful lesson to Linda to have her here. Linda asked her what she was going to do to celebrate New Year's Eve. She said "Honey, Ahm going home and have a talk with the Lord and ah'm goin to thank him for keepin old Nina alive & for all he's done for me." This really got to Linda and afterwards she said "How can I constantly gripe when I think what a wonderful Xmas you and Dad tried to give me and how lucky I am and Nina is thanking God." Guess this is as something we all do forget—to thank God just to be alive.

Thought you might like to put your renewal notice on your "wall of interest."

Had the nicest letter from Lucy & when Denny read about Dan & his adventures—he was green with envy. Dad told him—okay Denny—just stick it out one more year & then go ahead & take off on a ship some where—but don't jeopardize your future by quitting now. She just sounded so ecstatic about your R&R and we are all so grateful for this time you had together. Just keep plugging, praying & soon it will be through.

With all our love and
PEACE,
Mom & Dad

Jan. 8 1970

Dear Dail,

When I put this date down I couldn't believe it had been 5 days since my last letter. Think Dad and I are still recovering from the holidays. Not that they were riotous; but 3 or 4 nights until 2 in the morning and then the "piece de resistance" of getting Edie Davis back to her hotel & getting up at 5, is hard for me to take and I'm sure you can think of what your father is saying. In fact, he just told me "Next year I don't want to go anywhere or do anything, I just can't stand night life."

We have had a really rough two weeks regarding weather, with snow & more snow, sleet, and now 6° below zero. So tonite we went out & bought an electric blanket. I've never been too fond of sleeping under wires, but Dad has been wanting one for a long time. He's also been wanting to get himself a new stereo but Thank God so far he's just been looking. If he gets that stereo record player & the electric blanket & the TV up in that bedroom, I'll never get him out of bed. Then the thought of more noise coming into the house kinda' gets to me.

Well, the news in the paper hasn't been too good the last 2 nights what with the infiltration and shelling of LZ Ross and Tam Ky. Haven't heard anything since your letter from Chu Lai and of course I do get "up tight" wishing I knew exactly where you were. Winnie Bill called last night and we talked an hour. She, of course, worries about Wayne at Da Nang and it helps both of us to cry on each other's shoulders. She said that Wayne had written he had gotten to see the Bob Hope show & enjoyed it but he said he really had a "lump" when they wound up singing carols. As he said "it was the loneliest Xmas he ever spent—surrounded by thousands of people."

Went to church circle Tuesday and I hadn't used the car since Denny left. When I tried to open the door he hadn't fully shut it & the darn knob was frozen. Finally got a window open & then opened the door & couldn't shut it so drove up to Walter Weir's hanging on to the door with the window open at 4 below and muttering under my breath what I'd do to Denny if he were handy. Then I drove over to the gas station to return the owner's key to the station—which he had forgotten to give back—and Mr. Schmitt (Denny's boss) proceeded to tell me what a wonderful boy Denny was and how rare he found it to meet a hard working good young man. So I said "what if he does forget to close the door tightly."

Today I had what I call my "establishment" bridge club, and in keeping with my New Year's Resolution of tolerance, they aren't too bad. One of the women, Jean McCarthy, was quite thrilled as her son is returning home from Viet Naam the 1st week in Feb. Of course, he hasn't had a bad deal as he's been on a ship moored somewhere between Da Nang and Chu Lai. Couldn't help but wish I were the one making that announcement. I'll be so glad when your back in the "world," even tho it too seems to be shot to hell—

Well, this is Bill Colbert's last week of putting off and pulling deals and trying all angles. He leaves for Viet Naam, but he feels this duty will still be better than the "chopper" deal he would have had under ACS.

Linda called Sunday night because she felt so bad about not saying goodbye to her father & thanking him for all he did at Xmas. Dad had dropped the kids & me off at the airport entrance & they have the parking so loused up building that new garage that you walk almost 5 blocks. By the time he got to their flight gate, they have been told they had to board so no goodbyes. Anyway—she said she thinks she is over her flying fright, as she almost enjoyed this trip. Dennis had to sit in back of her and she said she kept turning around to say to him, quite loudly. "Now, you aren't afraid, are you Denny. Its really alright". She said he was about to kill her. Talked to Bob & he evidently had his usual over-indulged Christmas.

Don't know if I told you that I received a note from the Kreylings & they wanted to be remembered to you and to have you know that you are constantly mentioned in prayers.

Well, this has been a long bunch of nothing words—but guess it's the Holiday "blahs", where you know you should dismantle all the Xmas trimmings but your heart just isn't in it.

God be with you, take care and much, much love from
Mom & Dad

Peace

SP/4 Dail W. Mullins, Jr.
488-48-0511
CoA, 26th ENGR. BN.
APO SF, 96256

January 12, 1970

Dear Mom and Dad,

I hope, after what appeared to be quite a strenuous holiday season, you have enough energy to read this letter. It did sound, though, like you had a good time, even if you are tired as dogs now. Well, you have a whole four months to recuperate—until I get home and the next party begins. I am sorry I missed the party with all the military lifers—boy, how I'd like to go to one of those as a civilian.

Purely by coincidence, I, too, saw that rerun of the 21st Century on the Mystery of Life—they showed it through AFVN-TV Chu Lai. It is good, isn't it. I am not quite as pessimistic about the future of molecular biology and its impact upon mankind as I am about other aspects of our natural environment, but neither do I think we need avoid considering some important non-scientific implications of the work. I hope, at all costs, that this stuff is kept away from the military—God knows what obscene use they could derive from it.

Dan's adventures were certainly something, weren't they. He's a regular 20th century Tom Sawyer. Although I found his experiences interesting, they did not, in any way, make me envious. On the contrary—I am tired of "adventure"—"Fun, Travel and Adventure" as the army says. Hah! The only fun I'll have in the army is getting out! And rocket attacks are not my idea of adventure. As for the travel—I'd rather be in Hattiesburg, Mississippi at a Daughters of the Confederacy meeting.

As you can see, not much to tell. I just wanted to let you know I'm OK, counting days and appreciating your letters. Take care—think peace.

Love,
Dail

P.S. Did you ever send that care package?

Does p-CHLOROPHENYLALANINE MEAN ANYTHING TO YOU? 1984 IS COMING!

SP/4 Dail W. Mullins, Jr.
488-48-0511
CoA, 26th ENGR. BN.
APO SF, 96256

January 15, 1970

Dear Mom and Dad,

Well, if you're still counting days with me, you will observe that today, the 15th, marks the beginning of my 9th month in the sun-in-fun capital of Southeast Asia. I haven't said anything to Lucy yet, and I don't want to until I know for sure, but I think I'll be getting home a little sooner than I expected. As I understand it, beginning January 1, 1970, everyone in Vietnam will be getting a 5-day drop for every month they have left in country. Thus, after January 1, I had 4 months left over here—at 5-days per month, that's a 20-day drop. Translated into civilianese (a language I much prefer to the one I am, at present, forced to use), this means that I'll be arriving in the States on April 25 instead of May 14—if, as I said, all of this is true. And, I think it is, despite the fact that we've had so many false rumors in the past. I should know for sure tomorrow, however—as that's when, according to our CO, the orders on the matter are supposed to come down from Division. I think you can see what is accomplished by this—for those people arriving in Vietnam on, or after, January 1, their tour has been reduced from 12 months to 10—as 12 months, at 5-days per month, equals 60, or 2 months. Weird, I know, but if it means I'll get home 20-days sooner, I'm not going to ask any questions.

I was as surprised as you to learn that David Emerson had not been a Lieutenant over here—although I must admit that I was even more surprised when I first heard that he was! Since that time, however, I have learned that just about anyone who can tie his own shoelaces and yell loud can be a Lieutenant.

Barksdale was hospitalized this afternoon with suspected malaria—he had a fairly high fever and accompanying chills. I hope it turns out to be something else, although a mild case of the disease is not all that bad, and it is good sham (loafing) time. The weather is pretty nasty right now (cold, windy and rain—always rain), and I wasn't feeling too well myself. I had bunker guard tonight, but I thought I might really get sick sitting out in the rain all night, so another guy took it for me—sometime I'll take his. Actually, I feel much better now—I took a nap after supper, and that helped.

We haven't had any rockets in for several days, and things have been pretty quiet around here, although part of the 196th, I understand, has engaged a fairly good size NVA force down near Tam Ky. Tet is coming up the first of next month, as you know, and, although, this will be the first time that the enemy has called for a self-imposed Tet cease-fire, I expect the action will pick up somewhat. We're scheduled for another 3-day standdown beginning the 9th of February, my birthday and the last day of Tet—hopefully, if there is a large offensive, we'll be down in Chu Lai. I don't think things will be as bad as last year, though, and certainly not like '68. Knock on wood.

Got a letter from Lucy yesterday—they're really having some cold weather up there. Are you folks experiencing the same. Boy, I can't wait until next winter and snow again, instead of rain and rice. 'Course, I guess you all are praying for spring to come (me too, but for a different reason!). Well, beauty, I guess—and misery—is all in the mind of the beholder.

You know Dad's joke about introducing you as his first wife? Well, I have a similar one. When some fool lifer asks me which tour in 'Nam I'm on—I tell him it's my last! And I can't think of a better way to end this letter—except to say—take care, keep up the wonderful letters and keep a look of peace about you.

Love,
Dail

January 11, 1970

My dear Son,

    Just to let you know that you are not alone in suffering with the elements of nature, we have had without a doubt, the lousiest weather in years. In fact, we have broken the record for the number of days that snow has been on the ground—23 days and the previous record was 19. Of course the older you get the more you dislike cold, snowing sleeting weather.

    Saturday nite the Seiberts had asked us over to play bridge and as I go out to get into the car I took what could only be called a "pratt" fall. I went up in the air and came down flat—but thank heavens I hit my well padded rear end first or I think I would have had a skull fracture. Dad wanted to go back in and wait awhile, but I am under the theory that if you keep moving nothing too serious can be wrong. Anyway we went on.

    When we arrived at Seiberts Joan said "I'm so damn glad you could make it tonite as I don't think I could take being alone with my thoughts tonite." After asking her what had happened, she told me that about six months she thought she had a boil on her rear end and then sort of forgot about it. Last week it began to bother her so badly and she felt it had really grown and she was beginning to have pains in her groin and leg and of course, imagination always plays a big part in something like this. Anyway, Friday night she called Charlie in to look at it and I'm sure you can hear her describing his lewd examination and as she was looking into the mirror and screaming "Charlie, what the hell are you doing", she said a look of Machiavellian glee came over his face and he said "it's a cancerous growth." Well, I'm sure you know how she was feeling, and your father didn't help matters when in trying to ease her mental turmoil—he said "Joan, I wouldn't worry, because that is the easiest cancer to treat and if they do have to do a lot of cutting, you can be known as our half-assed friend." Anyway, she is seeing a plastic surgeon today, but I haven't heard what he had to say. You know, it really gets pretty rugged, growing old, just keeping up with symptoms.

    Sat with Winnie Bill at church and not seeing her husband which was unusual, I asked her what had happened to Don. She said he had also fallen the night before, but it was a little more serious than my fall, as they thought he might have broken a couple of ribs. Wayne's wife had come up from Springfield to spend the week end with them and they were so glad that Wayne and Betty have definitely decided to go to Hawaii. Think he is going to put in for R and R around March so he only has 5 months to go then.

    Dr. Nickle always has provocative sermons and this one was entitled "Look up or LOOK OUT." And the new testament text was Luke, Chapter 21, verses 20 thru 28. Read it if you have some source over there. Sometimes the propheticness of the Bible can be quite frightening.

This week I have had a lot of little jobs to do around the house and in trying to make dreary jobs interesting, I look at a lot of television. And believe me, it has left me quite confused. First I listened to Margaret Mead on the Today show talking about the uniqueness of the present age and the ridiculousness of the term generation gap. In her words, there is no generation gap just a complete abyss. There has never been a situation in history such as this, and parents must just give up there children and not even try and understand some of the problems. Then today I listened to Dr. Mortimer J. Adler, a philosopher, who has just written a book entitled "The Ethics of Common Sense", and what a switch. By the way I am going to try and get a copy of this book to send you for your birthday.

He really condemned the new avant grade professors and the new breed of students and their failure to know what the past was like and he felt it was cruet and stupid of the dissident youth to condemn without any knowledge of history, and he felt their ignorance was massive. He felt youth made no attempt for the long run but the short tomorrow. He said we are suffering from "Spockitis", which is a generation brought up in permissiveness, no rules, no regulations and a society cannot exist like this. Even Aristotle explained that the surest sign of immaturity is an unexamined life and an unplanned life. He felt that if all the protesters against this life were to do a detailed study of history—Cicero, the reformation, some of Dicken's social documentaries of his time—they would find that this is a pretty good time for all men. He said it is the first century in which man has conducted World Wars, but it is also the first time that man has talked about World Peace.

Then I have been listening to Mervin Belli, the criminal flamboyant lawyer—and you should hear some of his theories about army trials. As he explained—a good boy in Viet Naam is a dead boy and he felt the Green Beret incident was nothing but the normal course of any war.

Then for the light side, listening to Laugh In tonight where the minister says—"Bible study can be termed—cramming for the finals." And Goldie when asked how the population explosion affected her, and she replies—"it didn't bother me because I wore ear plugs." And their statement that Myra Breckenridge is bi-partisan.

After a few days of this type information being spewed out at you, it begins to make you feel like a whirling dervish.

Just heard from Joan Seibert and they removed the growth from her spine and he sent it in for a bi-opsy. He felt it was cancerous but told her not to worry as he felt they had been able to remove all of it.

Then I heard Dr. Paul Ehrlich on Johnny Carson's program the other night. He is a biologist and after listening to him on the state of the ecology of the world and all the other ramifications therein, you want to go out and shoot yourself.

Well, they announced the outfits being brought home next month and I didn't hear a word about the 196th, but we keep praying.

Right after I dropped your letter in the mail box the other day, the postman delivers two letters from you—which needless to say, were welcomed. I knew if I mentioned I hadn't heard from you for a while, I'd get two in a row. I'll still feel better when we get a letter after the new bombings of Tam Ky.

You are on our minds constantly and we too, count off each and every day and pray for Peace.

With much love,
Mom & Dad

P.S. Don't forget that Lucy has a birthday the 27th.

———————————

SP/4 Dail W. Mullins, Jr.
488-48-0511
CoA, 26th ENGR. BN.
APO SF, 96256

January 18, 1970

Dear Mom and Dad,

Well, believe it or, that rumor I told you about in my last letter turned out to be true—and not just for our division either; for all of 'Nam. I think I miscalculated a little when I told you what my new DEROs date would be as a result of the drop, however—nevertheless, I will be getting out on, or around, April 24, which, you must admit, is better than May 14. Did you ever receive that shorttimers calendar I sent to you? Well, if so, you can start marking it off now—as of tonight, the 18 of January, I have 95 days left! 95! I am short.

You will be distressed to hear, I'm sure, that your son has been playing tunnel rat again. Yes. On the 16th of this month Sgt. Hileman, "Pigpen" Hagan and I all went out to the field with D Company, 2/1, 196th infantry—they had uncovered a 500 ft. NVA tunnel complex (recently used) that they wanted us to blow up. With our .45 pistols cocked and flashlights glaring, then, "Pigpen" went in one entrance while Sgt. Hileman and I went into another. He and I soon had to split up, though, as our tunnel forked—I went to the left, down deeper, into an enlarged area. I walked down one tunnel, about 50 yards—unbelievable what those Vietnamese can do with a spoon. Rather soon I came to another exit and crawled out. Meanwhile, "Pigpen" and Hileman met each other somewhere off in the other direction—scaring each other half to death, I might add. Here's a drawing of the thing—

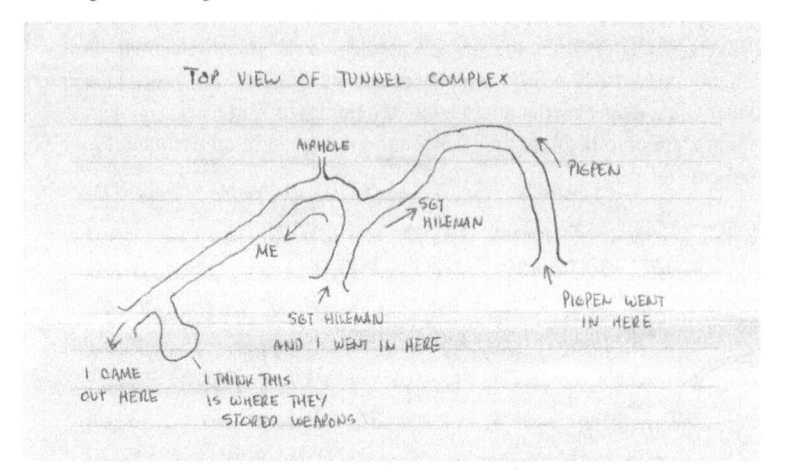

TOP VIEW OF TUNNEL COMPLEX

AIRHOLE
PIGPEN
SGT HILEMAN
ME
SGT HILEMAN AND I WENT IN HERE
PIGPEN WENT IN HERE
I CAME OUT HERE
I THINK THIS IS WHERE THEY STORED WEAPONS

Well, anyway, after we had checked it out for enemy soldiers and booby traps, we set about 200 lbs. of explosives in it and really did it a job—much to the delight of the infantry, who had been getting mortared from the area—they figure Charlie would sneak out during the night, lob a couple of rounds onto them, and then hightail it back into the tunnel before they could call in artillery on him. No more, however—he'll have to find a new tunnel.

I know this stuff really makes you mad—but blowing up tunnels is better than killing people, isn't it? And it is interesting in a strange, perhaps macabre, sense—but that's something I'll have to talk to you about in order to explain. I guess one reason I don't really mind these missions to much is because of the confidence and trust that the three of us, Sgt. Hileman, "Pigpen", and myself, have in each other. We all know what were doing with demolitions, know we all trust and respect each other, and, consequently, we make a safe, compatible team. If they tried to send me out with our new lieutenant, Lipps, alias Lippy the Lion, Lt. Fuzz,; well, that's a different story. You're right in one respect, though—I am getting too short for that stuff, and I may drop my demo pay before too long. We'll see.

I took your advice and read Luke 21: 21-28, although it was from the New American Edition and not the King James version. While I think I can see why he made reference to it in regard to these troubled times. However, if the good Doctor's idea was to frighten his parishioners, he would have failed miserably with me. The Bible is, and always will be, good literature, and nobody but a complete fool would deny that it contains some truths that, if followed, would enable man to live in greater peace and, perhaps inner contentment, than he does today (not saying much, granted)—but to say that it is a prophetic work—No, I cannot buy that. As an example, let me quote from the passage you requested I read—

"There will be signs in the sun, the moon, and the stars."

Now, this appears to me to be a rather direct and uninhibited reference to astrology—granted, there has been an upsurge of interest in medieval rot, but aside from the fact that "The Dawning of the Age of Aquarius" makes a good anti-war slogan, I don't dig stargazing as a means of predicting the future. I hope you understand why, as someone trained in a science, I cannot. Nor, I might add, do I dig men of the cloth who go around quoting scripture in order to scare ignorant people who don't know enough not to disregard it. It wouldn't surprise me if half-a-dozen people in that church went home and started making out a will. Well, enough said.

I was terribly sorry to hear about Mrs. Seibert—I know that must have frightened her, as it would anybody; I couldn't help but chuckle about some of it, though. Wouldn't you know that Mrs. Seibert, with all of her subconscious and conscious sexual and anatomical paranoia, would get a cancerous growth on her hind end. That's kind of like Emily Post getting arrested for drunken and disorderly conduct, huh? Or Ann Lauders getting caught in a raid on a teen-age pot orgy. Seriously, though—please tell her that I was sorry to hear that she was ill—I hope everything turns out alright.

Your comments about Dr. Mortimer J. Adler interested me a great deal—while I am somewhat familiar with him, I have not read, nor heard of, "The Ethics of Common Sense." I would, indeed, appreciate a copy of his book. Also, I have been trying to get a copy of Leonard Cohen's "Spice Box of Earth" and Rod McKuen's "And Autumn Came"—both of them are books of poetry. Do you think you could get them for me?

Well, I guess I'll close now. No, I didn't hear anything about the 196th or the Americal Division being pulled out either—I guess that was another bum rumor.

Take care, keep warm in that cold weather—you hate it, but I miss it—and keep writing—keep a look of peace about you—

Love,
Dail

January 16,

My dear,

Every time I write the 14, 15, or 16 of January I mentally cringe. That is school tuition dates, income tax, and christmas bill dates and I know I am in for a two week low mental depressed siege with your father. In fact, I can almost quote verbatim the remarks I will hear, such as "when am I going to enjoy the fruits of my labors"—(not realizing these bills are part of that), "I don't know how much longer I can go on carrying the ball", "where does it go"; and then we start on the government and all the "horses' asses" salaries he is paying with his taxes. And don't laugh because someday you will be doing the same thing.

Before I forget—I contacted the Registrar's office of the Grad school at Washington University and before I was through I became quite friendly with the woman in charge. Anyway she is going to see that you get all the necessary information and forms and will mail them to you at your present address. She wasn't too sure that a Doctorate in Genetics was available at Washington University, but she did know about the moleculare biology degree. Anyway she is going to check on the other. If you do not get this information in about 2 1/2 weeks let me know and I'll contact them again. I have no idea how long it takes our mail to reach you.

Of course, we would be over-joyed to have you near while you finish your schooling—but I must not allow myself to get too convinced that this will be. I know Lucy wrote and mentioned this possibility and told me to keep an eye out on the employment possibilities in St. Louis; and not necessarily in Social Welfare as she would be afraid of this in St. Louis. I talked to Mrs. Kinsey, who is working in Social Work since her husband was killed, and she said that if Lucy applies in the county it is not bad at all. Also was talking to Mrs. Vermillion and she said to talk to her husband about doing social work in connection with the hospitals—that many of the young social workers like this type phase of this career. Anyway, Dr. and Mrs. Vermillion are coming over to play bridge tonight and I'm going to ask him about the types of jobs available with regard to the hospital. Anything else I can do, please let me know.

Just when I am beginning to get really concerned about not getting a letter from you, the mail man comes through. Just as I started to write this letter I received your letter in which you had pulled bunker duty and then had an alert. These are the shellings we have been hearing about that really get me up tight. We had heard that Da Nang, LZRoss, and Tam Ky were being bombarded by enemy shell fire and infiltrations on January 5th and 6th. So your letters always make my (and your father's) day.

Well we have had another earth shattering event in the Mullin's family. Oscar died. Now I am now not being sarcastic (or am I.) I am sorry he died at

82, because I do think he was a decent individual all his life. He probably never changed any laws, he didn't stand up to be counted, but he worked hard all his life, was good to his wife, and educated and raised four children. This is Dr. John's father, and his wife Maitie was Grandma's Nemesis in that everything your grandmother ever told about what she did or what Dail or Basil did, Matie had something to top it. Anyway Oscar's dying started the round robin of telephone calls going among the survivors, which aren't too many now. Aunt Bonnie, Aunt Pearl, Jim, and Carl. Carl spends the winters in Arizona so he wasn't available and Jim insulted them when he told them to quit calling him on the phone. I had four phone calls from Icy within two hours wanting to know if I had gotten the paper and found out when the funeral was and if your dad and I were going to take her and she would sure like to go to the funeral also. They were always such good people and Oscar was so young and on and on. Well the children of Oscar really pulled the rug out from under them. They had a very private service with only his children and nothing was put in the paper until the services and burial were all over. This completely shook the women to their very toes. As Grandma said "they were always peculiar." Your father said they ruined the best social event the three old women were going to have in months. Sad, isn't it. What is really a sociological comment on aging, is that not one of these persons is more than fleetingly aware that there is such a place as Viet Naam, that we have civil unrest, and that the world is in a tremendous revolution. They know that dirty books are being written, that women are immoral, (because we have a cocktail now instead of slugging down Lydia Binkham's at 80 proof and Uncle John's Happiness Elixir), that children are rude and don't respect or care about their elders and the like—but close your eyes to the rest.

Perhaps your father and I and our generation are also being guilty of this in a small way. We do know things are going on, but we too, in many ways, do not want some of these changes to come. With most of us, very sincerely, it is our true fear that the changes being made in some areas are really not for the best. Values of marriage, children, family being tossed out the door—which could be due to a generation of children raised on Spockitis permissiveness.

Are getting an example of this in a recent letter from Linda. Don't know if you were told about this house deal of Lenny's and Bobs. Anyway, Athens College has a very rigid rule about no students living off campus unless they are married, and I am inclined to believe that the school has a very valid reason for doing this. Anyway, to circumvent this Lenny told them he was married and produced a fake marriage certificate and told the school officials that his wife would be down later. Now Bob is paying for his room at school which he occasionally sleeps in and he did not make any statements about a personal status. Well they finally caught up with Lenny and instead of then and there telling the truth, he makes it worse by saying his wife was pregnant and that was why she hadn't been down there. The school called Maryland to check on the marriage and that blew it. Instead of expelling him they are allowing him to stay provisionally:, turn his car keys in, back in a dorm immediately, a formal letter of apology to the school which will be printed in the school paper, to have dorm hours (which the boys do not have), and weekly meetings with his advisor until he graduates.

Now while he was getting away with this, all the kids who knew about it thought it was a gas, even overlooking the out and out stealing of anything he could get his hands on to furnish the house and his flagrant lying to all and sundry. Now it is a different story. They are all up in arms and Linda is just so upset stating "you think he had committed a murder." And they are all going to write letters to the Dean and on and on. Now this to me is a prime example of your father's old cliché which you are all inclined to laugh at, but which has so much truth to it—"you can do anything you please, as long as you are willing to pay the price". But don't cry and carry on when you are caught up with. I think Lenny is a very charming and personable boy, but it is time that someone caught up with him, before he did commit murder.

You probably do not get the local St. Louis news out yonder, but this snow, ice, sleet, and below zero weather, has caused a "national emergency" at Pruitt-Igoe housing complex. The cause was really started by the constant breaking of all windows, plus the pulling out of all plumbing facilities and heating elements from any apartment which is vacant for a day. Water pipes foze and broke and because so many outlets to toilets and sinks were open water flooded the entire set up with food supplies ruined, clothes gone and bedding a complete mess. Well, as usual, people have rallied around and food and clothes are pouring in from all agencies and churches, ours included. Spent Tuesday ironing mending, washing and repairing clothes and sheets to be sent down there. Many people donated brand new things. But when it came to delivering them, I stepped out. Funny how much of a coward you can become as the years grow short, but I am honestly afraid. There are snipers at windows there shooting at the trucks who are delivering these things. Now I think this is as bad as Biafara and I am not going to blame all their conduct on racial cleavage. This again goes back to no respect by anyone for anyone's person or possessions.

Hear the song "We've got to Love Everybody" so often. In fact almost every hour of the day on one station or another. Which is fine, but it just won't work. The word Love is wrong. Man is not made to LOVE everybody, he just can't. There will always be people—who try as you may—you cannot possible dredge up the emotion of love for. Now if they would use understand—that I'll buy. I cannot love many people, but I could make myself try to understand them—if I work at it—which I haven't done to the best of my ability. And by understanding them, doesn't mean I am going to accept all their kooky ideas and their behaviours. And society must have the right to rale up in anger against those who flagrantly break certain rules. Guess I'm thinking mainly of that Sharon Tate murder ritual which was all done in the name of a "Love" commune. Can this man be permitted to roam at will? What do people who want to do away with capital punishment suggest be done with his kind? I don't know and I hope your generation finds some answers to this and wars, famine and all the rest of the problems.

Spent Wednesday with Joan Seibert. She hasn't received the final pathology report but he was so positive of what it would be that she has accepted it. She really took it quite well after he removed it and told her not to worry. But sitting home thinking about her emphysema, arthritis, and now cancer—got her down, so we went out for the day. Just browsing, lungch, walking, and talking. As she remarked—"Christ, if I don't make it long enough to get this diploma I have worked so hard for, I don't think I can bear it." But Dr. Chamness told her he was pretty sure he had gotten it fairly early and that he didn't think she was going to have any trouble.

Saw the Bob Hope Special last night and while I have never been a big fan of his, he does do a tremendous job at this. Guess I was more interested knowing Wayne Bill and the Jost boy were in that mass of men around DaNang and Chu Lai. Dad said—"it's too bad Dail had to miss that" and I looked at him as though he had lost all his marbles and said—he couldn't have cared less.

You know most of the time I never re-read my letters that I write, but this one I have and all I can think is—what a lot of ranting and raving. But you know what I mean. And how interesting could a letter be if a typical housewife wrote anything entitled "My Day", (and welcome to it).

Anyway you can plow through the wordage and realize it is another typical "verbage" of your mothers. But I really mean well. Now I must call a halt as I still have your brother and sister to get a note off to—giving them a sermon and some well-meaning advice—which they probably won't take. They have mid-semester breaks starting next Tuesday the 23 until the 31, but we just do not feel like another $150 flying them home and Dad is so afraid of their driving at this time of year, so we are not encouraging them to come home. But Linda will probably start working on poor Bob to drive up.

Our love, prayers and PEACE,
Mom & Dad

SP/4 Dail W. Mullins, Jr.
488-48-0511
CoA, 26th ENGR. BN.
APO SF, 96256

January 24, 1970

Dear Mom and Dad,

As you said, Oscar Mullins was probably a fairly decent individual, and I guess it's always a shame when a decent person, even one 82 years old, passes away. Nevertheless, at the risk of seeming a bit indiscreet and not a little cruel, I must tell you that your account of the "double-cross" that his survivors pulled on Grandma, Bonnie and Pearl had Barksdale and me nearly rolling on the floor—I had to share that paragraph with him. He wanted me to thank you for bringing a little joy and laughter into an otherwise drab existence—olive drab, at that. And a tip of the Hatlo hat to Jim Mullins for telling them all like it is.

I may or may not have mentioned Eggen to you before—isn't that funny; he lives right next door to us and we're such good friends, and yet I can't even recall his first name (nobody has first names in the army—believe it or not, I have twice been called a queer by some sergeant for calling a friend by his first name!) Anyway, Eggen is our drafted hairdresser from Minneapolis—not really the hairdresser type, but then again, certainly not army material. Same as me. Eggen is 19, a young kid, really, and just a tremendous guy to be around—nothing ever seems to get him down. That is, until today, when the Red Cross, in their own inimitable way, notified him that his sister's second husband had been killed in a car wreck. He was 38. His poor sister's first husband died of a heart attack at age 33. She is now left with 6 children—4 by her first husband, 2 by her last. What is so disgusting about the whole thing is that the army won't let Eggen go home—he and his sister are very close, and he wanted to be with her now—but America's lonely vigil against the godless Commie pigs comes first, I guess. Where have all the flowers gone?

I received an application form from Washington University today—thanks for seeing to that matter for me. I'm going to wait until I receive a catalogue from them, however, before I fill out the application and order transcripts and GRE scores. Although, as you know, genetics (they aren't capitalizing it yet, Mom) is my thing, the degree in molecular biology would probably be more suitable for my plans and purposes. So often pure genetics becomes bogged down in chalkboard matings and fruit flies—it loses some of its excitement that way, I think. As I said, though, I want to look over what courses they have to offer in the field before I make formal application—I'll let you know if I don't receive a catalogue soon.

Spent an interesting (?) night last night—staring into the blackness of triple canopy jungle from a foxhole on top of Hill 459 about halfway between here and the Laotian border. Yesterday our platoon was choppered out there to help the first platoon finish the land clearance of a new fire support base—LZ Marge. We weren't able to complete the job before dark, however, so we had to spend the night. We divided our perimeter into three sectors—the engineers covered one, the infantry another and the artillerymen the third. I'll say right off that I do not like jungle. I must have thrown 50 hand grenades every time I heard a twig snap. LZ Marge will be providing artillery support for us when we go out with the infantry to destroy that NVA tunnel complex. I don't know just when we'll be leaving on that operation—but I'll try and get a letter off before we go.

Your letters always contain so many things to comment on, I never know where to begin.

No, I cannot laugh at Dad for having to pay all those taxes—unfortunately, I am, at present, one of those "horse's asses" whose salary the public must pay—and that's just about what I feel we in the military are—the unwilling doing the unnecessary for the ungrateful.

Although I'm afraid I failed to see the connection between Grandma's naiveté about world problems and your generation's trepidations about the future, I do sympathize—to a point—with you and the rest of the "children of the depression." Your specific example of being somewhat hesitant about finding favor with the new values dealing with marriage, children and the family have prompted me to enclose an article from Psychology Today magazine on Children of the Kibbutz—read it and let me know if it helped to allay your fears. Don't you agree after reading the article that, if you still think such a system removes much of the joy of parenthood, those very things you complain most about are, in fact, part of that joy?

As for Denny's current crisis. I will say that I find his lying both sophomoric and humorous. However, the school's attitude about off-campus housing is, to say the least, somewhat ridiculous. The sexual connotations of their rule are quite obvious—southern womanhood cannot triumph in a system that allows young "studs" to live outside the school's sphere of quasi-parental influence; ie., an apartment off-campus. Likewise, I find it unfortunate that Lenny and his friends had to steal furnishings for his house—such a thing is inexcusable, and rightly deserves punishment. If the school ignores this aspect, however, and chooses to press the matter of his having an illegal residence instead, they will, in all probability, not only antagonize the student body even more, but also raise the coed's laundry bills for grass stain removal. Where there is a will, there's a way, you know.

No, I cannot blame you at all for not wanting to deliver the items that you donated to the Pruitt-Igor housing project in their special time of need. I think it's enough that you gave. As for the sniping—something like that, I know, is very hard to understand. While every man at a window or roof-top with a rifle has his own feelings and reasons for doing what he, no doubt, feels he must, I think, perhaps, as a phenomenon in itself, such action can be generally attributed to frustrated and obviously misguided self-pride and disdain for "Them That's Got." The self-pride and disdain were there 20 years ago—but those emotions, remember, have had those 20 years in which to seek an outlet, a way out—a path paved by Martin Luther King and, yes, Eldridge Cleaver. White America kept the blacks from having a real identity for 400 years—now that they have begun to find themselves, it's going to cost the country a little—I hope not too much.

Although the Bible says "Love Thine Enemy" and not "Understand Him", I'm afraid that I am more inclined to agree with your views—as are, interestingly enough, Leakey and Morris. Human beings are as incapable of loving each other, except on an individual basis, as they are of loving their God—although very few "Christians" will admit to this truth. Love is too powerful an emotion, too uniquely human, to be diffused among a species—a concept humans are disdain to accept. Let us hope that understanding is not.

Well, I guess I've rattled on enough. Please continue to write as often as you can, take care, and keep a look of peace about you—

love
D.

January 19

My dear Dail,

Received your letter today dated January 12 and first off—No, p-chlorophenylalanine doesn't mean anything to us, and what in the world is 1984. I said to your father—"I really finally think he has flipped his lid in the God-forsaken hole." There is no source in the house that even gives me a hint—dictionary, encyclopedia, or medical reference books, so you'll have to elaborate.

Now, where to start in relating all the varied, interesting and glamorous events that have happened in my life since I last wrote you. That's a joke, son! I really have trouble sometimes in remembering what I have told you from one letter to the next, so forgive and bear with me if I sometimes repeat.

Did I tell you that Uncle Bob called me last Wednesday? It really frightened me when he told me he was calling from Louisville, as getting a call around 10 in the morning from him only means bad news to me. But he assured me everything was fine and he was just calling to see if it would be alright if he sent Aunt Dot up to visit me for awhile, and he was just checking to see if I was involved in anything that would prevent me from having company. Of course I told him if I did it would keep and I'd love to have her any time. He said she misses the children very much but on the whole is accepting it very well (I know what she is going through), but the thing that bothered him was that he has two big telephone installations going now that keep him out of town 4 and 5 days at a time and that when he is home he has to spend even most of his evenings at the office. Aunt Dot goes down with him but he said it gets pretty boring for her and he thought this would be a good time for her to visit me. Now he hadn't discussed this with her but he was going home and tell her and he'd call me. Well, it happened Aunt Dot had finally gotten some man out to do some repair work and she had the whole kitchen torn apart and had just started papering and painting and just couldn't walk away from this mess. Being very much like her, I could understand this, but neither your father or your Uncle Bob did.

Then Saturday I get a phone call from Linda wanting to know if I thought it would be alright for Denny, Linda, Bob, and some girl to drive up to Aunt Dot's and spend their semester break there. I hit the roof. We had told both of them that we just could not afford to pay their way by plane so soon after flying them home at Xmas and that as long as the school isn't closing they could stay down there, which many of the students are doing. Well this just crushes them and they are looking around for someplace they can sponge. Then Denny calls us last night to ask if it is alright if he went with four other guys to visit some girls at a school in Bristol, Virginia. I could Just die. His father said—"what are you going to do for money?" And Denny said that each of them had about $20 and if they managed to stop in towns that had a Delt house they figured that is all they would need for 4 or 5 days. Then I think of Dan travelling half way around the world on nothing and figure—"What the he**!" We'll probably see Linda and Bob dropping in before the semester break is over.

Sunday morning we had young Mr. Mulley preaching and I really always enjoy his sermons, altho you can sure hear some obvious mumbling from the fundamentalist, old, section of the church. He is the young fellow who is working with students on the various college campuses. I really think he has more thought provocation in his messages than the other alternate minister—Dr. Nickle and if he just had Dr. Nickle's looks and ability of oration, he'd be hard to beat. But he looks like a subdued Woody Allen. Anyway, he mentioned that he had just gotten back from Birmingham, Alabama where he had the privilege of attending a seminar between the medical profession and clergy. I went up to speak to him afterward and asked him what he thought of the set up down there. He said he had been quite tied up in this clinic in which they evidently are trying to instigate a closer working relationship between the minister, doctor, and patient; so he wasn't able to see the entire set up down there, but he claims they have bought up another six square city blocks for more expansion and he was quite surprised at the scope of the whole operation down there.

Today I took Eloise shopping as she is quite crippled with arthritis and it is difficult for her to drive some days, but after a day like this I'm really ready to forget my New Year's resolution of Tolerance, Love, Understanding—the whole—bit and revert back to my nasty self where I can tell everyone to go to he**. Really she tires you to the point of desperation and I just keep wondering what in the world that man ever saw in her.

Tomorrow I do my good deed by going over and setting and decorating the tables for the Women of The Church Meeting. I sometimes wonder if I am as useless as I feel I, but I've got to keep busy at something and I am scared to death to go down into the ghetto pockets. I've never been exceptionally brave and I figure my heart just isn't in good enough shape to stnad up under the fear of someone coming up and just saying BOO! Wish there was something I could do in my house where I would feel I was contributing.

Anyway, while shopping today I was able to pick up a couple of things for Lucy's birthday. I got her a really colorful wool poncho—which should keep her warm until you get home. I also got her some stationary and I want to pick up a few other small things. Wish I knew what I could send you for your birthday. Do you have anything special you need or want?

Well my day has worn me out and I'll say Goodnight and Godbless—

With all our love and PEACE,
Mom & Dad

P.S. Mrs. Bill had a picture that Wayne just sent her and it shows him sitting on top of a great big fat artillery gun or cannon. And guess what—he also is sprouting a hank of hair on his upper lip. Is that the first thing everyone does over there—grow hair? On the news tonight they said the VC's were recruiting 9 year old boys to fill in with regular North Vietnaamese soldiers. Isn't this whole thing sickening?

———————————

January 24

My dear Dail,

This has been the dreariest, coldest, bleakest month I can remember and every one seems down. Linda is griping because her finals were so hard and she had only six hours sleep in four days; Denny, as I think I told you, took off for Virginia, because he couldn't stand a semester break staying in Athens, your Sis still down in the mouth - and all in all it's jolly. When things get like this I get a paint brush in my hand and get busy. Don't know if I told you, but Dad bought me a mirror for over the fireplace at Christmas. For some reason I just didn't like the way it looked, and I don't dare hurt his feelings by taking it back, so I wound up painting the fireplace and I think that did it. Then I painted my kitchen chairs and table a bright yellow - that's cheery anyway.

I have my church circle and my new bridge club coming here the first week in February and Dad says I have to redecorate the whole house. Anyway, between my working at the church and the house I keep real busy and that makes the time go faster and that makes it nearer to the day when you will come home.

I'm a little shook up about that new draft law, as it does not seem to be working out. They have been told not to touch any numbers beyond 60 as of now, but boards like Webster find they do not have enough under this 60 to call upon and they are asking what to do. Now I see there is a move afoot to cancel all college deferments. If they take Denny right after we get you back I really don't know what I'll do. Did I tell you that Barber Kenney's husband was leaving for V.N. next month. She is evidently going home to live with Jack and Mary, not because she wants to - but because it is one way she can save some money.

Sent Lucy's birthday present off today - got her some stationary and a wool knit poncho. Nothing much, but am still recuperating from Christmas. I'm getting your birthday package off Monday and the birthday cake is not the kind I'd like to send you - but I had to think of something that would keep and ship. Hope you get it by the 9th. Got Aunt Dot's and Uncle Bob's birthday in February too.

Listened to a young fellow on a TV show the other day - named McAllister. He seemed quite young but was supposedly an expert on Viet Naam, it's history, social problems and the events leading up to the present conflict - which he said go back to 1945. He has written a book which I am trying to get. I sometimes get very -not discouraged - but rather frustrated in not being able to listen to all the authorities on various vital subjects and determine, for myself, on what points they are right and make sense and what part of what they say should be ignored. It seems that every vital question has such strong and concrete evidence for both sides and the more I listen the more confused I become.

For example, Dr. Margaret Mead has caused such a stir about her remarks concerning making marijuana available to 16 year olds and over - what I think she really meant was not to make it a criminal offense - but everyone has taken her remarks out of context. She, of course, states it is not harmful. But then the other day they had a panel of drug addicts on and they felt it would be most serious to make it legal and easily available, as they had all started on this drug and of course, after a few years were not getting the reaction desired so they all go on to the harder drugs. Looking at this group of rather young people, girls and boys, and listening to them tell what depths they had gone down to and what they had done to pay for these habits was horrendous.

Then the Viet Naam question. You hear capable, intelligent well-documented men stating both sides of this question.

Then the population and pollution problem. I know the other night we played bridge with the Meachams and I think I have told you that one of the few points that I think he makes sense on is his complete frustration over population and pollution. But your father cannot agree. Of course, he still is in that rosy-hued dream that "God will take care of it." But he really gets to Meacham when he says - "Now, Ken, you know the first law of physics is that "Matter cannot be produced or destroyed." Your father feels there is nothing more on earth now than there has ever been, so what is the sweat. Wish I had paid more attention to my one year of physics so I could have a rebuttal.

The other day I signed a petition which a group of high school youngsters brought around, asking to reduce the voting age to 18, and don't think I haven't had some remarks about this from people. But I believe in this. Not without some thinking but through a very well prepared and excellent program that KSD put on. They showed that the average person over 40 had not read ONE book in the past 10 years and that only 25 percent of that group ever read the daily newspaper. They showed so definitely that the average high-school senior was more aware of how the government operates and of the issues at hand, than any idiot over 50. When I think of some of the senile s-o-b's, I know, voting because they don't like the cut of clothes of a candidate - that I feel we need the younger vote.

I talk about going back and taking some courses and I really would like to, but it is not cheap even going to Meramec Junior College and I wouldn't think of burdening your father with any more school expenses. He gets almost hysterical sometimes when he talks about "only one more year of college fees." And I cannot blame him. It's been a heavy load.

The Meachams are going to Chicago in February for the Dental Convention and asked us to go along, but we told them we couldn't possibly afford it. Anyway, in talking about it - Ken remembered the year you and Dad went up there and you went on over to Lake Forest to look over that school. He asked us why we had never followed through on sending you there and we said that there really wasn't any definite reason except we felt it was too close to Chicago. Ken mentioned how a little thing like that could alter someone's whole life and it is true. You probably wouldn't be interested in Genetics and you wouldn't have Lucy. Makes you think sometimes, doesn't it.

Did I tell you I had a nice letter from Ray Wintker, in answer to a card and letter I sent him at Xmas. In the letter I mentioned you and Lucy going to Hawaii and that Denny and Linda were still in school and how she had decided not to get married - and just family news. His answer was almost entirely on how wonderful it was that Linda had decided not to get married and how so many people felt this was the way to answer personal inadequicies and that she had so much going for her and to ruin it with marriage would be bad and on and on. I'm glad she didn't get married when she had planned, because she was too emotionally wrought up about the whole deal, but I really hope that some day she will grow up enough to make an intelligent choice and realize that marriage is not fun and games.

Well, I must go and feed the inner man. Sometimes I think it will be wonderful when a pill is taken at meal times but then I think UGH!, how horrible. Say, speaking about pills, what about that controversy about birth control pills? Think you had better give some thought to other ways of controlling your family - but that's your business - as I light up another cancerfilled cigarette.

Well, as usual, we are praying, loving, and thinking of you alwasy. Everytime I look over these letters I type to you children I see the real reason I don't go out and get a job. What a typist; but as usual my thoughts are always ahead of my hands and my big mouth.

With love,

Mom & Dad

Sometimes when I sign Dad's name to these birdies, I get a little irritated. Why he can't write you children is beyond me. Dad *what really gets me is when he says — "Say, you haven't written the kids for a couple of days, you'd better get busy". If looks could kill.*

January 24

My dear Dail,

This has been the dreariest, coldest, bleakest month I can remember and every one seems down. Linda is griping because her finals were so hard and she had only six hours sleep in four days; Denny, as I think I told you, took off for Virginia, because he couldn't stand a semester break staying in Athens, your Dad is still down in the mouth—and all in all it's jolly. When things get like this I get a paint brush in my hand and get busy. Don't know if I told you, but Dad bought me a mirror for over the fireplace at Christmas. For some reason I just didn't like the way it looked, and I don't dare hurt his feelings by taking it back, so I wound up painting the fireplace and I think that did it. Then I painted my kitchen chairs and table a bright yellow—that's cheery anyway.

I have my church circle and my new bridge club coming here the first week in February and Dad says I have to redecorate the whole house. Anyway, between my working at the church and the house I keep real busy and that makes the time go faster and that makes it nearer to the day when you will come home.

I'm a little shook up about that new draft law, as it does not seem to be working out. They have been told not to touch any numbers beyond 60 as of now, but boards like Webster find they do not have enough under this 60 to call upon and they are asking what to do. Now I see there is a move afoot to cancel all college deferments. If they take Denny right after we get you back I really don't know what I'll do. Did I tell you that Barbar Kenney's husband was leaving for V.N. next month. She is evidently going home to live with Jack and Mary, not because she wants to—but because it is one way she can save some money.

Sent Lucy's birthday present off today—got her some stationary and a wool knit poncho. Nothing much, but am still recuperating from Christmas. I'm getting your birthday package off Monday and the birthday cake is not the kind I'd like to send you—but I had to think of something that would keep and ship. Hope you get it by the 9th. Got Aunt Dot's and Uncle Bob's birthday in February too.

Listened to a young fellow on a TV show the other day—named McAllister. He seemed quite young but was supposedly an expert on Viet Naam, it's history, social problems and the events leading up to the present conflict—which he said go back to 1945. He has written a book which I am trying to get. I sometimes get very—not discouraged—but rather frustrated in not being able to listen to all the authorities on various vital subjects and determine, for myself, on what points they are right and make sense and what part of what they say should be ignored. It seems that every vital question has such strong and concrete evidence for both sides and the more I listen the more confused I become.

For example, Dr. Margaret Mead has caused such a stir about her remarks concerning making marijuana available to 16 year olds and over—what I think she really meant was not to make it a criminal offense—but everyone has taken her remarks out of context. She, of course, states it is not harmful. But then the other day they had a panel of drug addicts on and they felt it would be most serious to make it legal and easily available, as they had all started on this drug and of course, after a few years were not getting the reaction desired so they all go on to the harder drugs. Looking at this group of rather young people, girls and boys, and listening to them tell what depths they had gone down to and what they had done to pay for these habits was horrendous.

Then the Viet Naam question. You hear capable, intelligent well-documented men stating both sides of this question.

Then the population and pollution problem. I know the other night we played bridge with the Meachams and I think I have told you that one of the few points that I think he makes sense on is his complete frustration over population and pollution. But your father cannot agree. Of course, he still is in that rosy-hued dream that "God will take care of it." But he really gets to Meacham when he says —"Now, Ken, you know the first law of physics is that "Matter cannot be produced or destroyed." Your father feels there is nothing more on earth now than there has ever been, so what is the sweat. Wish I had paid more attention to my one year of physics so I could have a rebuttal.

The other day I signed a petition which a group of high school youngsters brought around, asking to reduce the voting age to 18, and don't think I haven't had some remarks about this from people. But I believe in this. Not without some thinking but through a very well prepared and excellent program that KSD put on. They showed that the average person over 40 had not read ONE book in the past 10 years and that only 25 percent of that group ever read the daily newspaper. They showed so definitely that the average high-school senior was more aware of how the government operates and of the issues at hand, than any idiot over 50. When I think of some of the senile s-o-b's, I know, voting because they don't like the cut of clothes of a candidate—that I feel we need the younger vote.

I talk about going back and taking some courses and I really would like to, but it is not cheap even going to Meramec Junior College and I wouldn't think of burdening your father with any more school expenses. He gets almost hysterical sometimes when he talks about "only one more year of college fees." And I cannot blame him. It's been a heavy load.

The Meachams are going to Chicago in February for the Dental Convention and asked us to go along, but we told them we couldn't possibly afford it. Anyway, in talking about it—Ken remembered the year you and Dad went up there and you went on over to Lake Forest to look over that school. He asked us why we had never followed through on sending you there and we said that there really wasn't any definite reason except we felt it was too close to Chicago. Ken mentioned how a little thing like that could alter someone's whole life and it is true. You probably wouldn't be interested in Genetics and you wouldn't have Lucy. Makes you think sometimes, doesn't it.

Did I tell you I had a nice letter from Ray Wintker, in answer to a card and letter I sent him at Xmas. In the Letter I mentioned you and Lucy going to Hawaii and that Denny and Linda were still in school and how she had decided not to get married—and just family news. His answer was almost entirely on how wonderful it was that Linda had decided not to get married and how so many people felt this was the way to answer personal inadequacies and that she had so much going for her and to ruin it with marriage would be bad and on and on. I'm glad she didn't get married when she had planned, because she was too emotionally wrought up about the whole deal, but I really hope that someday she will grow up enough to make an intelligent choice and realize that marriage is not fun and games.

Well, I must go and feed the inner man. Sometimes I think it will be wonderful when a pill is taken at meal times but then I think UGH!, how horrible. Say, speaking about pills, what about that controversy about birth control pills? Think you had better give some thought to other ways of controlling your family—but that's your business—as I light up another cancer filled cigarette.

Well, as usual, we are praying, loving, and thinking of you alwasy. Everytime I look over these letters I type to you children I see the real reason I don't go out and get a job. What a typist; but as usual my thoughts are always ahead of my hands and my big mouth.

With love,
Mom & Dad

Sometimes when I sign Dad's name to these tirades, I get a little irritated. Why he can't write you children is beyond me. And what really gets me is when he says—"Say, you haven't written the kids for a couple of days. You'd better get busy." If looks could kill.

SP/4 Dail W. Mullins, Jr.
488-48-0511
CoA, 26th ENGR. BN.
APO SF, 96256

Jan 28, 1970

Dear Mom and Dad,

So you're redecorating the house again? That place must have more coats of paint on its walls than a Rolls Royce! Well, if it makes the time pass more quickly for you, all well and good—and as much as you may complain, Mom, I know how much you really enjoy that kind of work. Lucy and I are planning to take a trip of some sort down your way during my 30-day leave in May, so I'll be able to see what you've accomplished then. Of course, for our homecoming, you'll probably decide that the house needs redecorating again. . . .

I am aware of the current draft controversy back home. I still have hopes that Denny's birthdate lottery number will protect him unless, as you say, they do away with college deferments altogether. I was under the impression, however, that only freshmen and sophomores would be enslaved—this would enable Denny to at least finish college. After that—well, there's always Canada. If I had to do over, that's probably what I would do, believe it or not, I've given much belated thought to that matter since I've been over here and I've decided that the reason I chose not to "flee", as they say, to Canada in the first place was because of the embarrassment and sorrow it would have caused you and Lucy's parents, particularly among your more establishment-oriented friends. I now feel, however, that what grief you might have experienced as a result of my actually going North would not have been as great as the apparent fear and anxiety both you and Lucy have suffered because of my being over here. Patriotism—the territorial imperative alá Homo sapiens—figures little or not at all. Hindsight, of course.

I am not familiar with this McAllister fellow you mention. What is the title of the book he's written? While I was aware of the fact that the causes of the current Vietnam fiasco were not of very recent origin, the 1945 date puzzles me. Are you sure he didn't say 1954? That was the year, you may recall, that the Geneva Conference, while never recognizing Vietnam as anything other than one state, referred to the two zones, North and South, as having been "temporarily established" (their wording) by the ceasefire of the French-Indochina War. The Conference also called for an election to be held in 1956 which would firmly establish the union of the two zones—and this is what really started it all. "North" Vietnam sought to arrange for the proposed election for three years. They were thwarted in this attempt, however, by John Foster Dulles—one of the most inept and incorrigible Secretaries of State the United States has ever had. Dulles and his lackies, realizing that Vietnam would go communist (an even dirtier word then than now) under the leadership of its most popular leader, Ho Chi Minh, in such an election, encouraged the Diem government of "South" Vietnam to obstruct such an election. This insane manoeuvre resulted in the "North" seeking to effect the union by supporting the Viet Cong, the guerrilla communists of the "South"—an understandable move in light of the circumstances. After Diem was assassinated, of course, the conflict between the Diem loyalists and the Viet Cong grew more intense—the "North" sent in NVA troops while the "South", of course, asked for, and received, American military aid. It is my opinion that hostilities in South Vietnam, whether between loyalists and the VC or loyalists and the NVA, constitute civil warfare and that intervention by non-Vietnamese forces is, and always was, illegal. The United States, as you know, is in Vietnam today under the pretence of honoring SEATO—the Southeast Asia Treaty Organization. This treaty was made in agreement with the Diem regime (which ceased to exist in 1963, prior to the big U.S. buildup) representing South Vietnam (which, according to international law—the Geneva Conference—never existed).

As I said, that's my opinion—and the United Nation's—so take it for what it's worth.

Perhaps the most ironic thing about Vietnam is the fact that the United States, through its antiquated policies of foreign supervision under John Foster Dulles, have succeeded in doing exactly what they had intended not to do. The United States policy of communist containment worked well in Europe following World War II. The mistake came when our state department began to regard all communist countries as being subservient to Russia, including Communist China. They assumed that they could apply our postwar European policies to mainland Asia, and contain China's growing influence through military means.

Vietnam and China are, and always have been, racial enemies—just as are China and Japan. Had Vietnam gone communistic, they would never have aligned themselves with China, as we so feared they would. On the contrary, they probably would have been fairly independent—much like Tito's Yugoslavia—which is almost as much of a headache to the Russians as China is now. By attempting to force "American Democracy" on Vietnam, however, we only succeeded in forcing the North Vietnamese to do what they would never have done had we left them alone—namely, seek aid from China. 40,000 American soldiers later, we still are determined to see to it that Vietnamese rice farmers remember George Washington instead of Karl Marx—and those poor people could care less.

As for the marijuana question—you already know my feelings about that. I like what Schlesinger says about it—"Parents are advised not to lecture to children on the evils of smoking pot after they've had four martinis." I always get a kick out of that statistic—"90% of all drug users started by taking marijuana." That beautiful statement fails to mention how many people who smoke pot don't go on to harder drugs, doesn't it? How many alcoholics (who outnumber drug addicts in the United States ten to one) began by sipping beer at fraternity parties? That statement about drug addicts and pot is like saying that 100% of all alcoholics began by drinking water—quite true, but completely irrelevant.

Remarkably enough, I must admit that, for once, Dr. Meacham makes sense when he expresses concern over our exploding population and misuse of natural resources. Without a doubt, all of the problems facing mankind—including the threat of nuclear warfare and (in America) the "colored" situation—pale before our population and ecological mismanagement. If God is going to take care of it, he best get busy—now! There is a quotation by Sir Dugald Baird (?) that I like and which is relevant here—"I would suggest that it is time to consider a fifth freedom—freedom from the tyranny of excessive fertility."

As for Dad's arguments. Contrary to what the physics books of 1932 said, the people of Hiroshima and Nagasaki would, I'm sure, if they were alive today, testify most emphatically to the fact that matter can, indeed, be destroyed. Sixty billion tons of matter are destroyed every minute in the sun. Matter is destroyed—completely and undeniably—resulting in the production of energy according to the now famous $E=mc^2$ formula. There is no reason why the reverse should not be true (energy destroyed in the production of matter), although such has not been detected yet. Yes, matter can be destroyed—and, as a matter of fact, there is probably less matter is the earth now then there was yesterday because of this fact. That, however, is hardly the point with regard to population control. The simple fact remains that human beings are reproducing too much—screwing themselves to death, if you want to use Dr. Meacham's off-color, but rather apt, phrase. There are just too damn many people on the planet. Except possibly from a psychological standpoint, it is not merely the number of people on earth that is so important—rather, it is the number of people in proportion to another type of matter—food—that is the critical factor. Food—and air and water. You say the amount of water on earth never changes? Wrong! Look at this formula—

$$6CO_2 + 6H_2O \xrightarrow{\text{LIGHT}} C_6H_{12}O_6 + 6O_2$$

That is the general formula for photosynthesis, whereby green plants convert carbon dioxide (CO_2) and water (H_2O) into sugar ($C_6H_{12}O_6$) and oxygen (O_2). Notice that for every molecule of sugar produced, the plant uses six molecules of water. That water is gone—it will never again evaporate from the surface of the earth and fall again as rain.

The most optimistic estimate of the number of people that could be fed by modern science is 50 billion. Since there are only 3 billion people on the earth right now, it would appear that we have little, if anything to worry about, at least for awhile. Besides, by the time the number 50 billion is reached, either science or God will have intervened to save us all. Ah—but let's see, in fact, how long it will be before the earth has a population of 50 billion people.

Between the time of the first couple (Adam and Eve, if you wish) and the year 1650, our population grew to 1/2 billion. By 1850, 200 years later, it had only grown by another 1/2 billion, to 1 billion. In just 75 short years—from 1850 until 1925—we doubled that to 2 billion. During the next 45 years we added another billion, so that by 1970—now—we have 3 billion. In the year 2000—which is only 30 years away—the figure will be 7 billion (I'll be 56, my children should be through college). By the year 2050—I'll be dead but my son will have kids in school—there will be 25 billion humans—all of them still requiring at least one bowl of rice per day. Five years later, in 2055, the magic number will be reached—50,000,000,000. And more crying, hungry babies being born every second than are born every hour now. My grandchild will begin to be ready to start looking for a job—after he finds some room and a bowl of rice. No doubt, too, he'll be waiting for God to intervene at any minute. By then, every minute will count. If it is true that the world is going to end, not with a bang, but a whimper—it will be as a last, pitiful cry for something to eat—anything—even another human.

Homo sapiens—wise man?

Peace,
Dail

SP/4 Dail W. Mullins, Jr.
488-48-0511
CoA, 26th ENGR. BN.
APO SF, 96256

January 29, 1970

Dear Mom and Dad,
 Well, as you can plainly see, my stationary situation has again reached a critical level, and I have been forced to employ this ridiculous paper, so blatantly a product of the capitalist war machine. Oh, well—
 The remark I made about para-chlorophenylalanine was intended partly to amuse you, partly to comment on the fantastic age we're living in. Since you don't subscribe to Newsweek magazine, I guess you couldn't have really understood what I was talking about—accordingly, I have enclosed a clipping from

the January 5 issue of that weekly journal which should help clean up part of the mystery. 1984, as you should know, is the title of George Orwell's classic novel of life in the future, where everyone and everything (including sex) is controlled by Big Brother and his physio-chemico-psycho machinations. No, I'm not cracking up—yet—which may be unfortunate, since I could probably get a 212 (unfit for military service) discharge if I were.

It has always puzzled me how someone could be psychologically unfit for service in the military—these lifers around here are all crazy anyway. Anybody who would make this kind of life a career can't be all that psychologically ideal.

You will be fascinated, I'm sure, to hear what our platoon has been doing these past few days. LZ Hawk Hill is the headquarters of the 196th light infantry brigade, one of the three infantry brigades (including the 198th and 11th) making up the Americal Division. The commanding officer of the 196th is a full-bird colonel—Colonel Lee—who is assisted in his duties (which include, for the most part, walking around with his hands clasped behind his back, frowning, returning an occasional salute—not from me, however—and generally getting in the way) by Lt. Colonel Meyer (a short, fat, red-headed guy who leaves the hill by chopper during every enemy shelling or attack). Anyway, these two jokers live over near the BTOC (Brigade Tactical Operations Center) in—believe it or not—a 36 foot mobile home, complete with electric range and flush toilet—which, unfortunately, they are not able to use, being forced by the lack of plumbing to defecate in empty 55 gallon oil drums—a humiliating experience for a colonel, I'm sure. Well, with TET coming up, I guess these guys got a little nervous about having to live in a house trailer during possible rocket and mortar attacks. Did they send the trailer back to Chu Lai and move into a bunker like the rest of us? Of course not—the engineers built a bunker over their trailer! Naturally, the 2nd platoon was called upon to complete this important mission. You should see this thing—I don't think anything the NVA have got could penetrate that roof—it would take a thermo-nuclear warhead, I'm sure. But, as Barksdale said, at least we can all sleep well at night knowing that our beloved leader and father-image is safe. Just thought you'd like to hear where your taxes are going—we used 3 bunker kits to build that gargantuan thing, and at $8,000 a kit that's a cool $24,000—which doesn't, of course, include the cost of the trailer, which, I know, costs at least $15,000. And what is really ironic—here these two guys have all that protection when, after an attack, they're both gone before the echo of the first incoming round has faded. This isn't a war—it's a Peter Sellers movie, isn't it?

As you can sense, I'm rather hard-up for news—which, however, may be a blessing in disguise. I hope I can stay bored for about 100 more days.

As far as I know, our company is still scheduled to go on standdown the 4th of February—it will be a nice break, I guess. I thought we'd be there over my

317

birthday, but we come back the 7th. However, as you know, schedules change in the army as fast as officer's minds do.

As a footnote on that bunker we built for the colonel, you'll be thrilled to learn that on January the 24th they had decided not to put walls on it. On the 26th they decided it should have walls. On the 27th our CO decided that, actually, it didn't need walls at all, just two mounds of dirt alongside of it. However, tomorrow we're going over to put walls on it because the Colonel thinks it should have walls. I suggested we just put up one wall and leave the other side open—a compromise, you see—but that idea wasn't accepted with a great deal of enthusiasm. "Whoever heard of a bunker with only one wall?" Sgt. Hileman said. "Whoever heard of a house trailer inside of a bunker!" I said.

No, I'm not cracking up. Why do you ask?

Love—
and peace, if that's possible
Dail

P.S. Could you possibly call Washington U. again and see if they've sent me a catalogue? Thanks much—

January 28

My dear Dail,

I don't know what is happening to the mail. We don't receive any of your letters for about eight or nine days and then 3 are delivered at once, dated several days apart. Before I start in on a tirade against your being a tunnel rat at this stage, will you please tell me why anyone is named PigPen? The ramifications are endless, but certainly there is a very uncomplicated explanation—but who would tolerate the nickname "PigPen", without a fight.

I'm sure you know what a letter from you explaining in detail your excursions into the "underworld" does to us, and I really think it is about time you got out of this. This is the detail I worried about several weeks ago and you answered and said you couldn't get out of it, now you tell me it is volunteer duty. Let's quit.

Had a letter from Lucy today and was glad to hear that Dan was back under the fold. As she said, "he's the only boy in the state of Virginia who could leave the states with 30 dollars and return with 300." I'm sure his parents breathed a sigh of relief when he returned, but they are probably holding their breath—wondering what he has in mind now.

Yesterday I received a phone call from Mary Kreyling. She was called into town by the nursing home where her Mother is staying. She said this is the third time since the first of the year she has gotten an emergency call from the doctors, and they now tell her they cannot put up with much more of her behaviour and she is in a bind wondering what to do with her. Twice she was called down because she had put turpentine in her eyes and they thought she had blinded herself. Evidently she really gets quite unmanageable for a nursing home and the only recourse is a state asylum. Mary can't accept putting her in this type institution—but this seems to be the choice. Anyway she wanted you to know that she and Ed are thinking of you so very much and Carole wanted to be remembered. Carol got her degree this December and she is starting a job teaching Speech Therapy the first of February. Evidently she had enough of housekeeping and is very emphatic about any more children, and wants to start a life of her own.

Then last night we were sitting at Charcoal House having dinner with the Meachams and Mrs. Kreyling walked in with her Aunt and A friend. She still looks as glamorous as ever and I though old Meacham would fall on his face—asking "how come I've never met her before." In many ways Ken so reminds me of the original "dirty old man"—but that's feminine logic.

Mrs. Keitel called today and asked me to come over and have some coffee with her. She was telling me that Bob Karasek finished his 6 month reserve committment and because he enrolled in a Reserve Unit out of San Antonio he has to stay there until he can find another Reserve Unit to accept him. Anyway, through the influence of one of his Princeton friends he got on the staff of Trinity College and is teaching in the School of Architecture there and has a part time job at night in an Architect's office. Mrs. Karasek is working for Dr. Vest—the chest surgeon who has taken care of your father when he has run into trouble—and evidently likes it very much. She is evidently the same old Mrs. Karasek. While I was having coffee with Mrs. Keitel she called and said some fellow was coming by tonight and she wanted Mrs. Keitel to drop by around 9 o'clock, as she was afraid to be alone with him, he was so amorous. The fact he had a wife and three children didn't deter him. I really find these women hard to understand. What in the hell was he coming by for at all? Certainly she could prevent this.

Talked to Joan Seibert the other day and the final results on her posterior came in, and it wasn't cancer—but some very rare skin condition. She said she couldn't pronounce it but she looked it up in Merck Manual and the definition sounded like some locker room disease.

Last night, or Monday night (my days are so filled with fun and frolic, can't remember just what day it is) we went to see a movie. The first one in 5 months. We saw the Cactus Flower, simply because your father has had a lot of his colleagues and patients telling him he must see it. Now I don't know if you are aware of this story but it is about a gay Dentist who has a Mistress whom he has told he is married with 3 children—just to prevent her from putting the hooks into him. The plot evolved from there with his having his office receptionist take the part of his "wife" when the mistress starts breathing down his neck. Goldie Hawn from Laugh In, and Ingrid Bergman take the part of mistress and receptionist respectively and Walter Matheau is the Dentist. Whether it is because I haven't laughed in so long or what, but I almost became hysterical. It is the funniest thing I have seen in ages. It is a must for you and Lucy when you come home to the "World". Meacham saw it and said the fact that it was a Dentist was irrelevant to the story and I agree; but the fact that it was a tooth puller—made it so much more pertinent to me. Anyway, it was a fun movie—and there aren't too many of them around any more.

Anytime your time in Vietnaam is reduced is call for a big celebration, and we couldn't be more elated that you have 10 more days knocked off—your little count down calendar is marked off each day.

Let us know if you receive the package we sent and forgive our first attempt at recording. I told your father there is nothing more deflating than hearing your own voice on tape. I sound just like Kate Smith—and I'M not bragging. It has made me very aware of how horrible I sound and I'm working on it.

Were thinking of you and praying for PEACE,
Love,
Mom & Dad

P.S. Just received a phone call from your sister and she is quite in a turmoil, wondering how to handle Bob. She doesn't want to hurt him anymore than she has (it's a little late) but she is tired of his possessiveness and feels she has grown beyond him. I was very much aware that this might happen. Bob is a good decent fellow but could be a bore and Linda is just beginning to have that "spark" which could make her very critical.

P.P.S. Just heard a funny joke on tv. Did you hear about the fellow who crossed birth control pills with LSD. He didn't know what he had produced but it was one way to take a trip without the kids. Ha!

SP/4 Dail W. Mullins, Jr.
488-48-0511
CoA, 26th ENGR. BN.
APO SF, 96256

February 8, 1970

Dear Folks,

    I feel terrible about not having written sooner to thank you for the terrific birthday package—the food, the Rod McKuen book and especially the tape were just tremendous. The sausage, by the way, lasted about 35 seconds—that was after Barksdale and I learned that they were having Chu Lai Steak (army roast beef) in the mess hall that night.

    I guess I enjoyed the tape the most—well, I know I did. And I don't understand what you mean, Mom, when you say that your voice sounds bad—it sounded like you—what more could I ask. And thanks for taping Ron for me—that was out of sight. While I'm afraid, Dad, that I can't completely agree with your taste for WGNU and that chicken pluckin' music, I do know that C&W sounds are really coming back strong.

    AFVN radio has two hours of the Nashville sound on every morning here—they have this fool disc jockey who comes on at 5:00 am with "Gooooooood Morning, Vietnam!" You feel like picking up a gun and blowing the radio away.

    I found a mailing box for that tape you sent, and I found out we're allowed to send taped letters, FREE just like regular mail—so I'll tape my own message and send it back just as soon as I can. I'm afraid though, that my "program" will not be as elaborate as was yours—I'll try and tape a little of AFVN for you, though, to compensate for my being able to listen to KXOK.

    We were supposed to be choppered out to LZ Professional this morning to build bunkers—as usual, the building materials had not yet been delivered, so we had the mission postponed temporarily. We'll either go this noon or tomorrow morning—although neither Barksdale nor I will be there long, as we have to be in Chu Lai on the 12th to take a test for SP/5.

    We just got back from Chu Lai yesterday after a three-day standdown—it was a nice break, although the weather was rather nasty. Still, it's better than working.

    Well, I hate to close with so little news, but I suppose, in Vietnam, little or no news is preferable to something exciting to write about. Take care and keep those cards and letters coming in.

Love,
Dail

P.S. Peace

P.P.S. I thought you might find the enclosed clipping from our division newspaper of some interest.

February 3

Dear Dail,

I know it has been longer than usual since I have written you and when I stop and analyze why it seems superficial, but it has kept me tied up.

Have spent a little bit of time with Joan Seibert as she has really been down in the mouth, and I remember how good she was to me when I needed someone. Then Rosemary Meacham's mother died last Friday and while it was a blessing—not that she was in any pain, but she was just a breathing body, not knowing any of her children—but it is still hard to lose your mother.

Today I had the church circle and I'm still trying to figure out why, when I try to get outside the home, I wind up with the designated job of doing the same thing I'm doing at home. They decided I did such a good job of washing and ironing clothes from Pruitt Igoe, they want me to take over this complete responsibility. It's pretty discouraging when you have thought of yourself as a "sex symbol" (ha!) to wind up being thought of as the Irish washerwoman.

Dennis sent home a letter you had written him, in which you mentioned our proposed Easter plans. They are just plans and I don't know if they will materialize. The Vermilions go down to Panama City every Easter with their children and evidently there is a hughe group of Kirkwood and Webster people down there and one night they tried to get us interested and you know your father. Anyway, what we were thinking was that it costs us $120 to fly Denny and Linda home and Dad thought maybe he would take off a few days then and spend the plane fare on a vacation. But we have done nothing about reservations and I don't think we'll get any at this late date, and then it would be March 21 through the 29th—when the kids have to be back at school.

Am writing this while the Mike Douglas show is on and listening to a Barbar Seaman, some physicians wife, who has written the controversial book called "The Case against The Pill." Listening to her I don't know what to think. Mike's guest this week is Peter Lawford and he was trying to pin her down and she said "Mr. Lawford, would you take a birth control pill?" And he said—"not until I consulted Ralph Nader."

Last night on Laugh In they had the fellow who takes the part of the minister at the cocktail party. He said his picture was in the paper so much recently that his congregation was calling him "The Pray Boy of the Month." Jack Benny was their main guest and it was one of the funniest programs they have ever had.

We were with the Seibert's Saturday night and she gave your Dad a book she had seen in the Book Store, which she said she couldn't resist, as she felt it fitted him so. It is entitled "How to Make Yourself Miserable", and I think he was a little hurt, wondering why she felt he needed it. Anyway it is really funny—even its chapters; such as Misery about the past, present and future, methods to misery with others, how to lose your job, how to destroy romantic relationships, how to lose friends. It starts out by saying that most miserable people have a guilty complex. Now this could be about anything and their suggestions are—guilt about romantic feelings toward: 1, your locker make at the Y; 2, your sister; 3, your Doberman pinscher; 4, your umbrella. Then they spend some time telling you how you can create a first class anxiety and how to select a 3 dimensional worry. It winds up by saying—Alone at Last! Congratulations! You have driven everyone you know out of your life and you are unencumbered by job, lover or friends, and you are now free to brood twenty-four hours a day about how rotten life is, and you have now achieved the ultimate; Alone at last. It's pure satire, but oh so true. Think I'm going to keep it by the bedside and look at it whenever I get to feeling sorry for myself.

Well, the war news is certainly anything but good and believe me when I say we are thinking of you constantly. I have never seen anything get your father down, as your being in Viet Naam. He broods about it constantly, and as a result I must not say too much as it just makes him worse. I think he really feels badly about not being able to be their and take your place as he keeps saying "Hell, my life is over anyway, while he has everything before him". He still doesn't ever seem to realize how much he is needed by all of us.

Talked to Carole Neuwoehner the other day to invite her to a luncheon I am having Thursday and she was telling me that Jimmy is not at Denver anymore and is going to Normandy. She mentioned how unhappy he was as all of his friends are away at school and he has made no friends out there. Now this is a typical case of parents who will not lower their standard of living to send him to school and they found they just couldn't afford a school like Denver and maintain the home and social life they want. It really bothers me sometime wondering if Denny and Linda realize what he is giving up to keep them in school, and now Linda talks about going on to Vanderbilt, I guess at our expense. But we must call a halt someplace. I'm not saying we live like paupers—anything but—but I do say he has worked terribly hard, with very little chance to do some of the things he'd really like to. I know Charlie Seibert told us Saturday he is taking off with his brother Tuesday for Key West for deep-sea fishing and next month he has a big trip planned for turkey shooting (whatever that is) and Joan is planning on another trip to Europe and next Xmas they want to spend a month in Mexico, and we are trying to figure out if it is cheaper to take a few days off at Easter rather than spend plane fare. Oh well, we really do not regret it—but I wish the kids would just once in a while let him know they understand what it takes to keep them in school—instead of always telling us how much all the other kids have. I'm beginning to think Dentistry is the hardest way to earn a living that I know of.

Did you ever get the Xmas cookies I sent and were they edible, and also did you get your birthday package?

Must close as I asked Meachams to come by for dinner and I had better get it started and I promise not to wait as long on my next letter.

What can we say about the present escallation but that we pray constantly and think and love you always

Mom & Dad

SP/4 Dail W. Mullins, Jr.
488-48-0511
CoA, 26th ENGR. BN.
APO SF, 96256

February 13

Dear Mom and Dad,

Barksdale and I are down in Chu Lai right now, slumming. We came down the day before yesterday to take that promotion test and, having taken it, we're in no big hurry to get back. We'll probably catch a chopper out tomorrow.

The test was absurd. It's actually an oral exam, taken before a board of lifers (in our case, a Major, two Lieutenants and a First Sergeant). The questions they asked about my MOS—demolitions—were easy and I only had trouble answering one. However, your performance on that area of the test accounts for only about 25% of your total score. The remaining 75% is based upon, among other things, your personal appearance, your attitude and interest and your time in service.

When I was out at LZ Ross back in August, this ARVN out there gave me a Vietnamese friendship bracelet—I was to discover later that he was more interested in food than my friendship, as he stole my pet parrot and ate it one morning when we were on a sweep. Anyway, I still wear the bracelet—mainly because not everyone has one—unfortunately, its value, sentimental or otherwise, didn't impress the board. Neither did the fact that my boots weren't spitshined nor my fatigues pressed. I was also informed that my moustache was too long and shaggy.

I probably failed the thing because of these "gross" inadequacies. As Barksdale said—do they want a good demolitions man or an olive drab robot? With 90 days left—I'm afraid I don't even care.

I bought a book in the PX yesterday by some Canadian disc jockey named Al Boliska entitled The Mahareeshi Says . . . . It's a humorous take-off on the current guru fad. Some of Boliska's philosophical beacons are really funny. For example—

The Mahareeshi Says . . . . (on the ages of man)

Middle age is when the girl you smile at thinks you are one of her father's friends.

No matter how old you are, you can still be someone's dreamboat; even if your anchor is dragging and your cargo has shifted.

Middle age is that time of life when you can feel bad in the morning without having had fun the night before.

At middle age you can still do everything you used to—but not until tomorrow morning.

When a middle-aged man gets a gleam in his eye, its only the sun hitting his bifocals.

Middle age is when you proposition a good-looking girl and she turns you down, and you certainly do appreciate it.

Often the difference between "she's good looking" and "she's looking good" is about 20 years and 40 pounds.

Pretty good, huh?

Well, just wanted to let you know I'm OK. Did you get the tape I sent? Did it sound OK? I hope so.

Take care, all—I'll write more in a few days.

Love, peace
Dail

90 DAYS!

———————————

Sunday February 8

My dear Dail,

Received a letter from Lucy and she seemed so happy and thrilled about your phone call. We were glad that for once you were able to get through, even tho, as Lucy said, half the army was listening in.

Have "Laugh-In" on while trying to type this and it is still as wild as ever. They just said that Tin Tim is the only person where the Army burned his draft card.

Some of your letters are so darn amusing to us and we doubly appreciate the fact that you can still laugh; you know if you can still get or see something funny about the situations you are in—you've got it made. Your description of the two colonels and their mobile bunker was hilarious and sounder also like Colonel Blimpton in that English publication Punch. A rather ironic sidelight—I received this letter the day I was having a bridge club I belong to. Ruth DuBois couldn't make it so I had asked Carole Neuwoehner in her place. She is always so interested in you children and of course asked about you. I gave her this letter and she was reading it aloud to Jean Brown and a couple of the other women who had gotten here early. Anyway, a woman named Mary Lou O'Neill came in a little later. She is the gal whose son is a Citadel product and left New Year's Day for his second tour of Viet Naam—a gung ho patriot. Someone asked her if she had heard from her son and she said she had gotten a letter this week and he was the envy of his camp or wherever he is, because he has a flush toilet. There was a rather prolonged silence with everyone wondering where to look—after hearing about your colonel and his flush toilet.

Saturday night we went to the wedding of Dr. Vermillion's son, which was quite an affair. The reception was held at the Colony Club in Clayton in their ball room. We arrived and knew no one there, so we just sat at an empty table, thinking we would have one drink, eat and run. About five minutes later seven young darling girls came up and asked if we were saving the extra seats for anyone, and if not, could they join us. Well your father perked up immediately (by the way, he has read that clipping you sent several times and I think is trying to find a source of supply,) and said—"No, we were just waiting for all of you." Ha! Anyway they were all students from William Woods College, and former classmates of the bride. In talking to one little girl she said she was staying with the parents of her fiance, who lived in Webster Groves. Anyway, do you remember Sue Leeman who graduated with you and whom I think you took out a couple of times? This little girl is engaged to Sue's brother Neal—who is now in Viet Naam. This girl is a senior in Sociology and extremely bright and articulate. She mentioned spending this summer in Russia, Poland, East Berlin, and Yugoslavia on a student exchange basis of some type. The rather interesting point is her views in comparison to Bob Karasek's conversation about his feelings and experiences about Russia. She has changed her entire thinking about our involvement in curbing communism since spending a few weeks behind the so-called iron curtain. She claimed she was interrogated and held for 24 hours for just using the wrong door in a school they were visiting. She claims you can smell the fear and that she saw not one person smile the entire time she was over there. Another confusing commentary on the pros and cons of one of the issues of our times. She said to her it would be horrendous to think of the plight of negroes if they lived in Russia but that Europe can sit back and condemn us because they just do not have a black problem. Well, this is one view.

Well, St. Louis has started a Woman's Crusade on Crime and maybe this will be the answer. Usually if you get enough women mad enough things can happen. They are trying to get 100,000 women signed up to investigate the courts and why confirmed criminals are being released while the arresting policeman is signing the docket, how much judges are involved in graft, what to do about the juvenile delinquency problem, what to do about the increasing "hard drug" problem, complete relighting of all streets and alleys in St.Louis; the list goes on and on and they are fighting mad. Last Friday a nurse was leaving Firmin Desloge Hospital at 4 in the afternoon and as she was getting in her car, four colored teen-agers grabbed her and killed her. She had been married just a couple of months ago. One of the 17 year old boys was out on bond for a previous serious conviction. We are really living in a jungle.

Received a letter from Linda and she is having a talk from some professor from Nashville, Tennessee regarding graduate school in Sociology and seems quite serious about going on and Dad just thinks it is ridiculous. I'm beginning to hate the idea of her going into this field at all, especially if she has any idea of using it in a city like St.Louis. And, of course, these are the cities where is is really needed the most. As usual, somebody has to do it—but I don't want my daughter taking these chances. What she is doing about Bob is anybody's guess. I know Lucy seems to have had the social work deal and I can fully understand this.

I'm enclosing a piece that was in our church newspaper—which really applies to many things besides a minister—and which seems so apropos—sides lining up against each other. We are now in the process of visiting churches to recruit a new minister and someone thought this would be the right time to remind everyone to not expect a super-human being.

Did you hear about the fellow who told his wife to go upstairs and take her clothes off and lie down on the bed and he'd be right up. She said—"Honey, we just went through that an hour ago." He said "Well, Thank God it's my memory I'm losing first."

Well, it's late and I've promised, to be over at church early tomorrow. They had an emergency call for cancer bandages, which our circle furnishes to several agencies and I promised to help make them tomorrow.

Keep smiling and counting those days. I told Dad I went by Bill Colbert's house the other day and his father—who is the epitome of establishment—was getting in his car. On the back bumper he has a very prominent PEACE sign displayed. What a difference it makes when you have someone over there.

We're thinking Peace and about you and all our love.
Mom & Dad

"Many Christian churches have become split into liberal and conservative camps by the "polarization" now sweeping this nation.

When such division strikes your congregation, the following satire may help to promote reconciliation.

"The man you select should be moderately dynamic, charismatically calm and progressively conservative.

He should agree to handle all baptisms, weddings, sick calls, and funerals personally—freeing his staff to monitor the switchboard.

He must not take any position that might jeopardize the Annual Fund Drive. If a new church is built, he should, favor "Contemporary Gothic".

He and his wife should be "teetotalers who hold their martinis well." Their children must relate cooperatively to all peer groups. Their dog must like cats.

Each Sunday the service will open with all hands singing "Onward Christian Soldiers."

Above all, the man you recommend must be a flexible fellow, equipped with a multi-dimensional mind and a forked tongue—programmed to please all element's in our Passionately Polarized Parish.

The new head minister will stand tall in the pulpit and announce, "Conservatives to the Right, Liberals to the Left."

When the congregation is properly re-seated, a velvet curtain will descend down the middle, so the Right won't know what the Left is doing.

The minister will then face the Right and preach? "Christ's Concern for Law and Order . . . Ten Commandments . . . Our Patriotic Heritage . . . Decline and Fall of America? . . . Communism is our Foe . . . School Prayer . . . Perils of Pornography . . . Riots are Ruinous . . . The Jensen Report. . . . Equal Responsibility? . . . Our Revolting Youth . . . America is Beautiful . . . Initiative Enterprise and Integrity . . . Our Spineless "Intellectuals" . . . Traditional Sex . . . And How We Can Win the War in Viet Naam."

At the same time, the minister will face the Left and preach: "Christ's Concern for Compassion . . . Are Absolutes Obsolete? . . . Right of Conscience . . . Situation Ethics . . . Civil Disobedience . . . Boston Tea Party . . . Pike's Pique . . . Dialectic Dialogues . . . Freud, Jung, and Kierkegaard . . . Relevance of Riots . . . Bigoted Brothers . . . Project Equality . . . The Walker Report . . . Police Brutality . . . The Pluralistic Pew . . . Poverty is OUR Problem . . . Where the Action Is . . . Modern Sex . . . and Why we Should Get Out of Viet Naam."

After 30 minutes a chime will chime and the sides will sin in their separate cells. On the Right we'll have "Faith of our Fathers" and on the Left "We Shall Overcome."

As the last strains die, the curtain will rise and the united congregation will harmonize "Blest Be the Tie That Binds", in seven different keys . . . It is respectfully submitted that it will take such a Man and such a Service to meet today's demands that the Church be all things to all people at once."

SP/4 Dail W. Mullins, Jr.
488-48-0511
CoA, 26th ENGR. BN.
APO SF, 96256

February 16

Dear Mom and Dad,

On or about the 18th of this month our whole company will be going into the field on a major operation with the infantry and artillery. They told us where we'd be going, but I can't remember those Vietnamese words for more than ten minutes—all I know is that its southwest of here and west of LZ Professional, about half-way between the ocean and the Laotian border. Some infantry will be flown in first, of course, to clear a preliminary LZ and set up a perimeter. We'll be right behind them, though, and it will be our job, apparently, to clear a larger area, build expedient perimeter bunkers and erect mortar pits and leveled areas for artillery pieces. It's supposed to be an eight day operation for the engineers, but I think they're going to try and cut it down to five.

The area where we're going is supposed to have a lot of NVA, and our intelligence has reportedly spotted enemy trucks moving about! Because of this, they are expecting to find an enemy arms cache as large as, or larger than, that one they just uncovered down south. While we're out there, elements of the 196th, F-troop 17th cavalry, 1/1 cavalry and the 1st and 2nd ARVN divisions will be carrying on a battalion sized operation all around us—I hope they push any NVA away from us. I am definitely too short for this stuff.

I still don't know whether I passed or failed that promotion test—no one does, yet. I'll let you know as soon as I hear.

Whenever the engineers go out into the field on a mission, they usually work from sunup to sundown, since the slower we work the longer we stay out—for that reason, it may be difficult for me to get a letter off, either because of a lack of time or light. I'm taking some writing material and I'll try my best, but if you shouldn't hear from me, don't worry—I'll write as soon as I possibly can.

I'm afraid that I don't have much more news than that right now, folks. The weather is improving—it still rains occasionally, but most days are sunny and quite warm. It will start to get good and hot just about the time I leave.

Take care of yourselves, keep writing and say hello to everyone for me.

Love and peace, always
Dail

Sunday, February 15

My dear Son,
    Always feel so badly when I haven't written you for a longer period of time than usual, especially when the excuse is so very invalid. Tuesday and Wednesday spent most of both days getting cancer bandages ready for an emergency call from a hospital, and repairing, washing and ironing some clothes that a family needed right away. Thursday and Friday I felt kinda lousy—thinking I was coming down with the flu which has been rampant in this area. Had the time to write, but for some reason couldn't make my brain function—and I couldn't help thinking of the joke I sent you where the guy was so glad his brain was the first thing leaving him. False alarm, evidently, on both counts—altho sometimes I'm not so sure.
    Went to church today, which I do every Sunday, and it probably won't make sense to you—but this quiet hour sets me up for the week, and sometimes stirs me to do some serious thinking. Today was communion and also communicant Sunday, wherein we take in the young children as members. This is now a two year study period in most churches, instead of the six week crash course you took. There is a special pattern followed in our church for this taking of communion. The table is set very close to the front pews with the perfectly ironed linen cloth and napkins with the silver chalice and trays. The organ begins to play and for this service the elders and deacons come down the center aisle en masse, with the young minister carrying the bible for presentation. To you and many of the younger people this all seems ritualistic, out of place, and perhaps even heathenistic; but I couldn't help feeling how good it is to have something you know has been done for ages and still can be executed without someone getting up and picketing about it. It presents, to me, a continuity of life that is really a haven in a world that is changing too fast for we who are in the "Golden Years" (that's a joke, son—what is golden about them is beyond me—more like Lead). Anyway, I'm serious.
    Then I always enjoy both of the young fellows we have now. Today it was the College Campus fellow—Earl Mulley. I, for one, am going to regret finding a permanent minister to take over our pulpit. Today, being the first Sunday in Lent, he spoke about Christ's knowledge of his crucifixion and how the disciples began to maneuver to be top dog. This lead to the inherent nature of man to compete for rewards whether they be monetary, a gold medal, or recognition in their fields

and this to him, is good and a must. Man must strive and compete and work, but it is what he does with his rewards that is the final and complete answer. In other words, no storing up and amassing of money for selfish and personal gains. What do you do with your wealth and knowledge to help your fellow man. This, of course, always goes over with a bang with most of the congregation. Not all. While I really am engrossed with this young fellow there are times when thoughts enter your subconscious and won't leave. And today right in the midst of his sermon a joke I had just heard came in to my mind and wouldn't leave. About the old pastor who was leaving his church and was giving his last sermon. He had invited his young replacement to come and listen. The old man was at his very best and really had his congregation sitting on the edge of their seats. At a high peak he stopped turned and took a gulp of what looked like water. After the service he asked the the young fellow what he had thought of the sermon. The young fellow said—"It was tremendous, but I couldn't help wonder why, when you had them in the palm of your hand, you took the chance of losing them by taking that drink of water." The old fellow being turned out to pasture said "That wasn't water, son, that was a martini." So the next Sunday came the time for the young fellow's first sermon and he remembered what the elder one had done. After his sermon, he asked the older man—who had come to do him honor—how it went. "The sermon was excellent", he said, "but when you turned for that little nip, you shouldn't have waved the tooth pick with the olive on it, to make your point". Ah, well, we all have our hang-ups.

 I'm sure you remember Walter Weir? Well he had a tragic death last week. It, of course, was mentioned on television and radio both—mainly because Walter has become widely known through his racing cars. Dad and I had known, from Mickey Davis, that Walter had had a serious drinking problem at one time—in fact, this was one of his reasons for going to Mayo's psychiatric clinic; but we thought he had it licked and whenever I saw him at the station he seemed extremely in command, of his help and himself. Well, evidently he has been getting worse and worse (in fact, Tommy quit the station last October and is working at the airport as a mechanic). Evidently Mrs. Weir called all the ten kids home, even those living in Florida and up east, to have a family meeting to decide what to do with their father. Last Tuesday the ten kids, 17 grandchildren, and Walter's mother and father were all gathered together to come to some decision (Frankly—a crowd of this kind would drive me to drink). At 1 o'clock in the morning Walter must have really gotten wild and he left the house—evidently going to find some place where he could get a drink. The boys had taken the car keys away from him months ago, so he was walking. He evidently got out in the middle of a traffic lane on 66 near Katz, waving his arms, and one fellow swerved and avoided him, but the next fellow plowed right into him. So the family now has the answer.

Received Denny and Linda's semester grades and frankly we were pleasantly surprised. We knew Linda has been doing well, with 4 "A's", 1 "B", and a "C" in anatomy again—which kept her off the Dean's list. But we weren't too sure about Denny—as he has been slightly hinting in all letters, not to get shook up. But they weren't bad. three C's, two B's, and a D in Old Testament. As he said to us—"I believe in God and think I like him, but I sure don't know why I have to do all this studying about him." But Dad is still a little "phased out" about Linda's desire to go on in school. As he says, a literary hobo who is afraid to get out and do something with her knowledge. If she is really serious I hope she can do it on her own, because we have got to quit financing school sometime. I notice your father getting more discouraged and cantankerous—not being able to do many of the things that his friends are doing in their late years. Like trips whenever the mood strikes. Meachams in Chicago for a week, Charlie Seibert just back from Kewy West, after two weeks of deep sea fishing, the dentist down the hall leaving for Europe with his wife and two of his children. He really gets discouraged. Of course, he's been having a little of his old trouble bothering him and has quit smoking again and this always makes him almost impossible to live with. Hope he sticks to it this time. I try to do my smoking in the bathroom or someplace where he can't see me. I wish to heaven I could quit—but it seems more than I have the guts for. This is why I get up-tight with kids about marijuana and all their blase arguments about it not being bad for you and not being habit forming. Bull****, and from the horse's mouth. The world is not made up of staunch-like characters who can try and experiment with mental stimulants and walk away from it, without wanting to go on to more explosive experiences—especially the young. And just the facts of what people will do to earn money for this habit is frightening. But this is one generation who can never reach the other on this subject. I know while I was at Mayo's for about 5 days after they operated on me, they kept me on morphine when the pain would get unbearable. Then this young doctor came by and said that was it—no more. I think for two days I would have done anything for the release I knew this drug would give me—and that in just five days.

Last night we played bridge with the Seiberts and it really seems all we do is argue with our friends lately. Old Spiro Agnew was in town last week and Charlie said last night "That's my man for the next President." I thought your father would literally choke. Tricky-Dicky is bad, but the thought of Spiro overwhelms him. What is truly, truly unfortunate is that many many people are beginning to think this way. He is saying what the wide corn belt is thinking and wanting again in this country. Pride of country, heritage, obedience to elders, moral standards (whatever they were) and the God given Good Old Days. Washington University has been having a symposium all week with different speakers and the enclosed article is a quote by a Kevin Phillips—and many people are wanting this. Eugene

McCarthy spoke the first day and while he appealed to a good many of the students—some of the older participants resented his remarks.

Then last Wednesday night I went to one of my bridge clubs and came home thoroughly bewildered in trying to accommodate people and problems. First Lucille Monroe tells us that Gail is expecting a baby, then Jay Eichhorn announces that her daughter Sandy is expecting, and then Letitia caps it all by announcing that Ronald's wife (they were married in 29th of November) had a baby girl the first week of January. We not only have a mass population explosion in one group of 8 women, but they are doing it in two months instead of the usual 9. Sex education and knowledge seems to be working in reverse as far as I'm concerned. I've never heard of so many pregnant brides, walking down the aisle in virginal white with the veil of chastity. And don't tell me that there are more young brides today so more chance of being pregnant. The proportion just is not there. I knew of not one girl during my "age of consent", who walked down the aisle pregnant. But then maybe I was sheltered. I was at Ronald's wedding and I can't think but what a farce the whole ceremony has become. 4 bridesmaids, an hour long mass, the words of fulfillment from the priest (and boy was she filled) the big reception—it's a travesty. I know Mrs. Vermillion was talking to me about their son's wedding, which we attended a week ago. She and Dr. Vermillion were not at all in accord with the grandiose affair of 8 bridesmaids and his whole fraternity, and all the hoop-de-la that went with it. Especially, as Mrs. Vermillions said, when his bride has been making week end trips to Rolla for six months and sleeping with their son. Not that Byron told them this—but they were not born yesterday and were very well aware of what was going on and just prayed the marriage would be consumated before the appearance of their first grandchild. Linda was telling me that 8 girls in her dorm alone have had to get married. I think these statistics are frightening and it makes you sick to think of what you children have ahead of you, in trying to raise a right thinking family. And believe me, take it from a woman, this will color the whole relationship of any man and woman—she will wonder all her life if he would have married her under different circumstances and he will always think he was tricked into this situation. Some things will never change.

I picked up a book the other day entitled "A Loving Wife" by Violet Weingartin. Never heard of it or her, but it sounded interesting and it's funny sometimes what little gems you can find that haven't been on a best seller list. It's modern, but good and I've enjoyed it. It has no astounding message but in a small way, to me, it is a critique of our times. It is the story of a middle aged woman who thought she was happily married to a scientist, who is completely absorbed in his profession, who has a grown college son who brings his girl of the moment home for the holidays and thinks nothing of having her sleep with him in his "old room" with the trophies and teddy bears his mother has kept intact, and her going back to social work and meeting a man who reaches her intellectually and with whom she can "communicate". Make that three children and you can see why I am enjoying it.

Well, hasn't this been a rambling bunch of nothing? I do go on. We were so glad you enjoyed the tape. The other night Ray Charles was on Johhny Cash's program and Dad was sick because he hadn't gotten another tape—but I don't think I could go through that again with him. Wish you would have been here the day we made that. It was something else again.

Well, I figure about 75 more days—and for each day less I thank God and we think about you so much. I really think Dad is going to wither away. He really takes what you are going through harder than any of us—because he has no release. I cry and storm and I'm sure Lucy does, but he suffers siletntly except when he is talking with Charlie or Ken.

All our love and PEACE,
Mom & Dad

P.S. Be on the lookout for a CARE package. Hope you just don't find crumbs.

Wednesday February 18

My dear Dail,

Let me tell you about Monday! It's always a rather let down day, but around lo:30 the mail man came with your tape, and I was so excited I started to tear it apart—but then I said "No, I'll ruin it or do something wrong as women have no sense of the mechanical." So I spent the whole day looking at it and wondering and waiting for yoour father to come home so we could play it. Of course I bowled him over as he came in the door and we put it on his recorder and guess what came out—our horrible voices and our message to you—interspersed with a few words from you that came through. We spent an hour running both sides and every once in a while we would be able to hear a very interesting and provacative remark by you and then—nothing. It was the most frustrating hour we have ever spent and we were just sick. Dad, of course, had to remark—"and he has a Master's Degree." I don't know what happened but the tape we sent has to be erased before it is used again. So what I am doing is sending you a new, unused tape and we are begging you to repeat your broadcast if this is possible. We'll then send it on to Lucy as I am sure she can find someone who has a tape recorder. In fact, I imagine her father's church might have one.

Received your letter from Chu Lai and of course my first reaction is—I wish you would quit flying around in those damn choppers. And, of course, your quotes from the book you picked up were so apropos—but you won't know what this is all about until you reach 50 = and then if you can laugh at quotes that are made about your inadequacies, you've got it made. In fact, while writing this I've just heard some by-play that is now going on in St.Louis. They have booked the play "Hair" at the American Theater and there is an alderwoman, Mrs. Bass, who is really stirring the Mayor's office, the public and anyone else she can get to listen, stirred up about allowing this obscene "trash" (her words) to be allowed in our fair city. Yesterday she had called a meeting with the Aldermanic Committee to have a law put in the city charter that would bar all types of obscentiy. Of course Webster College students heard about it and stormed the meeting place and it wound up in a free for all. Mrs. Bass is standing up to these students and saying—"don't be too cocky, some day you will all be 40." And some kid in the back yells—"God Forbid". Funny, but he really will—and then what. Wonder what he will be in a sweat about worrying about his children and the world in chaos.

This brings me to your relating your appearance before the board of the higher echelon, to determine your ability to be an Sp/5 or continue on at your present status. I, too, couldn't care less. The only thing which does upset me is this is typical of what you are going to face when you come back to the World. Whether you like it or not, some things are still circumspect—long hair, too way-out clothes, headbands, dirty sandals; they just do not make an impression on the powers that be—whether it's a university, a business firm, or the army. So it is going to be up to you as to how far out on the limb you are going to put yourself. Speaking of universitys, I've really gotten in a hassle with the Graduate Apartment at Washington". The women I first spoke to was so intelligent and cooperative, but for four days in trying to get through to someone about a catalog and course information I got no one but foreigners who speak very little English and that poorly. I was beginning to talk like your father—"those d*** foreigners, why don't they stay in their own country where they belong." Finally reached a Dr. Stocker who again, was most cooperative and said he would see that the necessary information was sent to you post haste. So let me know if you shouldn't receive it. I offered to go out and pick up the material and mail it myself, but he said that wouldn't he necessary.

Doesn't look as though we are going to Florida, which is evidently very upsetting to the kids— and us, although I don't think they are aware of this. I feel it might just as well to let the kids go down to Panama City with some of the others going down, as their plane fare home is not cheap—but don't think your father feels this way. So because he can't take off the time and doesn't feel we should spend the money—he goes out and buys himself a stereo FM/AM radio—which we needed like a hole in our head. I'll never understand the machinations of your dad's thinking if I spend even 20 more years with him. Should have been aware of this when he started telling me not to buy anything and to watch how I spent his money and on and on. This is always the prelude to a purchase of his. Oh well! I just go up to the bedroom and close the door and it reduces the blasting noise a little. No wonder he can't hear.

Talking to Mrs. Bill the other day and they were a little upset. Wayne's commander (or whatever you call the guy) has been after Wayne to put in for a rank raise and some more training, but this would entail extending his army service for at least 3 more years; in other words think about it as a career. As Winnie said, Wayne was not at all receptive until he heard from his wife, who is beginning to think that it wouldn't be a bad deal and feels that the economy and job situation being as bad as it is—he would be much better having this assured job and money. Of course, they don't feel as though they can interfere—but they are not at all happy about it. So you see how some men get entangled into situations. Her arguments are free medical expenses, retirement at around 46, travel—she's evidently got a lot of arguments.

Well, I want to get a letter off to Lucy and Aunt Dot. It seems like I spend a lot of time letter writing, but Dad says I get diarreaha of the mouth and typewriter and I needn't spend so much time doing a routine job. I sure don't see him doing any writing to anybody.

Let us hear when you can and much love,
PEACE,
Mom & Dad

SP/4 Dail W. Mullins, Jr.
488-48-0511
CoA, 26th ENGR. BN.
APO SF, 96256

February 24

Dear Mom and Dad,

I know you both must be fairly worried by now, not having heard from me in several days and knowing that I would be in the field. I believe I wrote and told you before we left that circumstances would probably not permit correspondence and, sure enough, they did not.

I believe I indicated in that same letter that this particular mission was big and fairly important. That fact, added to my customary pre-field depression and nervousness, probably didn't help calm either of you. Well, as is usual, the whole thing wasn't as bad as my imagination always says it will be. Nevertheless, it was pretty rough and fairly frightening at times. Our company lost two men and the infantry five—it was my first real association with friendly casualties, and it is not fun, believe me.

Our part in the mission lasted five days, which is relatively short for a field exercise, and I was really glad to see Hawk Hill. We were fifteen miles from the Laotian border during the entire operation—from our position we could see a mountain that stood right on the border. You have never seen such foreboding country in your life—miles and miles of jungle-covered mountains. It's fantastically beautiful and so desolate. I did manage to get some pretty good pictures, so you'll be able to see for yourself when I get home.

The operation, incidentally, was called Operation Mary Ann—our company was part of Task Force Mary Ann. If the whole thing was as big as they say, you may be reading about it back home in the papers—let me know what they say; I'd be interested to hear.

Incidentally, as a sidelight—you're aware, I'm sure, of the current Laotian crisis. There has been some talk about American B-52 raids over the Plain of Jars—whether or not we are actually making them? Well, I can assure you, from personal observation, that we are. B-52's and fighter escorts were flying back from Laos all night long every night we were out there. Sometimes you could hear the ground shaking from the runs.

Well, we're back now, anyway—I'm tired, both physically and mentally, but otherwise unscathed, so we can all relax.

I haven't heard whether my R&R request for Hong Kong went through yet, but I expect to any day now. You still haven't told me whether there is anything you want me to buy for you while I'm there.

I received your package yesterday—thank you very much. Barksdale inhaled the Vienna Sausages almost before I got them out of the box, but I managed to keep him away from the cookies by eating most of them myself. We also gave a few of them to several of the Vietnamese children who work around here—I don't think they had ever tasted anything quite like them.

By the way, have you found out whether Washington U. ever sent me a catalogue? I sure do need one.

Well, I just wanted to let you know that I am back and safe, so you wouldn't have to worry anymore. As I said, I'm still pretty tired, so you'll excuse me if my letter is a bit short and rambling. Take care, both of you—keep writing, and I'll see you in about 79 days.

Peace and love,
Dail

———————————

Monday [maybe soon after Feb 20, 1970, when Chicago 7 trial ended?]

Dear Dail,

Sitting here wondering what to talk, or should I say write about, and Chanel walks by. Now we have had some weird and neurotic pets in this house, but she tops them all. We have had quite a problem with this dog in defecating. In other words, or cruder, she just doesn't know how to take a crap. After several trips to the veterinarian at $12 a trip, your father decided the last time he would do the job. So he comes home with surgical gloves and electric clippers. Of course, he can't possibly do this alone so I am holding her gagging and really thinking I will throw up any instant. We finally de-plugged her and he said he thought he could clip the hair away. They were down there about an hour and I wish you could see her. Some places are shaved down to bleeding skin and other places have long clumps of hair hanging down in the most peculiar areas. She has the funniest legs I have ever seen and right now she looks like a hot dog walking around on 4 stilts. It really wouldn't bother me except when I realize what your father paid for this mongrel and his remark when he came home that the woman who sold her to him was so stupid. Stupid, like a fox.

Think I mentioned that Linda has been talking about going on and getting a master's degree in Sociology. The other week she talked about having a conference with a man from Vanderbilt, a professor from Memphis State and also checking into a criminology course in juvenile delinquency at SIU. Your father and I think it is utterly ridiculous and the thought of her prowling around a ghetto in some city just gets to me. But after being told by so-called experts that we have caused her untold harm by decision-making, I'm afraid to say a word. I will say these plans she is trying to make will, supposedly, be at her expense—as we really meant it when we told both Denny and Linda that four years was our limit. But we received a letter from her in which she mentioned Lucy had written her and I am so grateful for the advice your wife gave her. She felt Linda should work in the field for a couple of years before she spent the time, money and energy in getting a masters. Evidently Lucy is fed up with the sociology field. I know your father had lunch with Stan Hofmeister the other day and he was telling him that Judy is graduating this spring in Sociology, but she is going to apply for a job as an airline stewardess, because they refuse to have her working in the areas where sociology would take her. As your dad said—"4 years to be a stewardess when she could have gone to their school in Colorado for 9 months and gotten the same type job."

Sometimes I think Linda just wants to keep going on to school and really isn't thrilled about the thought of going out and applying her knowledge in a practical way. I really wish she would meet someone whom she felt was the ONE, and settle down somewhere. But not unless she is sure.

Listened to a fellow named Jay Richard Kennedy the other night. He has written a new novel about Mao, which while listed as fiction—is based on actuality and personal knowledge and acquaintenship. Kennedy was used in Kennedy's, Johnson's, and also Nixon's administration as an authority on the new Chinese regime and he certainly gives you something to think about. He says Mao is the most complex, un-selfconscious revered man he has ever met and has done one of the most remarkable jobs of leadership we could ever imagine. When he talks about dividing 800,000,000 people into communes of not over 80,000 people and all self-supporting and self-existing small cities with a complete replica of each commune 2 miles underground—even to water systems and how they have been placed in groups of trades. This, he claims, is why Mao calls the atom bomb a paper tiger and they really cannot be bluffed by this threat. Now if a backward country—which until he took over, were mostly peasants—can build a complex like this, what is the matter with our country? Kennedy is evidently one of the few people in the world who is allowed free access to China.

Guess you did get to hear the results of the Chicago Trial. Just another thing I wonder about. I would hate to live in a land where the judicial system was no more and we would have more of a jungle than we have. As one lawyer said the other day—laws will never make people good; they just protect one person from the actions of another—not that person from himself. Does that make sense to you? It does to me.

Well this is going to be short as I am going up to the Motor Vehicle office on Big Bend. Lucy sent your driver's license to me to see if I could have it renewed. I called them and they said to bring it up that service men's licenses can be renewed by someone other than the licensee. So I'll see what I can do.

Talked to Mrs. Bell the other day. Mr. Bell's mother dies last week and we sent flowers to them. She was telling me that the last month in Viet Naam they send the men to what they term a "safe" area. (if there is such a place.) Is that true? Anyway from what I can figure we have 60 more days. I too try not to count, but it's hard.

Let us hear when you can and all our love
PEACE,
Mom & Dad

———————————

SP/4 Dail W. Mullins, Jr.
488-48-0511
CoA, 26th ENGR. BN.
APO SF, 96256

March 1

Dear Mom and Dad,

I should apologize, I guess, for not having written a second time since our return from the field—however, I received the blank tape that you sent on the day that I had intended to write, so I let that suffice. I hope you received the tape intact—should you experience the same trouble this time as last, don't throw the tape away. Find someone who has a stereo tape recorder, and use it.

Hawk Hill is on special alert tonight. Intelligence has informed the powers-to-be that we can expect a mortar and/or ground attack sometime tonight—while I never get too excited or upset about these intelligence reports (90% of the time they turn out to be false alarms), I am always ready for any eventuality.

Well, it's the beginning of another month and, according to the calendar I now have 74 days left. Most of the men from this unit who are going home with some time still to serve in the States have been getting four or five day drops—while this may conceivably lower my count to around 70 days, I'm still going to go by the maximum figure. That way, as I said before, I can only be pleasantly surprised.

Other than the fact that I am getting short, nothing else of major importance has occurred around here. Our platoon is working over at the F-troop, 17th armored cavalry company area, building bunkers for them. While this work is hot, tiring and extremely boring, I'd just as soon continue such work until I leave—one alternative to this work, of course, being the field, something I can't even be messing with anymore.

You noticed, no doubt, that on the tape I sent, the reel ran out before I had a chance to say goodbye—I didn't realize I was so close to the end. While I'm quite sure that this recording didn't contain any provocative remarks, I do hope you enjoyed it—I know I had fun doing it.

Well, I guess I'll turn in, now. I hope Charles doesn't disturb my sleep. Take care, let me know what's going on back home, and I'll be writing again soon.

Love and, of course, peace.
Dail

SP/4 Dail W. Mullins, Jr.
488-48-0511
CoA, 26th ENGR. BN.
APO SF, 96256

March 7

LZ Professional

Dear Mom and Dad,
    It's been so long since I last wrote to you folks that I can't even remember when it was—I do seem to recall having written a few days after sending the tape, but I'm not positive. I hope I did, anyway.
    I guess, first off, you'd like to know where in the world LZ Professional is and what I'm doing here. Fair enough.
    You'll remember my telling you once, I'm sure, that Tam Ky, the largest city around here and province capital, was located on Vietnam highway one, approximately half-way between Hawk Hill, to the North, and Chu Lai, to the South. Well, LZ Professional is located about five miles due west of Tam Ky, in the higher foothills of the central highlands. Although it is the base camp for the first battalion of the 196th, it's a very small LZ, only about as large as three or four of the lots in your neighborhood. Everything is packed onto the top of a mountain overlooking a beautiful jungle valley—from the air the LZ almost resembles an anthill, an analogy not too far-fetched, since on these more remote firebases, one is almost forced to live like an ant—underground. All of the buildings here, at least those parts which protrude above ground, are constructed from empty artillery ammo boxes.
    Eight of us from the second platoon were sent out here three days ago to rebuild four of the LZ's perimeter bunkers and construct a new mess hall for the infantry—their old one burned down about two weeks ago. I would have written sooner, but last night and tonight are the first nights we've had any lights. We wouldn't have them now, except that Lt. Lipps thoughtfully included a few sockets and bulbs on our first resupply chopper yesterday. I had tried to borrow a candle, but those things are like gold here on Professional.
    Normally, when the engineers come to a fire support base like this, they're expected to pull bunker guard in one or two of the perimeter bunkers, and thus relieve some of the grunts from this task for awhile. Before we came out here, though, our CO informed the brass on Professional that, should we have to pull bunker guard every night, we'd take the authorized half-day off next morning, and thus slow down the work. Well, since the people out here are anxious to have their bunkers and mess hall completed, we're exempt from guard this trip.

The only empty hootch on the whole hill was a 10' x 20' structure constructed, as I have said, out of old ammo boxes. It had formerly been used to house refugees and POW's, so you can imagine what kind of shape it was in. The first night we were here, all eight of us had to sleep on the floor in the dirt. I made the comment to Barksdale the next morning that one night in the place world sure change a few minds about ghetto life and urban development. We had rats running over us all night. One big one, apparently liking our body heat, attempted to set up a temporary residence during the night right between Barksdale and me. We altered his plans quickly, however.

The next morning, not wishing to spend another night like that, two of us stayed back in the hootch and did some expedient carpentry work—we walled up all of the holes and cracks and built eight beds, bunk style. Since then, we haven't had any trouble, although you can sure hear the rats at night, scratching and chewing on the wood.

An LZ like Professional, unlike Chu Lai or Hawk Hill, is completely dependent upon the helicopter for its very existence. Everything—ammunition, food, water, mail, gasoline, oil, you name it—has to be brought in by chopper. Consequently, most items are at a premium, as you can well imagine. Water for example. While nobody ever really goes thirsty, the permanent inhabitants of a hill like this are, needless to say, quite reluctant to part with anything as valuable as, say, some of their bath water. As a result, all of us are beginning to itch. That's after only three full days—we're scheduled to be out here for two weeks, so you can imagine what I'm going to feel like when I return. Of course, I did manage to fill my helmet with some water this evening, so at least my hands and face are clean—and I was able to shave. Out at LZ Mary Ann, none of us saw any water (except to drink, of course) for five days—out there, however, we were so miserable in other ways, that we didn't really notice the dirt.

I don't really know why I'm going on about all of this, except that I can't really think of anything else to talk about. I suppose, though, that it is as interesting to you as anything else might be.

Your count of how many days I have left puzzles me. The last letter I received from you mentioned the number 60—that sounded nice, but I'm afraid it was somewhat low. As of tomorrow morning, the eighth of March, I have 68 days left. I may or may not get a short drop—until I know for sure, however, I'll still figure 68.

I'm sure Lucy told you that she, and two other girls from her office, drove down to Atlanta a few weeks ago to see the Henley's. Jennifer, as you know, is expecting again, and all of them, embryo included, are apparently doing fine.

Nothing of tremendous importance has occurred since you heard from me last. I am, of course, getting shorter by the hour—I can almost taste that Virginia air already. Ahh—if I never see another rice paddy again, it will be too soon.

Please keep writing—you only have a few more weeks to go, and your letters do help—as they have, so very much, since last May.

Take care, both of you, and say hello to the kids—love and, of course, peace—
Dail

SP/4 Dail W. Mullins, Jr.
488-48-0511
CoA, 26th ENGR. BN.
APO SF, 96256

March 9

Dear Mom and Dad,

I'm rather tired tonight, so this probably won't be long—I just wanted to let you know that everything is OK.

The eight of us are still out here at LZ Professional building bunkers for the freedom of men everywhere. None of us has had a bath yet, and, frankly, I'm beginning to feel a little raunchy. During the day, you don't notice the heat so much, because you're busy. At night, however, it's a different story—all you can do is lie in bed, sweating and itching. Because of the filth, mosquito bites soon become infected and red, and your arms become covered with open sores. The worst thing about it, I think, is your hair—it gets gritty and matted. And, of course, in my case, falls out faster. Each day I become more and more amazed at the fact that there are some people who actually reenlist—what are fools like that doing running around loose?

I had intended, when we learned we were coming out here, to catch up on my letter writing—unfortunately, I forgot to bring any address book, so the only two people I can write are you and Lucy. Oh, well—that's combat, I guess.

I've been reading John Updike's Couples out here—I enjoy Updike, but I had only read his short stories and essays up until now. Couples is an extremely well written book, I think, but somewhat depressing, at least to me. Have you read it? I got the impression that the incidents he describes are, in fact, probably more fact than fiction. "The sexiest primate alive" as Desmond Morris says.

It's fun being short, but rather nerve-wracking, if you know what I mean. A common disorder known over here as the shorttimer shakes. At night I just lie on my bunk thinking about Lucy, genetics and my new tape recorder—in that order. I'll sure be glad when my life is normal again.

I seem to recall your making the comment in one of your letters that soldiers in 'Nam were given a shorttimer's job for their last 30 days. Well, this all depends on the unit. C Company, 26th Engineers makes it a point never to send their men to the field if they have 30 days or less lift in country. Unfortunately, A Company has no such policy—like most infantry units, our men can stay in the field up until 5 days prior to their DEROS. There is always sick call, however.

Well, as I told you, this letter wouldn't be too long. Please take care, keep writing, and I'll do the same.

Love and, from Vietnam, where the word has lost its meaning, peace
Dail

Sunday [probably March 1, 1970—before March 4, 1970, when she started reading "The Perfect Day"; last letter from Dail was dated Feb. 16—got the letter on Feb. 25]

My dear,

As I was driving home from church today down Oak Tree I saw these three people with a little boy and after giving them a double take, I saw it was the Thoms and Mary and Little Chris; so I pulled over. Chris hasn't grown much but he is still really too pretty to be a boy. He is a doll. The Thoms wanted to know all about you and to be sure and give you their love. Mary said that Steve had been trying to reach me as he had written you two letters since the first of the year and they had been returned. I'm positive I gave him your complete address the last time I talked to him. The Thoms are fine altho I felt Mrs. Thoms was beginning to show a few age lines which I hadn't noticed before. Of course, they were not dressed up and perhaps this makes the difference. She said she had been in California to visit Sandy and take care of one of her children while the other two had tonsilectomies. Then Sandy decided to have a D & C taken care of while her mother was there—so Mildred said she really got to know the children.

Do you remember the McLellands? She was the nurse at Hixon for awhile and their son is the boy who graduated from West Point and because of ear impairment, due to close detonation on maneuvers, he was told he would never be sent to combat. He had been sent to Venice as his first assignment and was really loving the life when he came under the thumb of a Colonel who didn't like the way he parted his hair—so he has been re-assigned to Viet Naam. Anyway in talking to Dorothy she told me I must get Ira Levine's new book entitled "The Perfect Day." He's the author of Rosemary's Baby and I wasn't too thrilled about reading anything he had written but she said she thought I'd really enjoy this. Don't know it whether it is fiction or non-fiction, but it has a genetic theme. She said she was probably more interested than the usual person because of a few genetic problems they have had. You know her husband was born with a club foot, as his father had. It skipped their boy who is going to Viet Naam, but showed up again in his new baby who was born about 3 months ago (that is, Bart McLelland's child), so Dot said it was of tremendous interest to her. I am to pick a copy of the book up Monday at the library and if it is worthwhile I'll try and get you a copy. I still have a list of the books you have mentioned you would like to received, but I'm sort of hoping for paper back editions. When you buy these darn books in hard back they really "sock it to you."

Well last night we had the bi-monthly meeting of the running debate between the Seiberts and Mullins. Sometimes it really gets hot—but it is good to toss ideas back and forth, if no one gets too up-tight. Solutions to all our problems are really going to have to be a give and take between the revolutionists and the establishments. As Charlie said last night, many of us older people are well aware that serious things are wrong in the world, but we will never be able to see how burning college buildings, banks, ROTC buildings, destroying files is the way to go about it. He feels the young will furnish the gripes—but that it is going to take the money and the know how of the despised "establishment" to make any new ideas work. I cannot help agree with him as I have been trying to read, listen and evaluate all the riots, trials and protests going on and I have yet to hear a concrete, workable plan of operation from any of the dissidents. Let's overthrow everything seems to be their rallying call—but can't they see what chaos would result. This is why so many people are really fed up and feel this is all anarchy. And Joan has about 20 as she calls them "black bastards" in a civil government course she is taking at Webster College. They are allowing these students to attend classes but with no grading, no tuition, and assured graduation and don't think this hasn't caused some rifts. As Joan claims the rest of them are working their asses off and they come in and just take up space.

You know, I was reading over that article you sent me on Israel's Kibbutz program and to me this seems such a sensible and plausible way to handle the children of the ghetto—and also the rest of the neglected and unwanted children. I can remember Nancy Lake and the three children she had by her first husband. She didn't want them and he wouldn't take them, so they roamed Audobon Park at the mercy of anyone who would take care of them—and they were just one of many. We spend fortunes on welfare programs to no avail—why not huge communes where they have trained personnel to teach these children some moral values and also training in learning to work for a living instead of getting by on their wits. It would probably save enough in juvenile jail detentions to pay for itself. It could probably take care of the drug problem, a lot of the crime and a respect for themselves as individuals. These are the programs and ideas I keep wondering WHY about. Instead they would rather keep ten illegitimate children with a mother in some rat-infested tenement and pay her a stipend each month and then when they reach the age of 8 or 9, out on the street to mix with perverts, deviates and all the rest of the dregs of society. What are all these graduating sociologist doing with their training.

Well the last letter we received from you was dated the 16th of February and you said you were leaving the 18th on some pretty sad sounding mission. We didn't get this letter until the 25th and we could just pray that you had gotten back safely. I'll be so glad when you put your feet on some land within our borders. Talked to Judy and she wasn't sure but she thought Bill was somewhere in the Cam Ranh Bay area on a pretty safe desk job. That figures. David Emerson was in Dad's office the other day and they had a long talk about Viet Naam and he feels pretty bitter about it too. Dad asked him what he was going to do and he said he was trying to get in graduate school in Japan and try and study the Japanese language. He hated the war but he liked the far East and the people and would like to work and live in that part of the world.

Still don't know if the kids are coming home for Easter or not. Will probably get a call tonight from one of them. Your father just does not understand why anyone would want to go to Florida when they can come home. I just shake my head sometime at his thinking.

Went to your grandmother's for dinner Wednesday night and it was the first time I had been there for over two years. It is really sad to contemplate her existence. That house is so badly in need of all kinds of repairs and attention and your grandmother is old and simple housekeeping is almost too much for her. She spends her time looking out of the windows keeping tabs on the neighbors and talking about the man next door who knocks on her bedroom window at two o'clock in the morning. Reminds me of Mrs. Marsh, your former landlady. But what is the solution. It worries your father and I can understand this. But she would completely disrupt any household you would bring her in; in fact, your dad is with her about 5 minutes and they are at it tooth and nail.

Just spent an hour watching a television program entitled Experiment in Television—This is Al Capp, and what repercussions this is going to bring forth. He was at his most caustic, interspersed with unflattering shots of the editor of the underground "The Realist" and part of the writers for this publication—along with Andy Warhol. Capp tore apart all the, what he called, "unwashed, foul mouthed, sex obsessed youth who have contributed nothing but taking up space and living off the sweat of their stupid, ignorant, silent parents". He was brutal. Well, all of this just makes the rift grow wider and wider and I'm truly becoming so confused trying to understand the young and live with old that I walk around with a continual real headache. I've always said I was born 100 years too late and boy am I finding this out more and more. Of course, we are all conditioned by our past experiences and ever since I went through that damn strike at Century Electric I am extremely frightened of any mob violence—be it students, democratic convention gatherings, protest marches—any situation where a large group of people gather where the tensions mount and one voice can set off the spark for violent and inhuman behavior. The one statement Capp made today that I heartily agree with is that let's try the pen and paper for revolution. Which brings me to something I've been wanting to tell you—I've had more people who have read some of your letters and who most emphatically feel that you just must go into the journalism field.

Joan was telling us that the youngest Seibert boy, Jack—who has been at Fort Leonard Wood for about 6 months, is leaving for Viet Naam. His brother Jim who has been back for about a year was telling his brother that he must never, never turn his back on any Viet Naamese. This is a boy who received three purple hearts while over there. Please be careful and take care of yourself and don't be too trusting.

Thought you'd be interested in the latest happenings at Ft. Leonard Wood.

Take care and we count the days and pray for you and PEACE, With all our love,
Mom & Dad

SP/4 Dail W. Mullins, Jr.
488-48-0511
CoA, 26th ENGR. BN.
APO SF, 96256

March 12

LZ Professional

Dear Mom and Dad,

Well, we received our long-awaited resupply yesterday. Our mail, looking as inviting as any Christmas present I ever received as a child, and which included your letter of March 1, was actually the only worthwhile item on the whole chopper. Instead of cigarettes, a case of Coke and some clean fatigues, those yo-yo's back at Hawk Hill had the gall to send six shovel handles, two weed cutters, eight pair of spike-resistant men's tropical combat boots (all size 14 wide), four empty canteens, four mosquito net frames (but no mosquito netting), one pair of undershorts (size 46) and two empty duffle bags. The new action army!

Your letter, as usual, was both fun and interesting to read. It's interesting in itself, I think, to note that Lucy, who is not, by nature, a talkative individual, usually sends letters which, while certainly fun to read, are short and to the point. Our correspondence, on the other hand, is always rather verbose and almost Dostoevskian in nature—and, as you might guess, we're both rather talkative.

I was pleased to hear that all of the Thoms' are doing so well. I don't understand why Steve's letters haven't reached me—are you sure you gave him the correct APO?

I do vaguely remember Mrs. McLelland, yes. It's unfortunate that her son had to come to Vietnam after all—indeed, it's unfortunate that anyone has to come over here—however, I can never manage to feel as sorry for career men as I can for the draftee. Someone who has chosen "the profession of arms" as a career cannot, in my opinion, expect complete sympathy when that career begins to weigh down upon them. As Dad says, "They picked it."

I seem to recall having read something, somewhere, about Ira Levine's The Perfect Day—could it have been in Time?—but, of course, I haven't read it. Why do you not like Levine? Because of Rosemary's Baby? Have you ever read it? Reading "nice" books is probably a luxury one must forego if they want to read good books—not all books that are worth reading make pleasant reading—paradox? I mentioned, for example, that I had been reading Updike's Couples—a book with a more morally unpalatable theme would be hard to find, and yet, you cannot just dismiss it as another sex book. It is too well written, too careful and precise in its treatment of characters and so obviously preoccupied with saying something about modern man, his loneliness, his searchings for himself.

I always get a kick out of your accounts of, as you call it, the "bimonthly meeting of the running debate between the Seiberts and Mulllins". I wish I could be there to listen in on some of your discussions. I, too, agree with you and Dr. Siebert on the question of violence. No sane man can condone such actions as a means to a political or religious end, except, possibly, as a last resort. In this accord, one must almost certainly consider the American Revolution, the French Revolution, the Russian Revolution and the overthrow of the Roman Empire as last resorts—World War II, also, was very probably the only answer to Hitler and the Thousand-year Reich. Unfortunately, man, being the creature he is, will probably never have to worry about failing to employ violence as a final resort—indeed, what should concern him is attempting to avoid using it at the outset of a crisis.

I think what puzzles many Americans—puzzles and frightens them—just as it bothers Arthur M. Schlesinger, Jr., is the fact that, as evil and as horrible as the acts are, burning down buildings, banks and ROTC classrooms, and destroying files, is, whether we like it or not, getting results—and, more importantly, it is getting them fast. To me, what is horrible is not the acts themselves, but the fact that it has come to this—that the middle Americans didn't listen when they first heard the whispered rumblings of "Peace!" and "Freedom Now!" from the college students and blacks ten years ago. Hindsight is 20/20.

About all I can say in answer to your arguments on the American welfare system is amen. Your views make so much more sense and sound so much more moral than these jerks who just throw up their hands and say "Goddamn Niggers!"

I don't like Al Capp too much, so I'd better not get started on him. I do think he had a lot of nerve in referring to today's "unwashed youth" as being "sex-obsessed"—no American comic strip is as sexually suggestive as Li'l Abner; it fairly rivals Barbarella. And as far as being unwashed—does he know what I'd give for a bath right now? Of course, I'm fighting for America (hah!), so it's OK if I'm dirty and unshaven. I think Capp's wooden leg has got more sense than he does.

Well, kind people, I guess I'll close. Take care of yourselves, as will I, and look for me to be back home in around 63 days.

Love, peace
Dail

Wednesday March 4, 1970

My dear Dail,

About two hours ago we listened to the tape you had made on Friday the 27th and we can't complain about THAT mail service. You say you enjoyed the tape we sent you for your birthday—well it couldn't compare with the fascination which your father and I listened to you recording. It was so very good to hear your voice, nose sniffs and all. You're still doing that, just as Dennis will never get over saying "you know" before every sentence. Whenever Dennis starts explaining something—all I can think of is his standing in front of a classroom teaching. It seems incongruous. But I must tell you that the first side still has your voice superimposed on the second. Just talked to Winnie Bill—whose only communication with Wayne is through tapes that he and Keith send, and tomorrow I am taking your tape to Keith and see if he can tell me what is wrong. I'm beginning to think it is the Sony recorder we have. Anyway the second side you made came on loud and clear.

While I am typing this I am competing with Johnny Cash on television and your father's new stereo equipment blaring away. Last night Ken Meacham and I got into quite a heated argument about my negative attitude on stereo equipment. Typically a feminine view, to me it is just something that keeps communication from occurring and drives the wedge of separtness deeper. Your father turns that stereo on so loudly and he doesn't know that anyone other than himself is a part of this world. And you wouldn't believe what he listens to. WGNU coming out of Illinois somewhere with all the sad stories of unthwarted love—like A Boy Named Sue, Does My Wedding Ring Hurt Your Finger When You Go Out At Night, Folson Prison Blues and on and on.

Well I got Ira Levin's new book—The Perfect Day—and just started it, but I don't think it is going to be my cup of tea. It's theme revolves around a young man, a century and a half after the unification of the nations, who fights a desparate battle for freedom in a world taken over by chemistry and computerization. Everyone wears a number identification bracelet instead of a name—but he calls it a nameber. I have never been a devotee of novels about the future and I'm sure it is simply because I'm having enough trouble living in the present and literature is purely escape for me—to lull rather than stir up. But I think you would enjoy it.

We were able to get a bit of your Mary Ann mission from your tape—altho this was the side that wasn't too clear—and I won't go into details as to how we feel about it. Shall I say just pure horror and sickness that you have to be a part of this mess. Yes, we are getting the news of the Plain of Jars and it's causing quite a stir with old Laird coming on every night with his usual stereotyped statements.

You cannot realize how completely split, confused, and wrought people are. Dad came home from the office the other day really shook up. He had a patient in who has been coming to him for over 20 years. Both she and her husband. At one time she was a buyer for Famous Barr and had quite an exciting and glamorous job. She is now around 50 and decided to quit her job—having had no children and a husband with a good job. They live in Webster. Anyway, she is an avid and active member of the John Birch Society and is now spending her time going around giving lectures. Dad said this woman is sick, sick. He said everyone and everything is a communist or communist inspired. Of course, the Viet Naam War is Russia's supreme success story in enslaving us. (I was surprised at this, as I thought the John Birchers were behind the war 100%). The Mei Lai incident never happened and it is just the insidious lies being spread through the press medium—which she says is completely controlled by the Communists. She told your father they are just about ready to take over our country and the first people they will either kill or enslave are the proffessional people. She sent your father a bunch of their magazines and literature and wanted him to put them in his waiting room. Of course, he brought them home and told me to burn them. I'm going to send you one or two and let you see what some people believe in with all their hearts. Many people I know, while not professing to be Birchers, do believe a lot of what they are saying and telling. I know the last time I talked to Mary Kreyling she and Ed seemed to think along this line—and so many others. Well, anyway the "World" is really divided and it's difficult to keep your cool and think straight with so much being thrown at one. Dad and I both truly think that things must change, but then you have a group of irresponsible children burning banks, school, and public buildings and we swing to the other side. What purpose can be gained by wanton destruction is more than I can understand.

St. Louis too is having a rash of arson inspired fires at the Community Colleges, and last night someone burned the principal's office at Beaumont High School—where they have been having a little racial tension. Now how does this burning help. Tuesday St. Louis had a special election with three points to vote on. 1 was a 1% sales tax increase to be used for completely relighting the streets and alleys of the city, 1 was for the hiring of 150 more policemen with raises in pay, and the third was for a new juvenile detention home in the ghetto—and the whole package was called "Fight Crime in St.Louis." I'm sure you know how hard (almost impossible) it has always been to pass any kind of tax increase or bond issure in this city. Well, Tuesday every one of these programs passed with the largest majority ever recorded. People are frightened. Just last week two homes on our block were completely wired with burglar alarm systems, which are triggered to some kind of boards set up in police departments. But when I read William Desmond's new book "The Human Zoo", it all seems pointless because as he points out—as people pile up and up in restricted areas called cities or suburbs, there is nothing you can expect but crime, revolt and complete anihilation of what we have called "human compassion" for our own kind, and it's going to get worse.

One thing you have mentioned in your letters and you repeated in your tapes—is your exodus date of May 14. What happened to the 5 days a month after so much service in Viet Naam. We thought this was official and have been counting your time thru April 24. What happened?

We are keeping our fingers crossed on the Hong Kong deal and the only thing I'd be interested in would be material—either British woolens or chinese silks—but we probably won't know if you get your leave until it is too late to get a money order to you, so don't worry about it. The only thing I want from the Far East is you.

Well I must get over to the Skillings. Dr. Skilling has been put in the hospital with a suspected heart condition and she has completely fallen apart. I go over and turn all her lights on before she comes home from the hospital. You forget when you see him that he is 70 his next birthday and it seems sad that a professional man cannot afford to retire—when any little bank clerk quits at 65 with a good pension. Of course, your fahter says he doesn't retire because he would have to face a life of just Eloise and working at anything would be better than that. He seems to be coming along fine and it really is a good thing for her that he is. I know that most of the people who tolerate her do it for him.

We are going to get a tape and run one when Dennis and Linda are home and send it to you. Let me know if there is anything you need or want. Be careful and I think it is time you got out of the Demo business.

All our love and PEACE,
Mom & Dad

P.S. Heard a commentator last night say that the most exciting new fad of the year is heterosexuality. How does that grab you. He was serious.

SP/4 Dail W. Mullins, Jr.
488-48-0511
CoA, 26th ENGR. BN.
APO SF, 96256

March 15

Dear Mom and Dad,
Our resupply chopper came in today from Hawk Hill with, among other things, our mail—in it, your letter of March 4.

I was glad to hear that you had received the tape I made and that you enjoyed it so much. I don't understand why the first side was so distorted; were you able to understand—or even hear—my explanation of what had most likely distorted the first tape I sent? As I had explained, I recorded on a four-track stereo set, while your Sony, if it's one of those small, portable models, is probably only a two-track hi-fi recorder. Keith Bill, though, should be able to help you out.

Having just spent close to $700 myself on stereo equipment, I'm afraid I'm going to have to side with Dad and Dr. Meacham on the question of the worthwhileness of stereo sound gear. One can go overboard, of course, with this, as with anything.

I received a note from Elliott yesterday telling me that both of our R&R requests to Hong Kong had been approved, and both for the exact same days—April 27 through May 3. The possibility had existed, of course, that I might have to go alone, and for that reason I was seriously debating whether I should, in fact, go at all—I wouldn't have felt right staying with his friends alone; furthermore, it promised to be a fairly lonely trip, without Lucy, thinking, all the while, of Hawaii. Now, however, Elliott and I can go together, so I imagine I'll go. Besides, since he doesn't have much money to spend, that ought to help me keep my own expenses down. I've got you covered on the British woolens and Chinese silks—I'll see what I can do. Indeed, the only thing I want from the Far East is me, too!

Do you realize how short I'll be when I get back from Hong Kong? 11 days! No, that "official" drop I mentioned we were getting turned out to be not so official—since I only DEROS from 'Nam and don't ETS (get out of the Army, as is the case with Barksdale), it's quite possible that I will get a small drop (nothing like 20 days, however). I should have my DEROS orders before I leave for Hong Kong, however, so I'll know for sure by then. LZ Home, here I come!

The day before yesterday, at noon, a chopper landed on the VIP pad above our hooch and disgourged, in order, two heavily armed American infantrymen, an ARVN interpreter and four VC prisoners, two men and two women (one woman and one small girl, I should say). All four of them were gagged with adhesive tape and had their hands tied behind them with shoe lacing. I was going to run up and take a picture, but I thought there might have been some regulation against this, and I didn't want them to take my film away. Anyway, after a brief interrogation, all four were locked up in a CONEX (a CONEX, as you may recall from Ft. Bliss, is nothing more than a large—6' x 6' x 6'—metal shipping and storage box). Well, these people spent the entire day cramped in this dark thing—with temperatures pushing 100° outside, you can imagine how hot it must have gotten inside that thing—Geneva convention? About 8:00 o'clock that evening, one of the lifer's up in the TOC decided that those people ought to be given some fresh air during the night. However, since all of the infantry on the hill were busy on the bunker line, the engineers were given the job of guarding them all night. All we had to do was sit on the ground outside the CONEX and make sure none of them tried to escape—they were sleeping quite soundly when I came on guard at 2:30 in the morning, so there wasn't much to it—thank goodness.

If you can find a paperback edition of The Perfect Day—yes, I would enjoy reading it. Don't send me a hardcover copy, though, as I have enough of those to contend with as it is—weight is critical, you know, when the time comes to pack up and didi. I finished Couples—an excellent book, I must say, but awfully sad and depressing. Right now I'm reading Nevil Shute's No Highway—not as good as On the Beach, but interesting. It's quite similar to Airport, which I read upon your recommendation and enjoyed.

Do send the John Birch literature—Barksdale and I can always use a good laugh. If any lifer's catch me with it, they'll probably give me a promotion. I hope one of those people comes to visit me in one of their door-to-door campaigns after I get home—I truly do. I'll make them think my house is a working Communist cell.

I was very sorry to hear about Dr. Skilling—tell him hello for me if you see him and that I hope he's feeling well soon. I'm still puzzling over this statement of yours in your last letter—"It seems sad that a professional man cannot afford to retire—when any little bank clerk quits at 65 with a good pension." That's like the school teachers in New York who are griping because the sanitation workers get paid more than they do. Well, if they want to make as much as a garbage collector, then know what they can do. Similarly, if you want to retire at 65 with a nice pension, don't be a 'professional man'. In the army you get security, 3 square meals a day plus a place to sleep, and after 30 years you can retire with a monthly salary of about $400—do you think I'd do it? Hah!

I'll be watching for your next tape, folks. Until then, take care—love, and peace.
Dail

P.S.—The March issue of Playboy Magazine has an interview with Ray Charles in it—hint.

Monday night [probably March 9, 1970; Dail refers to it as letter of March 10]

My dear SP/5 (whatever that is),

Just finished dinner sitting in front of the TV watching the Laugh In and they came off with one pertinent remark—you know that section where they have the news of the past present and future? Well Dan Rowan came on with the News of the Future and said "Flash, 1975, Viet Naam just became the 51st state of the Union and now the boys won't have to worry about fighting on Foreign soil"— that's a joke, son!

Sunday night your father for some strange reason decided he wanted to go to the Ozark Theatre and see "Easy Rider". I said O.K., but no discussion about it. We go up to the box office and guess who is right behind us preparing to brave the generation gap—the Seiberts! An odder combination to see a movie that no one over 30 should view, you would have a hard time finding. Charlie was mumbling on the way in and he was there under duress. I don't know if you have been able to catch this one anywhere, but I do remember your mentioning how impressed Lucy was with it and so were Dennis and Linda—so perhaps I should let it go at that, but I just cannot. I, frankly, was shocked, sickened, and very sad. We used to have young people like this growing up with us, sans the hard drug scene, but I'm afraid we called them bums, hobos, or rail riders—in that they flipped trains, not being able to afford glamorous souped up motorcycles. Do your thing boys, and try to get by without ever earning an honest penny in your life. Live off the beautiful land or your brother, but please don't consider doing any labor to pay for a meal or a room. No, maybe they weren't hurting anybody (altho passing out marijuana and LSD to everyone they met is not my idea of doing good), but not once in that movie did they help or do anything for anyone. Is this how the new order of being your brother's keeper works, just take what is given? I really am trying hard to understand the scene but I'm much too old and I've had to work too hard to keep my end up to lay around and have freak out orgies with my soul brothers and sisters. They have an LSD scene which really frightened and puzzled me. I can remember once when I was small and very ill and I had a temperature of 105° and I experienced what seemed a similar experience, but believe me I wouldn't want to go around trying to find something to make me repeat that time.

And then I get with my own generation and there too I fumble. Last Tuesday we had our church service circle and they got into quite a discussion about some money that was available for the three families we are taking care of. Believe I have mentioned them before: they all live in Webster and they are all black; one woman with 15 children (her husband is a methodist minister who comes back from the calling of the Lord long enough to release his semen, one with 10 children, and one who is rather unfertile—she only has 8). We spend an hour wondering what to do with this money and I finally said—"Why don't we buy a two year's supply of birth control pills or contraceptives?" This went over like a lead baloon; so I don't fit in anywhere.

Received a letter from Dennis Saturday and both Dad and I are utterly amazed at the improvement in Denny's letter writing. He sent us quite an impressive poem and I would send it on to you, but he mentioned he was going to write and repeat it to you.

Last night, after our big time at the Ozark Theatre, your father and I got to bed about 10:30. We had been sleeping quite a while when the phone rang, and we both flew out of bed and banged into each other trying to reach it. Dad made it first and it was some guy asking for Linda. My first guess was old Pete, but your father said he would recognize Pete and it wasn't him. This was at 1 o'clock in the morning. Needless to say, we had a little trouble getting back to sleep—we are just too old for this stuff, and we still don't know who it was making that call.

Before I forget it, try and remember the name of the fellow who teaches in Hong Kong. Eloise was over today giving me some errands to run while Dr. Skilling is still recuperating in the hospital and she wanted to know what we heard from you. I mentioned your going to Hong Kong, if you could, and about the boy from Webster who lived on Spencer Road and she said that is the street Dr. Skillings parents lived on for 50 years and Dr. Skilling grew up there and they know every family on this short street and she is anxious to know who it could be over there. I do hope you get to make this trip but please be careful and stay in neutral area, PLEASE.

Had an appointment with Dr. Mortensen Friday and of course 3/4 of my hour appointment was spent in just talking. Then when I get home I remember all my ailments I forgot to mention. Anyway, he has just been elected to the top lay office in his church and has become quite active in a movement for bringing a unified people together. He said they want neither the way out lefts or the far rights, but the truly concerned thinking people who realize that the philosophy set down by Christ is the only working, principle and it has got to be used and worked out. He loses me in some of his thinking and he is firmly convinced that the hydrogen bomb, released by the mistake of some idiot is going to be the end of what we know as the "World". We got to talking about you being in Viet Naam and I told him how strongly you felt about our mistaken position in being over there. Anyway, he said he would like to see you and talk to you if you should get in St. Louis on your leave. He also mentioned something which I've felt and mandy others have voiced, and that is—your ability to express thoughts and views can have a more lasting effect on change than any field you could choose—to quote "The pen is mightier than the sword."

Well St. Louis youth is on nation wide television again. This time it is the affluent Clayton youths and the wide spread use of drugs and what the community is doing about it and why the kids are using it. Half the report I couldn't begin to understand simply because this is a new language—"bummers", acid, freak outs, prime beef, and on and on. Listening to these 12, 13, and 14 year old youngsters talk about climbing walls, turning on, bummer trips is, unfortunately, completely foreign to me and I really do not understand what they are talking about—this is NBC's new thing. If they would quit printing news about this and quit showing pictures like Easy Rider they wouldn't have so many kids wanting to experiment. Guess this is where censorship and I have a common meeting ground. I still feel that certain eroticism and perversion should be restricted to age groups. I know you won't agree with this and I really hope I'll be around long enough to see what you and Lucy do with the problems that you will face as parents. It'll make a BIG difference. It's so hard trying to do the right, thing and knowing every day that you have goofed somewhere—and believe me no generation like ours has been made to feel that we have failed all down the line. But I really think most concerned parents tried.

Keith Bill lent us his tape recorder over the week end and it brings through your tape much better than ours. He thinks you are using a 4 track stereo system over there and that is where we are getting the play back. I'm going to mail the tape to Lucy tomorrow and I know she'll enjoy it as much as we did. By the way, let me know if you haven't received Washington University's Catalog and I'll give them another call. They promised to get it right off to you about two weeks ago, but that might be second class mail and may take a little longer in reaching you.

Winnie Bill told me at church yesterday that another boy from your class is in Viet Naam. Someone named Richardson, whom I didn't recognize at all.

Well I'd better get to bed as I promised to be at church tomorrow by nine to sew on cancer bandages. And you know how I am, I can't leave the house until everything is straightened.

Take care and please take any short-term job that comes up. We are also getting the "short shakes".

All our love and PEACE,
Mom & Dad

SP/4 Dail W. Mullins, Jr.
488-48-0511
CoA, 26th ENGR. BN.
APO SF, 96256

March 18, 1970

Dear Mom and Dad,
Received your letter of March 10 yesterday in our resupply along with two from Lucy. Our mail service out here at LZ Professional, while certainly not the best, hasn't really been too bad—I am grateful for that, at least. I still itch, however.

You have heard Lucy speak, I'm sure, of Miss Goodwyn, her supervisor down at the welfare department. Well, apparently she is leaving to take another position (I was sorry to hear that, however—she is a nice person and Lucy seemed so fond of her)—anyway, Lucy had her over to their house the other evening, along with several of her other co-workers and their wives and husbands, for a farewell party. From what Lucy said, everyone seemed to have a rather good time, and since Clyde and Lena were out for the evening, the spirits apparently flowed quite freely. After her guests had all gone home, Lucy, probably feeling somewhat melancholy after her several drinks, wrote me a letter—or tried to. It was really hilarious, and a classic study in the effects of alcohol upon the human mind and hand. I shall save that one, I think, for a future chuckle.

Yesterday, around noon, the Commanding Officer of the Americal Division, Major General Ramsey, came out to LZ Professional in his chopper on one of his routine inspection tours of American fire support bases in the Division AO. About ten minutes after he left on his way back to Chu Lai, an NVA 51 caliber machine gun mounted on the side of one of the hills near here opened up on his chopper and knocked it out of the sky, killing one pilot and both door gunners, and seriously wounding the general. Some infantrymen managed to reach the chopper and get the wounded dusted off before any of the enemy could, though.

The incident really shook up the lifers around here—"A general shot down! Here!" They immediately brought in an ARVN Psyops (Psychological Operations) team, which set up huge loudspeakers all around the hill and began broadcasting Chieu Hoi messages into the valleys below us. I, of course, couldn't understand anything that was said (my knowledge of Vietnamese stops at "papa-san"), but somebody working with the ARVNS told me that the crux of the message went something like this: "Attention soldiers of the People's Democratic Republic of North Vietnam. Hello, hello, hello. You are soon to be informed by your fellow soldiers that an American general's helicopter was shot down by your gunner's today. That is another Communist lie. True, a helicopter was downed—however, it was only a decoy aircraft, designed to locate your positions. No one was injured, and the helicopter sustained only light damage. You would be wise to lay down your arms and surrender now, before it is too late." The broadcast was concluded with, I am told, an old Vietnamese chant, intended to stir feelings of homesickness and despair in the minds of the NVA. My only comment about the matter was, "I'm sorry for the pilot and door gunners." And I am.

Lt. Lipps came out this evening with a resupply. He said that after we finished here at LZ Professional, we would be going out to a place called "New" Hau Duc, a refugee village and ARVN compound, to build a command bunker for the ARVN commander out there, a Major T'ang (sounds like somebody out of Terry and the Pirates). This Hau Duc is not, of course, the same place we were just a short while ago—as a matter of fact, that place was "Old" Hau Duc. You see, when the Americans first moved into "Old" Hau Duc, about a year ago, there were so many NVA and VC around that, in order to accomplish anything at all, they had to move the civilian populace out (relocate them, as it were) and declare the whole area a free fire zone (meaning they could shoot anything that moved at night). Well, the local Vietnamese were moved about 15 miles to the East and resettled in a new valley—for simplicity, I guess, it was just called "New" Hau Duc.

Lt. Lipps said he went out to the ARVN compound (there are no American GI's there—we'll be the only ones) in "New" Hau Duc yesterday and talked with this Major T'ang about the bunker we're supposed to build for him. This Major must be some guy. He's head of an element of the 2nd ARVN Division, which is one of their best. The NVA have a price of 3,000,000 piasters on his head, he's that good. Lt. Lipps said he walks around with a jungle hat and a small swagger stick, supervising the construction of this relocation village, jabbering in Vietnamese to the refugees and his soldiers. Aside from the fact that I am getting too short for these field missions, this one should be rather interesting. I have always wanted to do some work with the ARVNS and refugees, and this next mission should prove to be interesting in that respect. I'll keep you posted on what happens when I know more myself.

I can't recall, at the moment, the name of that friend of Elliott's who teaches in Hong Kong, but I'll be sure and ask him when I get back to Hawk Hill. All I know about him is that he went to Dartmouth with Elliott and that his wife's name is Squirrel.

I am anxious to read Denny's poem—I hope he doesn't forget to send it. I've written several poems over here myself—many of them are, shall I say, rather "erotic" in tone, however, so I doubt if you'd enjoy them.

You hadn't mentioned Dr. Mortensen in any of your letters for so long—I wondered whether you were still seeing him. While I might disagree with his statement to the effect that the philosophy set down by Christ is the only working principle by which man can live, I do admire his concern and interest in matters not directly related to medicine. He is an interesting man, isn't he?

I thought Keith Bill's tape recorder would make my tape a little cleaner. I wish, though, that you had told me you were going to send it to Lucy—If I had known that, I'd have given her a little message. I don't think she has a tape recorder, though.

This letter sure is getting long, isn't it.

I'm sorry you didn't enjoy Easy Rider. As you mentioned, Lucy said she really liked it, and I've been anxious to see it myself. Even Clyde and Lenn seemed to like it—however, they also enjoyed 2001: A Space Odyssey, which you didn't, so—

Well, dear parents—I'll close now. Please take care of yourselves, and keep writing. Not too much longer now.

Love and, of course, Amouré-Paz
Dail

March 14, 1970

My dear Dail,

Where to start? Can never remember from one letter to the next, what news we covered.

We hadn't received any mail from you in over 10 days. You have been so good about writing, that it sometimes works in reverse; as when I don't hear for a week—my over-active mind begins to pour out all sorts of thoughts. Then today we get three letters and while the news of LZ Professional is horrifying to me—just hearing is so good. Please do not tell me anymore about the rats as I have been looking over my shoulder all day.

With your letters came one from Aunt Dot and as I hadn't heard from her since her aborted visit—and was concerned—I was over-joyed, until I read her letter. She has been in the hospital and typical of Aunt Dot, didn't want to worry anyone. About three weeks ago she discovered two good sized lumps in her right breast and said she wasn't too concerned, but Bob became quite upset. Dot never gets excited about something she can see and feel but the inner and unexplainable aberrations get to her. Anyway she went right in to her O.B. man and he told her that they would have to be removed immediately and he knew of three surgeons whome he would recommend and to pick any one. As she told him—"just someone who will have patience with a coward." She couldn't get in for two weeks so it wasn't until last Saturday that she entered the hospital. The surgeon came in and told her what he was going to do and that she had to sign some legal papers as in an operation of this type they do a complete mastodectomy if they find any abnormal cells. She said she just told him she had walked in with two and wanted to walk out with two. Thank God they were benign and she is home and feeling fine. She went in yesterday for another check of the surgery and he was giving her instructions as to what she could do regarding physical activity. He told her not to swing a golf club or play tennis, but that slow normal activity would be fine and she could drive her car. She said to him—"Good, wonderful because I couldn't drive before I had this done." He probably things she is a little fey. She is to go in Monday for removal of bandages and the stitches. I, of course, called her the minute I received her letter and spent the first ten minutes crying.

For some reason last week was a prolonged period of anxiety and an uncontrollable desire to spend most of my time staring out the window and crying. Probably is menopause. Anyway, not hearing from you and worrying about Denny—and Linda—had me pretty low. Linda called here last Tuesday morning about 9:30. I was just on my way to church to sew on cancer bandages when she called and my first reaction when I heard her voice was—"Dear God, now what" and then I tell my heart to quiet down. After a few pleasantiries we get down to "What's the matter" and the "Nothing" bit. She finally said—"Has their been anything in the newspapers up there about our school". I said what in the world are you talking about. And she tells me that they have hit all the southern towns. It seems that last Sunday night around 11 o'clock a barrarge of cherry bombs errupted from the boy's dormitory and then a bonfire. With that the local police force of about 3 cops, called on the highway patrol for help. The boys, or about 250 of them, then gathered (Linda, said quietly (?)) and en masse walked to the President's home for a confrontation and guess who was one of the leaders? Dennis Mullins. My first reaction was rage and a sickness that he would be expelled with just one more year to go and really jeopardize his entire future with misguided ideas of what it takes to make a college work (and you know, as well as I, that it is not a group of idealists with no idea of the money it takes to keep an institution like this operating). Their main hang up seems to be Dean Rankin, who is dean of women, but also the power behind a lot of thrones. I have never met her so this is just hearsay from the youngsters, but she is old (?) (probably 50), unmarried, a bigot, a fascist and anything else they can think of. For three years the students have been trying to get her out of the heading of the SGA and also relaxing of rules. Now these campus rules are the issues that I just cannot see eye to eye with, with the children. Why does it make that much difference to have the girls stay out until 11 instead of 10, and why do they have to live off-campus, and why must the boys get in the girl's rooms? This is all such nonsense to have riots and protest marches about. And this is why older people are getting so tired of much of this upheaval—because now they call a march over petty, almost asinine, reasons, and the vital objectives are going to be thrown overboard in the process. Anyway, she called us again Tuesday night and said that the President had met with them that afternoon and that a great many of their requests were going to be met—whether he included the firing of Dean Rankin wasn't said. All I could think of this week was "Shades of Southwestern at Memphis", when we sweated out your involvement. But isn't it rather funny that your problems concerned youngsters running the affairs and having too much power and now it is just the opposite—students not having power and not running the school—do you wonder we are a thoroughly mixed up generation.

Have been thinking about that damn movie Easy Rider, too. It just seems so completely insane to have two characters such as this the heroes of the younger generation. I'll admit there is something seriously wrong when our government is producing no leaders or heroes from their ranks. We had a brief flurry with the astronauts but that has been cast aside for the "easy riders". Last night we went out for dinner with the Seiberts and when we came home I just couldn't settle down and sleep—whether the worrying I've been doing or the 6 cups of coffee and dinner table discussion or a combination of all. Anyway I finally got up and turned on "the boob-tube" (your father's favorite description—while he raises your hair on end with all the country and western laments about sour romance and unhappy marriages. I watched the David Frost show—which should be on three hours earlier. He had Abbie Hoffman, one of the Chicago 7, as his guest (?). I'd hate to have this as a guest in my home. Now I really have desperately tried to keep an open mind about the thinking of your peers and at times feel complete empathy with many issues—but I do not want to live in any part of history that would have an Abbie Hoffman controlling my destiny. This is a sick sick person. Even his eyes are distorted and to come on stage and thumb his nose and stick out his tongue at an audience—which at first was going to be very receptive to him—was like watching someone in a mental institution.

David Frost tried to keep the whole interview on a really high thouqht provoking plane, but it was impossible with this idiot. He sat in the chair and then every few minutes he would run to the front of the stage and stick his tongue or thumb his nose at everyone. Is this the conduct of an intelligent human being. See why some people would take Spiro Agnew over this? The few intelligent things he said were obliterated by his obscene carrying on. Frost asked him if he and his compatriots were in a position to be in command (and as Frost said—"God Forbid), what form of living or existence, or government would he suggest and how this huge complex world would be run in order to have some semblance of sanity to it. He (Hoffman) said, "the first thing we would do would be get rid of that dirty four-letter word. Work." And then he was asked how could any recognizable form of social order could evolve out of a set up like this. And of course, he answered "everyone would do their thing". Frost said—"let's get down to a basic job, which we don't like to think about—but is terribly important—who would take care of the garbage?" The audience by this time was getting completely out of hand and a few veterans who had just gotten back from Viet Naam were going to tear him apart—when the screen went blank for about two minutes, and then we came back to Frost interviewing some young girl who was up for an Academy Award for her part in "Suddenly Last Summer". No explanation was made as to what happened to Abbie; they probably put him in a straight jacket.

Am sending you a package via the Easter Bunny and in it will be two tapes, one which we have recorded on and one which is blank. Hope you enjoy them.

Haven't heard from Lucy since her trip to Atlanta. Dad said "she isn't driving all over the country in that Volkswagon". It really upsets him—but I tell him it is none of his business. Sounds like the Henley's are going to fill up the yard until he gets his male counterpart. Have you tried to tell him about the population explosion.

Please keep your wits about you and see if you couldn't develop back trouble. That's always been a good illness because it is so hard to prove maligning. God be with you and all our loave and

PEACE,
Mom & Dad

Thursday, March 19

My dear Dail,

This letter was to be written last night, but for some strange reason your father decided he wanted to see a movie. Now what he really wanted to go and see was General Patton, but he knew better than to ask me to see a saga about war, so we looked through the paper and believe me the choice was slim. We finally settled on a mess called "Pussycat, Pussycat, I Love You", simply because they said it was the comedy of the year and it was rated General Public. My God!! What must an X movie be? After about ten minutes I thought we were looking at one of Fellinis mental blowouts. The thing was made in Italy and was just a series of married men in bed either with their wives (very seldom) or mistresses (occasionally) or someone they had picked up (most often). Then it went to the wives and the same sequence. You know after you see some many bosoms hanging out it becomes thrilling to see someone completely covered. What a bore a sham and a mess to allow young children to witness. This is when I believe censorship should be rigid, rigid, rigid. Or else have a set up where movies, books, etc. are graded according to age. 5 and under, 10 and under, 15 and under up to 20. Then have a gamut from 20 to 40. Then only certain things for those over 40. I really think it would be so much better than the present mess. I resented the time wasted (even thos we walked out), but more I resent the hard earned money spent. Well, after Easy Rider and this latest trash, we probably won't see another movie for another year.

Just got back from Famous to buy your Dad some ties and shirts and ran into Stan and Aud. and they said to tell you hello. She has been coming in to your father's office for dental work and they too are evidently feeling the burden of education costs. Judy is supposed to graduate this spring, but has now decided to go on to graduate school, and Aud is beginning to think nobody wants to get out and apply some of the knowledge they're supposed to have. They sent money down to Kent to come home over Easter and he has decided to use it to go to Acupulco. Nice, heh! Linda called Sunday night and they are finished with classes tonite, but Bob has to be in a wedding Sunday morning, so they are not leaving until then. Denny is not too happy about spending two days down there with nothing to do, but it seems foolish to spend air fare when Bob and Linda are coming up. It will be good to see them.

Well, I guess you've heard by now the latest Far Eastern crisis. I'm referring to the ousting of Prince Sihanouk of Cambodia. What this is going to do to our position seems to be anyone's guess. Some seem to be elated as it now gives us a chance to get troops in Cambodia. Really, if a day didn't go by without some extreme crisis plastered all over the newspapers and on T.V., I don't think anyone would know how to act. Just heard a fellow on T.V. say—"just one year ago everyone was asking—Who is Spiro Agnew? Today everyone is saying "Who does Spiro Agnew think he is?" And this is about it.

You know in a recent letter you mentioned that perhaps if you had this all to do over again, you might have entertained the idea of going to Canada more seriously, seeing how hard this year was on Lucy and myself. Funny thing, I think Lucy and I have borne up under the strain better than your father. He is really erratic and violent at times and I hope it is your being over there that is making him like this—and not age and genetics. Last Tuesday night we went out to dinner with the Meachams. Shortly after we were seated a man and woman came in and sat at a table next to us. As usual your father was really raving—at this time about the Laos situation and about that "bastard" Nixon. He gets so loud that I just want to crawl under the table. About this time the woman at the other table started singing America and quite loudly said she wished she had an American Flag to wave. I thought your dad was going over and actually start a fist fight. Now none of this type confrontation does one bit of good. Just like the youngsters who painted their faces white and wore the most outlandish outfits they could get together, to protest in front of draft boards today. People really begin to think that this type behavior cannot correlate with intelligence and sound reasoning—so they defeat and lose ground. We must get away from the John Birch Rights and the Hippie and Yippie Lefts. What we need so badly now is some cool-thinking, intelligent men who are not politically motivated, but who truly have a dedicated desire to right what has been so wrong. But where are they. We just seem to have "top-blowing" who cannot seem to bend.

Am enclosing a piece, that was in our neighborhood paper today. This group has been in the paper and talked about quite a bit here and some of the facts brought out are not included in this article. Most of the (98%) youngsters on LSD and heroin and the other hard drugs, all started on marijuana and they seem to be finding that the great proportion of marijuana users have severe mental or emotional problems. Another inability to face up to reality and stomach the cruel fact that life is no bowl of cherries and never has been and never was promised to be. You know when you come home—and you won't appreciate this no w—you can always know that you faced up to one of the cruelest and hardest problems in your life—which if you would have defected to Canada, might have bothered you the rest of your life.

I can realize your short term shakes as I'm getting them too. For a long time now (years, in fact) I go around talking to myself—but I still don't answer my questions—so I think I'm still not too bad. But the past couple of weeks I find myself saying—"he's been over there over ten months and you'd think they could let them home after that long", and then I go look at the calendar again and so it goes.

One thing that has me burned up is this postal clerk strike in New York, Maryland, and New Jersey and which is threatening to spread throughout the country. If I don't get your mail I'll really start screaming. Wonder what would happen if all the G. I.'s would strike.

Well Chanel became a lady this week and neither she nor I are enjoying it. I've got her rear end all tied up with pants and all she does is stand with her front half twisted entirely around looking at the back half. Thank God, we had another snow storm as I think it is helping to keep down her male admirers. Altho since that hair cut your father gave her, I don't think she'd be attractive to even a cat.

Keep counting, keep alert, and let us hear when you can. With all the love—
PEACE,
Mom & Dad

Am including an article about the big boy from Amcrical. It is going to be interesting to see what type punishment is handed down to the General and a few more down the line, whom they just named in that Mei Lai incident. We'll see.

SP/4 Dail W. Mullins, Jr.
488-48-0511
CoA, 26th ENGR. BN.
APO SF, 96256

March 23, 1970

Dear Mom and Dad,
 Although the Postal strike back home has all of us wondering whether there's any point in writing, I thought I'd get a letter off anyway, since St. Louis hasn't yet been mentioned as one of the cities affected. According to AFVN Radio, mail to Vietnam from San Francisco has been temporarily interrupted, though, of course, we haven't been affected yet.
 We're still at LZ Professional, although our lumber supply was exhausted several days ago and we really haven't done any work to speak of since then—I think I mentioned in my last letter that we were finally able to get a shower, so things haven't been too bad. Two days ago a rather heavy cloud cover set in, and with it some rain, which helped to settle the dust, so perhaps that's why none of us has felt quite so dirty as of late. Of course, the mud isn't exactly thrilling itself . . . (what would GI's do without something to gripe about).
 Since we arrived on LZ Professional, almost three weeks ago, the first battalion of the 196th, which has its headquarters here, has had four men killed . . . all by our own troops! Three days after our arrival here, an artillery round, fired from the 105 howitzer battery here on Professional, landed in the middle of C company's night laager, killing three men, one of whom had only 7 days left in country. Yesterday, at about 4:00 o'clock in the morning, E Company's recon patrol walked right into a night ambush that had been set up at the foot of this hill by elements of D Company—one man was killed and five were wounded in that fatal mishap.

No alcohol or pot was involved in any of these tragic errors—just sheer stupidity on the part of the brass in the FDC and TOC.

Home has been on my mind quite a lot lately, as you can imagine. In just 51 days I should be landing at Fort Lewis in Washington state for processing before my leave. I don't know how long I'll be there—there's some paperwork, a free steak dinner and a uniform fitting to endure—but it shouldn't be more than 48 hours, at the very most. After that, I'll be off for points East. As I said before, I'm going to try and get a flight that stops in St. Louis for a few hours—I won't be there very long, though. In fact, there may not even be enough time to leave the airport—but I would like to see you. If that's the case, would you want me to spend the money and call you from Seattle to let you know first when I'll be arriving in St. Louis? That way, perhaps you could be waiting at the airport. Of course, Lucy and I plan to visit you later on during my leave, so there will be plenty of time to chat—besides, I want to bring my new sound equipment and gloat over it!

I've been meaning to ask you in several letters how my filing cabinet is. I hope it's still in one piece and that none of the papers in it got wet during the winter.

That reminds me—I still haven't received that catalogue from Washington U., although I went ahead and finished the application anyway; it was late as it was. The only thing I haven't had sent is my GRE score—and that's only because I can't remember the address—It's Graduate Record Exams, Box "something", Princeton, N.J.—I don't know what the Box Number is nor the zip code. Do you think Washington U. would? I think when you order a copy of your scores from them you're supposed to include some kind of test number, but, for the life of me, I can't remember what that was. I just hope they can find it with my name, SSAN and test type. I took it twice, you'll recall—or maybe you won't—and I want the second set of scores to get there, too, since they were very high. I only hope these people at Washington U. realize how difficult it is to apply to school from a foxhole.

Well, I just wanted to let you know that your son is still OK. I did go to the medics this morning—for some time, now, I've been troubled with dizziness, an upset stomach, which troubles me mainly during the night, spells of giddiness and lightheadedness when thinking about home and a rather wide strip of yellow-pigmented skin down my back—the doc said I had militarium shorttimerus, a disease which inflicts most of the soldiers over here during their last few months. Unfortunately, they wouldn't dust me off—

Take care—love and, of course, ☮
Dail

Sunday May 22, 1970 [obviously the wrong date; probably March 22]

My dear Son,

Well, I'm sure you have heard by now about your "goof". I'm talking about your addressing a letter to your father and me with everything perfectly correct except Midlothian, Va., instead of St. Louis, Mo. With all the griping I've been doing about the poastal service the last week, with the threat of a nationwide strike—that's pretty good service to have Lucy get it.

Speaking of that strike. I've been livid about it purely because of the possibility that mail to the fellows in Viet Naam would not be delivered. Tonite on TV they had a special on about the Mail Service and the ramifications of non-delivery. Welfare checks, small mail order businesses completely folding, the stock market unable to operate, companies unable to mail out bills (I couldn't care less about this last); but then they went further and talked about the whole world watching this strike as it is a bastion of democracy. If civil service employees are able to tie up a democratic government—then it is definitely proven that a system of government such as ours cannot work and prove effective. In other words, in Russia, China, England, Sweden, Germany, you name it, this could not possibly happen because they would be forbidden. Just think—all because of the lowly Mailman—and here I thought it would be the garbage men who would cause our downfall.

Also made another startling discoverey today—I've decided we have made a big mistake in trying to understand our children and the younger generation. What must happen is that they must try and understand us. Just kidding—but there could be a little truth to it. Am reading a very light little novel called "The Best Is Yet To Be", by a fellow named Bentz Plagemann. It is supposed to be a little autobiographical concerning a middle aged couple whose only son has just gotten married and they are hoping they are free from the load and will have the strength to do some of the things they have had to put off—thus the title. Anyway he is reminiscing one day about raising this child and he says—

"Little good did it do to reflect that once we had danced the Charleston and the Black Bottom, even the Big Apple. An astonishing thing had happened; when my head was turned for a moment the world had gone on, and now this terrible chasm lay between me and this world I truly never made. Looking at them in what seemed their private ecstasies, as they gyrated separately on the floor in their own minute space, never touching or coming together, wonderfully young and beautiful and glowing with good health, I felt as dismayingly remote from them as if I had stepped out onto another planet. We had read or heard all manner of things about them, these young, lightyears away from us. They were said to be promiscuous, although that was our word, not theirs. They had sex together, so we heard, as casually as we had once smoked our first cigarettes together, and they seemed supremely self-confident and knowing. They challenged or dismissed all of our values and what values were they lived by they either could not, or would not tell us. From the ruins of what had been our institutions they arose triumphant and what would the brave new world be like? They didn't seem to need ours. Had we seemed so remote to our own parents, so beyond their understanding? Yet there were certain unchangeable Verities, and along with my awe as I observed them I wondered if they could escape. From sex came children, and because with our species it takes so long for a child to mature, it would be necessary to have a home. And someone had to provide that home. A man had to work. A woman had to raise her children. There were illnesses and tragedies. Sometimes men failed. Sometimes children died. There was a great big dreadful thing out there in the night, beyond this, and out there in the night, was life, and it would catch them all, and it really did not matter if I did not understand them now, for when they had come as far as I had come, then they would understand me."

Ah, well!

This morning I sat with Winnie and Don Bill at church and it was very obvious they had a difficult time keeping their minds on the service, as they knew at sometime that morning Wayne was meeting his wife in Hawaii. They were to stay at the Sheraton Surfer (I think that is the name). Winnie had been hoping that Wayne would plan to go back to school for his masters, thus enabling him to get out of Viet Naam in 9 months—as his full term of service is up in August, when he would ordinarily be finished in Viet Naam and going back to school would mean he would get out the first part of June. But for some reason Winnie says that Wayne is beginning to flag wave and said he would not ask for any early out, as he has been trained for a specific job and he is desperately needed. He's probably acquired some jungle fever which has attacked his thinking processes.

Well we found out that "the troops", as your father terms them, won't be coming in until Monday evening. Karen Keitel flew home Friday and called us to say that the wedding Bob is to take part in will be in Tennessee and is going to be more of an affair than they had thought, so they are not starting home until Monday morning. Denny will probably be ranting and raving when he comes in, because he had to spend 4 days of his spring break in Athens.

Last Tuesday the Woman of the Church luncheon had a Mrs. Wolfert, head of the St. Louis County Children's Detention Service, as their guest speaker. I, of course, was quite interested in what she had to say in that this is the type of social welfare work that Linda plans to do, and also because Lucy is involved in social work. Frankly, some of her information was a little sickening to many of us. She felt, that being an audience of just women, she would dwell mainly on the young girls who come through the detention center. What she wanted to get across to us was that a great portion of these children are not there because of criminal acts, per se. She mentioned that a great many of the girls have been taken from homes where they are constantly being criminally assaulted and molested by their own fathers, stepfathers, or brothers. Talk about man the animal. Because professional help and room for these youngsters is at a minimal, she is trying to canvass church woman to take these youngsters in their homes for 30 to 90 day periods until jobs can be found. These, of course, are the youngsters who have reached 18. They are also looking for tutorial help at night to enable these youngsters a crash course to pass a high school equivalency test. The more I hear about this field of endeavor, the less I can see Linda involved with problems of this type. She has a difficult time handling her own simple problems with equanamity.

Well, now they have just announced that Nixon is planning to have the Army move in to handle the mail and I am sure you know how the mobs of postal pickets are re-acting to this situation. I'm beginning to think communism or socialism or some ism had better take over this country. We are sure going to the dogs fast under so called democracy. They announced that 50% of the Viet Naam mail was being delayed—and I know that is going to make you feel gleeful.

This week end a group took over Brookings Hall and two other buildings at Washington University with their usual complete demolition. Supposedly this is in action against the continuance of the ROTC program, which was voted upon by the entire student body, and passed. What happens to the majority rule, I truly don't know.

This afternoon we took a ride over to your grandmothers and she is getting so fuzzy—about some things. Of course, to someone who looks at her through my eyes, her peculiarities are just an extenuation and an enlarging of a personality she has always had; but to your father it is just senility—and I know he worries about her. I would too, if it were my mother; but what do you do? So many times I am reminded of the Mrs. Marsh, whom you spent some time with in Memphis. Grandma must spend 10 hours of every day sitting in her front window spying, and that is the only word, on neighbors. I wish you could hear some of the tales she tells us about these people. Granted, all people in South St.Louis are a little peculiar, but I don't think they do some of the things she says she sees—like husbands meeting other women and very occasionally, the reverse. I always think of my father's remark about her neighborhood needing a really good "drunk", so they could talk about him and forget about the rest of the block. He also couldn't understand all these husbands straying and all the louzy men. His point was that if the men are having romantic entanglements, it would certainly be with a woman—and how come they're not discussed. As he felt, for every dirty old man there had to be a dirty old woman.

Well, as you remarked, our correspondence does ramble on and I'm afraid sometimes doesn't say much.

I'm going to pick up the Updyke book "The Couples", and reread it with an unbiased mind. Perhaps this time I will feel it deserves some of the merits you mention.

Well, must get busy and I promised to make some cookies to send to the County Detention home. I'd really like to try and take one of these youngsters in for a month or so but you should see your father's look when I even mention this. He said—"you can't handle your own family, why in the world would you think you could handle a situation like this." And I'm sure this is true, so I do my usual part—a piddly one—I bake a few cookies. Well some of us were meant to be heroes and some of us just mice.

If addressing our letter is an indication of the short shakes (I believe this is what you term it), please calm down and stay alert. I know Lucy said she is really getting up-tight too. Take care and all our love

Monday morning

Getting your letter ready, in the hopes that the mail man will drop by, and the phone rang. Now it is only 7:45 A.M., but it was your grandmother—who has already been busy with her phone calls to all and sundry. And does she have a BIG problem. Don't know if I mentioned previously, but last week we were lucky enough to have another funeral in the family. Aunt Bonnie's (one of the girls) daughter's husband (her third) died. Well this morning bright and early Grandma made her daily call to Bonnie and Bonnie is just sick because she has decided they have the wrong corpse in their cemetery lot. In other words, her daughter's husband was switched with someone else and they don't know where he is. This is the truth! It was so difficult for me to not say—"What the hell difference does it make?" You don't know how often I wish grandma wasn't speaking to me again.

Well just thought you would like to know of the big things going on in the WORLD.

SP/5 Dail W. Mullins, Jr.
488-48-0511
CoA, 26th ENGR. BN.
APO SF, 96256

April 3, 1970

Dear Mom and Dad,

A thousand pardons, dear parents, for having failed to write in quite some time—I told myself that that tape I sent you might satisfactorily take the place of a letter, but I'm afraid I let it go to my head. It has, by now, probably come to represent four or five.

I mentioned to Lucy not long ago, that as my tour in Vietnam drew to a close, I was finding it more and more difficult to bring myself to write—mainly because what I do over here becomes less and less important. In addition, I must plead "reserved excitement"—an amazing and paradoxical emotion, don't you think? Let me explain.

Do you remember my telling you (if, indeed, I did) that everyone who has been going home from our company has been getting drops, and that these drops seemed to be getting bigger every day?

Well, nothing has changed, and the trend is continuing. As a matter of fact, these drops are Division-wide, and not just restricted to our company. The reason for these drops seems to be this—our good President is apparently going to announce another troop withdrawal this month; some 50,000, we understand. Now,

The other evening our squad leader came in and told Barksdale and me to get our demo bags ready because we'd be going on a mission to the field the next morning. Some ARVN's had discovered a dud 250 lb. bomb in the middle of Sông Hòa, a village near LZ West. We were told that, when we arrived out there, the ARVN's would drag the bomb out of the village whereupon we would blow it up. No sweat. As usual, however, our operations screwed up—the bomb, far from lying in the middle of a vill, was buried up to its fins in the middle of the village chief's rice paddy. And it was armed. The Lt. who met us out there said we couldn't destroy it where it was, because the head papa-son's rice paddy would be wasted. This idiot wanted Barksdale and I to dig it up, disarm it, move it, and then blow it up. "Not me!" I said. "I've only got 42 days left, sir, I'm not EOD (emergency ordinance disposal) and I ain't even going to touch that thing!" So, he agreed and let us return to Hawk Hill. One point for me.

Not much else to report on, folks—take care of yourselves and I'll see you soon.

Love, Dail

Friday, March 27

My dear Dail,

It's been quite a few days since I posted your last letter and it really gets to my conscience when I miss more than 4 days in writing you, but I've sorta felt like a yo-yo all week. You know, up down—up down and then all around. The kids got in Monday night and even before they arrived the joint was jumping, at least for us. It's so quiet around here with just Dad and I that even the telephone ringing is furore. Denny walks in, as usual, with a laundry bag over his shoulder and another one dragging behind hime, filled with dirty clothes. Then Linda breezes in right after letting us know all she has to buy and all she has to do while she is home and Bob doesn't say a word.

About an hour after they are home Denny informs your father and I that he has a tape worm. We both stand their bug-eyed and mouths opened wondering if he has flipped. But he is very serious. He says he told me a year ago that he thought he had one but I just laughed at him, but he positively knows he has one—he has done a lot of reading up on it and he has seen it and he claims he could pick it out of any book on worms. This isn't meant to be funny and by this time I was about ready to faint and throw up all at once. Anyway we've been two days getting smears and fece samples to labs and we still haven't had the final diagnosis. Now you just stop and think—do you know of any other family besides us that would have a case of tape worm? I really get so discouraged. Dr. Emerson says that if it is a tape worm they can be quite difficult to get rid of. He also syas that this is probably why Denny is constantly hungry. As Dad says—"he's eating for two."

Last night at the dinner table Bob, Linda and your father started needling Denny about his unwanted guest—and I'm sure you can imagine how the conversation went—(and all this while we are supposed to be eating a delicious dinner I slaved over.) They decided to see how many song titles they could think of that would be apropos—like "I've got you under my skin", "I've grown accustomed to your fece", "Love me or leave me", "The worms crawl in and the worms crawl out", and it went on and on. Wish I could really think it was funny.

And then to really tie things up—for the past three weeks your grandmother has been calling your father to tell him that she has a snake in her house and it spends most of its time in her kitchen sink. When your Dad goes over and confronts her with wanting to see this reptile, she always has some story about it hiding in the basement or some other cranny. It doesn't seem to like company. I'm seriously beginning to think everyone has delirium tremens.

And this is why your letter telling about Lucy's letter to you in the throes of a slight "jag", was so funny. I could just picture her sitting in her room writing this, probably crying a little and hiccupping a lot. Well thank God, she'll soon have you home to cry on your shoulder.

Our church has no special service on Good Friday, but we did have the church open from 9AM until 9PM and several of us signed up to spend an hour greeting anyone that might want to just sit and meditate. I went over about 3:30 and was rather shocked when I walked in to see the two podiums draped in black cloth and black cloths on the long communion table. The lights were rather dim and they had stereo music playing and it was a peaceful and rather lovely hour to sit and pray and think about you, Lucy, the children and hope that some sanity comes to this world.

Today Diane Vogt Taylor (Linda's friend) came by with her 6 month old little boy and he is a perfect doll. Not a pretty child but such a pleasant, good, clean, happy, baby and you just feel like biting him. Diane looks wonderful and marriage has certainly changed her for the better. Her husband is a graduate geologist and is with an Oil Company and they are in town for their last visit for two years. His company is sending all of them to Australia for two years and they are both very excited.

Linda was telling me that Pete Merrill called her at school about two weeks ago and told her that Gulf Oil was sending him to Africa in about a month or two. He also tells her that he has his own apartment now and has purchased some outlandish, out-sized dog. Guess that's to keep the girls away. Tonite in the paper was an announcement of Marea Merrills marriage to some fellow in New Mexico. Can't you see Pete in his own apartment, in a smoking jacket, with his dog—writing that Xmas message of his I sent you?

Well we have been trying to get the details of the fracas at Athens College—but we still aren't quite sure what the hell it was all about. When you pin Denny down, he admits that spring and sheer sap rising in their veins probably was a good part of why it was done. In many ways I feel sorry for Bob DeCurtis. He was telling me he sometimes feels he fits in with no group. He's not of his parents thinking, but neither does he feel he wants to break laws and rules—so he is a bystander. But he's got lots of company. Sheer wanton destruction has never been my bag either. Washington University has been in the throes of a mess since last Sunday night when a group of 50 students out of a total enrollment of 15,000 students have taken over and bombed, broken windows, torn and demolished records, harassed teachers, broken into classes and done everything they possibly could to be noticed. They have had to dispense classes for the last two days because of possible danger. Now this is all over ROTC being held on campus. The thing I don't understand is that a month ago they had a vote on ROTC and 80% of the enrollment voted to keep it in operation. Now does this mean that 50 hopped up students are allowed to burndown buildings?

Speaking of hopped up. It has been rather interesting to listen to the latest testimony from men involved in the Mei Lei incident. A black seargeant the other day said his outfit of 20 men had 10 involved in the killings that were high on marijuana. Speaking about drugs—the March 20 issue of Life has an article about a father, who finds out his son is a drug addict and if this doesn't make you want to weep, then you just cannot understand until you are a parent. And this week's issue of Look with pictures of 12 to 21 year old children inducting heroin into their veins is pretty rough. Guess I'm a little over-board on this whole subject—because Linda tells me that it is rampant at Athens. And then Dennis tells me that he tried marijuana once. And guess why. Because the half-assed friends kept calling him chicken. I've had some long talks with him, and I pray I am not whistling in the dark, but he assures me that it was a one time thing and the whole deal he says is ridiculous. I must believe him or I couldn't bear it. To jeopardize his life and future to fool around with this is more than I can comprehend. I would rather see him dead in Viet Naam. Now you know how strongly I feel about this whole deal, and I'm sick of it. Please don't mention anything about this in letters to me as I haven't mentioned it to your father. Maybe this is wrong, but he has had so much to contend with lately—his mother, thinking about you, that office, keeping kids in school, his health—I just cannot put another burden on him. You know we all have a breaking point and I just don't know how he would handle this. The thing is, Denny has finally found himself—it seems—in studying. He thinks he has a 3.6 average this semester. Believe me it is tough being a parent.

Linda Beswick and her fiance just came by to pick up Bob and our Linda. They are going to see M.A.S.H. This is a picture that everyone coming into your father's office has been telling him he must see—so last Saturday night and Sunday night we scurried over to the Shady Oak, park about 5 blocks away, get to the theatre and a big sign over the box office—"Sold Out". Well, when this happens twice to him, he definitely makes up his mind that nothing in the world is worth going back a third time for—even a woman. It is a satire on a medical army hospital unit and is supposed to be cruelly hilarious—so I'm anxious to hear what the children think about it. Denny went to see "What do you say to a Naked Woman", last night and he came home and said "Mom, it was really funny and clever—but pretty filthy, so don't you go see it." Does that make sense.

This fiance of Linda's is the boy who has been back from Viet Naam about 5 months. He was telling us the other night that he spent his R and. R. in Hong Kong and he says it was the most beautiful sight he had ever seen, flying into this city. He things it is a fantastic city and that you will thoroughly enjoy it. I hope so, but please take care as I don't want one more thing to worry about.

The enclosed is a copy of that poem of Denny's, I mentioned. Now, he didn't compose it, but it was published in their school newspaper and he thought it was worth sending home—which I did too.

We weren't too happy about this new detail you have scheduled—and I just keep praying it will be called off. Bob went out to get that Play boy issue, but he brought home April—so I'll try and get the March issue.

Take care and know you are much loved and PEACE—
Mom & Dad

P.S. I think so much of Aunt Dotty's remark—when she says the next time around she is going to raise chickens instead of children.

SP/5 Dail W. Mullins, Jr.
488-48-0511
CoA, 26th ENGR. BN.
APO SF, 96256

April 4

Dear Mom and Dad,

Just a short note to let you know that I received your letter of 27 March and the enclosed poem—thank you very much; I enjoyed it.

In return, I am sending you one—it was written by Kahil Gibran, and you may find that it speaks to you in one way or another. I hope you enjoy it.

I'm OK, getting shorter by the day—take care and I'll write soon.

Love, Dail

Tuesday morning, Mar 31

My dear,

44 more days, I count. I think I'm getting more nervous now than I was several months ago. Of course there are many reasons for feeling this way, mainly the type duty you seem to always be on now and the heightening tension in that part of the world.

Wanted to get this off last night but so darn many things came up and then I thought I'd wait until the mailman came this morning and see if I had a letter from you, but I didn't. I sometimes feel I'd relax more if I knew exactly where you were at all times, but Dad says no. Right now I don't know if you are at LZ Professional, New Hue, or Hawk Hill and sometimes I get a little "up-tight". It shows in my relationship with people as my patience becomes very short and my tongue just the opposite.

The children are still here. Linda is sewing a dress for herself as, like your wife, "she has nothing to wear". Bob and Dennis stay up every night clearing the programs on the "boob tube" so they sack in every morning until noon. Isn't that the life? Then they both start eating and this is continuous until 3 in the morning. No one would BELIEVE the amount of food and cooking I have done in the last week. I'm looking into buying a cow.

Sitting here watching Jeopardy while typing this to you. Linda Beswick and her fiance have the newest version of this game and have been coming over almost every day and I find that I'm not as intelligent while playing this with the kids, as I seem to be while I'm all alone. In the TV version I win fortunes every day.

Well your father just called and Dr. Emerson got in touch with him to tell him that all the specimens, slides, and jazz is back from the labs on Denny—and he does have a tapeworm. The funny thing it is a fish tapeworm (I wasn't aware that there were different species of the stupid things) and they even are able to pinpoint the origin of the damn fish. (The worms go in the worms go out, the worms play pinochle on your snout)—that last line was put in by Linda. Anyway, Dr. Emerson said there is a very powerful drug on the market now that could possibly get it very quickly, but you have to get the head of the stupid thing. He would like him to stay an extra day so guess the kids will leave Thursday—which means they will miss a day's classes. But I've got to get rid of this worm as I'm beginning to dream about it at night. Now really, did you ever hear of a family that gets the things we do. Sometimes I get so discouraged. Denny said he probably got this when he went up to Canada with the Y group and that was four years ago. Can you imagine! He's had this thing living with him that long.

For about two weeks your father has been coming home and each night he tells about some other patient who has been to see the movie "Patton", and how terrific it is and that every American should see it—blah, blah. Now the point of this is that about a month ago he started asking me if I wanted to go the show and it was always to see Patton. I just told him to go ahead by himself (or take a date), that I just didn't want to see a movie of this type. Anyway, last night he said he was going, if necessary by himself, but that he'd pay the way of anyone who wanted to go with him.

Now you know the kids would go see a lecture on Temperance, if someone paid for it. Then they get on me for being a spoilsport, so I go. Maybe we needed a man like this at that time, and George Scott does a fantastic job in portraying him—altho the dialogue consists only of "son-of-a-bitch" and "bastards", all kinds of bastards—Russian, German, Montgomery was the biggest, in fact—anyone who didn't believe as he did. Never have I heard such language. Anyway, about a third of the way through it, I went and sat in the woman's room and enjoyed myself taking care of a two month old baby. The mother was in there because he had started getting fussy—so I took care of him while she saw the movie.

Am going to send you a tape and some pictures we all made on Easter Sunday, and I wouldn't run this with anyone listening in or they will think you come from a long line of half-wits. It really sounds like we were all drunk, but Grandma has spent the day with us—so you know it wasn't alcholic spirits—I think it was release from tension by the time she left. Anyway, take it in the right way. If you could see Bob when he does the impersonation of the "gay" ones, it is so funny

Wanted to ask Linda Beswick's fiance some special places to see and go to in Hong Kong, but I always forgot until after he had left. He really was impressed with it as a city—and this surprised me, as all I can picture is narrow streets teeming with thousands of little coolies and smells of all kinds. We do hope you enjoy your leave—I'll enjoy having you out of Viet Naam for a few days.

Have to bring this to a close as Bob is waiting to take us to the Zoo, We are wracking our brains trying to find things to do that do not cost any money and it is hard. Haven't been to the Zoo for so long so I'm looking forward to it.

Take care of yourself and let us hear when you can and much much love from all—

PEACE
Mom & Dad

* * * * *

Mullins, Jr.
13400 Kingsmill Rd
Midlothian, VA. 23113

April 28

Dear Mom and Dad,
    Believe it or not, I've written to you folks once already—as usual, though, the letter lay deposited not in a mailbox, but on the back seat of our car for almost a week, so that to mail it now would be pointless.
    Just as you enjoyed being able to write to both of us at the same address once again, I find it most pleasurable myself to have to affix a stamp to a letter—instead of having to write that abominable FREE!
    At the moment, Lucy and I are in Myrtle Beach, S.C.—which, if you'll recall, is exactly where we were this time last year. This time, though, the circumstances are considerably more pleasant.
    We spent this weekend in Atlanta, GA., with the Jacksons and Henleys. It was great fun, and we both enjoyed being with our old friends from Memphis. As I think I told you when I was in St. Louis, we had planned to drive to Atlanta—from there to St. Louis by way of Athens, Ala., and then on down to Texas. Well, I came down with a slight case of the flu—which is what the doctor always says you have when he doesn't know—in Richmond last week, so I thought it best to come back to Richmond before heading West, just to see if I was going to be OK. Well, I'm fine now, but we still have to go back up there to pick up our stuff. Lucy, of course, couldn't resist stopping off at the beach on the way home—hence, our side trek to Myrtle Beach. We'll leave for VA. tomorrow. We'll be there a few days—I want to go down to FT. Eustis on the 30th and get paid—but after that we'll pack up and head for St. Louis.
    Naturally, Athens will be somewhat out of the way, so I don't think we'll be stopping off there—however, we will be passing through Louisville, and can stop and see Uncle Bob and Aunt Dotty—do you think they'd mind? I'll write them and let them know we're coming.
    I'm awfully sorry I waited so long to write—you probably have been wondering what in the world happened to us. I'm not exactly sure when we'll be arriving in St. Louis—I guess you might ought to look for us around Sunday night—but don't panic if we don't get there then. We may not make it until Monday sometime.
    So, until then, folks—take care and we'll see you soon.

Love,
Dail & Lucy

Made in the USA
Coppell, TX
27 October 2021